Contents

Contents

*Abbreviations listed before the bibliography (pp. 223–4) are used throughout
the volume without other explanation*

Mrs Janet Godden has again given invaluable help with the editing

There will be an index to vols. 1–5

ANGLO-SAXON ENGLAND

4

Edited by
PETER CLEMOES

MARTIN BIDDLE JULIAN BROWN
RENÉ DEROLEZ HELMUT GNEUSS
STANLEY GREENFIELD LARS-GUNNAR HALLANDER
PETER HUNTER BLAIR JOHN LEYERLE
PAUL MEYVAERT BRUCE MITCHELL
RAYMOND PAGE FRED ROBINSON

CAMBRIDGE UNIVERSITY PRESS
CAMBRIDGE
LONDON · NEW YORK · MELBOURNE

Published by the Syndics of the Cambridge University Press
The Pitt Building, Trumpington Street, Cambridge CB2 1RP
Bentley House, 200 Euston Road, London NW1 2DB
32 East 57th Street, New York, NY 10022, USA
296 Beaconsfield Parade, Middle Park, Melbourne 3206, Australia

© Cambridge University Press 1975

Library of Congress Catalogue Card Number: 78–190423

ISBN: 0 521 20868 8

First published 1975

Printed in Great Britain
at the University Printing House, Cambridge
(Euan Phillips, University Printer)

Illustrations

ACKNOWLEDGEMENTS

By permission of the Trustees of the British Museum the design on the cover is taken from the obverse of a silver penny issued to celebrate King Alfred's occupation and fortification of London in 886

Permission to publish a photograph or photographs has been granted by the Syndics of the Cambridge University Library (pls. I and II); Durham University Library (pl. III*a*); Biblioteca Medicea Laurenziana, Florence (pls. III*b* and *c*); Domschatz, Aachen (pl. IV*a*); Merseyside County Museums, Liverpool (pl. IV*b*); Heinrich-Heine-Institut, Düsseldorf (pl. IV*c*); Musée van Maerlant, Damme (pls. IV*d* and VIII); Niedersächsisches Landesmuseum, Hanover (pl. V); and Bibliothèque Municipale, Rouen (pls. VI and VII)

Material may be submitted to any of the editors, but it would be appreciated if the one most convenient regionally were chosen (Australasian contributions should be submitted to Bruce Mitchell) unless an article deals mainly with archaeology, palaeography, art, history or Viking studies, in which case the most suitable editor would be Martin Biddle (archaeology), Julian Brown (palaeography and art), Peter Hunter Blair (history) or Raymond Page (Viking studies). A potential contributor is asked to get in touch with the editor concerned as early as possible to obtain a copy of the style sheet and to have any necessary discussion. Articles must be in English.

The editors' addresses are

Mr M. Biddle, Winchester Research Unit, 13 Parchment Street, Winchester, Hampshire (England)

Professor T. J. Brown, Department of Palaeography, King's College, University of London, Strand, London WC2R 2LS (England)

Professor P. A. M. Clemoes, Emmanuel College, Cambridge CB2 3AP (England)

Professor R. Derolez, Rozier 44, 9000 Gent (Belgium)

Professor H. Gneuss, Englisches Seminar, Universität München, 8 München 40, Schellingstrasse 3 (Germany)

Professor S. B. Greenfield, Department of English, College of Liberal Arts, University of Oregon, Eugene, Oregon 97403 (USA)

Dr L.-G. Hallander, Lövångersgatan 16, 162 21 Vällingby (Sweden)

Dr P. Hunter Blair, Emmanuel College, Cambridge CB2 3AP (England)

Professor J. Leyerle, Centre for Medieval Studies, University of Toronto, Toronto M5S 1A1 (Canada)

Mr P. Meyvaert, Mediaeval Academy of America, 1430 Massachusetts Avenue, Cambridge, Massachusetts 02138 (USA)

Dr B. Mitchell, St Edmund Hall, Oxford OX1 4AR (England)

Dr R. I. Page, Corpus Christi College, Cambridge CB2 1RH (England)

Professor F. C. Robinson, Department of English, Yale University, New Haven, Connecticut 06520 (USA)

Continental influence at Bath monastery in the seventh century

PATRICK SIMS-WILLIAMS

Referring to the reign of Eorcenberht of Kent, 640–64, Bede writes:

> At that time, because there were not yet many monasteries founded in England, numbers of people from Britain used to enter the monasteries of the Franks or Gauls to practise the monastic life; they also sent their daughters to be taught in them and to be wedded to the heavenly bridegroom. They mostly went to the monasteries at Brie, Chelles and Andelys-sur-Seine...[1]

Although Bede mentions a few Kentish, East Anglian and Northumbrian noblewomen who were associated with Brie and Chelles,[2] his treatment of the English connections of the Frankish monasteries remains tantalizingly brief. In an article directing the attention of English historians to the importance of studying the links between English monasticism and the Columbanan monasticism of northern Gaul, James Campbell concludes that 'it is probable that the relationships between England and Gaul were of much more importance in determining the progress of the church in England in the seventh century than emerges directly from Bede's text'.[3] New evidence of these relationships comes from the early history of Bath abbey.[4]

The assertion in the late-eleventh-century Life of St David by Rhigyfarch that David founded monasteries at Bath, Crowland, Repton and other places[5] is obviously invention. The true history of the monastery at Bath begins with the twelfth-century copy of the foundation charter in the Bath

---

[1] Bede's *Ecclesiastical History of the English People* (hereafter *HE*), ed. B. Colgrave and R. A. B. Mynors (Oxford, 1969) III.8. The three monasteries lay in the Seine and Marne valleys in the vicinity of Paris. Other abbreviations used in the course of this article are: *BCS* = *Cartularium Saxonicum*, ed. Walter de G. Birch (London, 1885–93); *EHD* = *English Historical Documents c. 500–1042*, ed. Dorothy Whitelock (London, 1955); Sawyer = P. H. Sawyer, *Anglo-Saxon Charters: an Annotated List and Bibliography* (London, 1968). *BCS* and Sawyer are cited by number not by page. [2] *HE* III.8 and IV.23.
[3] 'The First Century of Christianity in England', *Ampleforth Jnl* 76 (1971), 16.
[4] I have in hand a study of the monastic culture of the West Midlands and the Welsh border. I am indebted to Mr David Rollason and Dr Hunter Blair for two references. Dr H. M. Taylor referred me to the article by Beat Brenk cited below and very kindly lent me his copy of the Marquise de Maillé's *Les Cryptes de Jouarre* (Paris, 1971).
[5] Ed. J. W. James (Cardiff, 1967), c. 13; discussed by A. W. Wade-Evans, *Life of St David* (London, 1923), pp. 80–3.

cartulary, Cambridge, Corpus Christi College 111. According to this, the land for the monastery was granted by Osric, king of the Hwicce (the Mercian sub-kingdom subsequently served by the bishopric of Worcester[1]) to an abbess Berta ('Bertanae abbatissae') on 6 November 675.[2] Editors have not noticed that *Bertanae* is the oblique form of *Berta* (not *'Bertana'*), which is a continental, not an English, name;[3] the only other women of this name mentioned in pre-Conquest English sources[4] are Æthelberht of Kent's queen (late-sixth-century), who was, of course, a Frank, and a *berchtae* commemorated in the ninth-century Durham *Liber Vitae* in the list of queens and abbesses,[5] who may be the same or, less likely, the Bath abbess.[6] No one regards this foundation charter as genuine as it stands. Professor Finberg, noting a similarity with a regnal style first found in a West Saxon charter of

---

1 A. H. Smith, 'The Hwicce', *Medieval and Linguistic Studies in Honor of F. P. Magoun, Jr*, ed. J. B. Bessinger and R. P. Creed (London, 1965), pp. 56–65.

2 *BCS* 43; Sawyer 51 – best edited by William Hunt, *Two Chartularies of the Priory of St Peter at Bath*, Somerset Record Soc. (1893), no. 1.7, pp. 6–7. 'Bretanae' in M. R. James, *A Descriptive Catalogue of the Manuscripts in the Library of Corpus Christi College Cambridge* (Cambridge, 1912) is an error. Quotations have been checked against the manuscript. Abbreviations have been expanded. Kenneth Harrison ('The *Annus Domini* in some Early Charters', *Jnl of the Soc. of Archivists* 4 (1970–3), 553) has established the date of Osric's charter; previous writers had thought the AD dating and the indiction disagreed. I regret that I had already completed this article before noticing Mr Harrison's valuable discussion of *BCS* 43, in which he concludes that 'there is a case for thinking that a genuine charter underlies it' (p. 554). To demonstrate the authentic basis of *BCS* 43, he also notes the similarity between the sanctions and attestations of Leuthere in this charter and in *BCS* 107, without, however, extending the comparison to other charters. His comparison of the dispositive clauses of the two charters and his defence of the *anno recapitulationis Dionysii* dating clause of *BCS* 43 deserve especial mention. His defence of the verbose, quasi-historical proem of *BCS* 43 is more questionable, particularly the argument based upon the suggestion that 'the text of the charter implies a fairly recent relapse into heathenism' (p. 553). Charles Plummer (*Venerabilis Baedae Opera Historica* (Oxford, 1896) II, 247) suggested that this proem was inspired by the text of Bede.

3 See the forms quoted by Ernst Förstemann, *Altdeutsches Namenbuch* I: *Personennamen* (Bonn, 1900), cols. 281–2, and Christopher Wells, 'An Orthographic Approach to Early Frankish Personal Names', *TPS* 1972, 101–64 (Index Nominum, 153). Marie-Thérèse Morlet (*Les Noms de Personne sur le Territoire de l'Ancienne Gaule du VIe au XIIe Siècle* (Paris, 1968–72) I, 55) says that the element BERT- 'est très fréquent dans les noms franciques, mais selon Meyer-Lübke, *Rom. Nam.* I, 20 [W. Meyer-Lübke, *Romanische Namenstudien*, Sitzungsberichte der kaiserlichen Akademie der Wissenschaften, phil.-hist. Klasse 149.2 and 184.4 (Vienna, 1905–17)], il est rare dans les noms gotiques'.

4 William Searle, *Onomasticon Anglo-Saxonicum* (Cambridge, 1897), pp. 88, 104 and 543.

5 *The Oldest English Texts*, ed. Henry Sweet, Early Eng. Text Soc. o.s. 83 (London, 1885), 154.

6 Thorvald Forssner (*Continental Germanic Personal Names in England in Old and Middle English Times* (Uppsala, 1916), p. 46, n. 5) equates her with Æthelberht's queen. He also comments that 'the occurrence of this name in England will mostly be due to its having been borne by [her]' (p. 47). This hypothesis does not seem very likely. If the Anglo-Saxons named their children according to fashions of this sort – and Forssner advances no evidence that they did – one might expect more occurrences of the name than one, and occurrences nearer to Kent than Bath is. Moreover we should not assume that the queen was famous outside Kentish circles because she appears historically significant to us as readers of Bede. (The Durham entry is, of course, later than Bede.) The names of the other women cited by Forssner occur in the post-Conquest portions of the Durham *Liber Vitae*, in post-Conquest contexts, and are obviously OE *Berte*.

801, suggested that it reached its present form early in the ninth century;[1] this argument does not, however, seem to exclude any *later* date up to the twelfth century. Nevertheless, two considerations discourage one from explaining away the name of the first abbess as a late invention. Firstly, since the cartulary contains at least one late-seventh-century charter of undoubted authenticity,[2] which presumably refers to Bath,[3] it is clear that some records did survive from the earliest period and might have been available to the compilers of the foundation charter. Secondly, in this genuine charter the name Folcburg appears, which is attested otherwise only on the continent.[4] According to this charter, which must be dated by its indiction and witness-list to 681, a certain Æthelmod, with the consent of King Æthelred (of Mercia) granted twenty hides by R. Cherwell (Oxfordshire) 'Bernguidi uenerabili abbatissae et Folcburgi et per uos monasterio uestro'. The editor suggests that Folcburg 'was probably the *decana*, or, as she would be called later, the prioress, of the convent'.[5] The name of her abbess is English, Beorngyth.[6] The spelling *ui* for *y* preserves an early orthography.[7]

From the two charters taken together, then, we see a monastery founded at Bath in 675 by a sub-king of the Hwicce with a continental abbess at its head, who by 681 had an English successor, although the foreign element continued in the person of Folcburg. It was probably a 'double monastery' at first, no houses for women only being recorded at this date.[8] An exact parallel for these events occurs in the Life of Bertila, abbess of Chelles (*c.* 658–*c.* 705[9]), one of the Frankish monasteries mentioned by Bede:

[1] H. P. R. Finberg, *The Early Charters of the West Midlands*, 2nd ed. (Leicester, 1972), p. 174, citing *BCS* 282, Sawyer 268. The significance of this similarity is minimized by K. Harrison, 'The *Annus Domini* in some Early Charters', p. 553.

[2] Hunt, *Chartularies*, no. 1.8, pp. 7–8; *BCS* 57; Sawyer 1167; *EHD* no. 57. The other seventh-century charter (Hunt, *Chartularies*, no. 1.6, p. 6; *BCS* 28; Sawyer 1168) contains internal contradictions and seems in part to be modelled on the genuine charter. If 'loco...Slaepi' in it is rightly identified with Islip on the Cherwell (*Preparatory to 'Anglo-Saxon England'*, being the Collected Papers of Frank Merry Stenton, ed. D. M. Stenton (Oxford, 1970), p. 225; Sawyer 1168), it may have been produced as a geographically more specific version of the Cherwell grant. At a synod held in Bath in 864 Burgred of Mercia granted land at Water Eaton to the bishop of Worcester (*BCS* 509; Sawyer 210; cf. Sawyer 402). Water Eaton adjoins Islip on the Cherwell. If Burgred was in fact disposing of some Bath estates along the Cherwell, this might be the occasion for fabricating the Islip charter in its present form.

[3] Since it occurs in the Bath cartulary. The agreement of the names Berta and Folcburg noted below confirms this presumption.

[4] Förstemann, *Personennamen*, col. 549.   [5] Hunt, *Chartularies*, p. xxxvi.

[6] Searle, *Onomasticon*, p. 99. The name *Burnegundis*, for which Förstemann (*Personennamen*, col. 269), found two examples in the early-ninth-century Polyptych of St Germain-des-Prés, is hardly this name; nor, as Forssner (*Continental Germanic Personal Names*, p. 282) points out, is *Bernoidis* in the ninth-century Polyptych of Rheims (Förstemann, *Personennamen*, col. 272).

[7] Cf. A. Campbell, *Old English Grammar* (Oxford, 1959), §§42 and 199.

[8] Stenton, 'St Frideswide and her Times', *Preparatory to 'Anglo-Saxon England'*, p. 228, and Philibert Schmitz, *Histoire de l'Ordre de Saint Benoît* (Maredsous, 1942–56) VII, 47–8. On double monasteries in general see *ibid.* I, 298–300 and references.

[9] *Vita Bertilae*, ed. Wilhelm Levison, Monumenta Germaniae Historica, Script. Rer. Merov. 6, 96.

Such great profit for the good of souls did the Lord bring to pass through her that even those faithful kings from the parts of Saxondom across the seas would ask her through trusty messengers to send them some of her followers for teaching or sacred instruction (which they had heard she possessed to a marvellous degree), or even those who might establish monasteries of men and women in that region. For the good of their souls, she did not refuse this religious request; rather, with the counsel of the elders and the encouragement of the brothers did she send, with a thankful heart, chosen women and very devout men thither with great diligence, with both saints' relics and many volumes of books, so that through her the yield of souls increased even in that people and, by the grace of God, was multiplied.[1]

Levison dates the Life to the end of the eighth century or the beginning of the ninth;[2] but he and others treat this passage as reliable.[3] It would be wrong to jump to the possible conclusion that Bath was one of the monasteries established by Bertila's followers, for other Frankish houses besides Chelles may have played a similar rôle; but it suggests the sort of reality which lies behind the two charters.

In view of Bath's position on the West Saxon border of the Hwicce,[4] it may be significant that in 675 the West Saxon bishopric had been held for a quarter-century by three bishops of whom the first and third (Agilbert and Leuthere) were Franks and the second (Wine) had been consecrated in Gaul,[5] while the Hwicce had no bishop of their own as yet.[6] Leuthere (670–6) in fact appears second in the column of episcopal witnesses in the foundation charter, after Archbishop Theodore. The consistency of this witness-list has been defended by C. S. Taylor, and by Finberg, who regarded it as being drawn from a shorter, authentic version of Osric's charter.[7]

---

[1] *Ibid.* c. 6. [2] *Ibid.* p. 99.

[3] Wilhelm Levison, *England and the Continent in the Eighth Century* (Oxford, 1946), p. 132, n. 2; Finberg, *West Midlands*, p. 209; and J. Campbell, 'First Century of Christianity', p. 21. (On the abbess Liobsynd(a) in 'St Mildburg's Testament' mentioned by these last, cf. D. Whitelock's caution (*ASE* 1 (1972), 12): 'nothing is known of this abbess'.) Jean Guerout ('Les Origines et le Premier Siècle de l'Abbaye', *L'Abbaye Royale de Notre-Dame de Jouarre*, ed. Yves Chaussy *et al.* (Paris, 1961) 1, 48, n. 9) believes that the writer of the *Vita Bertilae* used earlier documents.

[4] On the shifting boundary see C. Hart, 'The Tribal Hidage', *TRHS* 5th ser. 21 (1971), 149–50; but note that the reliability of many of the charters used is doubtful.

[5] *HE* III.7. On the chronology see Plummer, *Baedae Opera Historica*, II, 144–8.

[6] No bishop of Worcester attests the 675 charter. The date 679 for the foundation of the see is first given by two related sources, the Appendix to Florence of Worcester, ed. Henry Petrie and J. Sharpe, *Monumenta Historica Britannica* (London, 1848), p. 622 (cf. Arthur Haddan and William Stubbs, *Councils and Ecclesiastical Documents relating to Great Britain and Ireland* (Oxford, 1869–71) III, 127–8) and an early-twelfth-century tract, *Monasticon Anglicanum*, ed. William Dugdale, re-ed. J. Caley *et al.* (London, 1846) 1, 607.

[7] C. S. Taylor, 'Bath, Mercian and West Saxon', *Trans. of the Bristol and Gloucestershire Archaeol. Soc.* 23 (1900), 135–6; Finberg, *West Midlands*, p. 173. Bishop Hæddi who succeeded Leuthere in 676 also attests. Taylor suggests that both signatures appear because arrangements for the foundation spanned the change of bishop; Finberg suggests that 'Hædde may well have been consecrated as an assistant bishop while Leutherius was still alive'. (For early parallels see Haddan and Stubbs, *Councils* III, 301, and Colgrave and Mynors, *Bede*, '*HE*', p. 144, n. 2; for

4

Leuthere is the only witness who uses the style of humility: 'Ego Leutherius acsi indignus episcopus subscripsi.' Comparison with two other witness-lists suggests that this style was characteristic of him.[1] A dubious Malmesbury charter, which may have been based in part on a genuine charter, has 'Ego Leutherius acsi indignus episcopus rogatus a fratribus hanc donationis cartam subscripsi'[2] and a similar attestation recurs in a probably authentic Dorset charter (undated) surviving in the fifteenth-century Shaftesbury cartulary: 'Ego Leutherius, quamvis indignus, episcopus hanc cartulam donationis subscripsi.'[3] Levison demonstrated from the presence of a Frankish formula[4] that the latter charter should be associated with Leuthere himself, who may have more or less dictated its wording, and his point has been accepted by Professor Whitelock and Sir Frank Stenton.[5] There seems to me to be a close similarity between its sanction clause and that of the Bath charter:

[*Shaftesbury*] Si quis vero episcoporum seu regum contra hanc definitionis cartulam propria temeritate, vel potius sacrilega debacacione venire temptaverit, inprimis iram Dei incurrat. a liminibus sanctæ ecclesiæ *sit* (MS et) separatus, et hoc quod repetit, vindicare non valeat.

[*Bath*] Si quis uero quod absit succedentium episcoporum seu regum contra hanc nostrae diffinitionis cartulam propria temeritate presumere temptauerit, sit sequestratus a communione corporis Domini nostri Ihesu Christi et a consortio omnium sanctorum in aeuum priuatus.

I have found no other seventh- or eighth-century English charter which resembles the Shaftesbury charter's wording so closely. In particular, the word *definitio* is rare in sanctions. It does occur, however, in the Malmesbury

later ones see Pierre Chaplais, 'The Authenticity of the Royal Anglo-Saxon Diplomas of Exeter', *Bull. of the Inst. of Hist. Research* 39 (1966), 27–8.) Another possibility is that *episcopus* after Hæddi's name was added later from hind-sight. This is also suggested by Harrison, 'The *Annus Domini* in some Early Charters', p. 553. The possible connection suggested by Harrison between Bishop Wilfrid, who attests, and the use of AD dating is another point in favour of the witness-list; cf. Nicholas Brooks, 'Anglo-Saxon Charters: the Work of the Last Twenty Years', *ASE* 3 (1974), 225 and n. 1.

[1] Cf. 'quamuis indignus' in the autograph of St Willibrord, *The Calendar of St Willibrord*, ed. H. A. Wilson, Henry Bradshaw Soc. 55 (London, 1918), 39v, and E. A. Lowe, *Codices Latini Antiquiores* (Oxford, 1934–72) v, no. 606a. On the frequency of *indignus* in scribal signatures see P. Meyvaert, *RB* 71 (1961), 283–4; for examples of *indignus* in documents not concerning Leuthere see Harrison, 'The *Annus Domini* in some Early Charters', p. 554, n. 20.

[2] *BCS* 37; Sawyer 1245; *Aldhelmi Opera*, ed. R. Ehwald, MGH, Auct. Antiq. 15, 507–9.

[3] *BCS* 107; Sawyer 1164; *EHD* no. 55.

[4] 'Et hoc quod repetit, vindicare non valeat.' Pierre Chaplais ('The Origin and Authenticity of the Royal Anglo-Saxon Diploma', *Jnl of the Soc. of Archivists* 3 (1965–9), 55) describes the clause as 'of continental and probably Frankish origin'. He notes that it occurs elsewhere in England only in a grant by Edward the Confessor to Leofric (Sawyer 1003), where it may be attributable to Leofric's Lotharingian upbringing ('Diplomas of Exeter', p. 26).

[5] *England and the Continent*, pp. 226–8; *EHD*, p. 441; and F. M. Stenton, *The Latin Charters of the Anglo-Saxon Period* (Oxford, 1955), pp. 23–4. Chaplais ('Origin and Authenticity', pp. 55–6) is non-committal.

charter witnessed by Leuthere[1] and in a charter of Ine[2] written by Winberht, the scribe who wrote the Shaftesbury charter – he names himself in both according to continental practice.[3] An Abingdon fabrication referring to the eighth century in which the word occurs[4] seems to me to be based on the Ine charter. This leaves only one seventh- or eighth-century sanction independent of Leuthere's circle containing the word, a charter of Offa in favour of the bishop of Rochester in 764.[5] The resemblance between the Bath charter and the Shaftesbury one leads me to conclude that the later compiler(s) of the Bath foundation charter used at least the sanction and witness-list of an earlier charter which had been not only attested by Leuthere but also drafted by him or by one of his circle. We can, therefore, associate the Frank Leuthere with the beginnings of Abbess Berta's monastery at Bath.

There is no direct information about Leuthere, except for the little in Bede. Yet, as Bede states that he was the nephew of Agilbert, his predecessor but one, about whom there is further evidence in continental sources,[6] one may gather the sort of background and contacts he had. According to the *Généalogie des Fondateurs*, whose accuracy in details is controversial, Agilbert was the cousin of Adon, who founded the monastery of Jouarre *c.* 635,[7] and the brother of Telchilde (d. 664 + [8]), who later became its first abbess.[9] The family was a noble one with connections with le Soissonnais.[10] After a long

---

[1] 'Quodsi quis haec scripta et decreta nostrae definitionis [*variants:* diffinitionis; et definita et decreta nostra] irrita facere nitetur sciant se ante tribunal Christi rationem redditurum' (*Aldhelmi Opera*, ed. Ehwald, p. 509).

[2] 'Si quis vero contra hæc nostræ diffinitionis decreta propriæ temeritatis pertinacia fretus violenter venire nisus fuerit. noverit se in tremendo ultimæ discussionis examine coram iudice Christo æqua discretionis lance singulorum facta librante rationem redditurum' (*BCS* 100; Sawyer 239). Chaplais's comment on this charter is mistakenly quoted under Sawyer 243.

[3] Levison, *England and the Continent*, pp. 227–8; *EHD*, pp. 341–2; and Chaplais, 'Origin and Authenticity', p. 55 ('probably to be also attributed to continental influence').

[4] 'Si quis ergo diffinitionem hanc a me factam una, concorditer, canonice et ecclesiastice a rege Ini, necnon ab episcopo Daniele roboratam, irritam facere temptaverit, sciat se coram Christo rationem redditurum' (*BCS* 29; Sawyer 1179).

[5] 'Quicunque uero sequentium regum aut principum aut aliquis seculari fretus potestate hęc nostrę definitionis scripta irrita facere quod absit nisus fuerit. sciat se in presenti uita domini benedictione esse priuatum. et in nouissimo maledictione subiacere. ut a consortio sit separatus sanctorum et cum impiis et peccatoribus flammis ultricibus esse damnandum. excepto si digna satisfactione emendare curauerint quod iniqua temeritate deprauarunt' (*Charters of Rochester*, ed. A. Campbell, Anglo-Saxon Charters 1 (London, 1973), no. 6, pp. 7–8; *BCS* 195; Sawyer 105). Stenton ('The Anglo-Saxon Coinage and the Historian', *Preparatory to 'Anglo-Saxon England'*, p. 381) notes that 'it contains ancient formulas which we get in earlier Kentish charters – formulas brought, as I would think, by Archbishop Theodore from the continent'.

[6] P. Grosjean, 'La Date du Colloque de Whitby', *AB* 78 (1960), 250–2 and 269–71; Guerout, 'Les Origines', pp. 38–9, 45 and 51–3; and Marquise de Maillé, *Les Cryptes de Jouarre* (Paris, 1971), pp. 74–7.

[7] Guerout, 'Les Origines', pp. 11 and 33 and Marquise de Maillé, *Les Cryptes de Jouarre*, p. 70.

[8] Guerout, 'Les Origines', p. 52.

[9] *Ibid.* pp. 11 and 47 and Marquise de Maillé, *Les Cryptes de Jouarre*, pp. 77–8.

[10] Guerout, 'Les Origines', pp. 23 and 38.

period spent in Ireland, probably in the south in view of his 'Roman' stance on the Easter question at the Synod of Whitby,[1] Agilbert came to England. He was bishop to the West Saxons from 649 or 650 until 664, when he quarrelled with King Cenwalh (who had decided to divide the diocese, wanting an English-speaking bishop, Wine, at Winchester), and returned to Gaul, where he became bishop of Paris in 668 or earlier.[2] According to what has been regarded as reliable tradition he was responsible for building the crypt of St Paul at Jouarre, the mausoleum where he himself was buried.[3] Bede states that Cenwalh invited Agilbert to return but that he sent instead his nephew, the priest Leuthere, who proved an acceptable alternative.[4]

Jouarre is less than twenty miles from Chelles, whose influence on English monasteries has already been mentioned. The two monasteries must have been more than geographically close. Both were double monasteries and Columbanan in character.[5] Balthild, the English widow of Clovis II, had introduced the abbess Bertila and the other nuns from Jouarre in the course of refounding and enlarging Chelles between 657 and 664 (in 658 or 659 according to Levison); she lived at Chelles herself from her retirement (before 667) until her death (after 677).[6] Her presence may have encouraged an English orientation of both houses. Through his family ties with Jouarre, Leuthere must have been familiar with both. His participation in the foundation of a continental monastery in the kingdom of the Hwicce, outside his own diocese, can plausibly be related to this background. It may be concluded, at least, that the Bath nuns Berta and Folcburg probably came from the group of Frankish monasteries in the Paris region.

For an impression of the possible effect of the cross-Channel connection

---

[1] So Grosjean, 'La Date du Colloque de Whitby', p. 270. He thinks Agilbert may have been consecrated bishop in Ireland, but it is equally likely that he had already been consecrated 'évêque *pérégrin*' in Gaul as Guerout ('Les Origines', p. 45 and n. 54) thinks.

[2] See *HE* iv.1 and Guerout, 'Les Origines', p. 51.

[3] Guerout, 'Les Origines', pp. 51 and 38–9; Jean Hubert, *Les Cryptes de Jouarre* (Melun, 1952), pp. 4 and 7. The doctrine that the present crypt is a twelfth-century enlargement of a Merovingian original has been questioned by Jean Coquet, *Pour une Nouvelle Date de la Crypte Saint-Paul de Jouarre* (Ligugé, 1970). Dom Coquet argues that the crypt was constructed in Carolingian times, in part from Merovingian materials whose provenance cannot be proved. 'Certes [les chapiteaux] peuvent avoir appartenu, ainsi que les colonnes, à un décor plaqué de l'ancien sanctuaire...mais ils peuvent tout aussi bien avoir des origines diverses et partant des temps d'exécution différents' (p. 31). His scepticism is not shared by the Marquise de Maillé, who argues that the crypt is an eighth-century enlargement of the original mausoleum built by Agilbert (*Les Cryptes de Jouarre*, esp. pp. 145, 151, 267 and n. 1, and 274–5).

[4] *HE* iii.7.

[5] Guerout, 'Les Origines', pp. 6, 34–9 and 46, and Levison, *Vita Bertilae*, pp. 96–7.

[6] Guerout, 'Les Origines', pp. 38 and 47–8; Levison, *Vita Bertilae*, pp. 95–6 and c. 4; Marquise de Maillé, *Les Cryptes de Jouarre*, pp. 49–50 and 72–3; and *Vita S. Balthildis*, ed. B. Krusch, MGH, Script. Rer. Merov. 2, 475–508, cc. 7–8. On Balthild see Levison, *England and the Continent*, pp. 9–10 and references.

on cultural life at Bath it may be noted that Chelles was a source of books and teachers in Bertila's time, as her Life mentions,[1] and continued in importance for manuscript production and biblical study into Carolingian times;[2] Jouarre's history immediately after the early eighth century is obscure, but for the earlier period it may be relevant to refer to Agilbert's stay in Ireland *legendarum gratia scripturarum*[3] ('l'école d'exégèse autour de Lismore était alors à son apogée', comments Père Grosjean[4]), to his standing with such men as Wilfrid, Alhfrith and Theodore[5] and to the magnificence of the crypt of St Paul and its tombs, if these indeed belong in part to Jouarre's Merovingian period.[6] Comparisons have in fact been made between the remarkable relief work on Agilbert's own tomb and that of the sculptured crosses he could have seen in the British Isles,[7] though M. Hubert would rather consider that both are manifestations of a common renaissance, of which the Anglo-Frankish links mentioned by Bede are a part.[8]

There is no sign of a continental connection after the 681 charter, though it is inherently unlikely that this would have been dropped immediately. But various internal and external changes affecting the monastery in the eighth century probably did not encourage a permanent relationship. The next charter is dated 808 but must belong to 757–8: the West Saxon king Cynewulf grants North Stoke 'fratribus in monasterio Sancti Petri', Offa confirming.[9] This implies that Bath had now become an all-male community.[10] By the time of the next document, the report of a synod in 781,[11] the monastery is seen to have passed into the possession of the see of Worces-

[1] See above, p. 4.
[2] Levison, *Vita Bertilae*, pp. 96–7; Bernhard Bischoff, *Mittelalterliche Studien* (Stuttgart, 1966–7) I, 16–34; and Lowe, *Codices Latini Antiquiores* VI, xxii.
[3] *HE* III.7.
[4] 'La Date du Colloque de Whitby', p. 270.
[5] *HE* III.25 and IV.1.
[6] See Jean Hubert *et al.*, *Europe in the Dark Ages* (*L'Europe des Invasions*), trans. S. Gilbert and J. Emmons (London, 1969), pls. 77–91.
[7] E.g. M. Aubert, *L'Abbaye Royale de Notre Dame de Jouarre*, ed. Chaussy *et al.*, p. vii. The Marquise de Maillé (*Les Cryptes de Jouarre*, pp. 213–15, 273–4 and 281) speculates on contact between Agilbert and Theodore as a possible channel of influence between Jouarre and England.
[8] *Les Cryptes de Jouarre*, p. 7. Beat Brenk ('Marginalien zum sogenannten Sarkophag des Agilbert in Jouarre', *Cahiers Archéologiques* 14 (1964), 106): 'Mit diesem orientalischen Impuls stehen auch die angelsächsischen Steinkreuze von Ruthwell und Bewcastle in engstem Zusammenhang.' The doubt implied in Brenk's title is dispelled by the Marquise de Maillé (*Les Cryptes de Jouarre*, pp. 201–3). Francis Salet (*Bulletin Monumental* 128 (1970), 136) mistakenly quotes Dom Coquet as redating Agilbert's tomb to the ninth century. In fact Coquet does not question the traditional dating; the redating concerns the tomb of *Agilberte*. A seventh-century date for Agilbert's tomb is supported by Brenk and by the Marquise de Maillé (pp. 203–6).
[9] Hunt, *Chartularies*, no. 1.19, pp. 23–4; *BCS* 327; Sawyer 265.
[10] It has been argued that the charter has suffered 'improvement', Cynewulf of Wessex being confused with Cynewulf of Mercia (as in the abstract in Hunt, *Chartularies*, no. II.808, p. 153), because of the date given; see Hunt, *Chartularies*, p. xxxiv and Sawyer 265. However the date is more simply explained as a misreading of DCCLVIII as DCCCVIII.
[11] *BCS* 241; Sawyer 1257; *EHD* no. 77.

ter, as many of the early foundations did. This, however, was now reversed. Offa maintained at the synod that the church of Worcester was holding the inheritance of his kinsman, King Æthelbald, without hereditary right, including Bath and various other 'places', most, and perhaps all, of them monasteries. There is no evidence, in fact, that Æthelbald had possessed any of the places claimed, except for Stour-in-Ismere,[1] and Offa himself had consented to the reversion of this property to the see.[2] Stubbs's suggestion that Offa, with his eye on Bath, was claiming more than he expected to get as a matter of strategy is therefore plausible.[3] The synod's decision allowed him only 'that most famous monastery *æt Baþum*', but he was also compensated by the church of Worcester with 'thirty hides on the south side of the river nearby, which is called Avon, which land we bought at a proper price from Cynewulf, king of the West Saxons'. These transactions involving Bath could probably be explained if more were known of the political situation. Taylor pointed out that Offa defeated Cynewulf at Bensington in 779[4] and suggested that Offa wished to secure personal control of Bath and its lands because of its strategic importance on the West Saxon border.[5] Professor Whitelock comments that 'the purchase by the church from Cynewulf of Wessex on Offa's account of a stretch of land on the West Saxon side of the Avon is of great interest. It suggests that Offa is strengthening the southern boundary of his kingdom, and one wonders whether Cynewulf, who at times admitted Offa's overlordship, was an entirely willing party to the transaction.'[6] It must be noted, too, that the subject of Cynewulf's 757–8 grant, the estate of North Stoke, included Little Down Camp, a fort with obvious military possibilities four miles from Bath on the *north* side of the Avon.[7] The changing fortunes of Bath monastery may, therefore, mask some irrecoverable political adjustments. These manoeuvres do not seem to have led to the end of monastic life at Bath, for in 796 Ecgfrith of Mercia issued a charter 'in celebre monasterio quod Saxonice nominatur æt Baðun',[8] but they did make Bath a royal *Eigenkloster*. The transference of Bath from

---

[1] *BCS* 154; Sawyer 89; *EHD* no. 67. Cf. Sawyer 1826.

[2] *BCS* 220; Sawyer 1411. Cf. Taylor, 'Bath, Mercian and West Saxon', p. 139.

[3] W. Stubbs, 'The Cathedral, Diocese and Monasteries of Worcester in the Eighth Century', *ArchJ* 19 (1862), 250.

[4] *The Anglo-Saxon Chronicle*, *EHD*, p. 165.

[5] Taylor, 'Bath, Mercian and West Saxon', pp. 138–9.   [6] *EHD*, p. 466.

[7] On the bounds of *BCS* 327 see G. B. Grundy, *The Saxon Charters and Field Names of Somerset* (Taunton, 1935), pp. 230–2. For the 'prehistoric promontory fort' see *The Victoria County History of Somerset* II (1911), 480–1, and I (1906), 302 for Roman remains in the vicinity. For Bath's possession of North Stoke in the twelfth century see Hunt, *Chartularies*, nos. 1.49–50, pp. 49–51.

[8] *BCS* 278; Sawyer 148. *BCS* 277, which reads *vico* for *monasterio*, is merely a poor copy of *BCS* 278 and can be ignored; cf. N. R. Ker, 'Hemming's Cartulary', *Studies in Medieval History presented to F. M. Powicke*, ed. R. W. Hunt *et al.* (Oxford, 1948), pp. 65–7. On allegations that Offa refounded Bath see Taylor, 'Bath, Mercian and West Saxon', p. 138 and Hunt, *Chartularies*, p. xxxvii.

Mercia to Wessex in the tenth century[1] does not seem to have altered its status as such. Athelstan was supposed to have endowed the monastery;[2] the surviving charter is under suspicion,[3] but a book survives with a tenth-century inscription recording Athelstan's gift of it to St Peter's, Bath.[4] In 944 the monastery was in the gift of his successor, Edmund.[5] It was fitting, though Edmund may not have realized it, that he chose to give it to monks from across the Channel, from St Bertin's in Flanders.

[1] Discussed at length by Taylor, 'Bath, Mercian and West Saxon'. See also Joseph Armitage Robinson, *The Saxon Bishops of Wells*, Brit. Acad. Supplemental Papers 4 (London [1919]), 5.

[2] Cf. Hunt, *Chartularies*, no. II.808, p. 152, on the celebration of his anniversary.

[3] *Ibid*. no. I.9, pp. 8–11; *BCS* 670; Sawyer 414.

[4] BM Cotton Claudius B. v. Cf. P. Grierson, 'Les Livres de l'Abbé Seiwold de Bath', *RB* 52 (1940), 101, n. 5.

[5] *Ibid*. p. 104 and n. 3; *EHD*, p. 318 (*Gesta Abbatum S. Bertini*).

Linguistic facts and the interpretation of Old English poetry

BRUCE MITCHELL

In their admirable edition of *The Wanderer* Dunning and Bliss give the meaning 'as when' for *swa* in line 43b

> þinceð him on mode   þæt he his mondryhten
> clyppe ond cysse,   ond on cneo lecge
> honda ond heafod,   swa he hwilum ær
> in geardagum   giefstolas breac (41–4)

and defend their gloss in the following words: 'Here literary considerations must outweigh linguistic arguments.'[1] And in his latest book, Stanley B. Greenfield approves: 'Thus Bliss–Dunning...can properly say that though usage of *swa* meaning "as when" here "would be unique", but [*sic*] "literary considerations must outweigh linguistic arguments".'[2] I do not approve. I would say that Dunning and Bliss have let literary considerations outweigh not linguistic *arguments*, but linguistic *facts*. Hence my title.[3]

What, then, is a linguistic fact for the reader of Old English poetry? We can perhaps say generally that it is a statement which limits his choice of interpretations; for example, that a particular metrical pattern is impossible, that a given inflexional ending is unambiguous, that the word being discussed means 'x' and not 'y', that a conjunction expresses a particular relationship – contrast *oþþæt* and *þenden* – or that a certain word order is found only in principal clauses. We might agree that general statements such as these – and any particular statements about individual examples properly based on them – are, or could be, linguistic facts. We might also agree that we are entitled to expect consistency in their application. This is not the case in the Dunning–Bliss edition of *The Wanderer*, where the editors

---

[1] *The Wanderer*, ed. T. P. Dunning and A. J. Bliss (London, 1969), p. 113.
[2] *The Interpretation of Old English Poems* (London and Boston, 1972), pp. 118–19.
[3] The word 'linguistic' is used in its ancient sense – 'of language' – and has no reference to its present-day use by practitioners of a 'science' which has hijacked the word and which in many of its aspects will (I believe) prove to be one of the great non-subjects of the twentieth century – though I do not deny that it has valuable techniques in the analysis and teaching of current languages. It is with pleasure and gratitude that I acknowledge my debt to Professor Peter Clemoes for his cogent criticisms of earlier drafts of this paper.

accept *swa*, 'as when', while admitting that it is unique, but in lines 53–4 reject certain figurative meanings of *swimman* and *fleotan* because they are unique. Greenfield condemns what he calls this 'double-dealing'.[1]

But how reliable are these linguistic facts when we really need them? Are we like the critic of whom A. E. Housman said 'all the tools he uses are two-edged, though to be sure both edges are quite blunt'? In seeking to use facts, we have to discover first what generalization (or generalizations) is (or are) relevant to the problem (or problems) before us and second what relationship exists between the generalization(s) and the particular instance we are considering. These two questions demand separate discussion.

Establishing acceptable generalizations about the Old English language is less easy than is sometimes believed. We are perhaps most aware of difficulty in the realm of semantics. But even here assumptions are too often regarded as facts. Fred C. Robinson has recently warned us how a lexicographer, by the way in which he treats a certain word in his dictionary, can become a literary interpreter and influence generations of critics.[2] A particular case in point is whether the last word in *Beowulf* – *lofgeornost* – must be pejorative. I do not propose to go into this much discussed topic. But it is noteworthy – in view of *mildust ond monðwærust* in the preceding line – that even now no one discussing this word seems to have mentioned the fact that in Blickling Homily VI Christ is called *milde ond monðwære*.[3] Opinions may differ about the significance of this, but it is hard to deny that the fact ought to be mentioned. The new *Dictionary of Old English*, to be edited by Christopher Ball and Angus Cameron, will of course be invaluable. Meanwhile, a little less anxiety to *prove* – or to assume that it has been proved – that a word *must* mean 'x' and not 'y' would be welcome.

The danger of treating *assumptions* about the meaning of a series of individual words as if they were *facts* is that the process gets cumulatively more and more out of hand and leads ultimately to what I must describe as the arrogance implicit in such titles as 'The Meaning of *The Seafarer* and *The Wanderer*' and *The Mode and Meaning of 'Beowulf'*, which seem to me to involve the further assumptions that every poem has one fixed meaning and that that meaning has been revealed to a modern Cædmon.

Another assumption which, I believe, is too easily accepted is that there are rules which hold for Old English metre. I am becoming increasingly reluctant to admit metre as a decisive criterion, especially when it comes to dismissing the reading of a manuscript in favour of an editorial emendation. I am going to content myself here with one statement and one question on

---

[1] *N&Q* 215 (1970), 115.
[2] 'Lexicography and Literary Criticism: a Caveat', *Philological Essays: Studies in Old and Middle English Language and Literature in Honour of Herbert Dean Meritt*, ed. J. L. Rosier (The Hague, 1970), pp. 99–110. [3] But see below, Postscript, p. 28.

this topic. First, then, the statement. In Table II of Appendix C of his book on the metre of *Beowulf*,[1] A. J. Bliss lists all the types of half-lines in *Beowulf*. If we exclude hypermetric lines, we find that there are 130 acceptable types, of which twenty-nine occur only once. But Bliss also has eleven half-lines which he classifies as 'remainders' and eight which he calls 'defective'. This seems to mean that he finds in *Beowulf* forty-eight half-lines which occur only once, of which twenty-nine are acceptable and nineteen are not. Now the question. If twenty-nine acceptable types occur only once, on what grounds can we be sure that one of the remaining nineteen is not an acceptable thirtieth?

There are superstitions about word order too. Some six years ago I wrote,

[it] seems clear to me that word order is not conclusive in the poetry, that it cannot be used to prove that a certain clause must be subordinate and another principal. But this, of course, does not stop an editor from suggesting that a poet may deliberately have arranged his clauses so that those with S. . . . V. were subordinate and those with V. S. were principal. Nor does it mean that such a suggestion is wrong; it merely means that it cannot be proved right.[2]

I still believe this and remain unconvinced by arguments that, for example, the word order Subject–Noun Object–Verb proves that a clause in poetry must be subordinate. They can still be heard. But one has only to point to the opening of *Beowulf* to see the folly of this:

> Hwæt, we Gardena   in geardagum
> þeodcyninga   þrym gefrunon... (1–2)

In using this argument, critics are relying on a useful guide inherited from their student days which does not always hold even in Old English prose. On the other hand, a tendency to rely too much on the modern feeling that the subject comes first concealed the meaning of line 51 of *The Wanderer* – 'þonne maga gemynd mod geondhweorfeð' – and created consequent difficulties until it was suggested that *mod* was the subject, not the object, of *geondhweorfeð*.[3] There are sentences with the order Object–Verb–Subject, which runs directly counter to the instinct of modern readers. One such occurs in *Genesis A* 2887b, where the poet is describing the approach of Abraham and Isaac to the mountain where the latter was to be sacrificed: 'Wudu bær sunu, / fæder fyr and sweord' (2887b–8a). This particular example provides a striking illustration of a difficulty which

[1] *The Metre of 'Beowulf'* (Oxford, 1962), pp. 123–7.
[2] 'Some Syntactical Problems in *The Wanderer*', NM 69 (1968), 190–1.
[3] This conclusion was reached simultaneously and independently by Dunning and Bliss (*The Wanderer*, pp. 21–3) and by Peter Clemoes, '*Mens absentia cogitans* in *The Seafarer* and *The Wanderer*', *Medieval Literature and Civilization: Studies in Memory of G. N. Garmonsway*, ed. D. A. Pearsall and R. A. Waldron (London, 1969), pp. 74–5.

dogs the student of Old English syntax and indeed literature. One can readily see that Anglo-Saxon hearers used to the word order Object–Verb–Subject, alive to variations of intonation, and familiar with the book of Genesis, would have had no doubt that *wudu* was the object of *bær*. A few ignoramuses may have missed the point, and very likely, at the other extreme, there were a few theologically trained hearers (or perhaps more likely readers) on the alert for subtle implications who would have relished the ambiguity detected by R. P. Creed:

Wudu, placed first for purposes of alliteration, is generally and correctly translated as an accusative. But it can also be translated – or rather, *heard* momentarily in Old English – as a nominative. The case of *sunu* is similarly ambiguous. The verse, then, can be caught both ways: 'son bore wood' and 'wood bore son'; or 'the Son bore the Cross', and 'the Cross bore the Son'. In this remarkable punning line the offering of Isaac not only prefigures the crucifixion of Christ, it sharply figures – images – the later drama of Christianity. Isaac becomes the Son sacrificed in order to mediate between man and God.[1]

What we must not assume is that such a reading was intended by the poet. Alliteration (as Creed says) and rhetorical chiasmus would be enough to account for the word order Object–Verb–Subject. But it would be hazardous indeed to claim that no Anglo-Saxon ever read the passage in the way Creed does. We have no native informants for Old English. This is difficulty enough. We make things even worse by tacitly assuming that there was one standard 'mann on þæm Cloppames wæne' who represents all Anglo-Saxons of all periods. Such assumptions seem to me implicit in remarks about the effect of a certain word or phrase on 'the audience of the poem' and in the two titles quoted above.

Difficulties can arise even in the realm of inflexions, where we might think that the generalizations were fairly firmly established. The intractable riddle of *hryre* in *The Wanderer* 7b

> Swa cwæð eardstapa,   earfeþa gemyndig,
> wraþra wælsleahta,   winemæga hryre (6–7)

is one. The adjective *gemyndig* can take the dative, e.g. 'gif we gemyndige beoð Cristes bebodum',[2] as well as the genitive. But the genitives which precede *winemæga hryre* in the passage from *The Wanderer* seem to rule out the possibility (suggested in the Bosworth–Toller *Supplement, s.v. gemyndig* IV (1) (b)) of taking it as a dative on *gemyndig*. We must agree with Dunning and Bliss that Old English idiom is against the simple emendation to genitive

---

[1] 'The Art of the Singer: Three Old English Tellings of the Offering of Isaac', *Old English Poetry: Fifteen Essays*, ed. R. P. Creed (Providence, R.I., 1967), p. 80.

[2] *The Homilies of the Anglo-Saxon Church: the First Part Containing the Sermones Catholici or Homilies of Ælfric*, ed. Benjamin Thorpe, 2 vols. (London, 1844–6) (cited henceforth as 'Thorpe') I, 312, line 34.

plural *hryra* – the distributive singular seen in 'æfter deofla hryre' (*Beowulf* 1680a) is the norm – and that to emend to *hryres* is too violent.[1] Their unwillingness to take *hryre* as accusative after *cwæð* is understandable. Examples like '...lofsang cweðan', 'Drihten cwæþ word' and '...of ðam welerum ðe wom cweðen' – all cited by Bosworth–Toller, *s.v. cweðan* I – offer indifferent support for *cweðan hryre*, 'to speak the fall', because the accusatives describe what is uttered – words, a song, or the like – and not the topic or theme of the utterance. The closest parallel is perhaps Ælfric's *Arrius se gedwola cwæþ gemot ongean ðone bisceop*,[2] 'Arrius proclaimed a synod' (again from Bosworth–Toller). But it smacks of Latin influence. Dunning and Bliss accept as 'the most plausible explanation'[3] Miss Kershaw's notion that '*hryre* can hardly be taken otherwise than as a loose causal or comitative dative',[4] and offer the translation ' "remembering the fierce battles accompanying the deaths of his kinsmen", i.e. "the fierce battles in which his kinsmen died" '. I should like some evidence for the proposition that it can be so taken. However, the mention by Dunning and Bliss of the 'possibility...of taking both *hrusan* for *hruse* in [*The Wanderer*] line 23 and *hruse* for *hrusan* in line 102, as examples of the levelling of endings in late Old English'[5] provides a speculative foundation for further speculation. If such confusion between -*e* and -*an* is possible in the weak feminine noun *hruse*, is it possible that the strong masculine noun *hryre* acquired analogical weak forms in the oblique cases and that *hryre* is in fact a levelled form of an aberrant genitive singular *hryran*?

Those whose immediate reaction is to utter a snort of disbelief are invited to consider the various forms recorded in Bosworth–Toller and A. Campbell's *Old English Grammar* for words like *ewe* and *wange*, to remember that the masculine forms *sunna* and *mona* exist alongside the feminine *sunne* and *mone*, and to note that Bosworth–Toller distinguishes the words *will, well, wyll,-es* (masc.); *wille,-an* (fem.); and *willa,-an* (masc.). To this last group J. E. Cross rightly adds the proviso 'if these distinctions are valid'.[6] But even if we reject them, the confusion of forms remains real. Of course, if we took literally the surprisingly suspicious remark made by Klaeber that 'lack of concord as shown in the interchange of cases...should cause no surprise or suspicion',[7] the problem would disappear. So too would much else.

---

1 *The Wanderer*, p. 106.
2 Thorpe I, 290, line 12.
3 *The Wanderer*, p. 106.
4 *Anglo-Saxon and Norse Poems*, ed. N. Kershaw (Cambridge, 1922), p. 162.
5 *The Wanderer*, p. 108.
6 'The Metrical Epilogue to the Old English Version of Gregory's *Cura Pastoralis*', NM 70 (1969), 382, n. 4.
7 *Beowulf and the Fight at Finnsburg*, ed. Fr. Klaeber, 3rd ed. (Boston, 1936), p. xciii.

No matter how we solve it, we must agree that *hryre* is a real difficulty. But there are times when failure to apply a simple and obvious generalization leads to the creation of a pseudo-problem. This, I believe, is the case with *bræc* in *Beowulf* 1511b

> ac hine wundra þæs fela
> swencte on sunde,   sædeor monig
> hildetuxum   heresyrcan bræc,
> ehton aglæcan (1509b–12a)

and with *wehte* in *Beowulf* 2854a

> He gewergad sæt,
> feðecempa   frean eaxlum neah,
> wehte hyne wætre;   him wiht ne speow (2852b–4),

in both of which Klaeber detects an 'imperfective' use, translating *bræc* as 'was in the act of breaking', 'tried to pierce' and *wehte* as 'tried to rouse'.[1] These man-made difficulties, arising as they do from unwillingness to accept the linguistic facts, demonstrate the soundness of Zandvoort's observation that 'the attempt to transfer the category of "aspect" from Slavonic to Germanic, and from there to Modern English grammar, strikes one as an instance of misplaced ingenuity'.[2] Klaeber's suggestions embody not only the transfer of the notion of 'aspect' to Old English but also a violent extension of the idea of 'imperfective' as opposed to 'perfective' so that it embraces 'non-perfection' in the sense of failure. But they need not be accepted. There is no real reason why *bræc* should not be translated 'broke' or 'pierced' – the objections are those of a modern scholar who, having swallowed the idea that Beowulf could descend for *hwil dæges* without a snorkel outfit,[3] cavils at the suggestion that the sea-monsters' tusks achieved what the fingers of Grendel's dam could not – while in *wehte . . . speow* 'rousing him with water, but without success', it is clear that *wehte* cannot mean 'succeeded in rousing', and unnecessary to think that it ought to; compare the Modern English sentence 'He gave him the kiss of life, but without success.' In the first instance we can do with a less shrill demand for literal consistency, in the second with deeper consideration of the semantic fields of *weccan*.

Whatever the obstacles, however, we neglect the search for sound

[1] *Ibid.* pp. 186 and 221.
[2] R. W. Zandvoort, 'Is Aspect an English Verbal Category?', *Contributions to English Syntax and Philology*, ed. F. Behre, Gothenburg Stud. in Eng. 14 (1962), 19.
[3] I must now say (June 1974) that I am convinced by F. C. Robinson's defence of S. O. Andrew's explanation of *hwil dæges* in *Beowulf* 1495b as 'daytime'; see *Old English Studies in Honour of John C. Pope*, ed. Robert B. Burlin and Edward B. Irving, Jr (Toronto, 1974), pp. 121–4. But this does not affect my point; as Robinson rightly says, most critics have explained *hwil dæges* as either 'the space of a day' or 'the large part of a day'.

generalizations at our peril. Let me illustrate this from two past tense verb forms – *Ongunnon* and *Het* in *The Wife's Lament* 11a and 15a:

> Ærest min hlaford gewat   heonan of leodum
> ofer yþa gelac;   hæfde ic uhtceare
> hwær min leodfruma   londes wære.
> Ða ic me feran gewat   folgað secan,
> wineleas wræcca,   for minre weaþearfe.
> Ongunnon þæt þæs monnes   magas hycgan
> þurh dyrne geþoht,   þæt hy todælden unc,
> þæt wit gewidost   in woruldrice
> lifdon laðlicost,   ond mec longade.
> Het mec hlaford min,   herheard niman,
> ahte ic leofra lyt   on þissum londstede,
> holdra freonda.   Forþon is min hyge geomor,
> ða ic me ful gemæcne   monnan funde,
> heardsæligne,   hygegeomorne,
> mod miþendne,   morþor hycgendne. (6–20)

Both have been explained as pluperfects. Here we must ask: what general statements can be made about the use of a simple past tense to express a pluperfect sense?

The standard comment on this problem is typified by the laconic observation in my own *Guide to Old English*: 'The preterite indicative is used...for the pluperfect, e.g. *sona swa hie comon* "as soon as they had come" and (with a strengthening *ær*) *and his swura wæs gehalod þe ær wæs forslægen*.'[1] There are similar remarks by P. S. Ardern,[2] N. Davis,[3] and R. Quirk and C. L. Wrenn.[4] All the examples of a past tense without *ær* as a pluperfect which are given by these writers and by F. Th. Visser[5] are in subordinate clauses, where (as Quirk and Wrenn point out) 'the pluperfect time-relation is often implicit by reason of the type of clause'.

On the strength of these observations or others like them, readers of Old English poetry (including myself) have in the past been willing – sometimes indeed eager – to accept that any Old English past tense can be taken as the equivalent of a Modern English pluperfect in any kind of clause whenever it suits a reader's interpretation of the passage in question. So it is perhaps not surprising that I was comparatively unmoved when I first read the following statement by Douglas D. Short:

With its sophisticated system of verbal phrases, Modern English can accommodate elaborate inversions of chronology without confusing a listener, but Old English

---

[1] 2nd ed. (Oxford, 1968), §197.
[2] *First Readings in Old English* (Wellington, 1948), §40.
[3] *Sweet's Anglo-Saxon Primer*, 9th ed. (Oxford, 1953), §92.
[4] *An Old English Grammar*, 2nd ed. (London, 1958), §127.
[5] *An Historical Syntax of the English Language* II (Leiden, 1966), §808.

had to function with a far simpler system and therefore was not nearly so flexible a language in indicating time relationships. The pluperfect time relation was usually expressed in Old English by the use of the preterit of *habban* with the past participle of transitive verbs and the preterit of *wesan* with the past participle of intransitive verbs, although as the language developed *habban* gradually began to be used with intransitive verbs as well. Occasionally, in certain adverbial clauses where the adverb actually indicates the time relationship, a simple preterit can have a pluperfect sense. Similarly, in a non-adverbial dependent clause in which the action clearly precedes the action of the independent clause, a preterit alone has the force of a pluperfect. However, in line 11 of *The Wife's Lament* none of these conditions exists.[1]

After giving this what seemed to me at the time proper consideration, I still had the feeling that *Ongunnon* in *The Wife's Lament* 11a could be taken as a pluperfect; the examples in subordinate clauses already mentioned and the fact that the periphrasis with *wæs/hæfde* was not completely established in Old English provided, I felt, a *prima facie* case for this view. But I am now beginning to realize that I failed to appreciate both the acuteness and the importance of Mr Short's remarks. For, when recently (November 1972) pressed by a pupil to agree that this *Ongunnon* could indeed imply – as Pei and Gaynor have it in *A Dictionary of Linguistics* (New York, 1954) – that 'the action was completed by the time another action occurred', I came out with the old platitudes and the answer 'yes'. But, as I walked home, I pondered: 'Did I have any indisputable parallels?' I did not. So my search began.

There is no doubt that the Old English past tense can be used where today we would or could use a *perfect*. Often an adverb makes this time reference clear, e.g. *nu* in *Beowulf* 1337b–9a[2] and *ær* in *Beowulf* 655–7. But there are numerous examples with no adverbs both in principal clauses, e.g. *Beowulf* 38 and 247b–8, and in subordinate clauses, e.g. *Beowulf* 426b–30 and 442–5a. But the undoubted existence of examples without an adverb in which a past tense expresses what we may take as a perfect relationship cannot be used as an argument for the unrestricted use of the past tense as the equivalent of a pluperfect.[3]

I have two reasons for this statement. First, the distinction between the past tense implying that an action is completed and the perfect implying that the state resulting from an action still continues seems not to have been felt by the Anglo-Saxons as fully as it is today; compare *Beowulf* 1–3 with *Beowulf* 443–4, and the verb in the *nu* clause in *Genesis B* 730b–31a

[1] 'The Old English *Wife's Lament*: an Interpretation', *NM* 71 (1970), 588–9.
[2] To economize in space I give only the line references to the numerous illustrative passages from *Beowulf* which follow. So those accompanying me further will need a copy of the text. I ask their indulgence.
[3] On the use of a past indicative to refer to a future perfect, as in *The Ruin* 9, see my 'Some Problems of Mood and Tense in Old English', *Neophilologus* 49 (1965), 44–6.

> Him is unhyldo
> Waldendes witod,   nu hie wordcwyde his,
> lare forleton (729b–31a)

with that in *Genesis B* 836b–7a

> Nis me on worulde niod
> æniges þegnscipes,   nu ic mines þeodnes hafa
> hyldo forworhte,   þæt ic hie habban ne mæg (835b–7),

and note that Ælfric gives the following glosses in his *Grammar:* 'PRAE-TERITVM TEMPVS ys forðgewiten tid: *steti* ic stod'[1] and

ac swa ðeah wise lareowas todældon þone PRAETERITVM TEMPVS, þæt is, ðone forðgewitenan timan, on þreo: on PRAETERITVM INPERFECTVM, þæt is unfulfremed forðgewiten, swilce þæt ðing beo ongunnen and ne beo fuldon: *stabam* ic stod. PRAETERITVM PERFECTVM ys forðgewiten fulfremed: *steti* ic stod fullice. PRAE-TERITVM PLVSQVAMPERFECTVM is forðgewiten mare, þonne fulfremed, forðan ðe hit wæs gefyrn gedon: *steteram* ic stod gefyrn. forði is se forðgewitena tima on ðreo todæled, forðan ðe naht ne byð swa gemyndelic on gecynde, swa þæt ys, þæt gedon byð.[2]

I shall discuss the pluperfect gloss later. But let us note that, when glossing the perfect *steti*, Ælfric does not use a periphrasis with *wesan/habban* – which he does use in his homilies – and that, when he writes *ic stod fullice* for the perfect, he is using a pedagogic formula which, as far as I know, occurs nowhere else in Old English. My second reason is that no displacement in time of the events described is involved by taking a past tense as a perfect. The usual translation of *Næfre ic...geseah* in *Beowulf* 247b is 'I have never seen...', but 'I never saw...' is (almost) equally acceptable and its adoption has no effect on meaning or time sequence.

What limitations, then, are there on the use of the Old English past tense as a pluperfect? There is no doubt that the simple past tense can have a pluperfect sense in the situations outlined by Short in the passage already quoted. However, I would augment these undisputed categories and state the position thus. (My main concern at the moment is with the poetry, so my examples are taken from *Beowulf*. But I have the impression that what I set out below applies to the prose too.)

The past tense may serve as a pluperfect in:

(i) a principal clause when the time relationship is expressed by an adverb, e.g. 1612–16a, or by another clause, e.g. 262–5a, or by a *habban* periphrasis in a parallel sentence, e.g. 828b–31a;

(ii) in an *ac* clause, either without an adverb, e.g. 2826b–9, or with one, e.g. 2971–3;

---

[1] *Ælfrics Grammatik und Glossar*, ed. Julius Zupitza (repr. Berlin, 1966), p. 123, lines 15–16.
[2] *Ibid.* p. 124, lines 1–11.

(iii) in a parenthesis, either without an adverb, e.g. 53–7a, or with one, e.g. 898–902a;

(iv) in an adverb clause of time, e.g. 115–16a, 138–42a, and 716b–17;

(v) in other types of subordinate clauses, either without an adverb, e.g. 142b–3, 841b–6, 1333b–7a and 1397–8, or with one, e.g. 756b–7, 1355b–7a, 1465–7a and 1618–19;

(vi) in a conditional clause, where a past subjunctive may express impossibility in the past, e.g. 963–6 and 1550–3a.

The category missing is the principal clause with a simple past tense which occurs in a sequence of such clauses with no specific indication of a change in the time relationship, the category to which, if pluperfect, *Ongunnon* and *Het* in *The Wife's Lament* 11a and 15a would belong. Is it possible for us to decide whether such isolated forms can be taken as pluperfect or, in other words, whether such forms can disrupt the obvious time sequence without any contextual or grammatical hint?

Let us here reconsider the statement by Mr Short quoted above. Two points arise. First, it seems possible that for certain clauses at least (for example, those introduced by *siþþan*) the adverb 'occasionally' can be replaced by 'often' and perhaps even by 'regularly'. Second, we may note the ambiguity of the word 'usually'. Does this mean that the only exceptions are those specified in the sentences beginning 'Occasionally' and 'Similarly'? Or does it mask the old fallacy that 'because something is rare, this cannot be an example'?[1] Mr Short has clearly done us a service by showing that we have too easily taken for granted the proposition that one simple past tense in a series of past tenses can – with no immediate contextual or grammatical hint – interrupt the narrative flow by referring further back in time. He has not, however, succeeded in demonstrating that we are wrong to do so.

It may be difficult for us – lacking as we do intonation patterns and native informants – to make such a demonstration. Indeed Visser shows clearly that there is a difference of opinion about how the past tense and the pluperfect are used in Modern English.[2] But two questions can be asked. First, exactly how widespread is the use of the *habban* periphrasis for the pluperfect? Second, are there any examples in which the wider context of a poem demonstrates that the simple past tense can be used as a pluperfect in a principal clause without any immediate contextual hint? I hope it will not be taken as an indication of idleness or lack of interest if I confess that I have not the time at present to re-read the Old English corpus with a view to

---

[1] I have drawn attention to two specific examples of this fallacy in operation in the sphere of Old English syntax in 'Two Syntactical Notes on *Beowulf*', *Neophilologus* 52 (1968), 297, and 'The Narrator of *The Wife's Lament*', *NM* 73 (1972), 224, n. 4.

[2] *An Historical Syntax* II, §810.

answering these questions fully. I have already confessed to neglecting them in the past. But I can assay tentative answers.

As to the first, the *Beowulf* poet uses the periphrasis with *hæfde/hæfdon* thirty-three times. Twice, at 202–9 and 1292–5, it can be taken as the equivalent of a past tense because it does not seem to denote a break in the time sequence (though I would not press the point in either example).[1] That it is sometimes used *metri causa* is suggested first by 3074–5 and 3164b–5, where it is reinforced by *ær*, and second by 2103b–4, where the periphrasis and the past tense are used in parallel clauses, both with a pluperfect reference.

Analysis of the thirty-three examples shows that (*mutatis mutandis*) the periphrasis appears in *Beowulf* in the six situations described above in which the past tense functions as a pluperfect – with the exception of (iii). Examples follow. Only two – both of them in category (v) subordinate clauses – have *ær*. It is important to note that in category (i) principal clauses, none of the periphrases is accompanied by *ær*.

(i) In principal clauses the periphrasis *alone* denotes a change in time sequence. Good examples are 665b–7a and 893–5a.

(ii) So also in *ac* clauses, e.g. 691–6a. The periphrasis also occurs after *ond* in 2706–8a and after *nealles* in 2144–6a.

(iii) The absence from *Beowulf* of examples in this category is the result of chance. The nearest example is 2401–5, where the *hæfde* clause is semi-subordinate rather than semi-parenthetical.

(iv) We find the periphrasis in adverb clauses of time in 106–7a and 219–20.

(v) It occurs in other subordinate clauses in 116b–17, 1598b–9 and (with *ær*) in 3074–5 and 3164b–5.

(vi) It expresses impossibility in the past in 1550–3a.

For the convenience of any reader who wishes to pursue the matter, I list below all the examples of the periphrasis in *Beowulf*.[2]

But the fact that in principal clauses the simple past tense has a pluperfect reference only when this is made clear by a grammatical or contextual hint, whereas the *hæfde* periphrasis needs no such hint, emphasizes the obvious fact that the Old English past tense was not a direct equivalent of what we think of as a pluperfect. This is confirmed by Ælfric's use of *ic stod gefyrn* – not *ic stod* – for *steteram*.[3] A comparison of this gloss with *Widewe wæs ðeos Anna, þe we gefyrn ær embe spræcon*,[4] where a past tense + *gefyrn ær* has a past

[1] We may note here Davis's observation (*Sweet's Primer*, §92) that 'even the form with *hæfde* sometimes has the sense of a simple past'.

[2] (i) In principal clauses (15): 205, 665, 743, 825, 828, 883, 893, 1294, 2321, 2333, 2381, 2397, 2844, 2952 and 3046; (ii) in *ac* clauses (2): 694 and 804; in an *ond* clause (1): 2707; after *nealles* (1): 2145; (iii) in parenthesis (1): ?2403; (iv) in adverb clauses of time (6): 106, 220, 1472, 2104, 2630 and 3147; (v) in other subordinate clauses (6): 117, 1599, 2301, 2726, 3074 and 3165; (vi) expressing impossibility in the past (1): 1550. Total 33.

[3] *Ælfrics Grammatik*, ed. Zupitza, p. 124, line 9.　　　　[4] Thorpe I, 148, line 10.

or perfect – not pluperfect – reference, suggests that the phrase *ic stod gefyrn* was a pedagogic device rather than an idiomatic equivalent of *steteram.* That Ælfric did not use a periphrasis *ic wæs/hæfde gestanden* to explain *steteram* supports the proposition already advanced that even the periphrasis itself was not specifically pluperfect, though it could serve alone to indicate a change in time sequence just as the pluperfect does. (The Old English periphrasis is, I believe, of native origin and not the result of Latin constructions like *urbem captam habet.*[1] So it does not seem to me arguable that Ælfric avoided the Old English periphrasis in the *Grammar* because he thought of it as the equivalent of the Latin one – which he does not mention.) One is driven to the scarcely surprising conclusion that there was in Old English no perfect or pluperfect in the sense in which modern grammarians understand the terms and that the Old English past tense alone is unlikely to convey a pluperfect time reference.

I turn now to the second question: are there any examples in which the wider context of a poem – here *Beowulf* – demonstrates that the simple past tense can be used as a pluperfect in a principal clause without an immediate contextual hint? To answer this we have to fall back on individual examples. But the dangers involved for a modern reader in the analysis of particular examples can be demonstrated by considering two selected at random. 'Hwær cwom mearg?' (*The Wanderer* 92a) is usually translated 'Where has the horse gone?' But this (as I have suggested above) may be a concept not always present to the Anglo-Saxon mind. Why not 'Where did the horse go?' The *Exodus* poet's epitaph on the Egyptians drowned in the Red Sea is 'Hie wið God wunnon!' (515b). This could be translated 'They had contended against God.' But since their contending ended when they died 'they contended' – or even 'were contending' – 'against God [at the moment of their death]' cannot be ruled out. We must however attempt what may be impossible.

My rapid re-reading of *Beowulf* produced no convincing examples of principal clauses in which a past tense conveyed a pluperfect time reference with no immediate hint. What seemed to me the five most likely ones all proved illusory. In 12–16a and 415–21a a subordinate clause certifies the time reference of *ongeat* and *ofersawon.* In 2117b–20a the *fornam* clause is a parenthetic explanation for the actions of Grendel's dam and belongs, I think, in category (iii). In 884b–9 we may take *wiges heard* as referring to Sigemund or – by interpreting *æþelinges bearn* as 'the son of Sigemund' – to Sigurðr-Sigfrit. But whichever we do, *geneðde* takes its time reference from *acwealde,* a pluperfect equivalent after *syþðan*; see category (iv). A fifth example is

---

[1] The evidence which leads me to this belief is based on a long and complicated argument which is intended to form part of my *Old English Syntax,* now in progress.

1584b–8a, which contains (it is said) the only instance in Old English poetry of *to ðæs þe* meaning 'to the point where, whither' not preceded by a verb of motion. This has caused editors some concern; Dobbie indeed is 'tempted to believe that some of the text, containing a verb of motion, has been lost before 1585b'. This is quite unnecessary. Beowulf did not conduct his fight against Grendel from an armchair. We can take *forgeald* as pluperfect, *to ðæs þe* as 'to the extent that, so that', and translate – as Wrenn and Clark Hall have it – 'He, wrathful warrior, had given him his reward for that, so that he now saw Grendel lying in his resting-place, worn out with fighting, destitute of life, as he had been maimed erewhile in fight at Heorot.' But this does not justify our taking *Ongunnon* or *Het* in *The Wife's Lament* as pluperfect, for the preceding reference to Grendel's raids prepares us for a change in time reference and this is clinched by the *swa* clause in 1587b–8a.

So in the event I was left with no principal clauses in *Beowulf* in which a simple past tense interrupted the time sequence and so functioned as a pluperfect without any immediate grammatical or contextual hint. Is this really so surprising? Why should an Anglo-Saxon poet use a simple past tense in such circumstances rather than a past tense + *ær* or a *wæs/hæfde* periphrasis? Let those who believe that *Ongunnon* or *Het* could be pluperfect produce a Modern English principal clause in which a simple past tense in a sequence of simple past tenses has a pluperfect reference with no grammatical or contextual hint.

It is obvious that more work needs to be done before it can be said that this is the rule in either prose or poetry. And we must, I think, admit the possibility that the poet intended *Ongunnon* or *Het* to be taken as pluperfect by hearers whom he knew, or assumed, to have previous knowledge of a story of two lovers now lost to us, though here too I should like to see a modern example. But I must say that at the moment I have a lot of sympathy with Mr Short's proposition that *Ongunnon* in *The Wife's Lament* 11a cannot be pluperfect. The same applies to *Het* in 15a.

My use of evidence in this discussion demands a comment. The dangers of using material from one poem to *prove* something about another are – or ought to be – obvious. To some Americans ex-President Nixon was hounded out of office by his enemies. Imagine that in a thousand years' time the only surviving account of his resignation was one which took this line. We are in a similar position regarding Byrhtnoth's *ofermod* at the Battle of Maldon, for we have the testimony of only one man – the poet. What he says may give a distorted picture and seems uncertain evidence on which to base a theory about Beowulf's conduct when faced with the menace of the dragon. Yet parallels have been drawn. It is even dangerous to use one passage from a poem in an attempt to *prove* something about another passage from the same

poem, for this involves the assumption that Old English poems were con-
ducted on the lines of James Joyce's *Ulysses*. It is clear that this is not true
of *Beowulf* at any rate. It is difficult to reconcile the accounts of Beowulf's
youth in 2183ff. and 2428ff.; Hrothgar's claim in 1331ff. that he does not
know where Grendel's dam has gone contrasts strangely with his remark in
1357ff. that she and Grendel dwell in the haunted mere and with what seems
to me the suggestion in 1377ff. that Beowulf will be able to find her there;
and the statement at 2777ff. that Beowulf's sword had wounded the
dragon is contradicted in 2904ff., where the poet says that Beowulf could not
inflict any wound on the monster with a sword. Finally, I must admit that
I remain dubious about the validity of the time-honoured method of using
material from the prose homilists to *prove* that a passage in the poetry must
have Christian overtones when specific Christian references are lacking.

I would argue, however, that these instances concern literary matters and
that linguistic facts are different in kind. *Beowulf* may not belong to the same
period as *The Wife's Lament*. Ælfric almost certainly does not. Yet each offers
evidence about the Old English language at a particular time. There are no
examples in which the simple past tense expresses a pluperfect sense without
any contextual feature to make that sense explicit in *Beowulf*, in Ælfric, or
(as far as I know) in the earlier prose or in the later poetry. The idea that
there could be runs contrary to English usage of all periods. It seems to me
reasonable to regard it as a strong linguistic probability, to put it no higher,
that such a usage is not and never has been English. None the less, we must
bear in mind the point already made: that, while there are no examples to
support the notion that *Ongunnon* and *Het* could have a pluperfect sense, the
possibility exists that there was contextual evidence in a background story
known to the original audience but now lost.

The absence of any firm examples will not deter those who are willing to
tread the slippery path down which Dunning and Bliss have already taken
a tentative step, and down which Greenfield beckons us to follow,[1] towards
the proposition that there are times when 'literary considerations must
outweigh linguistic arguments'. There are times when a refusal to be so
deterred is justified. There are others when it is not.

Dame Helen Gardner's handling of an Old English phrase in her superb
translation of *The Dream of the Rood* provides us with a useful case in point.
In the course of her commentary she writes:

The word 'alone' occurs at the close (line 126) referring to the dreamer and the
litotes 'with a small company', meaning 'with nobody', or 'alone', is used of
Christ in the tomb (line 72). For this reason I have accepted the reading of the
runic inscription on the Ruthwell Cross in place of the reading of the manuscript

---

[1] See *The Wanderer*, pp. 112–13 and *Interpretation*, pp. 118–19.

[*to þam æðelinge*] at line 61 [= OE line 58], though it has been argued that there is no parallel for its syntax in extant Anglo-Saxon poetry.[1]

I think Dame Helen slightly mis-states the nature of the problem. It is true that there is no parallel in the poetry for the Ruthwell Cross's *æþþilæ til anum*. But M. Rissanen quotes sufficient parallels in the prose to make it (I should say) obligatory for us to agree that the *reading* is possible (though not necessarily preferable to that of the manuscript). The point is one of *meaning*. Rissanen carries conviction when he asserts that in view of the examples he quotes '– and in view of the total lack of such instances where *an* would be used as an exclusive pronoun "a solitary person" – it seems that *til anum* in *Ruthwell Cross* III 3 means "together", "to the same place", rather than "to the solitary one"'.[2] Yet, while the linguistic facts are on his side, Dame Helen could attempt to justify her translation by arguing either that poets sometimes use irregular syntax or that this happens to be the only surviving example of a construction which later became more common in the sense 'to a lone one'. But this is not really necessary. The fact that 'noble ones came together' could be said to emphasize by contrast the loneliness and aloneness of Christ on the cross. There is no contradiction here between literary considerations and linguistic facts. What Dame Helen has done is to emphasize her literary interpretation at the expense of literal translation when she renders *hweþræ þer fusæ fearran kwomu | æþþilæ til anum* by 'yet warriors from afar eagerly came speeding / to where he hung alone'. Here we can almost have our cake and eat it.

The problem which faces us when we turn to the passage which prompted Dunning and Bliss's remarks, *The Wanderer* 41–4, is quite different. At the end of my 1968 note on *swa* in *The Wanderer* 43,[3] I said that 'although I have no objection to admitting *hapax* usages when necessary, I do not feel that I need accept "as when" for *swa* in *The Wanderer* 43, despite the fact that it gives excellent sense'. Dunning and Bliss agree that their interpretation involves the acceptance of an assumption suggested by Leslie.[4] It is not immediately apparent to me why this assumption is so much less objectionable than some of those I suggested. But the important point is that, if we translate *swa* 'as when', we allow literary considerations to do impossible violence to linguistic facts. If this were a plausible use of *swa* and it were by chance that we have no examples of it (as Greenfield seems to imply in the passage I quote below), then we could accept it. But the notion that *swa* could mean 'as when' runs contrary to the whole pattern of English con-

[1] *Essays and Poems presented to Lord David Cecil*, ed. W. W. Robson (London, 1970), p. 33. The line numbers are those of Dame Helen's translation.
[2] 'Old English *þæt an*, "only"', *NM* 68 (1967), 286.
[3] 'Some Syntactical Problems', pp. 182–7.
[4] *The Wanderer*, ed. R. F. Leslie (Manchester, 1966), p. 74.

junctions at all periods of the language. The only single-word conjunction which has a composite meaning in Old English is admittedly *swa* – in the sense 'as if'. But I think I have shown in the note referred to that this is merely a convenient translation for an extended use of *swa*, 'as', in a comparative clause with a subjunctive expressing hypothesis, and that it provides no justification for *swa*, 'as when'. I do not believe that *swa* could have that double meaning.

In my opinion, we have here modern critics deliberately and unnecessarily flying in the face of linguistic probability because they like their interpretation better than any of those which the syntax suggests the Old English poet actually meant. Is there not a danger that, if this attitude spreads and is adopted by less reputable and sensitive scholars, it will harden into a form of impertinent (if not arrogant) sentimentality in which anything goes?

Greenfield does not seem to think so:

It might be well to emphasize here that, the corpus of the poetry and prose being relatively small in size, textual and analytical critics are often glad to find even *one* parallel syntactic or semantic instance to support their interpretation, let alone a 'norm'! Going further, we may note that statistically there is very little difference between one example and none. Thus Bliss–Dunning, after presenting and rejecting the various extant meanings Bruce Mitchell has ferreted out [!] for the conjunction *swa* in connection with lines 41ff. –

> þinceð him on mode   þæt he his mondryhten
> clyppe ond cysse   ond on cneo lecge
> honda ond heafod   *swa* he hwilum ær
> in geardagum   giefstolas breac

(it appears to his mind that he embraces and kisses his liege-lord, and lays hands and head on his knee *swa* he enjoyed favours from the throne formerly in bygone days) –

can properly say that though usage of *swa* meaning 'as when' here 'would be unique', but 'literary considerations must outweigh linguistic arguments' (pp. 112–13). In advancing this proposition, Bliss–Dunning are making an important point about the relation between textual, syntactic and literary concerns which bring us, in a way, back to the historical versus present meaning considerations raised in the first chapter. This is a point they make on several occasions, including the emendation to the singular *goldwine minne* in line 22, rather than accepting the syntactically possible MS. plural:

a decision must be made on literary rather than linguistic grounds. In line 22 the emendation to *minne* (a plausible emendation, since the scribe has made mistakes involving *n* in lines 14, 59, 89, and 102) seems desirable in the light of the meaning of the following line; though the wanderer may have lost more than one lord, he is not likely to have buried more than one (p. 108).[1]

Two points must be made here. First, the choice between the manuscript reading *goldwine mine* and the emendation *goldwine minne* in 22b

> siþþan geara iu   goldwine min[n]e
> hrusan heolstre biwrah,   ond ic hean þonan
> wod wintercearig   ofer waþema gebind... (22–4)

is, as Greenfield acknowledges, a choice between two syntactical possibilities. It is not a question of literary considerations outweighing linguistic 'arguments' here. It is merely a matter of allowing literary considerations to decide in favour of one syntactic possibility against another. The decision cannot be made on linguistic grounds. But taking *swa* to mean 'as when' is an entirely different kettle of fish. It means preferring a syntactical *impossibility* to several syntactical *possibilities* or indeed to several syntactical *certainties*.

As my second point will show, I do not use the word 'impossibility' lightly. I am not a statistical expert. My own view is that the importance of the difference between one example and none will vary with the circumstances; we may be more inclined to accept an inherently probable nonce-usage than an inherently improbable one. Linguistic expectation must come into it. If I have examples like 'ic mæg beon geclænsod' and 'he mæg beon geclænsod', it is reasonable for me to argue that '*þu miht beon geclænsod' was a living form and its absence is the result of chance. Here, I agree, the difference between no examples and one is not very significant. Indeed, I have already accepted this by saying that the absence of the *hæfde* periphrasis in parentheses in *Beowulf* 'is the result of chance'. At the other extreme, however, there are things which are contrary to the run of the language and to our expectation. *Swa*, 'as when', is, I believe, one. Here the finding of a single example would be decisive.

The importance of this can be illustrated from life. Ohthere and Wulfstan clearly had more justification for believing that they would find different ploughs, ships, garments and customs as they sailed north than for believing that they would find a dragon. Our attitude to the existence of the Loch Ness monster or the Abominable Snowman would be vastly different if we had one example rather than none.

There are, then, varying relationships between a generalization and any particular instance of it. One proposed solution may be the only possible one; for example *gemæcne* in 'ða ic me ful gemæcne monnan funde' (*The Wife's Lament* 18) must be acc. sg. masc.[2] Another may be impossible; for

---

[1] *Interpretation*, pp. 118–19. (Perhaps I may say that the logic of the Dunning–Bliss argument about the unlikelihood of the wanderer burying a second dead lord eludes me.)

[2] See my 'The Narrator', pp. 224–6.

example Conybeare's reading 'ða ic me ful gemæc ne monnan funde' of the same line.[1] In between there is a wide spectrum ranging from 'very likely' through 'possible' to 'very unlikely'. As an example of the 'very likely' I would cite Fred C. Robinson's defence of the manuscript reading *þone* in *Beowulf* 70a;[2] as an example of the 'very unlikely' the pluperfect interpretation of *Ongunnon* and *Het* in *The Wife's Lament* 11a and 15a. For the rest, argument will continue about such matters as the interpretation of *hryre* in *The Wanderer* 7b, the punctuation of *The Wanderer* 37–57 and the exact status of metrical 'rules'. This is as it should be; in Old English studies as in real life there is room for honest difference of opinion. The rôle of linguistic (and other) facts is to delimit this area.

[1] See *ibid.*
[2] 'Two Non-Cruces in *Beowulf*', *Tennessee Stud. in Lit.* 11 (1966), 151–5.

Postscript on 'milde ond monðwære' (above, p. 12)

While this volume was in the press, the article by Mary P. Richards, 'A Reexamination of *Beowulf*, ll. 3180–3182', *ELN* 10 (1973), 163–7, came into my hands. In it the author notes that in *Anglia* 50 (1926), 223–4, Klaeber drew attention to the fact that *milde ond monðwære* is used in the Blickling Homilies of Christ and elsewhere of saints or other good Christians. She interprets the phrase in *Beowulf* as a 'religious formula' and observes that 'the ending of the poem does not reveal a blend of Christian and pagan Germanic ideals. Rather, the poem concludes with the suggestion that Beowulf was as excellent a Christian as possible here on earth.' Obviously this is a possibility, but equally obviously it is not a certainty. (Reference to Mary P. Richards's article and to a short discussion on the same point in 1965 by Rowland L. Collins has now been made in *Old English Newsletter* 8.1 (1975), 35.)

The garments that honour the cross in *The Dream of the Rood*

JAMES SMITH[1]

In lines 14b–15a of *The Dream of the Rood* the cross is said to be honoured by a garment, or garments (*wædum geweorðode*) and in 21b–2a it is said to change (*wendan*) because of or along with or with respect to these garments. What they might be is a question which has racked many brains. The usual opinion at the present day is that they are some kind of cloth trappings.[2] Cook, for instance, was reminded of a streamer which, he said, formed part of the *labarum* (but in so saying he was misled either by memory or by mistranslation, for the only cloth which the *labarum* comprised might, from its size and shape, more properly be called an apron).[3] Ebert proposed silk cords or tassels.[4] Others prefer the veil or pall with which the cross is shrouded on Good Friday, to be dramatically revealed on Easter Sunday.[5] The weakness of all such explanations is that their proponents feel bound not to leave the spot without discovering an explanation: they scrupulously refrain, that is, from looking either backwards or forwards, with the result that, as the reference fails to explain itself, they are compelled to look outside the poem. They fail to take into account repeated references within the poem itself to coverings that, however unexpected and however diverse their materials, all agree in performing, to a greater or lesser degree, the principal office of a garment, that of enveloping the cross: in line 5b it is described as *leohte bewunden*, 'suffused, or wrapped round, with light' and in 16a, and again in 23b and 77, gold is said to 'clothe' it (*gyrwan*), the verb signifying, as it may,

[1] This article has been adapted by Peter Clemoes from part of an unfinished piece among the papers of the late James Smith, Professor of English Language and Literature in the University of Fribourg, Switzerland, by agreement with Professor E. M. Wilson, the literary adviser of the executors. Mr Peter Kitson, of Emmanuel College, Cambridge, has given invaluable help by deciphering the manuscript; Miss Rachel Rogers, of Newnham College, Cambridge, has kindly traced certain references; and Mr Paul Sorrell, of Corpus Christi College, Cambridge, has supplied the reference to Blickling Homily 1 in p. 33, n. 2.
[2] Cf. the discussion in the most recent edition, *The Dream of the Rood*, ed. Michael Swanton (Manchester, 1970), pp. 106–7.
[3] *The Dream of the Rood*, ed. A. S. Cook (Oxford, 1905), p. 17, where Eusebius's description of the *labarum* as including a purple streamer is quoted.
[4] A. Ebert, 'Über das angelsächsische Gedicht: *Der Traum vom heiligen Kreuz*', *Berichte über die Verhandlungen der königlich sächsischen Gesellschaft der Wissenschaften zu Leipzig*, philologisch-historische Klasse 36 (1884), 85.   [5] So Swanton's edition, pp. 106–7.

more than a sporadic embellishment. Nor is it to be overlooked that the first reference to the cross's *wæde* is in the immediate context of its glory: it is *wuldres treow* (14b) that is so clothed.

The 'flooding' of the cross with gold (*begeotan*, 7a) is a striking figure. According to 49a the cross is 'flooded' from the side of the dead Christ; in 48b it is 'drenched' (*eall...bestemed*) with Christ's blood, just as in 22b it is 'drenched' (*bestemed*) with blood – or rather with a 'moisture' (*wætan*) which is glossed in the following line as a flow of blood – that issues from itself. And as in 53a the dead Christ has been 'covered' (*bewrigen*) by clouds, so in 17a jewels have 'covered' (*bewrigene*) the cross. The import of these repetitions is likely to be structural to the poem – one of the parts, that is, which are essential to it as an organism. For the repetitions suggest a system of relations of the kind which idealist philosophers used to call 'internal' and which are as substantial, in a way, as the things they relate: for, as a consequence of their contact, the things themselves undergo a change in substance. In the poem, for example, gold not only liquefies but also, perhaps, liquefies into blood. Conversely, blood perhaps solidifies into gold. In any case, both blood and gold provide a covering for the cross – provide, that is, a garment. And although impenetrable as the darkness covering the saviour at the crucifixion, the garment may be composed, not of darkness, but of light. Here there would seem to be much for meditation. Little, however, for such as Cook, whose consideration of details one by one isolates each of them to such an extent that they are rendered incapable of bearing any save external relations: the second occurrence of *begoten* (49a), for example, he notes as procuring an 'artistic variation' on the first (7a), a variation merely decorative, that is, superficial not substantial, of no structural importance whatever.

Since external relations are accidental they are, when inconvenient, forgotten. A remarkable instance is the lack of importance attached to the *wæde* of 15a as tassels, pall or whatever, when related (20b–1a) to the anguish and fear of the visionary and (22a) to the changes which the cross displays.[1] The advocates of such paraphernalia now emphasize the *bleo* of 22a. Thus they slip from under the ridicule of supposing that a streamer or tassel originates an anguish, but only, at a cost at least equally great, by dissociating *wæde* and *bleo* and by attempting to supply what seems to them desirable denotations for *bleo* taken in isolation, namely the 'colours' of particular crosses that, according to an article by Patch,[2] had gained liturgical prominence by

[1] Cf. John C. Pope's percipient comment (*Seven Old English Poems* (Indianapolis, 1966), p. 65): 'Cook suggested that the *wædum* [of 15a] were some kind of streamers such as those with which processional crosses were decorated, and this seems possible. Yet when *wædum* is repeated at 22, it seems primarily to refer to the contrasted costumes, gold and jewels on the one hand, blood on the other. In that context streamers are either superfluous or positively distracting.'
[2] H. R. Patch, 'Liturgical Influence in *The Dream of the Rood*', *PMLA* 34 (1919), 233–57, esp. 235.

the eighth century – a reddened, presumably wooden, cross that was used during the early weeks of Lent, a 'more ornamental' cross, perhaps of the precious metals, which appeared on Palm Sunday, and a cross of crystal that was carried throughout Paschaltime. These 'colours' the commentators intend to be fed from their notes into the text much as nourishment is fed into a debilitated organism through a surgeon's tube.[1]

Surgical interventions earn gratitude only in so far as they are successful, and these can scarcely be congratulated on success. Whatever the nature of the changes manifested in or by the cross, they are not such as to shock or even surprise the visionary: if they were, his anguish, if only momentarily, would be relieved. He gives no hint of such relief, and it is difficult to believe that some change of mood would not follow the obliteration of a wooden cross by one of metal and of the metallic by a crystal cross. Obliteration would indeed seem an appropriate term for what is supposed to happen: the replacement of one of Patch's crosses by any other must be as sudden as it is total; the replacing cross must instantaneously dislodge and annihilate the one which it replaces. The impression upon an observer cannot be other than, hey presto, that of a transformation. And how are we to reconcile with such a substitution the description of the changing cross as *fus* (21b)?

Yet the meaning 'prompt, willing, eager' – required in 57a – harmonizes admirably in 21b with what, when extraneous features are not allowed to distort our understanding, must be recognized as an intransitive or at most a middle use of *wendan*. No compulsion of any kind is exercised upon the cross, and whatever phenomena the cross exhibits the visionary, and the reader with him, must be content to trace either to no cause or to the cross itself. The second proceeding, which is the more rational, amply justifies the application which is made of *fus*: the cross is prompt because, when human interests summon – interests in the first place of the visionary but also, in and through him, of mankind – it does not hesitate to change. It is willing because it changes, not once, but repeatedly – from bright to dark, from dark to bright again, and so on (*hwilum...*, *hwilum...*, 22b–3). It is so eager as to anticipate change (18–20a).

In these lines the poet propounds a mystery. 'Through the gold', says the visionary, 'I was able to descry an age-old strife of wretched men, that it [the cross] first began to bleed on the right side.' The mystery is the identity of dissimilar states, as a consequence of which they may be seen the one 'through' the other. Because of their dissimilarity, however, the states can be seen in their identity not by the eyes of the body nor even by those of the mind, but by those of faith alone. And such is man's inferiority to the angels

---

[1] Cf. the note in Swanton's edition, p. 111.

that, when he is under instruction, the eyes of faith cannot be completely opened by a single instruction, nor any number of instructions, however endless. With these eyes he never sees all that he might see; he does not always see what he sees sometimes; and occasionally, perhaps, he sees nothing at all. And so he falls back on that which the eyes of the mind and the body may provide. For most men, this is permanently available; nor, if properly controlled, need it impair, rather it must expand and dilate, whatever may be granted to the eyes of faith. From the identity of the states, therefore, the poet turns in the second place, as to something concealed, to their dissimilarity (22b–3). The eyes of the body are fully capable of distinguishing between gold and blood, those of the mind of appreciating the implications of the distinction – only too capable. But, by previously insisting on the ultimate identity of the blood and the gold, the poet has already taken one precaution against the implications overwhelming the reader; and now he takes another by making them continually replace one another. Thus he forestalls a premature satisfaction with the one, a premature despair at the other. Nor does his device operate only by a careful ordering of his ideas, but also by a careful choice of words in which the ideas are expressed. The visionary says that first it seemed that he saw (*Þuhte me þæt ic gesawe*, 4a) and then more boldly that he saw (*Geseah ic*, 14b) the cross in the splendour of light, gold and jewels; likewise (21b) he saw its change from splendour to the squalor of blood. But the identity of splendour and squalor, the squalor 'through' the splendour, this he was no more than 'able to descry' (*ongytan meahte*, 18b).[1]

Lines 14b–23 form part not of a stationary description but of an advancing narrative, an account not so much of something that the visionary discovers, as of his discovery of that something. When he first catches sight of the cross it might, for anything he knows, be an object like any other, save only for outward magnificence. That magnificence for a time monopolizes his attention: the light with which the cross is surrounded, the gold and jewels which radiate light (4–9a). But then he becomes aware (9b–12) of an ecstatic contemplation it commands from whatever exists: from holy spirits, men upon earth, and the august totality of creation. It all therefore must fall outside creation. Nor is the manner of bleeding which the cross manifests (22b–3a) known to nature, for this is so peculiar as, in addition to itself, to

---

[1] I offer 'descry' as the best available translation of *ongytan*, since, unlike 'perceive' and such words, it continues to denote a seeing and not merely a thinking even when contrasted with the verb 'to see' – a seeing which is not achieved without effort and which, however great the effort, is never fully achieved, since the eye remains conscious of falling short of a perfect knowledge of what it sees. Very much the same would seem to be the implication of *ongytan* in 18b, though secured by different, even by opposite means: by stressing not the shortcomings of an organ but the elusiveness of an object of sight. Yet suggestions of organic strain, of obstacles overcome, are contained within the auxiliary *meahte*; and, however slight, should not be neglected.

include an unbleeding (23b). That the cross, thus set apart, is identified with the crucified Christ is shown by its bleeding on its right side (20a).[1]

A cross that is soaked in the blood of the king of heaven and, because of that blood, is so bright that it overcomes all shadows as it stands before mankind at the Day of Judgement is an emblem of grief and shame to the sinful in the Old English poem *Christ III*.[2] But the golden, bleeding cross–Christ beheld by the visionary, 'synnum fah / forwunded mid wommum' (13b–14a), in *The Dream of the Rood* is possessed of, or possessed by, more of the mystery. The passion and the resurrection of Christ are the theological components of this mystery; for a poet's expression of his apprehension of the transcendent blood and gold there is the language of metaphor – more particularly a metaphor, not of the superficial, decorative sort, but elaborated in the earliest ages and cultivated down to the latest to serve for discourse about the glorious blood of Christ. Centuries before the passion, Isaiah foretold it as providing the saviour with a distinctive dress: that of those who trod the winepress (Isaiah LXIII.1–6). For Fortunatus in the sixth century, the blood covering the saviour on the first Good Friday – his bloody semblance, in other words – was 'regis purpura', a royal mantle. In the eighteenth century it still remained a 'crimson robe' for Isaac Watts. And if, on the first Easter Day, the saviour wore neither gold nor jewels, he was invested with the supernatural glory which, to finite apprehensions, gold and jewels serve, however feebly, to represent: as a psalm says of the lord in heaven, he was *amictus lumine sicut vestimento*, 'clothed in light as a garment' (CIV.2). Further, according to the commentary upon Isaiah by Jerome[3] – influenced perhaps by St Paul, of whom more in a moment – Christ's garment of blood and his garment of light, while remaining distinct, are also the same, so that the one can change into the other while still persisting as itself; the one can follow on the other and yet the two co-exist. This is a mystery and, says Jerome, because of their ignorance of the mystery the angels were appalled (*perterriti*) when Christ rose after his passion. For seeing him all bloody, they feared that filth, force, physical and moral ugliness were about to invade heaven. A moment's instruction however sufficed for them to see him as not only bloody but bright, like the beloved in the *Song of Songs*, 'rubicundus in passione, candidus in resurrectione'. Yet not parti-coloured,

---

[1] Cf. the note in Swanton's edition, p. 109.

[2] Lines 1081–9 (*The Exeter Book*, ed. G. P. Krapp and E. van K. Dobbie, The Anglo-Saxon Poetic Records 3 (New York, 1936), 33). Related (though different) imagery is used in Blickling Homily 1; there the cross is the throne of Christ the king and his blood a red jewel which he has given to make us participants in the kingdom of heaven: 'Drihten on middangearde bliðe wunode oþþæt he becom to þæm heahsetle þære rode on þæm upstige eall ure lif he getremede. He sealde his þone readan gim, þæt wæs his þæt halige blod, mid þon he us gedyde dælnimende þæs heofonlican rices; ond þæt geweorþeþ on domes dæge þæt he cymeþ to demenne cwicum ond deadum' (*The Blickling Homilies*, ed. R. Morris, Early Eng. Text Soc. o.s. 58, 63 and 73 (London, 1874–80, repr. 1967), 9–11).   [3] Migne, Patrologia Latina 24, col. 610.

but red in the white and white in the red, and whiter because of the red, the latter importing no prejudice to the former, but enhancing its perfection. 'The blood with which I am spattered', Christ informs the angels, 'does not disfigure but befits me.' Because preluded by the passion, the resurrection increases in glory; the passion shares in the glory and the increase, because it so preludes. According to St Paul, they remain so bound and so indebted to the end of time; for rather than an event, the passion is an aspect of history. Though Christ has risen, he remains as subject to the mockeries of sinners as 1900 years ago: constantly they trample him under foot, repeatedly they crucify him to their own ends. They do so to their confusion, should death or the Last Day overtake them unrepentant; but the blood continually flows, by which their repentance may be bought. The sufficiency of Christ as redeemer; the sacrifice to which nevertheless he deems it proper to submit in order to redeem; his unfailing promptness, willingness, eagerness for the sacrifice of himself – this mystery of acceptance of the Christian religion is given substance by his two garments, always distinct and yet the same.

Surely it is this traditional combination of thought and language that the poet of *The Dream of the Rood* adopts in investing the cross–Christ with garments that change without changing. The 'tree of glory', he says in 14b–15a, is honoured by a garment, and then, in the following line, begins to show its metaphorical quality: a parallel phrase informs the reader that the cross is 'clothed with gold'. It is 'covered in jewels' (16b–17a) and the jewels cover it 'honourably', just as the garment itself (15a) is 'honourable'. It would be difficult for the poet to express himself more clearly – or indeed, more carefully; for, as though to guard against any suspicion that by choice of metaphor he intended the outside to suffer degradation, he inserts (15b) between mentions of the garment and the gold the phrase *wynnum scinan*: the cross 'shines joyfully' in the full sense of the words, shines with things that are the cause of joy and, as such a cause, are the best of their kind. Having taken such measures, the poet may wait with confidence for the inside to reveal itself. It reveals itself as blood; and once revealed, this in turn becomes the outside of the cross. It must therefore rank as a garment; and accordingly, in 22–3, the poet places it alongside the garment of magnificence, dismissing the latter – already extensively described – in a single phrase and summing up its constituents, gold and jewels, in a single word 'treasure'. The squalid garment, on the other hand, is described twice over: it is constituted by a 'drenching with moisture', by a 'swilling with a flow of blood'. No poet has used the metaphor more subtly, more tellingly. It is integral to the partnership between Christ and the cross which is at the heart of the poem. The garment of blood that honours the cross manifests uniquely the truth of the claim:

Hwæt, me þa geweorðode   wuldres ealdor
ofer holtwudu,   heofonrices weard,
swylce swa he his modor eac,   Marian sylfe,
ælmihtig god   for ealle menn
geweorðode   ofer eall wifa cynn. (90–4)

Figural narrative in Cynewulf's *Juliana*

JOSEPH WITTIG

Old English saints' lives, as a group, have not generated a great deal of critical enthusiasm; and Cynewulf's *Juliana* has often been regarded as the worst of a bad lot. One of the poem's recent editors sees in it a 'uniformity verging on monotony' and finds it 'unrelieved by any emotional or rhetorical emphasis or by any other gradations in tone'.[1] While critics concede that all Cynewulf's signed poems have a smooth texture and contain 'fine passages', they regard *Juliana* as something of an embarrassment and generally assign it to the poet's adolescence – or senescence.[2]

In her article on saints' lives in a recent survey of Old English literature, Rosemary Woolf reveals what seems to be the key to this dissatisfaction with *Juliana* and with hagiography in general. While admitting that the saint's life is a highly conventional form, Miss Woolf feels the need to apologize for the 'dissolution' and 'distortion' of history in the genre.[3] Finding hagiography embarrassing as history, the Bollandist Hippolyte Delehaye made fashionable an explanation which saved the intelligence of the hagiographer at the expense of his audience: hagiography is not history, but homiletic literature for the popular mind; by hyperbole, oversimplification and repetition, it drives home basic truths of faith in a way which even the common man could not miss.[4] This attitude explains Miss Woolf's apology for distortion and her conclusion that *Juliana* is 'an uncomfortable mixture of the didactic and the spectacular'.[5] Such judgements reveal a twofold disappointment: *Juliana* offers neither a story which is psychologically credible and interestingly real, nor a history shaped by rational judgement and proportion such as the more sober medieval chroniclers at times produced. The purpose of this essay is to suggest that a critical understanding of the poem can best be achieved by emphasizing, not how it fails as realistic narrative or chronicle, but how it succeeds as something else: in a manner both deliberate and learned, Cynewulf uses biblical, liturgical and homiletic themes in an attempt to

---

[1] *Juliana*, ed. Rosemary Woolf (London, 1955), p. 17.

[2] *Ibid.* p. 19; Theodor Wolpers, *Die englische Heiligenlegende des Mittelalters* (Tübingen, 1964), p. 124; and C. L. Wrenn, *A Study of Old English Literature* (London, 1967), p. 125.

[3] Rosemary Woolf, 'Saints' Lives', *Continuations and Beginnings: Studies in Old English Literature*, ed. E. G. Stanley (London, 1966), pp. 40–5.

[4] Hippolyte Delehaye, *Les Légendes Hagiographiques*, 4th ed. (Brussels, 1955), p. 23; cf. pp. 88–9.

[5] Woolf, 'Saints' Lives', p. 45.

render the passion of the saint *significant*. This is achieved, it is true, without regard for realism, psychological probability or historical accuracy. But the poem's force arises from something other than convincing mimesis – from the connection of Juliana with central and potent Christian events, of which she is the imitator, embodiment and new exemplar.

The best rubric under which to discuss this sort of poetry is 'figural narrative'. Figural thinking, in Erich Auerbach's words, 'establishes a connection between two events or persons, the first of which signifies not only itself but the second, while the second encompasses or fulfills the first.'[1] Although the Christian use of this term originally pertained to the relationship of Old Testament to New (Moses is a *figura* of Christ), Auerbach thinks there is reason for using it in an extended sense; when the mind is called a *figura Trinitatis*, the mind and God are each claimed to be real, distinct from one another, and really related – a way of thinking clearly influenced by neo-Platonic analogism.[2] And there may be more than one *figura* of what is figured just as there may be more than one of what is figured – as the various levels of scriptural interpretation suggest. Thus the crossing of the Red Sea may be taken to refer to the historical event in Hebrew history, the redemption wrought by Christ, the imitation of that event in the church's sacrament of baptism and the individual act of spiritual conversion. All these events were regarded as both actually real and actually related.

In the following pages I will try to show how such a multi-term figural relationship operates in *Juliana* between Christ, the church, the saint and the individual Christian soul. Such a figural reading explains a number of the poem's details which make no literal sense; it grows quite consistently out of the poem's spiritual milieu; and it suggests how a poem which disappoints modern expectations might be understood in terms of the learning and preoccupations of an Old English religious poet.

Critics have noted Cynewulf's 'blackening' of Heliseus and his tendency

---

[1] Erich Auerbach, *Scenes from the Drama of European Literature* (New York, 1959), 'Figura', trans. Ralph Manheim, p. 53.

[2] 'The analogism that reaches into every sphere of medieval thought is closely bound up with the figural structure; in the interpretation of the Trinity that extends roughly from Augustine's *De Trinitate* to St Thomas 1, q. 45, art. 7, man himself, as the image of God, takes on the character of a *figura Trinitatis*' (Auerbach, 'Figura', pp. 61–2). The usefulness of the term *figura* for the following discussion is that it both suggests the scriptural model for comparing Juliana to Christ or his church and reminds one that each member of the relationship, and indeed the relationship itself, was regarded as actual and ontologically valid; cf. Elizabeth Salter, 'Medieval Poetry and the Figural View of Reality', *Proc. of the Brit. Acad.* 54 (1968), 73–92. 'Allegory', on the other hand, often connotes the relationship between a mere fiction and its 'meaning', or suggests the more whimsical varieties of Philonic exegesis. A. C. Charity has recently pointed out that figural validity was also claimed for what is usually called the tropological level (*Events and Their Afterlife* (Cambridge, 1966), pp. 152–3 and *passim*). He has also shown that figural thinking was very much utilized in relating the events of Christian times back to those of the New Testament (*ibid.* pp. 150–2 and *passim*).

to 'concentrate on the great spiritual struggle' between good and evil.[1] Thus it is evident from the poem's very beginning that it is so constructed as to derive impact from something other than realistic story-telling. The opening lines (1–31) make little attempt to portray the concrete or the individual: the events take place in the days of Maximian (2b–3a) and involve 'sum gerefa' (18–19a) and a 'fæmne' (27a), whose names almost incidentally are Heliseus and Juliana.[2] Much more attention is paid to the creation of a general background of pagan persecution (3b–17), while the heroine and her antagonist are so presented as to embody the city of God versus the city of men. Heliseus is immediately portrayed as a creature of Mammon and a worshipper of idols (22–4a), that is, of the devil, as ps. xcv.5 says: 'Quoniam omnes dii gentium dæmonia.'[3] Juliana, on the other hand, is immediately presented as a virgin pledged to the love of Christ (28b–31). This is the same mentality found in Tychonius's canons for the interpretation of scripture, canons used by Augustine in shaping his approach to history, which became commonplace habits of symbolic thinking. One of these rules was 'de domino et eius corpore', according to which scriptural statements were variously understood as applying to Christ or to his body, the church. Another was 'de diabolo et eius corpore'. As Wilhelm Kamlah succinctly phrased it: 'As the church is the body of Christ, so all the evil are the body of the devil.'[4]

The tendency to view Christian life in terms of such an absolute and all-embracing struggle is, of course, founded on the gospels themselves. The very passages in which Christ predicted persecution are either explicitly connected with the ultimate events of the second coming[5] or easily applied to them.[6] When these passages, or selections from the Apocalypse, are chosen to be read at Mass on the feasts of martyrs,[7] one can see evidence of how the

---

[1] Stanley B. Greenfield, *A Critical History of Old English Literature* (New York, 1965), p. 111; Woolf, *Juliana*, p. 15; and Wolpers, *Heiligenlegende*, pp. 122–3.

[2] The text quoted is that of *The Exeter Book*, ed. George Philip Krapp and Elliott Van Kirk Dobbie, The Anglo-Saxon Poetic Records 3 (New York, 1936), 113–33.

[3] Miss Woolf calls attention to this as 'a basic proposition of the saint's life' ('Saints' Lives', p. 41). It is found, e.g., in Ælfric's 'Life of Eugenia' (*Ælfric's Lives of Saints*, ed. Walter W. Skeat, Early Eng. Text Soc. o.s. 76, 82, 94 and 114 (London, 1881–1900; repr. in 2 vols., 1966), I, 26).

[4] Wilhelm Kamlah, *Apokalypse und Geschichtstheologie* (Berlin, 1935), p. 11. For Augustine's formulation of these two Tychonian canons, see *De Doctrina Christiana* III.31 and 37. On the widespread knowledge of the canons, see Kamlah, pp. 10–11.

[5] See, e.g., Matthew xxiv.1–12, Mark xiii.1–13 and Luke xxi.9–19.

[6] E.g., Matthew x.16–22, 26–32 and 34–42; Luke xii.1–8; and John xv.17–25.

[7] The passages cited in the two preceding notes were all gospel pericopes for the common of martyrs. From the Apocalypse, the following passages were pericopes for the first reading: iv.1–7 and 9–12, vi.7–9 and 17 and vii.13–17. Since Juliana's was not a feast with proper pericopes, these had to be selected from those in the *commune sanctorum*. Although Wolpers simply consults the *Missale Romanum* for evidence of ninth-century liturgy (*Heiligenlegende*, pp. 120–1), the *Missale* alone does not seem to be a reliable guide for the period. Cyrille Vogel (*Introduction aux Sources de l'Histoire du Culte Chrétien au Moyen Âge* (Spoleto, 1965), p. 321) points out that

church conceived each individual struggle in terms of the ultimate battle between the two bodies and the value-systems to which they pertain. Juliana, in as much as she is a martyr, is the archetypal Christian who suffers, then vanquishes the devil and the infernal powers which work through Heliseus and his idols.

The same deliberate concern for general significance, as opposed to realism, seems to shape Cynewulf's presentation of Juliana's virginity. This virtue could be considered in other than personal and literal terms, as is attested by the following passage from Ælfric's homily for the common of virgins:

Nis na gewunelic þæt mægðhad si gecweden on sinscipe, ac swa-ðeah ðær is þæs geleafan mægðhad, þe wurðað ænne soðne God, and nele forligerlice to leasum hæðengylde bugan. Eal seo gelaðung, ðe stent on mædenum and on cnapum, on ceorlum and on wifum, eal heo is genamod to anum mædene, swa swa se apostol Paulus cwæð to geleaffullum folce, 'Desponsaui uos uni uiro, uirginem castam exhibere Christo': þæt is on Englisc, 'Ic beweddode eow anum were, þæt ge gearcian an clæne mæden Criste.' Nis ðis na to understandenne lichamlice ac gastlice. Crist is se clæna brydguma, and eal seo cristene gelaðung is his bryd, þurh ða he gestrynð dæghwomlice mennisce sawla to his heofenlican rice. Seo gelaðung is ure modor and clæne mæden, forðan þe we beoð on hire ge-edcynnede to Godes handa, þurh geleafan and fulluht.[1]

'l'uniformité des livres liturgiques est inconnue de l'Église ancienne et de celle du moyen âge' and emphasizes that 'chaque évêque...est libre de créer le formulaire et d'ordonner les lectures'. Thus, while it is agreed that the English liturgy was 'Roman', this ought not be taken to imply modern uniformity. Klaus Gamber ('Die kampanische Lektionsordnung', *Sacris Erudiri* 13 (1962), 326–52) edits the pericopes of the Lindisfarne Gospels type and discusses their relationship to a continental model apparently brought to England by Hadrian, companion to Theodore (see Bede, *Historia Ecclesiastica* IV.1). For related manuscripts see Gamber, *Codices Liturgici Latini Antiquiores* (Freiburg, 1963), nos. 401 and 405–7. The pseudo-Bede homiliary seems to have been based on a lectionary of the Lindisfarne type; see G. Godu, 'Évangiles', *Dictionnaire d'Archéologie Chrétienne et de Liturgie*, ed. F. Cabrol and H. Leclercq, col. 900. The pericopes of Durham, Cathedral Library, A. II. 16 and A. II. 17 are printed by C. H. Turner, *The Oldest Manuscript of the Gospels* (Oxford, 1931), p. 217. Guided chiefly by Vogel's bibliography and by his discussion of the medieval lectionaries, I have consulted editions of epistle and gospel pericopes representing the chief medieval types. Also useful for the pericopes of the *commune* are Walter Howard Frere, *Studies in the Early Roman Liturgy* (Oxford, 1930–5) II and III, and Henri Barré, *Les Homéliaires Carolingiens de l'École d'Auxerre* (Vatican City, 1962), pp. 214–35. The edition of the *Missale Romanum* consulted was the Milan, 1474 (repr. Henry Bradshaw Soc. 17 (London, 1899)).
1 'Maidenhood is not usually spoken of in connection with marriage, but, nevertheless, there is a maidenhood of faith, which worships one true God, and will not adulterously bow to an idol. All the church, which consists in maidens and in youths, in husbands and in wives, it is all named as one maiden, as the apostle Paul said to the believing folk, "I have betrothed you to one man, that you may prepare a pure maiden for Christ." Christ is the pure bridegroom, and all the Christian church is his bride, by which he daily begets human souls to his heavenly kingdom. The church is our mother and a pure maiden, because we are in her born again to God's hand, through faith and baptism' (*The Homilies of the Anglo-Saxon Church: the First Part containing the Sermones Catholici or Homilies of Ælfric*, ed. Benjamin Thorpe (cited henceforward as *Catholic Homilies*), 2 vols. (London, 1844–6) II, 567). Cf. Augustine, 'Sermo 93 de Scripturis',

If Juliana's purity seems unrealistically adamantine, is it not because the poet wanted his audience to see, suggested in it, the virgin church and that absolute virginity which homilists took as a symbol for the Christian's relationship to the world?[1]

The description of Juliana's trial and persecutions can also be seen as an attempt to draw significance from the individual's sufferings by so portraying them as to recall for the audience that passion which each martyr imitates. Indeed, the likening of the martyrs to Christ is exactly what one would expect in medieval hagiography. As early as the Acts of the Apostles, Luke has the protomartyr Stephen say as he dies 'Domine Jesu, suscipe spiritum meum' and 'Domine, ne statuas illis hoc peccatum' (VII.59–60), thus echoing Luke's own gospel account of Christ's last words: 'Pater, dimitte illis', and 'Pater, in manus tuas commendo spiritum meum' (XXIII.34 and 46). Those gospel passages which urge the Christian to imitate Christ's death were naturally chosen to be read on the feasts of the church's first martyrs and later join the pericopes for the common of martyrs: 'Et qui non accipit crucem suam, et sequitur me, non est me dignus' (Matthew X.38); 'Si quis vult post me venire, abneget semetipsum, et tollat crucem suam, et sequatur me' (Matthew XVI.24 and Luke IX.23); 'Si quis mihi ministrat, me sequatur' (John XII.26). Passages in the same vein were chosen as epistle readings: 'Christo igitur passo in carne, et vos eadem cogitatione armamini' (I Peter IV.1); 'Quoniam sicut abundant passiones Christi in nobis: ita et per Christum abundat consolatio nostra' (II Corinthians 1.5). Homilies for the common of martyrs gather other scriptural injunctions on the same theme.[2] Ælfric's

---

Migne, *Patrologia Latina* 38, col. 574. The latter homily was included in Alan of Farfa's collection (pt II, no. 105, for the common of virgins), described by Réginald Grégoire, *Les Homéliaires du Moyen Âge* (Rome, 1966), p. 69.

[1] Virginity is a symbol for the renunciation of the world's goods. For instance, scorning a wealthy marriage for the love of God is explained by Haymo of Auxerre as purchasing the 'pearl of great price': 'Huius margaritae pulchritudinem, beatissima N., cuius hodie festivam celebramus festivitatem, multis divitiis datis comparavit, quando pro eius amore regni potentiam derelinquens, et thorum regalis matrimonii spernens, ad spontaneam paupertatem se contulit. Unde sine dubio quia regis terreni conjugium contemsit, sponsa effecta est regis coelestis: et quae noluit cum terreno rege regnare in mundo, regnat cum Christo in caelo' (PL 95, col. 1563, attributed to Paul the Deacon; Barré (*Les Homéliaires Carolingiens*, p. 160) lists it as belonging to Haymo's collection, pt II, no. 54). Renouncing earthly riches is, in fact, a commonplace in homilies for the feast of virgins and martyrs. See Paul the Deacon's collection, nos. 114, 117, 119 and 123 (here and throughout cited according to the revised list given by Grégoire, *Les Homéliaires*, pp. 110–12); and see also Ælfric's *Catholic Homilies* on Lawrence (I, 420–2), Bartholomew (I, 458) and Simon and Jude (II, 484). When Cynewulf introduces the saint's scorning of riches and power (42b–4a, 100b–2a and 114a–16) he is surely adapting this symbolic tradition.

[2] See, e.g., Rabanus Maurus's homily no. 36, 'In Natali Martyrum' (PL 110, cols. 68–78), and Caesarius of Arles's homily no. 223, 'In Natale Martyrum' (Corpus Christianorum Series Latina 104, 882–5). The currency of the latter is attested by its use in the homiliary of Alan of Farfa (pt II, no. 94) as well as in the Ottobeuren collection (no. 99); see Grégoire, *Les Homéliaires*, pp. 67 and 159.

homily on the protomartyr Stephen remarks that Stephen was the first man to imitate the death of Christ.[1] In the early arrangements of the church's liturgical year, moreover, Christmas did not belong to the proper 'of the time' (Advent, Christmas, Lent, Easter and so on); instead it began the cycle of the saints' feast days, for Christ was regarded as the first of the martyrs.[2] And Apocalypse I.5, which calls Christ 'testis fidelis, primogenitus mortuorum', was explained as meaning that Christ was the first of the martyr witnesses.[3] In sum, not only did Christ urge Christians to take up his cross, he himself came to be regarded as one of the martyrs: just as they die his death, he dies theirs. As the anonymous treatise *De Duplici Martyrio* expressed it: 'Vita Domini, qui summus fuit martyr, quique et hodie pugnat et vincit in martyribus plurimis, fuit offendiculo...Quemadmodum igitur ille suo mirabili testimonio clarificavit Patrem in hoc mundo, atque etiam in coelis, ita testimonium illius quodammodo consummatur testimonio sanctorum, quasi sit una passio Domini et servorum.'[4]

Given this body of tradition, the audience of *Juliana* might well be struck by the way in which her passion recalls that of Christ. The saint is interrogated and beaten by her angry father (89–129 and 140–3a); she is given over to Heliseus for judgement (158–60a) and scourged a second time on his orders (186b–8); she is then hung 'on heanne beam' (227b–30) where she suffers for six hours; finally she is taken down and shut in the dark prison (231–3a). Christ, one recalls, was first seized and taken before the Sanhedrin of his own people (Matthew XXVI.57ff., Mark XIV.53ff. and Luke XXII.54ff.); they beat and buffeted him (Matthew XXVII.67ff., Mark XIV.65 and Luke XXII.63ff.); he was then sent to Pilate for judgement (Matthew XXVII.2ff., Mark XV.1ff. and Luke XXIII.1ff.) who had him scourged again (Matthew XXVII.26ff., Mark XV.15ff. and John XIX.1ff.); he was then hung on the cross where, according to Mark, he suffered for six hours (XV.25–7); finally he was taken down and laid in the tomb. Even the interrogations of Christ by the Chief Priest and by Pilate, concerned as they are with blasphemy and the rights of Caesar, are echoed by the dialogues of the poem.

Juliana, of course, does not expire at this point; she is not Christ and

---

[1] 'Đone deað soðlice þe se Hælend gemedemode for mannum þrowian, ðone ageaf Stephanus fyrmest manna þam Hælende' (*Catholic Homilies* I, 50). [2] Vogel, *Introduction aux Sources*, p. 276.
[3] Ambrosius Autpertus, *In Sancti Johannis...Apocalypsim Libri Decem* (Cologne, 1536), p. 14: 'Nam cum omnis electorum ecclesia in sanctis praedicatoribus testimonium perhibeat de Christo, illi tamen principaliter dicuntur martyres, qui pro Christi testimonio mortem pertulerint. In eo ergo Christus martyr fidelis extitit...' Cf. Bede. *Explanatio Apocalypsis* (PL 93, col. 134) and pseudo-Alcuin *Commentariorum in Apocalypsim Libri Quinque* (*ibid.* 100, col. 1093).
[4] 'The life of the Lord, who was the first martyr, and who today fights and conquers in many martyrs, was as a stumbling block...Therefore, just as he glorified the Father with his own marvellous testimony in this world as well as in heaven, so his testimony is, in a way, consummated by the testimony of the saints, as if the passion of the Lord and that of the servants were one' (PL 4, cols. 965–6). This and all subsequent translations are my own.

cannot rise again to complete her work as he did. Nor is she nailed to a cross. But the imitation of Christ is not literal identity with Christ. Ælfric recounts the legend about St Peter's request to be crucified upside down, because 'ne eom ic wyrðe þæt ic swa hangige swa min Drihten';[1] and one recalls the legendary reason for the new shape of St Andrew's cross. Both remind us that there were reasons for avoiding exact parallelism. But taken in the whole context, Juliana's suffering 'on heanne beam' is enough to suggest the parallel with Christ's passion.[2]

The parallels between Juliana's persecution and the passion of Christ are, to some extent, present in Cynewulf's apparent source;[3] but it is worth noticing that he has so altered the Latin *Vita* as to make these parallels considerably more obvious. For example, in the Latin account the prefect simply orders Juliana to be suspended by the hair;[4] the Old English adds 'on heanne beam' (228b). In the Latin the suspended Juliana prays to Christ: 'Clamans dicebat: Christe fili Dei, veni, adjuva me';[5] by deleting this prayer, which calls attention to her individuality just at this moment, Cynewulf allows the saint's suffering to merge with Christ's in the audience's mind. In the Latin, when Juliana is taken down, the prefect immediately exhorts her to idolatry; upon her refusal he has her tortured and only then is she put in prison.[6] The Old English keeps the parallel with Christ's deposition by eliminating this scene as well.

The next section of the poem, in which Juliana triumphs over a demon, also seems largely shaped by the imitation of Christ's deeds. Towards the end of her confrontation with the devil he exclaims to her:

> Ic asecgan ne mæg,
> þeah ic gesitte   sumerlongne dæg,
> eal þa earfeþu   þe ic ær ond siþ
> gefremede to facne,   siþþan furþum wæs
> rodor aræred   ond ryne tungla,

---

[1] *Catholic Homilies* I, 382.

[2] The same phrase 'on heanne beam' is used later (309b) to describe the crucifixion of Andrew.

[3] The 'Acta Sanctae Julianae' in *Acta Sanctorum*, February (II, 875–9), is the closest extant 'source' and seems sufficiently like the Old English version to have supplied Cynewulf with his material. Three Munich manuscripts not used by Bolland are referred to by Anton Schonbach in his edition of Arnold's German version of the story; see *Mittheilungen aus altdeutschen Handschriften* V (Vienna, 1882). One can gather from Schonbach's 'Anmerkungen' (pp. 75–84) that these versions diverge more widely from the Old English one than does the Bollandist text. Krapp and Dobbie conclude: 'In the absence of any closer Latin version, the text in the *Acta Sanctorum* may be accepted, for all practical purposes, as Cynewulf's original' (*The Exeter Book*, p. xxxvii) and Rosemary Woolf concurs: 'The numerous verbal echoes of the *Vita* in *Juliana* make it seem probable that Cynewulf was following a Latin source, either identical with, or at least very similar to the text printed by Bolland' (*Juliana*, p. 17). For general discussions of the poet's alterations of his 'source' see *ibid.* pp. 15–16, and Wolpers, *Heiligenlegende*, pp. 119–23. Subsequent references to the Latin *Vita* are by page number to the *Acta Sanctorum*.

[4] 'Tunc praefectus jussit eam capillis suspendi' (*Acta* 875).   [5] *Ibid.*   [6] *Ibid.*

43

folde gefæstnad   ond þa forman men,
Adam ond Aeva,   þam ic ealdor oðþrong,
ond hy gelærde   þæt hi lufan dryhtnes,
ece eadgiefe   anforleton,
beorhtne boldwelan,   þæt him bæm gewearð
yrmþu to ealdre,   ond hyra eaferum swa,
mircast manweorca.   Hwæt sceal ic ma riman
yfel endeleas?   Ic eall gebær,
wraþe wrohtas   geond werþeode,
þa þe gewurdun   widan feore
from fruman worulde   fira cynne,
eorlum on eorþan.   Ne wæs ænig þara
þæt me þus þriste,   swa þu nu þa,
halig mid hondum,   hrinan dorste,
næs ænig þæs modig   mon ofer eorþan
þurh halge meaht,   heahfædra nan
ne witgena.   Þeah þe him weoruda god
onwrige, wuldres cyning,   wisdomes gæst,
giefe unmæte,   hwæþre ic gong to þam
agan moste.   Næs ænig þara
þæt mec þus bealdlice   bennum bilegde,
þream forþrycte,   ær þu nu þa
þa miclan meaht   mine oferswiðdest... (494b–521)[1]

Taken as a piece of realistic narrative this would indeed be an example of rather shrill hagiographic hyperbole: no one before Juliana has thus conquered the devil, instigator of all the crimes that men have ever committed. But Juliana's uniquely powerful chaining of the devil is surely meant to recall Christ's harrowing of hell. In the passage just quoted the devil concludes that no man had yet so boldly 'mec...bennum bilegde' and 'miclan meaht mine oferswiðdest'. In the Old English prose *Harrowing* Christ says to the devil: 'Nu þu scealt beon untrum and unmyhtig, and myd eallum oferswyþed.'[2] Earlier in *Juliana* the devil had asked the saint how it was

[1] 'I cannot declare, though I tarry for all of a long summer day, all the sorrow which I, early and late, treacherously caused, since the firmament was first raised up, and the course of the stars and the earth established, and the first of mankind, Adam and Eve. Them I deprived of life, and so taught them that they lost the love of the lord, eternal happiness, and bright paradise as well. That caused misery to both those parents, and to their offspring also, that darkest of man's works. Why should I count more of countless evils? I originated all the hateful crimes which ever occurred since the beginning of the world among mankind, the kin of men, the well-born upon earth. Nor was there any of them who dared lay hands on me so boldly as you now, holy one, nor was any man on earth this brave, through holy might, none of the patriarchs or prophets; although the God of hosts, the king of glory, revealed to them the spirit of wisdom, gift without measure, yet I could win through to them. There was not one of them who thus boldly bound me up with chains, overwhelmed me with punishment, before you, now, overcame my great power.'

[2] *Bright's Anglo-Saxon Reader*, rev. James R. Hulbert (New York, 1935), p. 134, lines 15–16. For

'þæt þu mec þus fæste fetrum gebunde' (433). Describing Christ's triumph over the devil, the prose *Harrowing* says: 'and he [Christ] Satan gegrap and hyne fæste geband'.[1] Thus both the concepts expressed and the very language of the poem suggest that the audience should compare Juliana's binding of the devil with Christ's binding of Satan.

Alerted by such clear echoes, a Christian audience should notice other parallels which confirm that the poem is imitating the harrowing. In the latter Satan expects to hold Christ easily in hell,[2] but his expectations are thwarted and the infernal powers are astounded by Christ's courage and prowess.[3] Similarly the devil expects to vanquish Juliana with ease (357–62a and 452b–3), but he is thwarted and marvels at her daring and strength (518b–22a). In the harrowing *Inferus* (OE *Hell*) sends Satan out to stop Christ's advance;[4] in *Juliana* the devil has been sent to the saint, obviously in an attempt to forestall her victory over death through martyrdom (321–2 and 523b–5a). During the harrowing Christ is repeatedly described in terms of light;[5] in the midst of the devil's interrogation Cynewulf calls Juliana 'seo wlitescyne wuldres condel' (454). At the end of the harrowing *Inferus* mocks Satan as a failure and receives him into his power;[6] and the devil of the poem expects to be mocked and punished in hell for his failure with Juliana (328b–41a and 526b–30a). And just as Christ immediately afterwards leads Adam and his children out of the stoutly barred prison of hell,[7] Juliana is immediately brought out of the narrow house of her jail (532).

Juliana, of course, does not literally harrow hell any more than she is literally crucified or buried. The barred work of hammers which shuts her in (236–7a) may be reminiscent of hell's barred gates,[8] but Juliana is neither dead nor in the lower world. Cynewulf seems to present a view of the harrowing deliberately inverted. Instead of Christ seeking out the devil, the devil seeks out the saint. The series of interrogations which the devils of the

---

the Latin version of the harrowing see *Evangelia Apocrypha*, ed. Konstantin von Tischendorf (Leipzig, 1876; repr. Hildesheim, 1966), pp. 389–416. All subsequent references to the *Harrowing* are to these editions, cited as 'OE' and 'Latin'.

[1] OE, p. 136, lines 14–15.

[2] OE, p. 132, lines 16–18; Latin, pp. 395–6.

[3] OE, pp. 135–6; Latin, pp. 399–400.

[4] OE, p. 133, lines 20–3; Latin, p. 397.

[5] 'þu þe hæfst þæt leoht hyder geondsend...and beorhtnysse hæfst ablend þa synfullan þystro' (OE, p. 135, lines 24–6; cf. Latin, p. 400). See also OE, p. 129, lines 3–7, and Latin, p. 391; and OE, p. 135, line 3, and Latin, p. 398.

[6] 'La ðu ealdor ealre forspyllednysse, and la ðu ord and fruma ealra yfela, and la ðu fæder ealra flymena, and la þu þe ealdor wære ealles deaðes, and la ordfruma ealre modignysse, for hwig gedyrstlæhtest þu...hæfst ealle þyne blysse forspylled' (OE, p. 136, lines 18–25; cf. Latin, pp. 400–2). Christ then gives Satan into hell's power forever and the mockery of him, in the *Harrowing* as in the poem, is a jubilant farewell to his powers.

[7] OE, p. 137, lines 3–5; Latin, p. 402.

[8] 'Belucað þa wælhreowan and þa ærenan gatu, and to foran on sceotað þa ysenan scyttelsas' (OE, p. 133, lines 24–6); 'Portas crudeles aereas et vectos fereos supponite...' (Latin, p. 397).

harrowing address to Christ, 'Who are you? Where are you from? How dare you venture among our powers?'[1] becomes Juliana's series of questions to the devil, 'Who are you? Who sent you? How do you dare come among the righteous?'. It is appropriate that the interrogations and the entire harrowing motif be thus inverted, for since Christ's victory the advantage in man's struggle with hell has shifted to the human soul, freed from Satan's power and no longer held by right; now hell must pursue. Indeed both Juliana and the devil refer to the redemption as an event in the past (427b and 448a). But just as Juliana's passion is described in details which fit a mortal, New Testament saint yet imitating the passion of Christ, so her victory over the devil is described in details suitable for her situation, which also recall the victory of Christ which she imitates. Admittedly the devil over whom she triumphs is only one of many, with brother devils (312a) and a father in hell (321a). Admittedly he calls Juliana 'mæg' (352a) and 'wigþrist ofer eall wifa cyn' (432), and implies that she is but one of the numerous stalwart Christians who will not forsake God (382–9a). Nevertheless in his last speech the devil becomes the power responsible for all the sins of history, becomes all devils; and he then describes Juliana's victory in terms that could only apply to Christ, and which force the audience to understand Juliana's deed as a re-enactment of Christ's harrowing.[2]

As with his references to the passion, so with the harrowing of hell Cynewulf seems to change his source in order to sharpen the audience's awareness of the figural comparison. For example, in the Latin *Vita* Juliana responds to the devil's initial and deceiving advice by weeping bitterly and begging God not to desert his handmaid. God's response begins, 'Confide, Juliana, ego sum tecum qui loquor ad te.'[3] These lines are omitted from the Old English; they would, at the very beginning of the scene, suggest that it is God, distinct from and beside Juliana, who overpowers the devil. In the Old English God, addressed clearly as the Father (274a), simply says to Juliana: 'Forfoh þone frætgan' (284a). In another instance the Latin text, a little more than midway through the scene with the devil, describes how Juliana binds the devil and beats him: 'Tunc Sancta Juliana ligavit illi post

---

[1] See OE, pp. 135–6; Latin, pp. 399–400.

[2] Another instance of a saint re-enacting Christ's harrowing can be found in Ælfric's 'Passion of Bartholomew'. The holy man's presence in a temple dedicated to the idol-devil Ashtaroth renders the creature dumb. Forced by Bartholomew to declare himself to the king of the country, Ashtaroth cries out: 'Geswicað, earme, geswicað eowra offrunga, ðelæs ðe ge wyrsan pinunge ðrowion ðonne ic. Ic eom gebunden mid fyrenum racenteagum fram Cristes englum, ðone ðe ða Iudeiscan on rode ahengon: wendon þæt se deað hine gehæftan mihte; he soðlice ðone deað oferswyðde, and urne ealdor mid fyrenum bendum gewrað, and on ðam ðriddan dæge sigefæst aras, and sealde his rode-tacen his apostolum, and tosende hi geond ealle ðeoda. An ðæra is her, ðe me gebundenne hylt' (*Catholic Homilies* I, 462). Thus Bartholomew binds Ashtaroth by virtue of and in imitation of the harrowing.

[3] *Acta* 876.

tergum manus, et posuit eum in terram, et apprehendens unum de vinculis de quibus ipsa fuerat ligata, caedebat ipsum daemonem.'[1] When Cynewulf eliminates these lines from his version, it is probably not just to exercise good taste, as some have suggested. The Old English Juliana does not beat the devil. She does not simply tie his hands behind his back. She herself is not bound. Rather it is at this point that the devil cries out to her: 'þu mec þus fæste fetrum gebunde' (433), and one imagines the devil bound since Juliana first seized him, under her power since that time, the whole scene expanding upon the moment of Christ's harrowing. To note one final instance, in his closing speech the devil of the Latin *Vita* exclaims that Juliana is stronger than the apostles, the martyrs, the prophets and patriarchs. He says that even Christ, when tempted in the desert and on the mountain, treated him more kindly. At last he exclaims: 'O virginitas, quid contra nos armaris?'[2] It is obvious that these details would distract the audience from the figural comparison, and the only part of this speech which Cynewulf retains is the reference to the Old Testament patriarchs and prophets. A reference to the loss of paradise by Adam and Eve is substituted[3] and the devil goes on to describe its effects among mankind since the fall. The deletion of the reference to Christ is especially noteworthy, since it might set Juliana and Christ side by side and distinct in the audience's mind just when Cynewulf is inviting us to see Juliana *as* Christ, or Christ *in* Juliana. The poet simply has the devil conclude:

> Næs ænig þara
> þæt mec þus bealdlice   bennum bilegde,
> þream forþrycte,   ær þu nu þa... (518b–20)

And so he presents Juliana re-enacting the victory, long awaited, which frees the entire race of Adam and Eve from the power of hell.

The argument to this point may be summarized as follows. Cynewulf has been concerned to retell Juliana's passion, not as a realistic story, but as an event which is assimilated through a combination of Christian themes to those central events from which martyrdom takes its inspiration and its meaning. The characters are 'flat' because they are deliberately generalized. Juliana's virtue is unrealistic because it is made into an emblem of the Christian's attitude towards the world. The details of her suffering are hyperbolic to remind the audience that Juliana's passion is a replica of Christ's. The apparently digressive scope of the devil's confession, indeed one reason for his very appearance in the poem, becomes clearer when seen

[1] *Ibid.* 877.   [2] *Ibid.*

[3] The reference to the fall of Adam and Eve is in the *Vita*, but occurs earlier (*ibid.* 876). It is impossible to tell what Cynewulf did with this earlier passage since the Latin here corresponds to the manuscript leaf missing after line 288.

as an allusion to the defeat of Satan by Christ. Juliana's life is not merely her own. It has a place in the context of salvation history; it achieves its full significance as it is imagined in terms of the archetypal life it follows and to which it bears witness.

Another aspect of Juliana's confrontation with the devil is fairly obvious: her behaviour in temptation is a witness for all tempted Christians. Her example constitutes an *a fortiori* argument – if Juliana can endure death (as Christ endured it for men), surely a Christian can bear the less ultimate inconveniences of slighter temptations. And it is logical that the devil should confess when and where he does, for Juliana, by her Christ-like strength and fidelity, holds the devil powerless just as the harrowing did: thus for the Christian who follows Christ the devil's wiles are exposed and his force vitiated. That the confession includes details which instruct the faithful in the psychology of temptation is indeed a homiletic touch; but it is one completely in harmony with the understanding of a martyr as 'witness' to a life which, after all, all Christians are called to imitate.

There is a tradition about martyrdom which supports this fairly obvious reading and which makes the intention of the poem perfectly clear. There were 'two kinds of martyrdom', one exterior and one interior. Exterior martyrdom was suffered by the body; interior martyrdom was suffered by the soul resisting temptation. A sermon of Gregory which found its way into Paul the Deacon's homiliary for the common of martyrs says that Christians suffer interior martyrdom 'si patientiam veraciter in animo custodimus'; it continues: 'Perfecte enim adversarius vincitur quando mens nostra et inter tentamenta eius a delectatione atque consensu non trahitur...'[1] Juliana's victory, then, is both a figural re-enactment of Christ's and a paradigm for every Christian's. The parallel between bodily and psychological martyrdom is drawn in terms almost identical to those the poem implies in the *De Duplici Martyrio*:

Neque enim semper saeviunt Nerones, Diocletiani, Decii, ac Maximini, nunquam tamen cessat diabolus exercere Christi militiam professos...Cum tyrannus dicit:

[1] From a homily of Gregory on Luke XXI.9–29 (PL 76, col. 1259) which is included in the homiliary of Paul the Deacon as no. 116 for the common of martyrs. The notion of the two martyrdoms was a commonplace. Cf. Paul the Deacon's homilies for the feasts of martyrs nos. 117 (from Maximus of Turin, PL 57, cols. 429–30) and 123 (from Gregory, PL 76, cols. 1115–16); see also Ælfric's *Catholic Homilies* II, 536, and 'Sermo de Memoria Sanctorum', *Lives of Saints*, ed. Skeat I, 352. (On the likelihood that Ælfric intended the latter piece as an introduction to the Lives of Saints as a whole, see P. A. M. Clemoes, 'The Chronology of Ælfric's Works', *The Anglo-Saxons. Studies in some Aspects of their History and Culture presented to Bruce Dickins*, ed. Peter Clemoes (London, 1959), p. 222.) Or see the commentaries on Apocalypse XI.3 where the 'two witnesses' are regularly glossed as interior and exterior martyrdom. So Haymo, PL 117, col. 1070; pseudo-Alcuin, PL 100, col. 1147; and Ambrosius Autpertus, *In Apocalypsim*, p. 205. The same notion probably underlies *The Dream of the Rood* 112–18, where he who 'for Dryhtnes naman deaðes wolde / biteres onbyrigan' is paralleled with him who 'in breostum bereð beacna selest'.

'Abnega Christum, et immola Jovi, et esto amicus noster; aut morere:' saepe lingua negat, corde reclamante, et manus adolet thus, cum animus intus adoret Christum: quanquam hoc quoque gravissimum est crimen, tamen aliquam impietatis culpam elevat humanae naturae imbecillitas. Ibi Satanas tibi loquitur voce tyranni; at quid tibi dicit idem per tuam concupiscentiam: 'Abnega Christum, et esto dives; sacrifica Mammonae, et Christo nuntium remitte...Oblecta oculos... Lucrare pecuniam...'[1]

The treatise then elaborates 'idolatry', in this metaphor, as various types of sin: gluttony, avarice, calumny, oppression of the poor and so on. The sufferings and temptations of Juliana's public trial, therefore, precisely parallel those of private temptation. Set within the exemplary argument of the saint's exterior martyrdom, the devil's confession exposes how he tempts to an internal idolatry; Christians must resist by imitating, in an unbloody manner, the martyrdom and victory of Juliana and of Christ.

After her release from prison and her reaffirmation of faith, Juliana is subjected to a series of further torments before being finally beheaded (559b–671a). Such multiple torments have vexed students of hagiography, and their presence here has been another embarrassment to the poem's critics. Hippolyte Delehaye explains this hagiographic habit in a way which tends to minimize the intelligence of both author and audience: not only is the hagiographer trying to impress his hearers with the bravery of the martyr and the power of God; he is also simply giving free rein to his imagination and memory, using up all the torments he can think of, knowing that an *angelus ex machina* can always save the victim for yet another round.[2] Granted that Christian patience and divine omnipotence are argued by the lives of the martyrs, one might wonder if some further rationale lies behind the presentation of these multiple sufferings. One is struck by the fact that homilies for the feasts of martyrs do not engage in this sort of hyperbole, nor do they use the lives of the martyrs to entice a *credo* from neophytes. (It might be objected that these homilies were intended for a different audience from that towards which 'popular' hagiography was directed; but then it would have to be shown that *Latin* hagiography was more 'popular' than, say, Gregory's homilies ' ad populum'.) Rather, in the manner of the *De*

---

[1] 'For Neroes, Diocletians, Deciuses and Maximians will not always rage; but the devil never ceases to attack the soldiers of Christ...when the tyrant says, "Deny Christ, and sacrifice to Jove, and be our friend – or die", then often the tongue denies, though the heart within protests, and the hand offers incense, though the soul adores Christ internally. And in spite of this being a most serious sin, nevertheless the fickleness of human nature alleviates somewhat the guilt of this impiety. But then, Satan speaks to you in the voice of the tyrant, and what does he say but the same thing addressed to your concupiscence: "Deny Christ and be rich; sacrifice to Mammon and renounce Christ...amuse your eyes...make money" ' (PL 4, cols. 971 and 975–6).

[2] *Les Légendes Hagiographiques*, p. 89; Wolpers (*Heiligenlegende*, p. 35) tends to accept this explanation, or at least rests content when he can explain something as having a generally 'homiletic' intent.

Duplici Martyrio, the homilies explore the meaning of the martyrs' lives in an effort to make them exemplary for the interior lives of Christians.[1] When a list of various tortures is given, it is presented as having been endured by the *church* in the age of martyrs, not by one individual.[2] A homily of 'Paul the Deacon', for example, exclaims: 'Quanti enim ab initio impugnaverunt Ecclesiam, cum fidei semina jacerentur, et arma contra eam commota sunt? Sed quanto impugnabatur, tanto clarior reddebatur.'[3] The homily then gives a list of tortures clearly regarded as testing, not a single martyr, but the collective church.

Given Juliana's figural imitation of the life of Christ, and considering the poem's paralleling of the saint's exterior martyrdom with the Christian's interior battle, it might be worth asking whether, in the final section of the poem, Juliana is meant to suggest the church. Thomas D. Hill has shown how in Cynewulf's *Elene* Helen's confrontation with the Jews is meant figurally to portray the conflict between church and synagogue.[4] It would not be all that surprising, therefore, if a Cynewulfian female saint 'bore the person' of *ecclesia*. Moreover, biblical women are frequently allegorized as representing the church, and suffering women as portraying the early, struggling church. John XVI.21 says: 'Mulier cum parit, tristitiam habet, quia venit hora eius; cum autem pepererit puerum, iam non meminit pressurae propter gaudium, quia natus est homo in mundum.' Alcuin interprets this woman as the church suffering in the world and adds that, historically, it happened during the time of persecution.[5] Apocalypse XII describes the woman clothed with the sun and the child she brings forth, both of whom are immediately menaced by a dragon. Although the woman is generally explained as the Virgin Mary, commentators also regularly interpret her as a figure of the church: Bede, pseudo-Alcuin and Haymo all explain that she is the church, persecuted ceaselessly but in vain. Bede writes:

[1] See, e.g., the pseudo-Bede homilies, PL 94, cols. 457–65; the collection is neither English nor eighth-century, but the homilies are from Bede's gospel commentaries, as is pointed out by Jean Leclercq, 'Le IIIᵉ Livre des Homélies de Bede le Vénérable', *Recherches de Théologie Ancienne et Médiévale* 14 (1947), 211–18. Or see the homilies collected by Paul the Deacon (Grégoire, *Les Homéliaires*, pp. 110–12) and Ælfric's 'Sermo de Memoria Sanctorum', *Lives of Saints*, ed. Skeat, I, 350.

[2] See Rhabanus Maurus, no. 36 (PL 110, col. 68) and the pseudo-Bede homily no. 73 (PL 94, col. 458).

[3] No. 74 (PL 95, col. 1540). This sermon is listed neither by Grégoire nor by Barré. The PL attribution suggests that it is ultimately from the Chrysostomus Latinus; I have been unable to trace it further.

[4] 'Sapiential Structure and Figural Narrative in the Old English *Elene*', *Traditio* 27 (1971), 165–9.

[5] 'Quod [the suffering described in the verse of the Gospel] primitiva quidem Ecclesia persecutionis tempore historialiter agebat; sed ea, quae nunc est Ecclesia, a Christo pace jam reddita, pia aemulatione spiritaliter repraesentat. Praeteritos igitur parturitionis ejus dolores, in vigiliis sanctorum, jejuniis et afflictione carnis imitamur: sequentem vero ejus jam enixae alacritatem, ipsius jucunditate festivitatis aemulamur' (*Liber de Divinis Officiis*, PL 101, col. 1215). Cf. Alcuin's *Commentarius in Sancti Ioannis Evangelium* (PL 100, cols. 955–6).

'Inextricabili astu diabolus Ecclesiam impugnans, quanto plus dejicitur, tanto magis persequitur.'[1] And Haymo, commenting on Apocalypse XII.13, says:

[diabolus] persecutus est mulierem, quae peperit masculum, id est fortem populum, sicut fuerunt sancti martyres, qui ante potuerunt mori quam a fide Dei separari . . . post adventum Filii Dei acrius persequi aggressus est, et ad argumentum persecutionis callidus semetipsum convertit alios per membra sua crucifigens, ut Petrum, alios lapidibus obruens, ut Stephanum, alios igne consumens, ut Laurentium, alios quoque serpentibus tradidit, ungulis laniavit, in mare praecipitavit, et per varia instrumenta similia transire coegit.[2]

If the suffering Juliana can 'bear the person' of the primitive church, there is a rationale for the multiple tortures. Instead of being merely an individual enduring repeated hurts, she might be meant to suggest the vigour of the community which the martyrs' witness established. One might hazard a further generalization. When he subjects a saint to a series of tortures, the hagiographer's aim is less to convert the naive through tales of marvellous deliverance than it is to reaffirm and celebrate the belief that the martyrs share and confirm Christ's victory. The world in which the hagiographers lived knew violence intimately, and often knew that an individual martyr's death was a bloody and unspectacular event. These writers give us, it might be argued, not naively believed and literally intended wonders, but a symbolic idealization of the event, an idealization which commemorates an individual by associating him or her with the whole church in the age of martyrs, suffering, witnessing and finally following Christ triumphantly to heaven. Indeed the collective assembly of martyr-witnesses *is* the church, according to a homily for the feast of martyrs. The homilist is speaking of Christ's words to Peter as the rock upon whom the church is to be built:

Sed forsitan interrogabis, utrum haec aedificatio suscipiat lapides aut ligna aut ferrum? Non, inquit: Nec enim est sensibilis aedificatio. Quod si talis esset, dissolveretur tempore. Confessionem autem pietatis, neque daemones, neque ulla creatura vincere potest. Testantur martyres quorum latera radebantur, sed fides

[1] Bede, *Explanatio Apocalypsis* (PL 93, col. 168); cf. pseudo-Alcuin, *In Apocalypsim* (PL 100, cols. 1152–3) and Haymo, *In Apocalypsim* (PL 117, col. 1083).

[2] '[the devil] persecuted the woman, who brought forth a son, that is, a strong people, such as were the holy martyrs, who were more easily slain than they were separated from God. . . after the coming of the son of God, she was attacked very sharply, and the cunning one busied himself with the argument of persecution: crucifying some in their members, like Peter; striking some down with stones, like Stephen; consuming some by fire, like Lawrence; others he gave over to serpents, some he tore with claws, some he cast into the sea; and he caused similar things to happen through various instruments' (PL 117, col. 1089). Elsewhere (on Apocalypse XI.7) Haymo applies a series of tortures to the church as a whole: 'Faciet autem contra Dei testes bellum, et corporale et spirituale, exhibebit cuncta quae in praecedentibus martyribus sunt adimpleta, id est virgas, fustes, plumbatas, candentes ferri laminas, ungulas ferreas, bestias, ignes, et carceres, et si qua sunt similia tormentorum genera' (*ibid.* col. 1073).

non frangebatur. O nova rerum materies! Paries effoditur, et thesaurus non aufertur. Caro scinditur et fides non rumpitur. Talis quippe est martyrum virtus.[1]

The *materies* of the church is the martyrs, whose *confessio pietatis* is enduring.

Therefore, when Juliana is led before Heliseus after her suffering on the *beam* and her victory in the prison, she seems figurally to suggest the church. There is really no question about the outcome of her further trials; the remainder of the poem merely confirms her victory, just as the church confirmed Christ's and the martyrs confirmed the church's. Although Heliseus, his idols and the devil all rage against her, they only enhance and spread her triumph. 'Sed quanto impugnabatur, tanto clarior reddebatur.'

This figural explanation might clarify another aspect of the poem which has annoyed critics: Juliana's 'preaching'. Judged as the literal behaviour of an individual, this may well make her seem a shrill and spectacularly stubborn person. But if she figures a collective *persona* the objection misses its mark. Even her speeches earlier in the poem, which have been called monotonous and monochromatic, might reflect what some commentators on the Apocalypse call the *arma ecclesiae*. These arms of the church are faith and innocence, which Ambrosius Autpertus explains as follows: 'Dumque [Christiani] falsa audiunt, vera praedicant: dum tormenta excipiunt, fidem proferunt.'[2] At any rate, in the final section of the poem Juliana's preaching seems well able to suggest the collective testimony of the church. The loss of at least one manuscript leaf between lines 558 and 559b makes detailed interpretation of the section impossible; but when the text resumes two third person plural verbs are used: 'heredon' (560a) and 'sægdon' (561a): 'they' are praising God. Now the Latin text corresponding to the gap tells how Juliana preaches to Heliseus, who responds by having her tortured by spiked wheel and fire. Delivered from these torments by an angel, Juliana proclaims a long thanksgiving prayer which recapitulates God's protection of his people – his church – through salvation history: from Lot, Jacob, Joseph, Moses and David down to the sending of Christ, Christ's death and resurrection and the mission of the apostles. In response to this prayer a large number of Nicomedian bystanders are converted, whereupon 130 are be-

---

[1] 'But perhaps you will ask whether this edifice consists of stones or timbers or iron. No, Christ says; for it is not a tangible edifice. If it were, it would be dissolved by time. But neither demons nor any other creature can conquer the profession of piety. The martyrs testified, whose sides were rent, but the faith was not broken. A new stuff, this! The wall is dug up, and the treasure not carried off. Flesh is torn and the faith is not broken. Such indeed is the strength of the martyrs' ('Paul the Deacon', no. 74, PL 95, col. 1541; see above, p. 50, n. 3).

[2] *In Apocalypsim*, p. 209, commenting on Apocalypse XI.7; cf. Haymo, PL 117, col. 1073. It might also be noted that Juliana's speeches, which continually counter the threats and promises of her father and Heliseus with references to God's controlling power, are paralleled in homilies. Compare, e.g., *Juliana* 111b–13a with 'Ego [qui mitto vos sicut oves...] sum qui coelum extendi, qui terram fundavi, qui mare infrenavi...' (PL 95, col. 1539).

headed for their faith. It is noteworthy that Juliana, also to be eventually beheaded, is not killed at this time. Does she remain, not because she is an indomitable individual, nor because the writer can think of more tortures to which he wants to subject her, but because she is conceived of as an embodiment of the triumphant and enduring witness of the primitive church, sowing the seeds of faith? All this is from the Latin text,[1] in which Juliana is next submitted to burning at the stake. The Old English poem resumes in the midst of this torture, and 'they', presumably bystanders converted by Juliana's preaching and witness, are praising God.

Just before being beheaded, Juliana preaches a last sermon – fitting, if she figures the primitive church. This homily urges Christians to apply the lessons of the martyrs to themselves: to establish themselves upon the rock of a virtuous life (647–52a) – compare the *confessio pietatis* of the martyrs – and to suffer one another in peace and charity (652b–7a), a standard homiletic application of the martyrs' example to a peace-time church.[2] Juliana is not the church, any more than she is Christ; she began as an individual virgin-martyr and she dies a mortal saint's death. But her trials and endurance have been so portrayed as to suggest the church spreading and confirming the faith in a hostile world.

One last remark about Juliana as *ecclesia*. Cynewulf has added numerous references to Juliana's wisdom.[3] Walter Howard Frere has pointed out that the sapiential books were used heavily for the first readings on the feasts of saints,[4] and selections from Proverbs and Wisdom, for instance, are frequently prescribed for the common of virgins and martyrs.[5] That the saints are wise is a commonplace. It is also a commonplace that the assembly of saints presents the collective wisdom of the church. Now the teaching of the church and the witness of the martyrs were thought to affect the good for their salvation, but to justify the damnation of the evil.[6] That Heliseus and

---

[1] *Acta* 877–8.

[2] See Rhabanus Maurus, no. 36 (PL 110, col. 69), and Paul the Deacon for the feasts of martyrs, nos. 112 (from Gregory's homily no. 37, 'In Evangelium', PL 76, col. 1277), 116 (from Gregory's homily no. 35, PL 76, cols. 1263–4) and 118 (from Gregory's homily no. 32, 'De Diversis', PL 76, cols. 1234–5).

[3] Juliana's wisdom is conveyed negatively, but unmistakably. She is called foolish by her adversaries (96b–8, 120, 145, 192b–3 and 202a), is urged by them to be 'wise' (144–5 and 251b–2), but she rejects their judgements (134) and their errors (138–9); later the devil confesses to being the source of these errors (301a and 368). The events of the poem prove Juliana's apparent folly to be wisdom, her apparent stubbornness to be fidelity. All of these references to wisdom and folly are added by Cynewulf.   [4] *Studies in the Early Roman Liturgy* III, 92.

[5] The following passages were common pericopes: Proverbs III.1–9, III.13–20, VIII.22–35, and xv.2–4 and 6–9, and Wisdom IV.7–11 and 14–15, v.16–20 and 22, VII.30 and VIII.1–4, and x.10–14.

[6] On the church's preaching see, e.g., pseudo-Alcuin on Apocalypse XI.5 (PL 100, col. 1148), Haymo on Apocalypse xv.5 (PL 117, col. 1122) and Ambrosius Autpertus on the same verse (*In Apocalypsim*, p. 287). On the witness of the martyrs see, e.g., the pseudo-Bede homily no. 74 for the feast of one martyr (PL 94, col. 460).

some of his followers perish at the end of the poem, while others are converted through Juliana, seems to put this idea into action. The very manner of Heliseus's death recalls a passage from the book of Wisdom, parts of which were read on feasts of martyrs:

Et reddidit iustis mercedem laborum suorum, et deduxit illos in via mirabili, et fuit illis in velamento diei, et in luce stellarum per noctem; transtulit illos per mare Rubrum et transvexit illos per aquam nimiam. Inimicos autem illorum demersit in mare. Et ab altitudine inferorum eduxit illos. Ideo justi tulerunt spolia impiorum; et decantaverunt, Domine, nomen sanctum tuum, et victricem manum tuam laudaverunt pariter.[1]

This notion might well underlie the poem's presentation of Heliseus's end. Juliana embodies the wisdom of God's people. On the one hand, she leads the good to baptism and salvation, even to the possession of Heliseus's city; on the other, she brings a watery death to those too perverse to survive the figurative crossing of the Red Sea. Behind her, she leaves an exultant and rejoicing people.

Cynewulf's *Juliana*, therefore, does not seem to be a piece of realistic fiction ruined by clumsiness and naiveté. It is certainly shaped, in rather definite ways, by themes of scripture, liturgy and homily. It seems to be aware of, and to sharpen the form of, figural tendencies already present in the Latin *Vita*. The poet was certainly deliberate, and most probably learned.

Whether or not Cynewulf's presentation of Juliana in such a way as to cause the audience to see in her Christ, the church and a Christian paradigm is a necessarily 'poetic' conception is another matter. Bede, commenting on Apocalypse XII.27, expresses fundamentally the same kind of idea when he connects the struggles of the woman, the church, Christ, the martyrs and the interior lives of Christians.[2] Yet one can at least insist that Cynewulf's imagination and his sense of intellectual symmetry were active in visualizing

---

[1] 'And [Wisdom] gave the reward of their labours to the just, and led them out on a marvellous way; and she was a shelter to them by day, and a starry light by night; she led them across the Red Sea and brought them through deep waters. The wicked, however, she drowned in the sea, and she summoned them from the depth of the infernal regions. Therefore the just bear off the spoils of the impious; and they praised your holy name, Lord, and together they praised your victorious hand' (Wisdom x.17–20). Cf. Wisdom v.21–3. Wisdom x.13–14 might incidentally bear on Juliana's victory in the dungeon: '[Sapientia] venditum iustum non dereliquit. Sed a peccatoribus liberavit eum; descenditque cum illo in foveam, et in vinculis non dereliquit illum...'. The fact that Wisdom v.16–20 and 22 and x.10–14 were pericopes for the common of saints would have drawn attention to these passages and their contexts.

[2] Apocalypse XII.17 reads: 'Et iratus est draco in mulierem: et abiit facere praelium cum reliquis de semine eius, qui custodiunt mandata Dei, et habent testimonium Iesu Christi.' Bede comments: 'Mandata Dei in fide Jesu Christi custodire, hoc est pugnare cum dracone, et ipsum provocare in praelium. Et gratias Deo, qui saevi draconis evacuavit incoeptus. Ecce enim, Dominum in carne natum exstinguere molitus, ejus resurrectione frustratur. Post apostolis fiduciam docendi refringere laborans, quasi mulierem, id est, totam Ecclesiam de rebus humanis auferre satagebat. Sed et hoc frustra nisus passim nunc singulas fidelium impugnat aetates' (*Explanatio Apocalypsis*, PL 93, col. 168).

Juliana figurally. Surely he believed that he was relating the real persecution of an historical martyr. He probably believed that the saint had endured protracted torture. But while he never denies her irreducible individuality, he also seems to have believed that her meaning could be fully expressed only if that individuality were seen in all its essential, complementary relationships. In the framework of salvation history and divine exemplarity, part of a *figura*'s very being points forward to, or back to, or up to, the fulfilment of its being. The human mind, therefore, only realizes the whole import of the individual when it is able to imagine the *figura*'s essential connections within the hierarchy of being and the flow of time. Cynewulf's imagination explores these relationships and manifests them so that his audience can realize them as well. And that last 'making real' is, of course, the rhetorical aim of the poem.

But in the last analysis, acknowledging that *Juliana* is consistently shaped by figural and rhetorical design will not promote the poem to the ranks of the greatest Old English poetry. That an intelligent Old English audience would have regarded it, according to the criteria of the age, as a 'just representation of general nature' will fail to satisfy an age whose criteria have so radically altered. One can only urge that its matter, which may not interest us, and its form, which may not meet our own expectations, need not obscure the care, learning and imagination with which Cynewulf composed it.

Old English composite homilies
from Winchester

M. R. GODDEN

Many of the homilies preserved in manuscripts of Old English are composite; that is, they are made up largely of passages drawn with little change
from other Old English writings (usually homilies) and not freshly composed or translated from Latin. Most of them exist in only one copy, compared with the several surviving copies of most original homilies, and they
were probably not given wide circulation. But such homilies can tell us a
great deal about the homiletic tradition in England: about attitudes towards
homiletic form and content; about the interests of those who read and
plundered the homilies of Ælfric and Wulfstan; and about the availability
of particular texts in particular areas, and the form in which they were
known.

Much of the essential groundwork for the study of these homilies, describing them and identifying their sources, has been done by N. R. Ker and
Karl Jost.[1] Two of the composite homilies published in A. S. Napier's
collection of homilies attributed to Wulfstan, items XXIX and XXX, have been
discussed by L. Whitbread,[2] who argues for common authorship for the
two pieces and suggests connections with other works of the period. And
Paul Szarmach has recently analysed a composite homily on Jonah which
was compiled from a Vercelli homily and a homily by Ælfric.[3] I want here
to look closely at two unpublished composite homilies in Cambridge,
University Library, Ii. 4. 6. They are particularly interesting to study because
they draw on a large number of Old English sources, about some of which
little is known, and because, as I intend to show, their composition can be
fairly definitely assigned to a particular place and period – Winchester in
the middle of the eleventh century. It is rare that composite homilies can be
placed in this way, and information about homiletic work at Winchester is
of particular value, because although Winchester was clearly a major literary
centre few late Old English manuscripts can be assigned to it.

[1] N. R. Ker, *Catalogue of Manuscripts Containing Anglo-Saxon* (Oxford, 1957), *passim* and K. Jost,
Wulfstanstudien (Bern, 1950).
[2] ' "Wulfstan" Homilies XXIX, XXX and some Related Texts', *Anglia* 81 (1963), 347–64.
[3] 'Three Versions of the Jonah Story: an Investigation of Narrative Technique in Old English
Homilies', *ASE* 1 (1972), 183–92.

Ii. 4. 6 has been described in detail by Ker, who dates it to the middle of the eleventh century,[1] and recently has been assigned to Winchester by T. A. M. Bishop, who points out that the manuscript includes the hand of a New Minster scribe who also copied parts of several other extant manuscripts.[2] It is a collection of homilies almost entirely by Ælfric, most of them from his *Catholic Homilies* but including some later works of his as well. The beginning of the collection is lost, and it now runs from the second Sunday after Epiphany to the Sunday after Pentecost, with extra items for Rogationtide at the end.[3] The only items not by Ælfric are two homilies for Rogationtide, articles 27 and 28 in Ker's description, which occur as part of the main series, not amongst the extra Rogationtide homilies at the end. It is these two homilies, both composite, which I wish to consider.[4]

The first, article 27, occupies twenty-five pages (215v–28r). Twenty-one of these are taken up by a continuous extract from a homily by Ælfric, the *Sermo ad Populum in Octavis Pentecosten Dicendus* printed as item XI in Professor Pope's collection.[5] To this extract the compiler of the homily did little more than add a general introduction and a brief conclusion, but by his choice of extract and by his additions he produced a very different kind of homily. He rejected Ælfric's lengthy explanation of the church year and the liturgy but picked out his discussion of death, the fate of the soul and the Last Judgement, and added to it passages of exhortation to repentance, prayer, fasting and almsgiving, to produce that combination of general exhortation with accounts of death and judgement which is characteristic of the many anonymous homilies in Old English produced for Lent and Rogationtide. For the additional material the compiler drew partly on existing Old English sources. The first three sentences are drawn from a Rogationtide homily by Ælfric (the correspondence is word-for-word).[6] The opening of another of Ælfric's Rogationtide homilies has possibly been used a little later: 'On ðisum dagum we sceolon gebiddan ure eorðlicra wæstma genihtsumnysse, and us sylfum gesundfulnysse and sibbe, and, þæt gyt mare is, ure synna forgyfenysse' (*Catholic Homilies*, ed. Thorpe I, 244, lines 12–14);

---

[1] *Catalogue*, pp. 31–5.

[2] *English Caroline Minuscule* (Oxford, 1971), p. xv, n. 2.

[3] The character of the collection is well described by John C. Pope (*Homilies of Ælfric: a Supplementary Collection*, Early Eng. Text Soc. 259 and 260 (London, 1967–8), 39–42).

[4] They have not so far been published in their entirety, but the second of them is included in the forthcoming collection of hitherto unpublished Rogationtide homilies by my colleagues J. E. Cross and Joyce Bazire. I am grateful to both of them for their comments on this article, and to Professor Clemoes for his generous help.

[5] The extract corresponds to lines 139–454 of Pope's text. This use of the Ælfric homily in Ii. 4. 6 was noted of course by Professor Pope, who collates this manuscript, and also by Enid M. Raynes in her unpublished Oxford University D.Phil. thesis (1954).

[6] *The Homilies of the Anglo-Saxon Church: the First Part Containing the Sermones Catholici or Homilies of Ælfric*, ed. Benjamin Thorpe, 2 vols. (London, 1844–6) II, 314, lines 1–8. The correspondence was pointed out by Ker (*Catalogue*, p. 32).

'...on ðysum þrym dagum ealra swyðost. we sceolon þone heofonlican drihten biddan þæt he us forgife eorðan wæstma genihtsumnyssa. and þyses lifes gesundfulnesse. and æfter ðam þæs ecan lifes myrhþe' (Ii. 4. 6, 216r 14–19). The correspondence is not close, but in view of the many other borrowings from Ælfric it is probably not coincidental, especially since the first two paragraphs of the Ælfric homily occur in Ii. 4. 6, immediately after the two composite homilies. A little further on there is a sentence from the *Old English Martyrology*: 'On þæm þrym dagum cristne men sceolon alætan heora þa woroldlican werc on þa þriddan tid dæges, þat is on undern, ond forð gongan mid þara haligra reliquium oð þa nigoðan tid, þæt is þonne non';[1] 'On þysum ðrym dagum cristene menn sculon forlætan heora þa woruldlican weorc. on þa ðriddan tid dæges. þæt is on undern sylfne. and forð gan mid þam halgum reliquium. oþ þa nigoðan tid þæt is oð non' (Ii. 4. 6, 217r9–15).

The other composite homily, article 28 (228r–38r), draws on a much wider range of sources, and no single piece dominates it in the way that the Ælfric extract dominates article 27. It is another typical Old English penitential homily. It begins with an exhortation to confession (228r11–229r1) adapted from the chapter on confession in Alcuin's *Liber de Virtutibus et Vitiis*.[2] This is probably the work of the compiler, for the Alcuin material has been adapted specifically to form the opening of a Rogationtide homily, with the quotation from St James (part of the epistle for Monday in Rogationtide) rearranged to come first. There follows a long section (229r1–231r18, ninety-eight manuscript lines in all) of exhortation and warning which corresponds very closely, as Ker has pointed out, with the last third of the anonymous Old English homily Napier xxx.[3] This too is a composite homily, and it is possible that the correspondence is due to two compilers drawing independently on the same earlier text (itself a composite one, since the passage in question uses at least five Old English sources). It seems more likely, however, that the material was put together by the compiler of Napier xxx, for it is very much of a piece, in subject and technique, with the rest of his homily, and two of the sources on which it draws, Vercelli iv and the *Institutes of Polity*, are used for earlier parts of Napier xxx as well.[4] The compiler of the homily in Ii. 4. 6 presumably took the material from a version of Napier xxx; his extract begins part way through a passage borrowed originally from Vercelli iv. Three short passages in the Napier text are

---

[1] *An Old English Martyrology*, ed. G. Herzfeld, EETS o.s. 116 (London, 1900), 72, lines 21–4.

[2] Migne, Patrologia Latina 101, col. 621.

[3] *Wulfstan: Sammlung der ihm zugeschriebenen Homilien*, ed. A. S. Napier (Berlin, 1883), pp. 143–52. (I refer to items in this collection as, e.g., Napier xxx.) The extract in Ii. 4. 6 corresponds to Napier xxx, pp. 149, line 14 – 152, line 6 (with omissions).

[4] For the sources of Napier xxx, see Jost, *Wulfstanstudien*, pp. 208–10.

lacking in the Ii. 4. 6 extract, and the conclusion is different, the Ii. 4. 6 extract here partly following a Wulfstan homily: 'utan don swa us þearf is, beon geornfulle ure agenre þearfe, geswican ure synna and forbugan ælc unriht and gebugan georne to rihte';[1] 'Uton don for ði swa us micel þearf is. beon geornfulle ure agenre ðearfe. geswican ure synna. and swærra gylta. and forbugan ælc unriht. and gebugan georne to rihte' (Ii. 4. 6, 231r11–16). These differences are probably due to the Ii. 4. 6 compiler; at least, the missing passages seem to be integral parts of Napier xxx. But there are signs that the text of Napier xxx used by the Ii. 4. 6 compiler was slightly different from the extant one: in a few minor respects the Ii. 4. 6 extract agrees with the antecedent sources against Napier xxx. For instance the words 'ne seo modor þære dehter ne seo dohtor þære meder' in Napier xxx (p. 149, lines 28–9) do not appear in Ii. 4. 6 nor in Vercelli homily iv, the source for this part. And Napier xxx's 'ealra cristenra manna' contrasts with the reading 'ure ealra' which is in the source for this section, Napier xxiv, and in Ii. 4. 6.[2]

The next sentence in article 28, after the extract from Napier xxx, corresponds almost exactly with part of a sentence in the anonymous homily Napier lviii: 'Ne sceal nanum cristenum men æfre to langsum þincean, þæt he his agene þearfe gehyre secgan and embe godes mærð smeage' (Napier lviii, p. 306, lines 15–17); 'Ne sceal næfre nanum cristenum menn to langsum þincan. þæt he his agene þearfe gehyre seggan' (Ii. 4. 6, 231r18–231v1). Napier lviii is also a composite homily, and this part of it is based on a Wulfstan homily (a source identified by Jost[3]): 'And ne þince nanum cristenum menn to langsum þæt he gehyre embe Cristes mærða secgan' (Bethurum viiiB, lines 10–11). Napier lviii may not be the actual source, but its wording is closer than Wulfstan's to the Ii. 4. 6 reading.

There next follows another long passage (sixty-five lines) of general exhortation and warning, about church attendance and prayer (231v1–233r5). Much of this is in the loose style characteristic of the compiler, but he may have been drawing partly on Old English or Latin sources, and at one point he has probably translated from the *Diadema Monachorum* of Smaragdus:

Venient enim angeli assumere animam, et separabunt eam a corpore, et perducent ante tribunal immortalis et metuendi judicis. At illa memorans operum suorum, contremescit, et videns et considerans actus suos, pro metu et timore horrendo egredi pertimescit. Tamen tremens et metuens ad æternum pergit judicium. (PL 102, cols. 680–1)

To uran forðsiðe cumað godes englas. and ure sawla fram ure lichaman totwæmað. and hi to drihtenes þrymsetle gelædaþ. þæt we þær underfon swa we ær geearnodon.

---

[1] *Homilies of Wulstan*, ed. D. Bethurum (Oxford, 1957), no. xiii, lines 53–5.
[2] See Napier xxx, p. 150, lines 24–5; Napier xxiv, p. 121, line 6; and Ii. 4. 6, 229v11.
[3] *Wulfstanstudien*, p. 263.

þonne beoð ure sawla gemyndige ure ærran misdæda. and swiðe forhtigað. and bifiað. and for þan micclan ege. and gryre. þe us þonne getenge byð unþances. and earhlice of lichaman gewendað and underfoð æt gode ecne dom. swa swa hi ær geearnodon; (Ii. 4. 6, 232r12–14)

The remaining half of the homily is drawn almost entirely from various works of Ælfric. First there is a single sentence from the Ælfric homily with which article 27 began: 'Se ðe æfre ðurhwunað on ánrædum geleafan, se bið gehealden' (*Catholic Homilies*, ed. Thorpe II, 330, lines 7–9); 'Ac uton... geþencan hu hit is gerædd on bocum. se ðe æfre þurhwunað on anrædum geleafan. se byð gehealden' (Ii. 4. 6, 233r3–8). This sentence, obvious though it is, must be original to Ælfric, since it fits into a pattern of rhythmical, alliterative phrasing in his homily. The next twelve lines of exhortation are taken almost unchanged from homily XII in Ælfric's *Lives of Saints*.[1] After one linking sentence there follows a long disquisition (116 lines) on love for one's fellow-men, drawn from Ælfric's homily on St Stephen.[2] Most of this homily has specific reference to the martyrdom of Stephen, but the compiler has picked out a passage of general application in which Stephen is not mentioned. There is only one substantial difference from Ælfric's text, the addition of two sentences towards the end:

þeah se mann habbe fullne geleafan. and ælmyssan wyrce. and fela to gode gedo. eall him byð idel swa hwæt swa he deþ. buton he habbe soðe lufe to gode. and to eallum cristenum mannum; Seo soðe lufu is. þæt gehwa his freond lufige on gode. and his feond for gode; (Ii. 4. 6, 235v8–15)

These two sentences are taken almost verbatim from yet another homily by Ælfric, for the twenty-first Sunday after Pentecost, the only variation in Thorpe's text of Ælfric,[3] apart from spellings, being *Seo is soð lufu* for *Seo soðe lufu is*. The Ii. 4. 6 homily continues with exhortations and warnings. The next seventeen lines come from item XII in Ælfric's *Lives of Saints*,[4] a source already used a little earlier. The next six lines are from item XIII in the same collection.[5] A passage on the duties of parents and children which follows is made up of short extracts, reproduced almost verbatim, from the Rogationtide homily by Ælfric used at the beginning of article 27 and again in article 28.[6] The next sentence is probably based on one occurring a little later in the same homily: 'Hi beoð gesælige, gif hi soð lufiað, and buton

[1] *Ælfric's Lives of Saints*, ed. W. W. Skeat, EETS o.s. 76, 82, 94 and 114 (London, 1888–1901; repr. in 2 vols., 1966). Ii. 4. 6, 233r8–19 = Skeat XII, lines 122–7 and 135–7.

[2] Ii. 4. 6, 233v1–236r16 = *Catholic Homilies*, ed. Thorpe I, 52, line 27–56, line 22. This parallel was noted by Ker.

[3] *Catholic Homilies* I, 528, lines 28–31.

[4] Ii. 4. 6, 236r16–236v12 = Skeat XII, lines 145–8, 152–3 and 268–72. Partly identified by Ker.

[5] Ii. 4. 6, 236v12–17 = Skeat XIII, lines 116–19.

[6] Ii. 4. 6, 236v20–237r16 = *Catholic Homilies*, ed. Thorpe II, 324, lines 27–9, and 326, lines 9–16.

hiwunge him andlyfan biddað' (*Catholic Homilies*, ed. Thorpe II, 328, lines 16–17); 'Hit is gerædd þæt þa beoð gesælige þe soðfæstnysse lufiað. and buton hiwunge farað' (Ii. 4. 6, 237r16–18).

After a linking sentence by the compiler, the next sentence renders Proverbs XXVIII.14, but in wording so close to that of Ælfric (in his homily for the eleventh Sunday after Pentecost) that it must be indebted to him: 'Eadig bið se man þe symle bið forhtigende; and soðlice se heardmoda befylð on yfel' (*Catholic Homilies*, ed Thorpe I, 408, line 29); 'Eadig byð se mann þe symle byð forhtigende and to gode clypiende. and soðlice se heardmoda befylð on yfele' (Ii. 4. 6, 237v8–11). The concluding passage, on the end of the world, is taken almost verbatim from the end of Ælfric's homily *On the Nativity of Holy Virgins*.[1] Thus altogether almost three hundred of the four hundred lines in this text are made up of identified borrowings from at least fourteen different passages from earlier Old English homilies.

The two homilies in Ii. 4. 6 were probably composed by the same man. They occur side by side as the only non-Ælfrician homilies in the manuscript, they are for the same occasion and they deal with essentially the same subjects without actually repeating each other. They use the same techniques of composition and they both make extensive use of Ælfric, including different parts of the same Ælfric homily. Moreover in both homilies passages that seem to have been written by the compiler himself include a characteristic phrase, *ealle gemænelice*. This occurs three times in the rather small amount of writing by the compiler in article 27 and once in article 28,[2] not in the usual sense ('all jointly', with reference to different classes of people separately specified) but simply as an emphatic way of saying 'all' or 'everyone'. The phrase also occurs in the only other piece of writing in Ii. 4. 6 that is not by Ælfric – a concluding passage occurring at the end of the first part of a long, two-part homily by Ælfric for Mid-Lent and not found in any other copy of the homily:

Uton eac ealle gemænelice urne leofan drihten biddan þæt he ure mod onlihte. and us him glæde gedo. and us his mildheortnysse geunne. and ure synna forgyfnysse. and þæs ecan lifes myrhðe. þam si wuldor. and lof. a to worulde. AMEN (1021)

('The phrase *and þæs ecan lifes myrhðe* also occurs in article 27, as the compiler's addition to a reminiscence from Ælfric.[3]) It looks as if the compiler was responsible for this passage too, and since the passage is clearly designed for the place it now occupies the compiler himself must have added it to the collection now preserved in Ii. 4. 6. No doubt he added his own two homilies to the collection too and perhaps used it as a source book, for it contains three of the Ælfric homilies from which he borrowed.

---

[1] Ii. 4. 6, 237v15–238r13 = *Catholic Homilies*, ed. Thorpe II, 574, lines 6–17.
[2] At 215v19, 227v11–12, 227v19 and 228r16.   [3] See above, p. 59.

The two composite homilies had not had a long history before they were copied into Ii. 4. 6, for the first of them still has traces of the preliminary drafting. On 215v the scribe began to copy out the beginning of an Ælfric Rogationtide homily, and originally continued with this at least as far as the foot of the page. But then he erased the last two lines on that page, leaving just the first three sentences of the Ælfric homily, and wrote over the erasure the beginning of a passage which is not by Ælfric but uses the characteristic phrase *ealle gemænelice*. This passage continues on the following pages until the long extract from Pope's homily XI begins. Thus the composite homily did not exist in its final form in the scribe's exemplar but was taking shape as he wrote. Presumably he was expected to copy from the Ælfric Rogation-tide homily until he came to the compiler's mark which would have referred him to the draft of the next section, but at first missed the mark and went on copying from the Ælfric homily.[1] It seems clear, then, that the homilies were actually put together at the New Minster at Winchester around the middle of the eleventh century, the time when the scribe was writing. One might note that one of the sources for the homilies, Wulfstan's homily XIII, occurs in a manuscript partly written by the same scribe.[2]

Altogether the compiler used thirteen identified sources in Old English: four homilies from Ælfric's First Series of *Catholic Homilies*, two from his Second Series, two items from his *Lives of Saints*, another Ælfric homily printed as item XI in Pope's collection, two anonymous composite homilies (items XXX and LVIII in Napier's collection), Wulfstan's homily XIII, and the *Old English Martyrology*, some of the briefer borrowings perhaps being through intermediaries. The fact that homilies by Ælfric and Wulfstan and the *Martyrology* were available at Winchester is not very surprising, since they are known to have had a wide circulation (though the *Martyrology* is not otherwise known to have been at Winchester). The anonymous homilies, though, are rather rarer. Napier XXX occurs only in one copy, Oxford, Bodleian Library, Hatton 113, which was written at Worcester in the third quarter of the eleventh century.[3] It has been argued that the homily was actually composed at Worcester,[4] but the main evidence, that many of the sources used have affiliations with Worcester, is not wholly convincing: Wulfstan's homilies were widely circulated and available at many other places; there is no reason to think that the Vercelli homilies were only or mainly known at Worcester;[5] and the parts of Cambridge, Corpus Christi

---

[1] Alternatively, of course, the scribe himself may have been the compiler, perhaps changing his mind after he started copying, perhaps simply missing his own earlier directions while he copied.

[2] See Bishop, *English Caroline Minuscule*, p. xv, n. 2.

[3] See Ker, *Catalogue*, pp. 391–9.

[4] Whitbread, ' "Wulfstan" Homilies', p. 362.

[5] See now D. G. Scragg, 'The Compilation of the Vercelli Book', *ASE* 2 (1973), 189–208.

College 201 which contain the only surviving copies of texts used in Napier xxx and its companion piece Napier xxix are quite distinct in origin from the part of the manuscript which has Worcester connections. It is intriguing to know that a slightly different version of the homily was available at Winchester rather earlier. Napier lviii also occurs in one manuscript only, BM Cotton Otho B. x. The manuscript was written in the first half of the eleventh century, but its place of origin is unknown.[1]

Given the availability of these texts at Winchester, the compiler's choice of sources is partly what one might have expected. Composing penitential homilies for Rogationtide, he turned to two Rogationtide homilies by Ælfric and the Rogationtide section in the *Martyrology*, and to some general penitential homilies very like what he himself produced. But the other Ælfric homilies – the ones for St Stephen's Day and the Nativity of Holy Virgins, and the three for Sundays after Pentecost – are very unlikely sources, unconnected with Rogationtide and primarily dealing with subjects unrelated to the concerns of the compiler. The compiler must have had a detailed knowledge of Ælfric's work to be able to abstract such appropriate passages from such inappropriate homilies. His treatment of these sources was fairly conservative. Of the three major extracts used in the two homilies, the one from Pope xi (in article 27) shows only a few additional phrases; the one from Napier xxx shows the omission of three short passages and the insertion of one sentence from another source, apart from minor changes of wording; and the one from Ælfric's homily on St Stephen has just two additional sentences. The shorter extracts sometimes show more change, but there is no radical rewriting, and in some cases sources have been copied verbatim (the sentence from the *Martyrology* in article 27 for instance).

Quite why the compiler used this method of composing it is difficult to say. The length of some of his borrowings and the accuracy of others prove that it was not merely a matter of reminiscence. And it was not for distinctive ideas and facts that he excerpted earlier writings; much of what he borrowed deals with homiletic commonplaces. He seems to have had a remarkable respect for the words of his predecessors. Ælfric in particular is treated almost as a learned authority: one of the sentences borrowed from him is introduced with the words 'hit is geræd on bocum' and another with the words 'hit is geræd'.[2]

The two homilies are like most Old English composite homilies in being mainly prescriptive and admonitory. Other examples are homilies xxix, xxx, xlvi and lviii in Napier's collection, or articles five and six in London, Lambeth Palace Library, 489.[3] Composite homilies made up mainly of

---

[1] See Ker, *Catalogue*, pp. 224–9. [2] See above, pp. 61 and 62.
[3] See Ker, *Catalogue*, pp. 344–5.

narrative, such as the one on Jonah discussed by Szarmach,[1] are rare, and I do not know of any composite homily which could be described as explanatory or exegetical. Like a number of his contemporaries, the Winchester compiler has picked out from the work of Ælfric and Wulfstan and others appropriate passages of injunction and warning and discarded the rest – the explanation and interpretation and narrative. The passages are skilfully woven together on a rather superficial level by inserting frequent connectives and using verbal associations, but there is rather less concern with an underlying thread of thought or argument. There is, though, a certain amount of independence in organizing the material. The homilies do not follow the structure of any one source but have their own organization and character, even though the first of them shows such a heavy debt to a single Ælfric homily. One can draw a contrast here with three composite homilies in manuscripts from Exeter – the two in the Lambeth manuscript and the one on Jonah in BM Cotton Cleopatra B. xiii.[2] Each of these takes one particular text as its base but omits some passages and adds others drawn from different texts so as to produce a homily of a different kind from the base text but still essentially following its structure. The Winchester homilies, with their greater freedom, are more like some of the composite homilies in Napier's collection.

In general these two Winchester homilies are fairly typical of what was being produced in England in the eleventh century. The topics to which the compiler gave most weight are those which dominate a large number of Old English homilies, and his technique of compiling homilies by weaving together passages lifted from a variety of Old English texts is evidenced by a number of homilies in other manuscripts. The distinctive feature is that these two homilies can be placed in a definite context – a place, a period, and an Ælfric collection into which they were immediately interpolated and for which they were possibly composed. The other feature that distinguishes them is their compiler's striking but perverse talent for ferreting out from unlikely texts by Ælfric the exhortatory and eschatological material that is in general so uncharacteristic of that author.

[1] See above, p. 57 and n. 3.
[2] For the place of origin of the manuscripts, see Ker, *Catalogue*, pp. 184 and 344–5.

The hermeneutic style in tenth-century Anglo-Latin literature

MICHAEL LAPIDGE

Some twenty years ago the late Professor Alistair Campbell observed that there were two broad stylistic traditions of Anglo-Latinity: the one, which he called the classical, was seen to have its principal proponent in Bede; the other, which he called the hermeneutic, was said to have its principal proponent in Aldhelm.[1] The following discussion is an attempt to clarify Campbell's broad distinction by reference to a variety of tenth-century Anglo-Latin texts which may be described as 'hermeneutic'. By 'hermeneutic' I understand a style whose most striking feature is the ostentatious parade of unusual, often very arcane and apparently learned vocabulary.[2] In Latin literature of the medieval period, this vocabulary is of three general sorts:[3] (1) archaisms, words which were not in use in classical Latin but were exhumed by medieval authors from the grammarians or from Terence and Plautus; (2) neologisms or coinages; and (3) loan-words. In the early medieval period (before, say, 1100) the most common source of loan-words was Greek. This was a result of the universal prestige which Greek enjoyed, particularly after the Carolingian period, when a very few exceptional men seemed to have a fundamental knowledge of the language.[4] But sound knowledge of Greek was always restricted to a privileged minority (prin-

---

[1] 'Some Linguistic Features of Early Anglo-Latin Verse and its Use of Classical Models', *TPS* 1953, 11, and (ed.) *Chronicon Æthelweardi* (London, 1962), p. xlv.

[2] So Campbell apparently understood the term, though he did not define it. It implies that the vocabulary is drawn principally from the *hermeneumata*, a name by which certain Greek-Latin glossaries are designated. But the term is not entirely satisfactory (cf. the usual meaning of ἑρμηνεύω); after some reflection I have adopted it because its use is sanctioned by earlier students of Anglo-Latinity. Another possible term would be 'glossematic'.

[3] See G. Goetz, 'Über Dunkel- und Geheimsprachen in späten und mittelalterlichen Latein', *Berichte über die Verhandlungen der königlichen sächsischen Gesellschaft der Wissenschaften zu Leipzig* 48 (1896), 62–92, and the discussion by U. Mölk, *Trobar Clus, Trobar Leu* (Munich, 1968), pp. 149–76.

[4] On knowledge of Greek in the Latin west see the judicious treatment by B. Bischoff, 'Das griechische Element in der abendländische Bildung des Mittelalters', *Byzantinische Zeitschrift* 44 (1951), 27–55 (repr. Bischoff, *Mittelalterliche Studien* (Stuttgart, 1967) II, 246–75), and more recently O. Prinz, 'Zum Einfluss des Griechischen auf den Wortschatz des Mittellateins', *Festschrift Bernhard Bischoff*, ed. J. Autenrieth and F. Brunhölzl (Stuttgart, 1971), pp. 1–15. The older study by A. Tougard, *L'Hellénisme dans les Écrivains du Moyen Âge du Septième au Douzième Siècle* (Paris, 1886), provides a great amount of information but frequently errs in assuming that the appearance of a Greek word implied a knowledge of Greek on its author's behalf.

Michael Lapidge

cipally because of the lack of an adequate and widely circulated introductory primer[1]); for the majority of medieval authors, acquaintance with continuous Greek came only through reciting the Creed, the Lord's Prayer or occasionally the psalter in Greek, and acquaintance with Greek vocabulary came through Greek–Latin glossaries. The most popular of the Greek–Latin glossaries – those based ultimately on the grammar of Dositheus – had originated as bilingual phrase-books in the bilingual world of Late Antiquity.[2] But as first-hand knowledge of Greek disappeared, these glossaries were inevitably carelessly copied, with the result that Greek words derived from glossaries often bear little resemblance to their originals ($\iota\chi\theta\hat{v}s$ becomes *iactis* in several glossaries, to choose a random example). Accordingly, Greek vocabulary derived from glossaries has a distinctive flavour, either in its bizarre orthography or its unpredictable denotation, and is usually readily identifiable. In the following pages I shall attempt to show how Anglo-Latin authors of the tenth century ornamented their style by the use of archaisms, neologisms and grecisms, derived for the most part from glossaries. One point should be mentioned, however: it is customary among certain scholars of insular Latin to describe a style in which unusual words are found as 'Hisperic'. But this term is often carelessly employed.[3] It ought to refer strictly to the exceedingly obscure and almost secretive language of the *Hisperica Famina* themselves, compositions which abound in grecisms and are characterized by a predictable kind of neologism – nouns terminating in *-men*, *-fer*, *-ger*; verbs in *-itare* or *-icare*; adjectives in *-osus*.[4] Unfortunately, however, the term 'Hisperic' carries with it some connotation of Ireland. The *Hisperica Famina* themselves were almost certainly composed in Ireland;[5] but all medieval Latin literature which displays neologisms and grecisms was not. Such literature usually has nothing in common with the *Hisperica Famina* save that it sends a modern reader to his dictionary. I would therefore urge the use of the more neutral term 'hermeneutic' and hope to show that the excessively mannered style of many tenth-century Anglo-Latin compositions has nothing to do with Ireland or the *Hisperica Famina*, but is in the main an indigenous development.

[1] Bischoff, 'Das griechische Element', pp. 39–40 (*Mittelalterliche Studien* II, 259–60).
[2] See *Corpus Glossariorum Latinorum*, ed. G. Goetz (Leipzig, 1888–1923) I, 1–34 (hereafter *CGL*). Vol. III of this collection contains a variety of Greek–Latin glossaries.
[3] For example, W. F. Bolton (*Anglo-Latin Literature* I (Princeton, 1967), 139) observes certain 'Hisperic traits' in Bede's poetry, notably the use of such compound adjectives as *altithronus* and *flammiuomus*; but these – and all such adjectives which Bolton cites – are common in Late Latin.
[4] See M. Niedermann, 'Les Dérivés Latins en *-osus* dans les Hisperica Famina', *Archivum Latinitatis Medii Aevi* 23 (1953), 75–101, and the extensive discussion by M. Herren, *Hisperica Famina* I (Toronto, 1974), 13–19, 38–9 and App. I. I am much indebted to Michael Herren for many detailed discussions of the language of the *Hisperica Famina*.
[5] Herren, *Hisperica Famina* I, 32–8.

The hermeneutic style in tenth-century Anglo-Latin literature

THE BACKGROUND OF THE STYLE

Because no thorough study or survey of the hermeneutic style in medieval Latin literature has ever been made, a few brief remarks on its earlier appearance may be useful. Perhaps the earliest florescence is in the diction of the *Metamorphoses* of Apuleius[1] in the second century. The characteristic features of Apuleius's style – particularly the long, tortuously convoluted periods, the penchant for rare and polysyllabic words, grecisms and neologisms – are found again in certain Late Latin authors: in Ammianus Marcellinus, Martianus Capella, Ennodius and Sidonius Apollinaris.[2] The difficult style of these Late Latin authors, and particularly their inclination to unusual vocabulary, is found in turn (in various forms to be sure) in several insular authors and works that stand at the threshold of the Middle Ages: Gildas,[3] Columbanus,[4] the *Hisperica Famina*, Virgilius Maro[5] and Aldhelm.[6] Aldhelm will concern us later. The hermeneutic style received a new impetus during the Carolingian period from the prestige which Greek learning then assumed.[7] Some of this prestige was due to the renown of John Scottus Eriugena and his Irish colleagues. John's knowledge of Greek was thorough, and he is known to have translated the Greek works of pseudo-Dionysius, Maximus the Confessor and Gregory of Nyssa.[8] But John's Greek transla-

[1] See P. Médan, *La Latinité d'Apulée dans les Métamorphoses* (Paris, 1925) and M. Bernhard, *Der Stil des Apuleius von Madaura* (Stuttgart, 1927).

[2] On Martianus's prose style, see W. H. Stahl, *Martianus Capella and the Seven Liberal Arts* (New York, 1971), pp. 28–39; Stahl (pp. 250–2) lists some 160 extremely rare words, many of them neologisms, used by Martianus. On rare words in Ennodius, see F. Vogel, 'Ennodiana', *Archiv für lateinische Lexicographie* 1 (1884), 267–71. On Sidonius Apollinaris see A. Loyen, *Sidoine Apollinaire et l'Esprit Précieux en Gaule aux Derniers Jours de l'Empire* (Paris, 1943).

[3] Gildas, *de excidio et conquestu Britanniae*, ed. T. Mommsen, Monumenta Germaniae Historica Auct. Antiq. 13. On Gildas's style see F. Kerlouégan, 'Le Latin du *de excidio Britanniae* de Gildas', *Christianity in Britain 300–700*, ed. M. W. Barley and R. P. C. Hanson (Leicester, 1968), pp. 151–76.

[4] Ed. G. S. M. Walker, *Sancti Columbani Opera*, Scriptores Latini Hiberniae 2 (Dublin, 1957); see also Walker's study, 'On the Use of Greek Words in the Writings of St Columbanus of Luxeuil', *Archivum Latinitatis Medii Aevi* 21 (1951), 117–31, together with the somewhat different view by J. W. Smit, *Studies on the Language and Style of Columba the Younger (Columbanus)* (Amsterdam, 1971). On Greek learning in Ireland in general see M. Esposito, 'The Knowledge of Greek in Ireland', *Studies* 1 (1912), 665–83.

[5] Ed. J. Huemer, *Virgilii Maronis Grammatici Opera* (Leipzig, 1886). On Virgilius see D. Tardi, *Les Epitomae de Virgile de Toulouse* (Paris, 1928) and R. Baccou, *Un Grammairien Latin de la Décadence: Virgile de Toulouse* (Toulouse, 1939). That Virgilius was an Irishman has recently been argued by M. Herren, 'Some Conjectures on the Origins and Tradition of the Hisperic Poem *Rubisca*', *Ériu* 25 (1974), 70–87.

[6] Ed. R. Ehwald, MGH Auct. Antiq. 15. Aldhelm's style has been much maligned but never studied in detail; see only the concise remarks by M. Roger, *L'Enseignement des Lettres Classiques d'Ausone à Alcuin* (Paris, 1905), pp. 295–6.

[7] See M. L. W. Laistner, 'The Revival of Greek in Western Europe in the Carolingian Age', *History* 9 (1924), 177–87. For the earlier period the standard account is by P. Courcelle, *Les Lettres Grecques en Occident de Macrobe à Cassiodore* (Paris, 1943).

[8] See the concise and accurate discussion by E. Jeauneau, *Jean Scot. Homélie sur le Prologue de Jean* (Paris, 1969), pp. 24–50.

tions do not concern us in this context as much as does his macaronic Greek–Latin poetry. One brief example may be cited:

> Si vis OΥΡΑΝΙΑΣ sursum volitare per auras
> ΕΜΠΥΡΙΟΣque polos mentis sulcare meatu,
> OMMATE glaucivido lustrabis templa sophiae,
> quorum summa tegit condensa nube caligo,
> omnes quae superat sensus ΝΟΕΡΟΣque ΛΟΓΟΣque.[1]

It should be stressed that all these Greek words were no doubt common coin to John himself, and that he may well have been using them without self-conscious ostentation. Nevertheless, his poetry had a great vogue at that time: it was lectured on and glossed at Laon,[2] and an anonymous student of Martin of Laon, one of John's Irish colleagues, compiled a glossary from one of Martin's lectures. These lecture notes, known as the *Scholica Graecarum Glossarum*,[3] had a considerable circulation and became a source of Greek vocabulary for later writers. Also at Laon were written a series of poems that are stuffed with grecisms (some are written entirely in Greek) in direct imitation of John's poetry.[4] Clearly the writing of Latin adorned with grecisms became a popular literary fashion at this time, and it is amusing to find Hincmar of Rheims decrying this fashion to his nephew at Laon (who was apparently a practitioner):

But when there are sufficient Latin words which you could have put in those places where you have put grecisms and abstruse words and even Irish words and other barbarisms (*Graeca et obstrusa et interdum Scottica et alia barbara*) – as you saw fit – which are bastardized and corrupt, it would appear that you have inserted these words most unfortunately not out of humility but for the ostentation of those Greek words which you wished to use – which you yourself don't understand – so that everyone who reads them may recognize that you wanted to vomit up words which you hadn't choked down.[5]

In spite of Hincmar's opposition, the hermeneutic style flourished in various continental centres during the tenth century. In Italy its principal proponents were Liutprand of Cremona,[6] Eugenius Vulgarius[7] and the *Polypticon* attri-

---

[1] Ed. L. Traube, MGH Poetae 3, 537.

[2] Laon 444, 294v–8r; see E. Miller, 'Un Glossaire Grec-Latin de la Bibliothèque de Laon', *Notices et Extraits des Manuscrits* 29.2 (Paris, 1880). On the school of Laon at this time see E. Jeauneau, 'Les Écoles de Laon et d'Auxerre au IXe Siècle', *Settimane di Studio del Centro Italiano di Studi sull'Alto Medioevo* 19 (1971), 495–560.

[3] They are printed by M. L. W. Laistner, 'Notes on Greek from the Lectures of a Ninth-Century Monastery Teacher', *Bull. of the John Rylands Lib.* 7 (1922–3), 421–56.

[4] Ed. L. Traube, MGH Poetae 3, 685–701.   [5] Migne, Patrologia Latina 126, col. 448.

[6] Particularly the *Antapodosis*, ed. J. Becker, MGH Script. Rer. Germ. pp. 1–158. Although Liutprand spent some time in Constantinople as a diplomatic emissary, he does not seem to have acquired a thorough knowledge of Greek (see M. Manitius, *Geschichte der lateinischen Literatur des Mittelalters* (Munich, 1911–31) II, 167). Liutprand explains at one point that he uses the grecism *cosmus* for *mundus*, 'quia sonorius est' (*Antap.* II.34).
Ed. P. von Winterfeld, MGH Poetae 4, 412–40.

buted to Atto of Vercelli.[1] In Germany, three works which seem to stem from Tegernsee display grecisms of various kinds: the anonymous *Gesta Apollonii*,[2] the letter-collection of Froumond of Tegernsee,[3] and the slightly later (*c.* 1050) and anonymous poem *Ruodlieb*.[4] The *Vita S. Christophori* of Walter of Speyer also abounds in grecisms.[5] From France of this time there are several works which display a hermeneutic style: the *Gesta Abbatum Fontanellensium*[6] written at St Wandrille in the early ninth century; the *Libellulus Sacerdotalis* of Lios Monocus,[7] possibly from Fleury; the *Bella Parisiacae Vrbis* of Abbo of St Germain-des-Prés;[8] the *Occupatio* of Odo of Cluny;[9] and the *Gesta Normanniae Ducum* of Dudo of St Quentin.[10] Of all these continental authors, Abbo and Odo concern us most: Abbo, because the third book of his *Bella Parisiacae Vrbis* was intently studied in tenth-century England; Odo, because he was the inspirational force behind the Benedictine reform movement which so profoundly affected English culture in the tenth century. The first two books of Abbo's *Bella Parisiacae Vrbis* are a detailed account of the siege of Paris by the Normans in 888–95. But Abbo wished

---

[1] G. Goetz, 'Attonis qui fertur Polipticum quod appellatur Perpendiculum', *Abhandlungen der sächsischen Akademie der Wissenschaften zu Leipzig*, philologisch-historische Klasse 37.2 (1922).

[2] Ed. E. Dümmler, MGH Poetae 2, 483–506. There is a discussion of the grecisms in this poem by E. Klebs, *Die Erzählung von Apollonius von Tyrus* (Berlin, 1899), p. 336, n. 2. Froumund of Tegernsee himself provided glosses to the grecisms in the poem; see G. Schepss, 'Funde und Studien zu Apollonius Tyrius...und zur lat. Glossographie', *Neues Archiv* 9 (1884), 173–94.

[3] Ed. K. Strecker, *Die Tegernseer Briefsammlung*, MGH Epistolae Selectae 1. On literary culture at Tegernsee see G. Zacher, *Das Kloster Tegernsee um das Jahr 1000* (Leipzig, 1935), and more recently C. E. Eder, 'Die Schule des Klosters Tegernsee im frühen Mittelalter im Spiegel der Tegernseer Handschriften', *Studien und Mitteilungen zur Geschichte des Benediktiner-Ordens* 83 (1972), 6–155.

[4] Ed. E. H. Zeydel (New York, 1959). On the grecisms in *Ruodlieb* (some of which are extremely curious and may have been derived from a native Greek-speaker), see F. Löwenthal, 'Bemerkungen zum Ruodlieb', *ZDA* 64 (1927), 128–34, and H. Ottinger, 'Zum Latein des Ruodlieb', *Historische Vierteljahrschrift* 26 (1931), 449–535.

[5] Ed. K. Strecker, MGH Poetae 5, 10–79.

[6] Ed. S. Loewenfeld, MGH Script. Rer. Germ., and also F. Lohier and J. Laporte, *Société de l'Histoire de Normandie* (Rouen/Paris, 1936). On grecisms in the work see Tougard, *L'Héllénisme*, pp. 25–6.

[7] Ed. P. von Winterfeld, MGH Poetae 4, 276–95 (from Paris, BN lat. 13386, saec. ix, perhaps from Fleury). On the vocabulary of this difficult little poem (which merits closer study), see only Winterfeld's notes, p. 277, and Manitius, *Geschichte* 1, 600–1. P. Grosjean ('Confusa Caligo: Remarques sur les Hisperica Famina', *Celtica* 3 (1956), 35–85) made the interesting suggestion that Lios Monocus, who is also known as the principal scribe of Rome, Vat. reg. lat. 296 (saec. ix, perhaps from Fleury) may have been the scribe of Rome, Vat. reg. lat. 81, the so-called A-text of the *Hisperica Famina* (pp. 39–40); this manuscript too is probably from Fleury (see below, p. 73, n. 1).

[8] Ed. P. von Winterfeld, MGH Poetae 4, 72–121. On Abbo's use of the *Scholica Graecarum Glossarum* and other glossaries, see M. L. W. Laistner, 'Abbo of St Germain-des-Prés', *Archivum Latinitatis Medii Aevi* 1 (1924), 27–31; on Abbo's own glosses to the poem see D. R. Bradley, 'The Glosses on Bella Parisiacae Urbis I and II', *Classica et Medievalia* 28 (1967), 344–56.

[9] Ed. A. Swoboda (Leipzig, 1900). To my knowledge, there has not yet been any detailed study of this long and interesting poem; on its bizarre vocabulary see only Swoboda's notes, pp. xviii–xix.

[10] PL 141, cols. 609–758, and also J. Lair in Mémoires de la Société des Antiquaires de Normandie 3 (Caen, 1865).

to make his work a 'trinity' (that is, to make it consist of three books), and so he added a short third book to the other two. This third book has nothing to do with the siege of Paris, but is a series of exhortations to the monastic life. It is written in a fiercely tangled and often inscrutable Latin whose vocabulary is nearly all glossary-based; as it survives, the third book is virtually an exercise book in arcane vocabulary. Abbo clearly intended it as such, since he provided glosses for the most difficult lemmata. A brief quotation may convey some impression:

> *dementis*   *os aureum habens*
> nomine limphatici careas, crisostomus ut sis;
> *minister secretorum*   *-to*   *breves sermones*
> apocrisarius ades; aforismos os tibi servet;
> *rex*   *sis*   *sobrius*   *cancellarius scriptor*
> basileus constes, abstemius antigraphusque
> *mundi descriptor*   *explorator*
> cosmosgraphus, solumque tui catasscopus esto.
> *nudus*   *s. sis*   *secularis, mundanus*
> gimnus ab inlicitis, ne sisque biotticus actor.[1]

The first two books of Abbo's work had virtually no circulation (they survive only in one manuscript, and that is from St Germain-des-Prés), but the third book became an extremely popular classroom textbook, particularly in England (I shall discuss its rôle in the curriculum below). Odo of Cluny's *Occupatio* (written *c.* 925) is a little known, difficult and fascinating poem which deserves to be better known. It is an extensive account of Christian history from the creation and fall up to the time Odo was writing. Again, a brief quotation may convey some notion of the style of Odo's poem (Odo is here discussing Satan's attempt to overthrow the divine kingdom from which he has been expelled):

> Cerberus iste neces horum insatialiter ardet.
> sed dentistupium dans criticus ille polorum
> armilla beluae rabida ora capistrat hiulcae,
> myctiron et rinos eius teyoten aduncans,
> nec nocet his rabies, quantum haud explebilis ardet.[2]

Even in so brief an excerpt there are several grecisms (*myctiron* = μυκτήρων, *rinos* = ῥινός and *teyoten* is a garbled version of θειότητα) and the one neologism, *dentistupium*. For all the fascination of its style and subject, Odo's poem had a very limited circulation (it survives in but one manuscript). But that as significant a figure as Odo of Cluny would choose to write his major work in such a style tells us a good deal about the prestige of the hermeneutic style in the early tenth century, particularly in Benedictine monastic circles.

---

[1] 3.24–8 (MGH Poetae 4, 117).   [2] 1.218–22 (ed. Swoboda, p. 9).

It is interesting to recall that Odo died at Fleury in 942 and that Oda of Canterbury, who had spent some time at Fleury and who was to become a principal motive force in the English Benedictine movement and a proponent of the hermeneutic style at Canterbury, may well have been personally influenced by the great Odo.

The cultivation of the hermeneutic style in northern France in the early tenth century is noteworthy; I suspect that further study might indicate that such cultivation was most extensive in those Benedictine centres associated with the Cluniac reform.[1] In any case, the four principal leaders of the tenth-century English Benedictine reform – Oda of Canterbury, Dunstan, Æthelwold and Oswald – all had intimate connections with continental Benedictine centres.[2] Of these four men, Oda, Dunstan and Æthelwold were personal practitioners of the hermeneutic style (as I hope to show); no extensive writings of Oswald survive, but it should be recalled that Oswald was a student of Frithegod at Canterbury, and Frithegod (himself a disciple of Oda) was an eminent practitioner of this style. One might surmise that the hermeneutic style was cultivated energetically in England in an attempt to show that English learning was as profound and English writing as sophisticated as anything produced on the continent. The impetus for the cultivation of the style in tenth-century England was therefore probably of continental origin.[3]

But if the impetus of this Anglo-Latin stylistic movement was of continental origin, the energy and thoroughness of its application and cultivation in England were unique. In Europe in the early tenth century some few writers affect a hermeneutic style; in England in the later tenth century virtually every Latin author whose works have survived is affected by this stylistic tendency. There is an obvious reason for this: the prominent rôle given to the study of hermeneutic texts in the tenth-century English curriculum. The study of difficult and hermeneutic texts was a traditional feature of the English curriculum since the days of Aldhelm. Already in the eighth century Aldhelm's prose writings were diligently studied by his fellow-countrymen, and the influence of his style is clearly discernible in the writings of his disciples and followers: in the poetry of Æthelwald,[4] in Felix's

---

[1] Both Odo of Cluny and Lios Monocus were associated with Fleury, and it is probable that the extant copy of the A-text of the *Hisperica Famina* was written there (A. Wilmart, *Analecta Reginensia* (Vatican, 1933), p. 31), possibly by Lios Monocus himself (Grosjean, 'Confusa Caligo', pp. 38–9).

[2] Oda and Oswald had studied at Fleury, Dunstan at Ghent. Æthelwold too had wished to study at Fleury but had been prevented by royal intervention; however, he sent his disciple Osgar to Fleury to learn monastic discipline and later imported monks from Corbie to Winchester. See J. Godfrey, *The Church in Anglo-Saxon England* (Cambridge, 1962), pp. 298–306.

[3] There is no evidence whatsoever that this impetus was of Irish origin. I am unaware that any of the principal English reformers had any contact with Ireland, nor can I think of any tenth-century Hiberno-Latin author (resident in Ireland) who affected such a style.

[4] Ed. R. Ehwald, MGH Auct. Antiq. 15, 519–37; cf. Ehwald's remarks on p. 521.

Vita S. Guthlaci,[1] in some of Boniface's prose,[2] and especially in the *Vita Germanuum Willibaldi et Wynnebaldi* by the English nun Hygeberg.[3] When Latin learning was reinstituted in the tenth century, Aldhelm became the principal curriculum-author. The immense popularity of his writings is revealed by the many surviving copies of them – particularly of his prose treatise *de virginitate* – which are of English origin or provenance and were written at this time. That his works were read painstakingly is revealed by the occurrence of tags and phrases from his works which appear everywhere in tenth-century Anglo-Latin sources as disembodied clichés; certain of the most ostentatious of the royal charters from this period are virtual centos of Aldhelm. His works were so well known at this time that he was often quoted without name: Byrhtferth in his *Vita S. Oswaldi*, for example, concludes a quotation from the *Enigmata* by saying merely 'haec de Philosophi verbis sufficiunt'.[4] The difficulty of understanding Aldhelm's Latinity, and particularly its bizarre vocabulary – his *densa Latinitatis silua* (to use his own words) – was what commended his writings to tenth-century teachers and students. It would appear that a session of study of Aldhelm was considered then (as it is now) a most taxing and invigorating mental exercise. There is the example of the English scholar (calling himself B) who wrote to Archbishop Æthelgar that he had been starving for intellectual food since the death of his patron at Liège and asked for Æthelgar's permission to proceed to Winchester and there satisfy his hunger by studying Aldhelm's *de virginitate*.[5] A more accurate index to the intensity with which Aldhelm was studied is the number of surviving manuscripts of his works that are extensively glossed. Of twenty-one manuscripts examined by Napier, for example, only two were found to be without glosses;[6] very often the glossing is in

---

[1] Ed. B. Colgrave, *Felix's Life of St Guthlac* (Cambridge, 1956); see Colgrave's discussion of Felix's style, pp. 17–18.

[2] Particularly in the preface to his *de octo partibus orationum*, which is printed and discussed by P. Lehmann, 'Ein neuentdecktes Werk eines angelsächsischen Grammatikers vorkarolingischer Zeit', *Historische Vierteljahrschrift* 26 (1931), 738–56. The great number of reminiscences of Aldhelm in this work led Lehmann to attribute the work to Aldhelm himself, but he later retracted this view and ascribed the work correctly to Boniface: 'Die Grammatik aus Aldhelms Kreise', *Historische Vierteljahrschrift* 27 (1932), 758–71.

[3] Ed. O. Holder-Egger, MGH Script. 15.1, 80–117. The name of the authoress was identified from a cryptogram in the work by B. Bischoff, 'Wer ist die Nonne von Heidenheim?', *Studien und Mitteilungen zur Geschichte des Benediktiner-Ordens* 49 (1931), 387–8. The vocabulary (especially the neologisms) of this work is most unusual and deserves closer study.

[4] Ed. J. Raine, *The Historians of the Church of York*, Rolls Series (1879), I, 418. On Byrhtferth's authorship of this work, see below, p. 91.

[5] Ed. W. Stubbs, *Memorials of St Dunstan*, RS (1874), pp. 387–8.

[6] A. S. Napier, *Old English Glosses* (Oxford, 1900). See also H. D. Meritt, *Old English Glosses* (New York, 1945). There are twenty-two manuscripts of Aldhelm containing English glosses listed by N. R. Ker, *Catalogue of Manuscripts containing Anglo-Saxon* (Oxford, 1957): nos. 8, 12, 16, 54, 61, 120, 143, 149, 184, 238, 252, 253, 254, 255, 259, 263, 267, 300, 314, 320, 349 and 378. There is also the earlier study by K. Schiebel, *Die Sprache der altenglischen Glossen zu Aldhelms Schrift 'De laude virginitatis'* (Göttingen, 1907).

English. Although syntactical glossing (the use of sequence letters, construe marks etc.) is frequently found in Aldhelm manuscripts as well[1] – further evidence of the study of Aldhelm in the classroom – the great majority of Aldhelm manuscripts with lexical glossing suggests that Aldhelm was principally studied for the interest of his unusual vocabulary. Often the glosses and lemmata to his works were separately collected.[2]

Aldhelm was the most prominent but not the only difficult and hermeneutic school-text in tenth-century England. I mentioned earlier that the third and difficult book of Abbo's *Bella Parisiacae Vrbis* had separate circulation. Of the nine complete manuscripts of the third book which survive, at least six were written in England and of these, five were written in the tenth century or the early eleventh.[3] The manuscripts themselves give some indication of how Abbo's third book was studied and what rôle it occupied in the English curriculum. In BM Harley 3271, which contains Ælfric's *Grammar* and other elementary Latin grammatical texts, two separate versions of Abbo's third book are found. In the first version, Abbo's poem is written out as if it were prose and is provided with a consecutive interlinear English gloss.[4] Following this version the text is written out again, properly as poetry this time, with Abbo's (Latin) glosses to the difficult lemmata. The purpose of these versions side by side is apparent: the student was intended to master the difficulties of the work with the help of an accompanying translation before he moved on to the authentic version of the work in Latin without a translation to help him. This occurrence of Abbo's work in a grammar book is also noteworthy. In another such grammar book, BM Harley 3826 (possibly from Abingdon[5]) which contains the *de orthographia* of Bede and that of Alcuin, Abbo's third book is found placed in the middle of an (unprinted) glossary which contains some very rare words indeed. The study of Abbo went hand in hand with the study of glossaries, apparently, and both were considered aspects of the study of Latin grammar. In Canterbury in particular, Abbo's third book seems to have been intensively studied. One complete copy of the third book is found in an eleventh-century manuscript from St Augustine's (Cambridge, University Library, Gg. 5. 35), but in another Canterbury manuscript from Christ Church of the late tenth

---

[1] Cf. Ehwald's notes, MGH Auct. Antiq. 15, 215, and the discussion by F. C. Robinson, 'Syntactical Glosses in Latin Manuscripts of Anglo-Saxon Provenance', *Speculum* 48 (1973), 443–75.

[2] E.g. Oxford, Bodleian Library, Auct. F. 2. 14 (S.C. 2657), 11r–19v, and Bodley 163 (S.C. 2016), 250r.

[3] There is a manuscript of this work which was unknown to Winterfeld in the National Library of Scotland (Edinburgh), Adv. 18. 6. 12, which is of the eleventh century from Thorney (a Winchester foundation). See *Scriptorium* 27 (1973), 84–5.

[4] See J. Zupitza, 'Altenglische Glossen zu Abbos *Clericorum decus*', *ZDA* 31 (1887), 1–27.

[5] T. A. M. Bishop (*English Caroline Minuscule* (Oxford, 1971), p. 31) has noted that the scribe who copies part of another Abingdon manuscript (Lincoln, Cathedral Library, 182) is also found in Harley 3826.

century (Cambridge, Corpus Christi College 326), the first seventeen lines of Abbo's third book are found, immediately followed by a list of (unprinted and untraceable) glosses, all beginning with A, B or C. The principal text in this manuscript, by the way, is Aldhelm's prose *de virginitate*. In still another tenth-century manuscript from St Augustine's, Canterbury (BM Cotton Domitian A. i, fols. 2–55) a list of *glose diverse* (37v–8v) is nothing more than the lemmata and glosses of Abbo's third book.

Aldhelm and Abbo seem to have been the most important of the difficult texts in the tenth-century English curriculum, but many other smaller works were studied as well. In many English manuscripts of the period one finds transliterated versions of the *Credo* or the *Pater Noster* in Greek, and several Hisperic poems (notably the *Rubisca* and the hymn 'Adelphus adelpha') are found as well. The prominent rôle in the curriculum occupied by difficult and hermeneutic texts such as these is conveniently illustrated by the composition of one well-known classbook from Canterbury (the above-mentioned ULC Gg. 5. 35): there the standard curriculum authors such as Juvencus, Caelius Sedulius, Arator and Prudentius are found together with Aldhelm, Abbo and a variety of shorter difficult pieces.[1] In this respect the English curriculum was quite distinct from any continental curriculum of the tenth century: at no continental centre was so important a position given to the study of hermeneutic texts, and even the works of Aldhelm had ceased being read anywhere in Europe except England by that time.[2] This is one reason why pre-Conquest Anglo-Latinity is so thoroughly distinct from Latin written in continental centres. It remains to consider those Anglo-Latin works of the tenth century which display this hermeneutic style.

THE PRINCIPAL HERMENEUTIC WRITINGS

The following discussion is necessarily confined to consideration of the unusual vocabulary which a particular work displays. In general this vocabulary was learned either from the study of the difficult school-texts – Aldhelm and Abbo – or was extracted from glossaries. In order to give some notion of the source of each unusual word, I have used the following symbols, printed in square brackets after each word:

[1] See the description of this manuscript by A. G. Rigg and G. R. Wieland, 'A Canterbury Classbook of the Mid-Eleventh Century', below, pp. 113–30.

[2] Cf. the general treatment of the medieval curriculum by E. R. Curtius, *European Literature and the Latin Middle Ages*, trans. W. R. Trask (New York, 1953), pp. 48–54, and the more recent discussion by G. Glauche, *Schullektüre im Mittelalter*, Münchener Beiträge zur Mediävistik und Renaissance-Forschung 5 (Munich, 1970). On Aldhelm's disappearance from the European curriculum by the tenth century, see M. R. James, *Two Ancient English Scholars: St Aldhelm and William of Malmesbury* (Glasgow, 1931), p. 11.

[A]: when the word is found in the writings of Aldhelm;[1]

[Ab]: when the word is found in the third book of Abbo's *Bella Parisiacae Vrbis*;

[G]: when the word occurs in any of the glossaries printed by Goetz, *Corpus Glossariorum Latinorum*.[2]

When no symbol is given, the word in question is not found in any of these sources. The reference to Goetz's *Corpus Glossariorum Latinorum* gives only an approximate notion of what words might have been found in a glossary. Clearly no single medieval glossary ever contained all the words which are listed in Goetz's indices, which are based on dozens of separate glossaries. Further, many of the glossaries printed by Goetz are much later than the tenth century and the majority are found in continental manuscripts. But with the present state of knowledge – given that many glossaries in English manuscripts are as yet unprinted – nothing more than an approximate indication can yet be given. For this reason, too, it is seldom possible to identify a particular glossary which an English author may have been using. I have not given page or line references to the words I have cited. Such documentation would make the discussion nearly unreadable, and in most cases the works in question are short enough for the words to be quickly located. For the sake of convenience I have grouped the various Anglo-Latin works of the tenth century according to the monastic centres in which they were produced.

Canterbury

The archbishop of Canterbury in the middle of the tenth century was Oda (941–58), an extremely able and learned man of Danish extraction who had received the monastic habit at Fleury.[3] The principal pre-Norman source for Oda's life, Byrhtferth's *Vita S. Oswaldi*, makes no mention of Oda's early studies, save to note that he was raised in the household of one Æthelhelm where he received instruction from a man of religion.[4] The later life of Oda by Eadmer (precentor at Canterbury in the early twelfth century) notes that, at an early stage of his life, Oda learned Latin and Greek so that 'he became so very competent in either language that he could compose poems and prose and whatever else came into his head in the most resplendent language'.[5]

---

[1] Ehwald compiled an excellent and exhaustive *index verborum* to his edition of Aldhelm, MGH Auct. Antiq. 15, 555–738.

[2] *CGL* VI and VII are indices to the glossaries printed in II–V.

[3] The only detailed study of Oda is that by J. A. Robinson, *St Oswald and the Church of Worcester*, Brit. Acad. Supplemental Papers 5 (London, 1919), 38–51.

[4] Ed. Raine, *Historians of the Church of York* I, 404.

[5] PL 133, col. 934. Eadmer's statement is not above suspicion, since there is no evidence that Greek was taught anywhere in England during Alfred's reign or in the very early tenth century when Oda was young, and we have no trace of the 'disciples of Theodore' whom Eadmer

Only three brief Latin writings by Oda survive. Two of them, the *Constitu-tiones* and a letter to his suffragan bishops, are written in an unadorned business-like style.[1] The third is a prose preface composed for the versification of Eddi's *Vita S. Wilfridi* which Frithegod undertook at Oda's command to celebrate his removal of Wilfrid's remains from Ripon to Canterbury in 947.[2] This little preface is a striking exemplar of the hermeneutic style. It displays many grecisms (e.g. *collema* ('union') [G], *epithema* ('covering') [G] and *philantropia* [G]) as well as many words which were extremely rare in earlier periods – *aggeratim*, for example, or *insopibilis* [G]. Oda was also fond of archaic forms such as *quaquauersum* [G] or *quorsum* [G] which he may have learned either directly from Terence or indirectly through glossaries. Similarly the word *floccipendo* [G] which derives from a confusion of two separate words in Terence;[3] whether Oda learned the term directly from Terence or not, he is the first of many Anglo-Latin authors to use it. I have suggested above that Abbo's third book was studied diligently at Canterbury, and several of Oda's difficult words appear to derive from Abbo: *aporia* ('distress') [Ab], *decusare* ('to ornament', from *decus*) [Ab], *diametrum* [Ab] and *entheca* ('store') [Ab]. But much of Oda's very recondite vocabulary cannot be found elsewhere, and one is left to conclude that he created it himself. Such words as *dictionalitas* (a word appropriately used by Oda to describe Frithegod's style), *giganticida* and *primicola* are straightforward coinages from Latin elements. Others are hybrid forms, such as *brachilexium* ('brief utterance': $\beta\rho\alpha\chi\dot{\upsilon}s + \lambda\dot{\epsilon}\xi\iota s + -ium$) or *angilogia* ('troubled expression': Latin *angi-* + Greek $\lambda o\gamma\acute{\iota}a$). But certain of Oda's neologisms are inscrutable, such as *phisilega* (from Greek $\phi\acute{\upsilon}\sigma\iota s$ + Latin *lex*?). So, although Oda's surviving writings are few, it is probable that the energetic cultivation of the hermeneutic style at Canterbury received its initial impulse from him.

Oda's stylistic influence – and particularly his penchant for neologism – is best seen in the work of his disciple Frithegod.[4] Frithegod's work, the *Breuiloquium Vitae Wilfredi*,[5] may be dubiously described as the 'masterpiece' of Anglo-Latin hermeneutic style. It is without question the most difficult Anglo-Latin text. Some beginnings have been made towards solving the

mentions. Eadmer's statement may be nothing more than an impression received from the number of grecisms in Oda's preface to Frithegod's poem; it seems more probable that Oda learned Greek (if at all) at Fleury.

[1] PL 133, cols. 945–52.
[2] Ed. A. Campbell, *Frithegodi Breuiloquium Vitae Wilfredi et Wulfstani Narratio Metrica de S. Swithuno*, Thesaurus Mundi 1 (Zürich, 1950), 1–3.
[3] Terence, *Eun.* 411; cf. also Donatus, *in Ter. Eun.* 303.
[4] Frithegod is mentioned among Oda's clergy and monks in a charter relating to Christ Church, Canterbury (*Cartularium Saxonicum*, ed. W. de G. Birch (London, 1885–93) (hereafter *BCS*), no. 1010); the evidence of this charter dispels Manitius's erroneous assumption that Frithegod was a monk at Ripon (*Geschichte* II, 499).
[5] Ed. Campbell, *Frithegodi Breuiloquium*, pp. 4–62.

lexical and textual difficulties of this text,[1] but the bulk of its extremely obscure and hermeneutic vocabulary awaits explanation. It seems clear from the nature of certain glosses in the surviving three manuscripts that the author provided some glosses to his most obscure neologisms (after the manner of Abbo), but by no means all the surviving glosses are by Frithegod himself, and many of the most difficult words have no gloss whatsoever. Given this situation, any remarks on the nature of Frithegod's vocabulary must be considered extremely tentative.

Frithegod adorned his *Breuiloquium Vitae Wilfredi* with hermeneutic vocabulary of every kind. To begin with, he employed a wild profusion of grecisms: *adelphus* [G], *agalma* ('image') [G], *agius* ('holy') [G], *agon* [A, G], *anathema* [A, G], *apocriphus* ('hidden') [A], *apodicticus*, *archon* [Ab, G], *artemon* ('ship') [G], *aulicus* ('courtly') [Ab, G], *basileius* ('royal') [G], *biblus* [A, G], *caeroma* ('web'), *cathegoro* [G], *cathorthoma* ('success') [G], *cauma* ('heat') [A, G], *chelis* ('lyre') [G], *chorea* (χωρία, 'places') [G], *clinicus* [G], *cleronomus* ('heir') [Ab, G], *cosmicus* [G], *creagra* ('flesh-hook') [G], *desmos* ('bond') [G], *dexia* ('right hand') [G], *dias* (δύας, 'two') [G], *dinamis* ('power') [G], *diorisma* ('ordinance') [G], *dissologia* ('hesitation') [G], *emblema* [G], *ennea* ('nine') [G], *ephebus* ('a youth') [Ab, G], *ephibate* (ἐπιβάται, 'laymen') [G], *epistasis* ('superstition'?), *epistile* (ἐπιστολή, 'letter') [G], *ethnicus* [A, G], *eucharis* ('gracious') [G], *eudoxus* ('honoured') [G], *eupraepia* (εὐπρέπεια, 'majesty') [G], *eusebius* (εὐσεβής, 'pious') [G], *eutiches* ('fortunate') [G], *exoticus* [G], *extasis* [A, G], *gigarton* ('grape-seed') [G], *glossa* [G], *gramma* [A, Ab, G], *idea* [G], *imera* ('day') [G], *iota*, *kakia* ('evil') [G], *kalo* (καλέω, 'to call') [G], *karis* [G], *latria* ('service') [G], *limma* (λῆμμα, 'assumption') [G], *loethargus* [G], *macharius* ('blessed') [G], *mandra* ('sheep-fold', 'flock') [G], *mathites* ('pupil') [G], *mekotes* ('greatness'), *melicus* ('lyric') [G], *metamorphosis* [G], *monas* [G], *monogramma*, *neutericus* [Ab, G], *nous* ('mind') [G], *oechonomus* [G], *olimpia* [A, G], *orama* ('vision') [A, G], *organicus* [A], *orgia* ('rites') [A, G], *ormiscus* ('necklace'), *palinodus* [Ab], *parafrasticus* [Ab, G], *parma* [G], *periergia* ('over-elaboration') [G], *phantasma* [G], *philocompos* ('fond of boasting') [G], *phronimus* ('wise') [G], *pichria* ('bitterness') [G], *pinax* ('list') [G], *pisticus* ('faithful') [G], *poderes* [G], *porisma* ('bonus') [G], *prognosticus* [G], *prothema* ('exordium', 'a theme'), *psaltes* [G], *reuma* [G], *ristes* ('saviour') [G], *scamma* [A, G], *scisma* [A, G], *sicophanta* [Ab, G], *sinergus* ('co-worker') [G], *singraphe* ('decree') [G], *sinmistes* ('initiate') [G],

---

[1] See the notes by Manitius (*Geschichte* II, 499) and the very sparse and cryptic notes by Campbell scattered throughout the apparatus of his edition. There is also an excellent study by D. C. C. Young, 'Author's Variants and Interpretations in Frithegod', *Archivum Latinitatis Medii Aevi* 25 (1955), 71–98. Young occasionally errs, however, in failing to recognize the agency of glossaries in transmitting Greek learning to the Middle Ages: there is no point whatsoever in imputing to Frithegod an Aeolic or Homeric form.

sintagma ('composition') [G], *sinthema* ('agreement') [G], *sistema* [G], *soma* ('body') [G], *sophisma* [G], *sperma* [G], *spermologus* [G], *stemma* [A, G], *stigma* [A, G], *stroma* ('trappings') [G]. *tegna* (τέχνη, 'craft') [G], *tetraplasticus* (τετραπλάσιος, 'fourfold'), *thema* [G], *theorema* [G], *theosophus*, *tiphus* ('arrogance') [G] and *ʒoe* ('life') [G]. The majority of these Greek words might have been found in one or more Greek–Latin glossaries of either the Philoxenus or the pseudo-Dositheus type. But several of them are not found in any extant (that is, edited and printed) glossary, and these particular words are rare even in Greek – *caeroma*, *epistasis*, *mekotes* and *ormiscus*, for example. It is impossible to say where Frithegod found such words, but I incline to think that he had some first-hand knowledge of Greek. One cannot estimate how thorough this knowledge was, but at least he was able to decline Greek nouns competently. His familiarity with Greek is further witnessed by his fondness for coining words from Greek elements (see below). It is a possibility worth entertaining, then, that he may have learned some of his Greek vocabulary from reading in Greek sources.[1]

Archaisms of various kinds are found in Frithegod: the verbs *ascio*, *caecutio* [G], *displodo* [A, G], *exanclo* [A, G], *friguttio* [G], *ineptio*, *manticulor* [G], *promico* and *sentisco*; the nouns *claxendix* [G], *corculum* [G], *deliquium* [G], *funabulum* [G], *glos* [G] and *silicernium* [G]; and the adverbs *aliorsum* [A, G] and *opipare* [G]. Not all these words are found in glossaries. Some were probably culled by Frithegod from his reading of the grammarians (especially Nonius Marcellus) or Terence. Here too the sources of his vocabulary require detailed investigation: the word *timefactus*, for example, is extremely rare and is found in the classical period only in Lucretius (it did not find its way into medieval glossaries). Frithegod can scarcely have read Lucretius, but where he found the word is not clear.

The most striking aspect of Frithegod's hermeneutic vocabulary is his flair for neologism. There are so many varieties of neologism in his poem that it is scarcely possible to classify, and often impossible to explain, them. Sometimes he simply combines existing Latin elements to form unproblematic compounds, such as *benigniuolus*, *malesanus*, *multipetax*, *pompisonus*, *prauicola* or *quadripatens*. In a similar vein are the adjectives *lacerus* (from *lacero*), *polinus* (from *polus*) or *uafrinus* (from *uafer*). Or he may produce feminine agentive nouns simply by replacing the masculine *-or* termination with *-rix*: *grassatrix*, *latrix*, *multatrix*. He also favoured diminutive terminations, such as the adjective *pandulus* (from *pando*, 'manifest') or the nouns

---

[1] In the earliest catalogue from Christ Church, Canterbury (*c.* 1170), there is an item 'Donatus grece' (M. R. James, *The Ancient Libraries of Canterbury and Dover* (Cambridge, 1903), pp. lxxxv and 7). This was probably a copy of pseudo-Dositheus, not Dionysius Thrax as James suggests. If this Greek grammar was pre-Conquest, it indicates that Greek may have been studied at Canterbury.

casella and *ornaculum*. In the same way he produced unusual but straight-forward adverbs: *fidentius, latiatim, longule*. Frithegod also delighted in coinages from Greek elements. Some of these, too, are relatively straightforward: compounds beginning with *archi-* such as *archiierarchus, archileus* (ἀρχι- + λαός, 'the chosen people', presumably), *archipater, archipolites* ('arch-citizen') and *archistrateios* ('arch-general'), or words such as *Christotoche* ('Christ-bearing') and *pseudotheosebia* ('false piety'). On the model of the glossary word *cliothedra* ('renowned seat') [Ab, G] he produced *cliaulia* (κλέος + αὐλία, 'renowned hall'). Each of these words retains its Greek aspect. Other words were Latinized by Frithegod: *chrismalis* (from χρῖσμα), *condolomatus* (from κονδύλωμα, 'swelling'), *fronime* ('wisely', from φρόνιμος) or *kirialis* ('lordly', from κύριος). More problematic are certain Latinized forms apparently but not certainly based on Greek elements, such as *opicizus* (from ὀπικίζω?) or the two adjectives terminating in *-eus*: *cleanteus* (from κλαίω) and *apopempeus* (from ἀποπέμπω). But in a great many cases it is impossible to detect the source of a coinage, save by guessing. The word *arpa* seems to derive directly from OE *hearpa*. The word *fasma*, though apparently a transliteration of φάσμα ('phantom'), means 'speech' in context and would seem to derive from Latin *fare*. The word *adeps* ('suet', 'lard') is stretched by Frithegod to mean 'light', possibly on the assumption that candles were made from animal fat. The word *creperum* ('darkness') means 'sin' in Frithegod, whereas *pallens* (properly 'pallid') seems to mean 'brilliant'. But there remain perhaps a dozen words or so whose meaning is totally obscure and whose context is of no avail in discovering the meaning; I would mention *catillatus, coragia* (apparently from either χορηγία or χορηγεῖον, but neither is appropriate in context), *effeuum* (perhaps meaning 'honied', perhaps from *fauum*), *excolicus, pilotria, serranus*, and others. This list does not exhaust the unusual and obscure words in Frithegod. With the present state of knowledge concerning glossaries and Greek learning at tenth-century Canterbury, such a list is necessarily tentative. But at least it may indicate why Frithegod is to be regarded as the foremost proponent of the hermeneutic style in tenth-century England.

Near the very end of the tenth century the *Vita S. Dunstani*[1] was dedicated to Ælfric, archbishop of Canterbury (995–1005). The author of this work, who describes himself as a *vilis Saxonum indigena*, was an Englishman[2] whose

---

[1] Ed. Stubbs, *Memorials of St Dunstan*, pp. 3–52, from two manuscripts: BM Cotton Cleopatra B. xiii and Arras, bibl. munic. 1029.

[2] Stubbs argued (*Memorials*, pp. xii–xviii) that B was a continental Saxon and doubted that the form *Saxones* would ever be used by an English writer without a qualifying prefix such as *Angul-Saxones*. But *Saxones* was a common term for 'English': Æthelweard (*Chronicon*, ed. A. Campbell (London, 1962), p. 56) describes King Edgar as stemming 'ex stirpe...Saxonum' and earlier the English nun Hygeberg had described herself as being 'indigna Saxonica de gente' (*Vita Willibaldi*, MGH Script. 15.1, 86). At a later point in the life, while describing

name began with the letter B. A revised form of B's *Vita S. Dunstani* had been sent by Wulfric, abbot of St Augustine's, to Abbo of Fleury before Abbo's death in 1004;[1] the *termini* for the composition of the *Vita S. Dunstani* are therefore 995 × 1004. Since the work was dedicated to a successor of Dunstan, and since two of the surviving manuscripts of the work were written at Canterbury, it is reasonable to assume that B wrote the work at Canterbury as well. It is written very much in the manner of Oda and Frithegod. There are a number of grecisms: *agonista* [A, G], *archon* [Ab, G], *charisma* [A, G], *chyra* (χείρ, 'hand') [G], *ebeninus* ('ebony'), *eulogium* [G], *eucharistia* [G], *frenesis* [G], *rima* (ῥῆμα, 'word') [G], *schema* [A, G], *theologus* [Ab] and *theoricus* [A, G]. None of these grecisms is particularly unusual. What is unusual about B's vocabulary is his neologisms. Like Frithegod, B very often Latinizes Greek forms and so produces new words: the adjective *crisidineus* ('dazzlingly golden', from χρυσός + δινέω + *-eus*?), or the noun *cleptor* ('thief', from κλέπτης) with the Latin termination *-or* where one would have expected *-es* (cf. his word *dogmatizator*, from δογματίζω). Frequently he rehabilitates very obscure words from earlier periods, such as the nouns *consessor* [G], *insessor* and *praevisor*, and the adverbs *gemmatim* (perhaps a neologism) and *tenuatim*. But the most striking feature of B's vocabulary is his coinages from existing Latin elements: from the verb *imbuo* he produces *imbutor* ('instructor': cf. his use of *imbutio*, 'the process of instruction' [G]); from *invideo* he produces *invisorius* ('an envious man'), or from *ictus* the verb *ictuo* ('to strike'). Of a similar kind are the adjectives *angoreus* ('narrow'), *augmentabilis*, *decibilis* ('comely', from *decus*), *favoreus* and *gemabilis* ('lamentable') as well as the adverb *cordatius* ('heartily'). Like Oda and Frithegod before him, B seems to have taken a special delight in coining words; if his coinages are less eccentric and unpredictable than those of Frithegod, they are nonetheless distinctive.

The distinctiveness of B's neologisms is a helpful indicator in considering the authorship of another anonymous work. There exists a letter (in a manuscript probably from Canterbury) that is addressed to Æthelgar, archbishop of Canterbury (988–90) from a correspondent who designates himself as 'B. omnium faex Christicolarum'.[2] This letter too is written in a consciously difficult style. There are again several grecisms: *agius*[G], *cardia* ('heart') [G], *dagma* ('bite') [G], *sophia* [A, G] and *stoma* ('mouth') [G]. As in the *Vita S. Dunstani* there are coinages from existing Latin elements: the adjective

---

Dunstan's musical training, B writes '...cytharam suam quam lingua paterna hearpam vocamus'. The Old English form of the word is *hearpa*, as here; the Old Saxon form is *harpa*. That is to say, B's native language was English.

[1] Wulfric's letter to Abbo accompanying the revised version of the *Vita S. Dunstani* is printed by Stubbs (*Memorials*, p. 409). The revised version survives in St Gall 337; a collation of it is printed by Stubbs (*Memorials*, pp. 458–72).

[2] BM Cotton Tiberius A. xv, fol. 162; ed. Stubbs, *Memorials*, pp. 385–8.

lectoreus (cf. *angoreus* and *favoreus* in the *Vita S. Dunstani*) and the adverbs *ignetenus* and *solotenus* (cf. *fundotenus* in the *Vita S. Dunstani*, a word previously used by Frithegod). One highly unusual adjective, *basilitius*, appears to be a hybrid form based on Greek βασιλ- and Latin *-itius*, very much in the manner of *crisidineus* in the *Vita S. Dunstani*. But one neologism in particular points to the common authorship of these works: the words *imbutor* and *imbutio* based on *imbuo* were used in the *Vita S. Dunstani*; in the letter to Æthelgar is found the word *imbuimen* ('instruction'). All these characteristic neologisms suggest that the same B wrote both the letter to Æthelgar and the *Vita S. Dunstani*. From evidence within these two works, one may reconstruct B's career as follows: he was of English origin; he studied abroad at Liège but sometime after the death of his patron there returned to England during Æthelgar's archbishopric (perhaps going first to Winchester); later, during the archbishopric of Ælfric, he wrote the *Vita S. Dunstani*, probably at St Augustine's, Canterbury.[1]

The writings of Oda, Frithegod and B provide ample evidence that the hermeneutic style was practised with considerable flair and enthusiasm at Canterbury. I suggested earlier that textbooks of the hermeneutic style, and particularly Abbo's third book, were diligently studied there as well. Given this intellectual atmosphere in tenth-century Canterbury, it is worthwhile to ask whether various poems found in contemporary Canterbury manuscripts may also have been composed there. The first of these is a macaronic poem in Old English and Latin that is prefixed to a copy of Aldhelm's prose *de virginitate* (the principal textbook of hermeneutic style).[2] The poem is known to Old English students as 'Aldhelm' and begins as follows:

> Þus me gesette   sanctus et iustus
> beorn boca gleaw   bonus auctor
> Ealdelm, æþele sceop,   etiam fuit
> ipselos on æðele   Anglosexna,
> byscop on Bretene.   Biblos ic nu sceal,
> ponus et pondus   pleno cum sensu...[3]

This brief poem is stuffed with grecisms: *biblos* [A, G], *boethia* ('help') [G], *cosmus* [G], *dinams* (δύναμις, 'power') [G], *encratea* ('mastery') [G], *euthenia* ('prosperity') [G], *ipselos* (ὑψηλός, 'high') [G] and *ponus* ('work') [G]. It has a stylistic flavour quite unlike that of any other surviving Old English poem, but very much in the spirit of contemporary Canterbury.

---

[1] Cf. the accounts of B's career by Stubbs (*Memorials*, pp. x-xxvi) and D. Whitelock, *English Historical Documents* 1 (London, 1955), 826.

[2] CCCC 326 (saec. x²), pp. 5-6.

[3] Ed. E. V. K. Dobbie, The Anglo-Saxon Poetic Records 6 (London and New York, 1942), 97-8. Dobbie's comments on the style of the poem are amusing: he mentions Oda, Frithegod and the author of the *Vita S. Dunstani* whom he takes to be 'Byrhtnoth [*sic*] the author of the *Handboc*' (p. xci).

A similar estimate may be made of two unusual poems which are found in a slightly later manuscript from St Augustine's (ULC Gg. 5. 35, saec. xi med.). These poems have never been edited; because they are relevant to the present discussion, I have printed them below in Appendix I. In the first of these two poems (Appendix I(*a*) below), a master taunts a student to explain – by providing two synonyms each – a series of medical terms:

> dic duo que faciunt pronomina nomina cunctis;
> omnia dic que sunt uerbi, que silliba signet.[1]

The master then lists some twenty-seven Greek medical terms (with the riddle of the phoenix thrown in for good measure). If the student fails to provide explanations, he'll go away unrewarded: 'sinon exposueris, indonatus abibis!' A list of glosses written out in simple prose follows the poem; possibly these constitute the student's reply or perhaps are the master's crib.

The other poem from this manuscript (Appendix I(*b*) below) is more unusual still. At first sight it appears to be nothing more than a string of Greek medical terms ingeniously set in hexameters. The poet's obvious intention was to display his ingenuity, not to impart any precise medical knowledge. This is confirmed by a closer inspection: all the words are nouns except the last, which is an imperative verb. So the nouns (forty-seven of them) are listed relentlessly for ten lines until we come to the blunt command at the end: *tricocinare*! – 'sort it out for yourself!' The poet's challenge even today is a difficult one: for the most part the nouns bear little resemblance to their Greek originals, and many seem to be totally incomprehensible. But for once we can match the poet at his sport: the glossary from which he compiled his 'poem' is – because of the extraordinary nature of its vocabulary – identifiable. There is a short medical glossary printed in Goetz's *Corpus Glossariorum Latinorum* from two manuscripts (one tenth-, the other early-eleventh-century).[2] This short glossary was principally compiled from the writings of Cassius Felix, a fifth-century African medical writer, with additions from Isidore, Oribasius and Caelius Aurelius.[3] Of the forty-eight words in the poem, forty-one are found in this glossary. The charac-

---

[1] 'Tell me two nouns which provide synonyms for all (the following terms); tell all things about each word, what every syllable signifies' (below, p. 103). These two lines are derived *verbatim* from an *enigma* of Alcuin (MGH Poetae 1, 282). The spirit of this brief poem may be compared to an *altercatio magistri et discipuli* from tenth-century Winchester (ptd *ASE* 1 (1972), 85–137) in which the student taunts the master to expound his knowledge of musical theory; the master replies instead with an exposition of computistical theory.

[2] *CGL* III, 596–607, from Rome, Vat. reg. lat. 1260, 177r–8r, and Berne, Bürgerbibl. 337, 8r–14v. I have been unable to examine these manuscripts, but it would be interesting to see whether on palaeographical grounds either of them might have been written in England.

[3] See O. Probst, 'Glossen aus Cassius Felix', *Philologus* 68 (1909), 550–9, and M. Niedermann, 'Sur les Gloses Médicales du Corpus Glossariorum Latinorum', *Recueil de Travaux...de la Faculté des Lettres* 7 (Neuchâtel, 1918), 87–97.

teristically mangled forms of many of these words in the glossary are exactly reproduced in the poem. An examination of the brief commentary I have printed with the poem will leave no doubt that this medical glossary was the poet's source. Here, then, is no attempt to disseminate medical information;[1] the poem is a witty, hermeneutic *jeu d'esprit*, the doubtful end-product of years of study of glossaries and absorption of arcane vocabulary. And it is precisely the sort of literary *jeu d'esprit* which would have been nurtured in the intellectual atmosphere of the tenth-century Canterbury school.

Winchester

Æthelwold was promoted from the abbacy of Abingdon to the bishopric of Winchester in 963. For at least a decade before his accession, the see had been occupied by bishops of no distinction, and the monasteries were inhabited by clerics who – according to Æthelwold's biographer and student Ælfric – were thoroughly corrupt.[2] With the support of King Edgar Æthelwold expelled these clerics and replaced them with his own monks from Abingdon. From that time Æthelwold devoted his huge energy towards establishing Winchester as the pre-eminent English religious centre. His enterprises to this end were vast and numerous: he imported monks from Fleury and Corbie to instruct his native monks in plain chant; he attempted to establish and publicize the shrine of St Swithhun at Winchester with the translation of the saint's remains in 971; though we have no extensive records, a similar intention must also have inspired his translation of St Birinus's remains. Perhaps his most ambitious undertaking was the construction of a new cathedral at Winchester, which was then one of the largest churches in Europe.[3] This cathedral was fitted with a huge, lavish (and very noisy) organ.[4] In all these undertakings there is a concern with display and ostentation. This concern is seen also in the illuminated manuscripts which were produced under his direction at Winchester.[5] Of these, the most famous and splendid is the Benedictional of St Æthelwold.[6] From

---

[1] It has been suggested by J. D. A. Ogilvy ('Paraphrases Attributed to Albinus of Canterbury', *Univ. of Colorado Stud. in Lang. and Lit.* 9 (1963), 1–3) that these medical poems are related to the medical treatise found at various places in the manuscript. But this treatise was added in blank pages by a considerably later hand, and in any case the basis of the poems was a glossary, not a medical text.

[2] *Vita Athelwoldi*, c. 12, ed. M. Winterbottom, *Three Lives of English Saints* (Toronto, 1972), p. 22.

[3] See R. N. Quirk, 'Winchester Cathedral in the Tenth Century', *ArchJ* 114 (1957), 28–68.

[4] Wulfstan, *Narratio de S. Swithuno, praef.* 141–70, ed. Campbell, pp. 69–70.

[5] See T. D. Kendrick, *Late Saxon and Viking Art* (London, 1949), pp. 1–38; on Æthelwold's influence see esp. pp. 4–8; also F. Wormald, 'Decorated Initials in English Manuscripts from A.D. 900–1100', *Archaeologia* 91 (1945), 107–35, and 'Late Anglo-Saxon Art: some Questions and Suggestions', *Studies in Western Art* 1: *Acts of the Twentieth International Congress of the History of Art* (New York, 1963), 19–26.

[6] BM Add. 49598. There is a facsimile edition of this manuscript by G. F. Warner and H. A. Wilson, *The Benedictional of St Æthelwold*, Roxburghe Club (Oxford, 1910); see also the earlier

a poem in the manuscript that is lavishly written in gold capitals, we learn that the author of the poem and the scribe of the manuscript was one Godeman. It is probable that this Godeman was the monk of that name who was Æthelwold's chaplain at Winchester and who later became abbot of Æthelwold's foundation at Thorney, probably after Æthelwold's death in 984.[1] The poem has previously been consulted only as a means of dating the manuscript and has not been printed except in the facsimile edition of the manuscript.[2] I would suggest that the extremely ornate, hermeneutic style of the poem itself was considered by Æthelwold and Godeman to be the appropriate literary accompaniment to the lavish artistic production of the manuscript; I have consequently printed the poem in Appendix II. Within its brief compass Godeman's poem contains a number of grecisms – *agalma* ('image') [G], *biblos* [A, G], *Boanarges* (βοανηργές) [G], *craxare* ('to write') [A, G], *iconomos* [G], *heresis* [A, G] and *soter* ('saviour') [G] – as well as some other unusual forms (e.g. *baptizator* and *lurcon* [A, G]). The occurrence of such vocabulary in Æthelwold's personal benedictional strongly suggests that he was himself a sponsor of the hermeneutic style.

The extensive use of grecisms may be seen in another work which was almost certainly commissioned by Æthelwold: Lantfred's *Translatio et Miracula S. Swithuni*. This work is a simple record of the many miracles effected by the translation of St Swithhun's remains to within the new cathedral in 971, and the propagandizing tone of the work suggests that its principal function was to publicize the saint's newly founded shrine. Lantfred himself was from the continent and conceivably had been invited to Winchester by Æthelwold. His *Translatio et Miracula S. Swithuni* has never been fully or adequately edited,[3] but some observations on its vocabulary may not be premature. There are abundant grecisms: *adelphus* [G], *anastasis* ('resurrection') [A, G], *basileus* [Ab, G], *bioticus* ('secular') [Ab, G], *charisma* [A, G], *cosmus* [G], *cleptes* ('thief') [G], *dema* (δέμας, 'body') [G], *didasculus* ('teacher') [A, G], *doxa* ('glory') [A, Ab, G], *echonomus* [G], *empyrios*, *eucharis* ('gracious') [G], *eulogitus* ('blessed') [G], *forniforus* (φερνοφόρος,

---

study by J. Gage, 'A Dissertation on St Æthelwold's Benedictional', *Archaeologia* 24 (1832), 1–117, and the brief treatment by F. Wormald, *The Benedictional of St Ethelwold* (London, 1959), pp. 7–15.

[1] Warner and Wilson, *Benedictional*, pp. xiii–xiv. However, it has been suggested by J. B. L. Tolhurst ('An Examination of two Anglo-Saxon Manuscripts of the Winchester School: the Missal of Robert of Jumièges and the Benedictional of St Æthelwold', *Archaeologia* 83 (1933), 27–44) that the scribe of the book was one Godemann of Ely who had earlier been a monk of the New Minster, not the Godemann who afterwards became abbot of Thorney. The distinction is not essential to the present argument, since either Godemann was a monk at some time at Winchester under Æthelwold's direction.

[2] Warner and Wilson, *Benedictional*, p. 1.

[3] I have prepared an edition of this work as part of a forthcoming volume of tenth-century Anglo-Latin saints' lives, which will also include editions of Byrhtferth's *Vita S. Oswaldi* and *Vita S. Ecgwini* and the anonymous *Vita S. Rumwoldi*, all mentioned below.

'gift-bearer', hence 'teacher'?), *glaucoma* [A, Ab, G], *hierarchus*, *idalma* (εἴδωλα, 'images', influenced by *agalma*?), *idea* [G], *imera* ('day') [G], *machaera* ('knife') [A, G], *macharius* ('blessed') [G], *mathites* ('pupil') [G], *melota* ('sheepskin') [A, G], *omousios* ('of similar substance') [G], *onoma* ('name') [A, G], *pneuma* [G], *proseuca* ('chapel') [G], *rema* ('word') [G], *soma* ('body') [G], *sperma* [G], *stoma* ('mouth') [G], *symposium* [Ab, G], *trapezita* ('money-changer') [A, G] and *zoe* ('life') [G]. In addition to these grecisms, Lantfred uses the rare and archaic adverbs *opipare* [G] and *polose* [G], as well as the two verbs which were especially favoured by tenth-century Anglo-Latin writers: *floccipendo* [G] and *parvipendo* [G]. The unusual form *cecaumen* ('heat') was apparently coined from Greek καῦμα and the Latin termination *-men*.

Another student of Æthelwold at Winchester was the Wulfstan who is known as the author of several Latin works: the *Narratio de S. Swithuno*,[1] a metrical version of Lantfred's prose account of the miracles effected by the translation of Swithhun's remains; a short prose *Vita S. Ethelwoldi*;[2] some paracteric hymns are possibly his as well.[3] None of these works displays hermeneutic vocabulary as ostentatiously as do the works of Godemann and Lantfred; nevertheless, a considerable number of grecisms occur. Since in his *Narratio de S. Swithuno* Wulfstan was following the text of Lantfred closely, there is no point in listing again the numerous grecisms used by Wulfstan that he had found in Lantfred. But a few occur in Wulfstan that are not found in Lantfred, such as *agape* (meaning specifically 'alms') [A, Ab, G], *cauma* ('heat') [A, G] and *numisma* [A, G]. There are also a few common grecisms in the *Vita S. Ethelwoldi: basileus* [Ab, G], *crisma* [G] and *mandra* [A, G].

Three poems found in a late-tenth-century manuscript from Winchester may reasonably be assigned to the school of Winchester during Æthelwold's episcopacy. Two of the poems are a debate (*altercatio*) between a master and student; the third (which seems to have been addressed to Æthelwold himself) is a more philosophical reflection on the problem of free will.[4] Although the three poems are probably not by one author, it is convenient to consider them together. Like the other Winchester products of this period, they abound in grecisms: *adelphus* [G], *cleptes* [G], *clima* [A, G], *cosmicus* [G], *cosmus* [G], *epilenticus* [A, G], *idion* [G], *myirmica* (μύρμηξ, 'ant') [G], *paradigma*

---

[1] Ed. Campbell, *Frithegodi Breuiloquium*, pp. 65–177, and also M. Huber, *S. Swithunus: Miracula metrica auctore Wulfstano monacho*. Beilage zur Jahresbericht des humanistischen Gymnasiums Metten (1905–6), pp. 1–105. (Campbell's edition was not, as he thought, the first.)

[2] Ed. Winterbottom, *Three Lives*, pp. 33–63; cf. also Winterbottom's remarks on Wulfstan's prose style, p. 3.

[3] PL 137, cols. 81–105; also C. Blume, 'Wolstan von Winchester und Vital von Saint-Evroult', *Sitzungsberichte der königlichen Akademie der Wissenschaften in Wien* 146.3 (1903), 1–23; cf. discussion by H. Gneuss, *Hymnar und Hymnen im englischen Mittelalter* (Tübingen, 1968), pp. 246–8.

[4] See my edition of these poems: 'Three Latin Poems from Æthelwold's School at Winchester', *ASE* 1 (1972), 85–137.

[A, G], *pneuma* [G], *rema* [G], *scamma* [A, G], *scisma* [A, G], *sicophanta* [Ab, G], *sirma* [G], *sintagma* ('arrangement') [G], *sintheca* ('composition') [Ab, G], *sophisma* [A, G], *sophista* [A, G], *usia* ('substance') [G] and *ymera* ('day') [G]. At one point the poet of the *Altercatio* even lapses temporarily into Greek: *lempiris cruttonempiris* (probably for ἐμπείροις κρύπτων ἔμπειρος). There are also several archaic verb forms in the poems (*conquinisce, infi, inqui* and *siet* for *sit*). Other words appear to be neologisms, such as *cunctisator, pallade* ('wisely', 'after the manner of Pallas'?) and *serranus*,[1] though it is always possible that they were extracted from glossaries which either have been lost or are not yet printed. But the poet of the *Altercatio* took a great delight in coining words, and no glossary could account for a line such as 'spulpus eris, spulcus fueris spulsusque manebis'. Here the stylistic tendency to coin words results in an ingenious and imaginative invention.

Since all these tenth-century Latin compositions from Winchester are in some way directly connected with Æthelwold, it is reasonable to assume that Æthelwold himself was a sponsor of the ostentatious style affected in them. We know also that, among the books which he sent to his newly-founded monastery at Medeshamstede (Peterborough) was a book entitled 'de litteris grecorum' (no doubt a Greek–Latin glossary) and also a copy of Abbo's poem ('descidia Parisiace polis', probably only the third book).[2] From this it may be inferred that the Winchester curriculum (like that of Canterbury) included the study of difficult texts and the cultivation of the hermeneutic style, and that Æthelwold was anxious to establish a similar curriculum in his newly founded monastery. Given Æthelwold's personal interest in this style, it is worthwhile to re-examine some documents that were possibly composed by him. The first of these is a letter from an English bishop to Arnulf count of Flanders which is found in an epistolary collection (possibly from Canterbury).[3] The author of the letter calls himself 'Sancti N⟨ominis⟩ confessoris adque pontificis coenobii archimandrita'. As Stubbs noted, none of the English cathedrals has such a dedication except Winchester, which might be considered the church of St Swithhun, confessor and bishop.[4] There were two counts of Flanders named Arnulf: the elder (918–65) and his grandson (965–88); either might have received a letter from Æthelwold, whose episcopacy (963–84) overlapped both reigns. The letter is written in a very ostentatious style, including several grecisms (*archiman-*

---

[1] Because I was unable to explain the form of the word *sarranus*, I obelized the word in my edition (pp. 130–1). But the word was apparently familiar to students of the hermeneutic style in tenth-century England: it is found in Frithegod 349 (spelled *serranus*) and in an unprinted series of *glossae collectae* (from Abingdon, perhaps) in BM Harley 3826 (saec. x), 70v–71r and 150r–67v. Until glossary material of this sort in manuscripts of English origin is printed, the full extent of English hermeneutic style cannot be thoroughly studied.

[2] *BCS* 1128. The donation also included an *expositio Hebreorum nominum* (probably Jerome's) and a *sinonima Isidori* – two further source-books of obscure vocabulary.

[3] BM Cotton Tiberius A. xv, 155v; ptd Stubbs, *Memorials*, pp. 361–2.   [4] *Memorials*, p. 361.

drita [A, G], *catalogus* [A, G], *orthodoxus* [A, G], *sophista* [A, G], *theologus* [Ab] and *theoricus* [A, G]; from glosses in the manuscript we can infer that other grecisms in the letter have been obliterated); it ends with a prayer *pro policrati amore pantorumque agiorum*. The word *policrates* ('very mighty') is not found in glossaries. This letter should be compared with another document from Winchester: the foundation charter of the New Minster. This unusually fulsome and extensive document is dated 966, and survives in a separate manuscript which is very lavishly written in gold letters.[1] The Latinity of the charter matches the lavishness of the manuscript, particularly in its display of grecisms: *aporio* [A, G], *carisma* [A, G], *cataclisma* [A, G], *macrobius* (possibly a coinage from μακρός + βίος), *melancolia* [A, G], *policrates*, *pompaticus*, *singraphe* [G], *thema* [G] and *tirannos* [A, G]. The occurrence of the word *policrates* here is striking: except for this occurrence and the one in the letter from the bishop of Winchester mentioned above, it is not found anywhere else in Anglo-Latin. This may well suggest common authorship of these two documents. It has been argued on independent grounds that the New Minster foundation charter was composed by Æthelwold himself.[2] The hermeneutic style of both works, together with Æthelwold's known sponsorship of such a style, argues strongly in favour of Æthelwold's authorship. This stylistic argument is further strengthened by consideration of two charters which were composed and written by Æthelwold when he was abbot of Abingdon.[3] These two virtually identical charters also display a variety of grecisms (*agius* [G], *alogia* [G], *anagogicus*, *basileus* [Ab, G], *epilenticus* [A, G], *eulogium* [G], *microcosmus*, *philargiria* ('love of silver') [A, G] and *sintagma* [G]). A later charter 'dictated' by Æthelwold when he was bishop of Winchester is in a similar style.[4] He clearly considered that hermeneutic vocabulary was an appropriate stylistic ornament for the language of a charter. His influence (and possibly his actual authorship) may therefore also be suspected in a series of hermeneutic charters from Winchester during his episcopacy.[5] In any case, the use of grecisms in charters from Abingdon and Winchester that were certainly composed by Æthelwold exactly

---

[1] BM Cotton Vespasian A. viii (saec. x²), 3v–33v; ptd *BCS* 1190. See F. Wormald, 'Late Anglo-Saxon Art', pp. 19–26, and E. John, *Orbis Britanniae* (Leicester, 1966), pp. 271–5.

[2] D. Whitelock, 'The Authorship of the Account of King Edgar's Establishment of Monasteries', in *Philological Essays: Studies in Old and Middle English Language and Literature in honour of Herbert Dean Meritt*, ed. J. L. Rosier (The Hague, 1970), pp. 125–36, esp. 131.

[3] *BCS* 1046 ('Ego Aþelwold abbas hoc eulogium manu propria apicibus depinxi') and 1047 ('Ego Æþelwold abbas Abbandunensis coenobii hoc sintagma triumphans dictavi'). On these charters see E. John, 'Some Latin Charters of the Tenth-Century Reformation', *RB* 70 (1960), 333–59, and also P. Chaplais, 'The Anglo-Saxon Chancery: from the Diploma to the Writ', *Jnl of the Soc. of Archivists* 3 (1965–9), 160–76, esp. 163–5.

[4] *BCS* 1138 ('Ego Athelwold Wintoniensis ecclesiae episcopus hanc cartam dictitans rege suisque precipientibus prescribere jussi').

[5] *BCS* 1147 and 1149–59. Grecisms in these charters include *agiographus* [A, G], *cleronomia*, *dyrocheus*(?), *kalo* [G] and *sinthema* [G].

Michael Lapidge

resembles that in the letter to Arnulf of Flanders and the foundation charter of the New Minster, and it is not fanciful to see all these compositions as the work of Æthelwold. If so, it is interesting to have even this small corpus of Latin writings[1] in the hermeneutic style by the man who was in so many ways the agent of publicity and ostentation at tenth-century Winchester.

Ramsey

The monastery at Ramsey was founded in 969 by Oswald, then bishop of Worcester. The renowned French scholar, Abbo of Fleury, taught there briefly (986–8) at the invitation of Dunstan, but the best known native English scholar from Ramsey in the late tenth century was Byrhtferth, who had been a student of Abbo and who is known as the author of two extant works: the *Manual*,[2] an extensive discussion of computistical theory (and related material) partly in Latin, partly in English; and the brief *epilogus*, as Byrhtferth calls it, that was written to accompany a manuscript of Bede's computistical works.[3] The purpose of the *Manual* is plainly didactic – it attempts to explain the complexities of computistical theory to novitiates whose Latin is rudimentary – and it necessarily includes a certain amount of technical vocabulary of Greek origin (e.g. *embolismus*, *epacte*, *epagomene* etc.). One would not expect a display of hermeneutic vocabulary for its own sake in a primer of this nature. And yet there is in Byrhtferth's style a remarkable inclination towards uncommon words. I note the following grecisms which are not technical terms: *biblitheca* ('the bible') [A, G], *caraxare* ('to write') [A, G], *metron* [G], *onoma* ('name') [A, G], *oroma* ('vision') [A, G], *peripsema* ('off-scouring') [A, G], *philacterion* ('security') [G], *senpecta* (συμπαίκτης, 'older monk') [G], *sophisticus* [G], *stema* [A, G], *tetrarcha* [A, G] and *theologia* [G]. He also prefers rather uncommon adverbs: *concorditer* [A], *diatim* [G], *enerviter* [A], *opipare* [G] and *peramplius*. Often he twists the sense of a common word to give it a completely new meaning: *euiscero*, 'to disembowel', is made to mean 'to set out clearly'. So although the intention of the *Manual* is didactic, there is some discernible predilection for hermeneutic vocabulary.

[1] In addition to these Latin works, the *Regularis Concordia* (ed. T. Symons (London, 1953)) is generally agreed to be by Æthelwold. It is written (as one would expect) in a simple unadorned style appropriate for a manual of monastic discipline.

[2] Ed. S. J. Crawford, Early Eng. Text Soc. (London, 1929). Crawford's second volume of commentary never appeared; see instead the *corrigenda* by H. Henel, 'Notes on Byrhtferth's Manual', *JEGP* 41 (1942), 427–43, and the further studies by Henel, *Studien zum altenglischen Computus*. Beiträge zur englischen Philologie 26 (Leipzig, 1934), and C. Hart, 'Byrhtferth and his Manual', *MÆ* 41 (1972), 95–109.

[3] Oxford, St John's College 17; ed. G. F. Forsey, 'Byrhtferth's Preface', *Speculum* 3 (1928), 505–22. It has been argued that this epilogue was in fact intended by Byrhtferth to be the epilogue of his *Manual*: H. Henel, 'Byrhtferth's Preface: the Epilogue of his Manual?', *Speculum* 18 (1943), 288–302.

90

This predilection may be more fully revealed by a consideration of two further works which are conceivably by Byrhtferth.

There is a *Vita S. Oswaldi* preserved in a single eleventh-century manuscript from Worcester which appears from internal evidence to have been written sometime between 997 and 1005 by a monk of Ramsey.[1] Crawford suggested, on the basis of some undeniable verbal parallels with Byrhtferth's *Manual*, that the author of this *Vita S. Oswaldi* was Byrhtferth himself.[2] Although certain reservations have been expressed,[3] Crawford's identification has on the whole been accepted. There is no need to rehearse Crawford's evidence and arguments here; rather, I suggest that the identification may be confirmed by consideration of another saint's life perhaps by Byrhtferth: the *Vita S. Ecgwini*.

In the above-mentioned manuscript from Worcester which contains the unique copy of the *Vita S. Oswaldi*, there is found, immediately following the *Vita*, a unique copy of a life of St Ecgwine, an early-eighth-century bishop of Worcester (*ob.* 717) who was the founder of the monastery at Evesham. This *Vita S. Ecgwini* is generally unknown and has been printed only once, more than a century ago, in an edition that is totally unreliable.[4] The author of the *Vita S. Ecgwini* tells us that he is writing just after the year 1000,[5] but gives no further clue to his identity. However, there are so many striking verbal parallels between the *Vita S. Ecgwini* and the *Vita S. Oswaldi* that one is led to assume some relationship between the two. Here briefly are some of the most convincing parallels:

Vita S. Ecgwini, ed. Giles	*Vita S. Oswaldi*, ed. Raine
quis urbana fretus eloquentia potest pleniter investigare? (p. 349)	quis urbanitatis fretus eloquentia potest proferri? (p. 447); quis urbanitate fretus

---

[1] BM Cotton Nero E. i, Pt 1, 1r–23v; ed. Raine, *Historians of the Church of York* 1, 399–475. On the dating see F. Liebermann, 'Zur Geschichte Byrhtnoths', *ASNSL* 101 (1898), 23, and Whitelock, *English Historical Documents* 1, 839.

[2] S. J. Crawford, 'Byrhtferth of Ramsey and the Anonymous Life of St Oswald', *Speculum Religionis. Studies presented to C. G. Montefiore* (Oxford, 1929), pp. 99–111.

[3] J. A. Robinson ('Byrhtferth and the Life of Oswald', *JTS* 31 (1930), 35–42) pointed to certain differences in the use of the relative pronoun and D. J. V. Fisher ('The Antimonastic Reaction in the Reign of Edward the Martyr', *Cambridge Hist. Jnl* 10 (1950–2), 254–70) has observed certain chronological errors in the *Vita S. Oswaldi*, such as the placing of the Battle of Maldon before Dunstan's death, which would be improbable in a work produced at Ramsey. D. J. V. Fisher suggests that the work by Byrhtferth was partially rewritten by a later author unfamiliar with the events of Oswald's life at first hand. See further E. John, *Orbis Britanniae*, pp. 290–1.

[4] BM Cotton Nero E. i, Pt 1, 24r–34v; ed. J. A. Giles, *Vita Quorundam Anglo-Saxonum*, Publ. of the Caxton Soc. (London, 1854), pp. 349–96. Fisher ('The Antimonastic Reaction', p. 259, n. 18) drew attention in a footnote to certain similarities between the *Vita S. Oswaldi* and the *Vita S. Ecgwini*, but did not pursue the question.

[5] Ed. Giles, p. 387: 'nos vero, qui in ultima millenarii sumus parte et ultra progressi'.

Michael Lapidge

Vita S. Ecgwini ed. Giles	*Vita S. Oswaldi* ed. Raine
	potest edicere? (p. 456; cf. p. 428: urbana fretus facundia)
Gregorii antistitis Romuleae urbis (p. 349)	egregii Romuleae urbis Gregorii patris (p. 433)
Leviathan tortuosum serpentem (p. 352)	Leviathan serpentem tortuosum (p. 433)
genitores Jordanico sacro flumine tingui (p. 353)	Jordanico flumine abluti (p. 400); tincti Jordanico flumine (p. 422)
tum miles praecellens Christi...praesul quoque flagrans superno desiderio undisonos fluctus maris pertransit, et ad sanctorum limina pervenit gaudens apostolorum (p. 358)	miles praecellens Christi, flagrans... superno desiderio, undisonos fluctus salsi maris pertransit, et ad sanctorum limina pervenit gaudens apostolorum (p. 435)
reversus almus praesul tripudians ad proprium solum, odas reddidit summo Jhesu, qui sibi destinavit suae sedis ministrum sanctum Raphaelem archangelum (p. 360)	reversus almus pater ad solum proprium, odas reddidit summo Jhesu, qui sibi destinavit suae sedis ministrum Raphahelem archangelum (p. 436)
quem ego levi petitione a rege Aethelredo...adquisivi (p. 363)	quod leni a rege petitione adquisivit (p. 420)
rex autem armipotens Koenred (p. 378)	rex autem armipotens Eadgar (p. 425)

The list could be prolonged considerably. There are also numerous smaller phrases – one might almost say formulae – which are common to both works: old age is normally *cygnea canities*, Rome is always the *Romulea urbs*, the sun always *aureus sol* and the moon always *vaga Lucina*; the distinction between earthly and heavenly life is invariably expressed by the parallel *in arvis...in astris*. All these common phrases and expressions, together with the common store of hermeneutic vocabulary (see discussion below) suggest incontestably that the author of the *Vita S. Ecgwini* is that of the *Vita S. Oswaldi*.

Since Byrhtferth has been proposed as the author of the *Vita S. Oswaldi*, one is obliged to ask whether there is evidence of common authorship between the *Vita S. Ecgwini* and Byrhtferth's *Manual*. Here, again, the parallels are many and striking:

Vita S. Ecgwini, ed. Giles	Byrhtferth's *Manual*, ed. Crawford
constat istius vita breviter edita, et in bis binis partibus divisa; quae quatuor partes demonstrant quid in pueritia vel adolescentia sive in juventute atque in senectute gessit (p. 350)	sunt loca bis binorum temporum, veris aetatis, autumni et hiemis, et qualitates vel aetates hominum, id est, pueritia, adolescentia, iuventus et senectus (p. 10; cf. p. 204)
regali diademate ornatus (p. 379)	suffultus regali diademate (p. 204)
in parte anatolae quae est oriens, duo principes...mansitabant. in mysimbri climate, quae est meridies, bini duces... accumbebant. in disis loco, qui est occidens, complices duo manebant. in	ipsi quoque orientem appellant anathole, et occidentem disyn, et aquilonem arcton, et meridiem misymbrion (p. 202)

92

Vita S. Ecgwini, ed. Giles	Byrhtferth's *Manual*, ed. Crawford
arctonis climate, quae est septentrio, dominatum possidebant bini comites (p. 382)	
(quinarius) significat unitatem quae est in Deo, quia unus est Deus; duoque sequuntur dilectionem Dei et proximi (p. 386)	quinarius: ternarius ad sancte Trinitatis pertinet mysterium, binarius vero ad dilectionem dei et proximi (p. 204; cf. *Vita S. Oswaldi*, p. 416: dilectione Dei et proximi)
fructum opimum et opipare quod nos splendide dicere possumus (p. 386)	qualiter fructuosus duodenarius numerus sit opipare, id est splendide (p. 222)

These verbal parallels are striking enough in themselves, but they become more striking when one considers how unusual the appearance of scientific material (such as the names of the four *climata*) is in a saint's life. There are many more similarities between Byrhtferth's *Manual* and the *Vita S. Ecgwini*, such as the citation of particular lines from Arator or the tendency to numerological explanations, but it would protract the argument unnecessarily to present them all here.[1] Perhaps enough evidence has been presented to allow the conclusion that Byrhtferth was the author of both the *Vita S. Oswaldi* and the *Vita S. Ecgwini*.[2]

Given that these two saints' lives are by Byrhtferth, we may return to the question of his Latin style. I suggested above that, even within the restricted didactic scope of the *Manual*, there is a perceptible predilection for hermeneutic vocabulary. The saint's life, particularly in tenth-century England, was a medium much more suited to the display of such vocabulary, and it is not surprising, perhaps, to see so wide a range of hermeneutic vocabulary in Byrhtferth's *Vita S. Oswaldi* and *Vita S. Ecgwini*. These two works (taken together here for the sake of convenience) exhibit many grecisms: *agonista* [A, G], *agonitheta* [Ab, G], *algema* ('pain') [Ab, G], *anastasis* ('resurrection') [A, G], *antismos* (ἀστεϊσμός, 'urbanity') [G], *archiatros* ('principal physician') [A, G], *archisterium* ('monastery') [Ab, G], *caraxo* ('to write') [A, G], *cataplasma* ('poultice') [A, G], *emplastra* ('salve') [G], *epicedion* ('dirge') [A, G], *epitaphion* [A, G], *exoticus* [G], *flebotoma* ('blood-letting') [A, G], *geron* ('old man') [G], *glaucomia* [G], *gymnosophista* [A, G], *hierarchus* [G], *machaera* ('knife') [A, G], *onoma* ('name') [A, G], *orgia* ('rites') [A, G], *oroma* ('vision') [A, G], *paraclitus* [A, G], *paranymphus* [A, G], *poderes* ('priestly

---

[1] I have considered Byrhtferth's authorship of the *Vita S. Ecgwini* in greater detail in a forthcoming article: 'Byrhtferth and the *Vita S. Ecgwini*'.

[2] These proposed additions to the canon of Byrhtferth's Latin writings should be seen in the context of recent research on the canon of his English writings. It has been suggested, for example, that he compiled a vernacular Hexateuch, using whatever translations by Ælfric were available and himself translating the rest; see Peter Clemoes, 'The Composition of the Old English Text', *The Old English Illustrated Hexateuch*, ed. C. R. Dodwell and Peter Clemoes, EEMF 18 (Copenhagen, 1974), 42–53. I am extremely grateful to Peter Clemoes for discussing Byrhtferth with me.

robe') [G], *soma* ('body') [G], *stema* [A, G], *synaxis* ('assembly') [A, G], *tetrarcha* [A, G], *theca* [A, Ab, G], *theophilus, theoricus* [A, G], *tiriacis* (θηριακός, 'antidote') [A, G], *topographia* and *uranicus*. It will be seen that some of these words were also found in the *Manual*. Byrhtferth was clearly pleased with his display of Greek vocabulary. At one point in the *Vita S. Oswaldi* where he wishes to retrace his steps to an earlier argument, he writes, 'utendum puto anabibazon (=ἀναβιβάζων) verbo, quod significat sursum scandens'. The tendency to use rare adverbs that was noticed in the *Manual* is exceptionally pronounced in the two saints' lives: I note *affabiliter* [A], *agiliter* [G], *amicabiliter* [G], *concorditer* [A], *dapsiliter, diatim* [G], *digniter, enerviter* [A], *festine, fiducialiter* [A, G], *gratanter, honorabiliter, immarcessibiliter, immisericorditer, indigniter, inedicibiliter, ineffabiliter, irreprehensibiliter, magnanimiter, manipulatim* [A, G], *modulanter* [G], *opipare* [G], *optabiliter, paternaliter, praesentialiter* and *regaliter* [G]. Many of these adverbs appear to be coinages. Byrhtferth also uses the archaic adverbs *susum* [G] and *iosum* (for *sursum* and *deorsum*). His predilection for adjectives is less pronounced than that for adverbs, but there are none the less some extremely curious forms which are probably coinages: *beliabus* and *Beelzebutinus* (both meaning 'devilish' and neither occurring elsewhere), *confessoricus, dulcibilis, inedicibilis* and *lurconus*. Finally there are a few nouns which seem to be neologisms: *archiptes, malignatio, prototestis, pubetinus, strucio* (which normally means 'ostrich' but refers in Byrhtferth to some ecclesiastical order: 'quondam mansitabant diacones et struciones') and *urbecula*. Byrhtferth's Latin is difficult, though not nearly as difficult as that of Frithegod. But that as pedantic a schoolmaster as Byrhtferth (as we know him from his *Manual*) would consciously cultivate the hermeneutic style indicates that the Ramsey curriculum, like that of Canterbury and Winchester, included the study and imitation of hermeneutic texts.

Before leaving Ramsey one more brief work should be mentioned. There is a short poem by one 'Osuuoldus' in an eleventh-century manuscript from St Augustine's, Canterbury.[1] This poem has never been printed, but because it provides some further evidence for the cultivation of the hermeneutic style at Ramsey, I have printed it below as Appendix III. There are two possibilities for the identification of this Oswald. First, St Oswald himself, who was bishop of Worcester and York and was the founder of Ramsey (*ob.* 992). The poem exhibits several unusual words, and it will be remembered that St Oswald was the nephew of Oda of Canterbury and had been the student of Frithegod;[2] he presumably would have been conversant with the hermeneutic style. But a somewhat stronger case may be made for a younger

[1] ULC Gg. 5. 35, 419r–v.
[2] *Historia Ramesiensis*, ed. W. D. Macray, RS (1886), p. 21.

The hermeneutic style in tenth-century Anglo-Latin literature

Oswald who was the nephew of St Oswald, who like him had studied at Fleury, and who was later a monk at Ramsey and a contemporary of Byrhtferth. We learn from the later *Historia Ramesiensis* that a volume of poetry by him was extant at the time the compiler of this chronicle was writing,[1] though it has not survived. Leland ascribed to this Oswald several works (now lost) including a *Liber sacrarum precationum* and the treatise *de componendis epistolis*.[2] It will be seen that the poem itself (in Appendix III) is concerned with the process of composing poetry: 'Osuuoldus' sets out the requirements by which a poet may be considered 'Vergilian' and then confesses his own ignorance of the art of poetic composition, finally asking the reader to correct whatever poetic peccadilloes he may have committed. It is, in short, just the sort of poem an author of a treatise *de componendis epistolis* might have written. The poem is interesting for stylistic reasons: it contains some grecisms (notably *pneuma* [G] and the hybrid *doctilogos* [G]) and some archaisms (*ergo* as prep. with gen. and *mismet*). Most striking is the occurrence of the archaisms *iosum* and *susum* in the last line; these two words also occur in Byrhtferth's *Vita S. Ecgwini* but (as far as I know) in no other Anglo-Latin source.[3] This would tend to confirm the location of the poem in the Ramsey of Byrhtferth's time, and the identification of its author as the younger Oswald who wrote the treatise *de componendis epistolis*. But it suggests that there were more authors at Ramsey cultivating the hermeneutic style than Byrhtferth, and that St Oswald, who had earlier been a student of Frithegod, had ensured that the study of hermeneutic texts formed part of the curriculum in his new foundation at Ramsey.

Glastonbury

It is from the monastery at Glastonbury that the English Benedictine reform movement appears to have begun: Dunstan was abbot there from 940, and shortly afterwards Æthelwold studied there with him. Unfortunately, there are very few surviving literary documents which were composed at Glastonbury. More unfortunate still is the fact that no extensive Latin writings of Dunstan himself survive from the period of his Glastonbury abbacy. We have seen how the other principal leaders of the English Benedictine reform movement – Oda, Æthelwold and Oswald – had personally endorsed the study of the hermeneutic style, and it is interesting to ask whether Dunstan too had encouraged the imitation of it. In this connection two brief poems which appear to have been composed by Dunstan at Glastonbury may be

[1] Ed. Macray, p. 160: 'habetur hodieque in archivis nostris liber ejus versificus, multiformis peritiae ipsius et perspicacis ingenii testis'.
[2] *Commentarii de scriptoribus Britannicis*, ed. A. Hall (Oxford, 1709) I, 172.
[3] Cf., however, Odo of Cluny, *Occupatio* 1.206: 'figitur haec iosum, comit uas tonsio susum'.

considered. Because these poems have not previously been brought into discussion of Dunstan's scholarly achievement (and, oddly enough, are both omitted from Stubb's *Memorials of St Dunstan*), I have printed them below as Appendix IV. The first of these poems (Appendix IV(*a*)) is a distich in which Dunstan simply asks for Christ's protection; it is found on the first folio of a manuscript which was at Glastonbury in the tenth century and which is known as 'Dunstan's Classbook'.[1] The second poem (Appendix IV(*b*)) is found in a late-tenth-/early-eleventh-century manuscript of Augustine's *Encheiridion*;[2] it is in the form of an acrostic on O PATER OMNIPOTENS DIGNERIS FERRE DONANTI. The final letters of each line spell out the sentence INDIGNVM ABBATEM DVNSTANVM XPĒ RESPECTES. This sentence establishes that the poem was composed during Dunstan's abbacy (940–*c.* 957) by Dunstan himself, for no one else would address him as *indignus*, 'unworthy'. Given this, the poem assumes importance as a virtually unique witness to Dunstan's literary and scholarly ability.[3] It is evidently the production of a poet who took pride in his command of Latin and delight in his ability to outwit his readers. The syntax of the poem is so disordered that its meaning may be discovered – if at all – only with immense difficulty. Some of the syntactical disorders were caused perhaps by the exigencies of the acrostic form. But one gets the impression from working with the poem that most of its obscurities are fully intentional and that Dunstan wrote it as a deliberate challenge to his readers' wits. I have made some attempt in the notes accompanying the poem to rearrange the syntax and to decode its meaning, but such attempts are by no means founded on certainty, as anyone who spends a moment or two with the poem will quickly discover. For the purposes of the present discussion, however, the vocabulary of Dunstan's poem is noteworthy. It includes several grecisms, such as *logia* (for λογία, n.pl. of λογίον, or perhaps even λογεία) [G] and *neofilax* (ναοφύλαξ, 'custodian of the temple') [G], as well as the possible neologism *tetrificus*. These words clearly indicate – notwithstanding the poem's manifold syntactical difficulties – that Dunstan was familiar with the hermeneutic style. Although one poem is

---

[1] Oxford, Bodleian Library, Auct. F. 4. 32; see R. W. Hunt, *St Dunstan's Classbook from Glastonbury: Cod. Bibl. Bodl. Auct. F. 4. 32*, Umbrae Codicum Occidentalium 4 (1961).

[2] Cambridge, Trinity College O. 1. 18, 112v–13r (see M. R. James, *The Western Manuscripts in the Library of Trinity College Cambridge* (Cambridge, 1900–2) III, 19–22. A partial copy of the poem (the first twenty-two lines, without initials) is found also in a manuscript from Christ Church, Canterbury (Cambridge, Trinity College B. 14. 3, 65v (saec. x/xi)); see James, *Western Manuscripts* I, 404–6.

[3] The only other surviving Latin work by Dunstan is a rather unexceptional charter (*BCS* 880) which he claims to have composed: 'Ego Dunstan indignus abbas rege Eadredo imperante hanc domino meo hereditariam kartulam dictitando composui et propriis digitorum articulis perscripsi.' It is perhaps noteworthy that here too he addresses himself as *indignus abbas*. Other works attributed to Dunstan by T. Wright (*Biographia Britannica Literaria* (London, 1842), pp. 458–62) are spurious.

admittedly slender evidence, it suggests that Dunstan, like the other principal leaders of the English monastic reform movement, was a sponsor of difficult and hermeneutic style, and that this style was cultivated at Glastonbury where the reform movement effectively began.

From later in the tenth century there are two letters from Glastonbury which were written by Abbot Ælfweard (*c.* 975–?1009). Both are addressed to Sigeric, archbishop of Canterbury (990–4); the authorship of one is specified and that of the other is to be inferred from shared vocabulary and similarity of style.[1] Both are written in an extremely tortuous style which includes several grecisms such as *ciriceus* (κηρύκειος, 'herald's wand', 'pastoral staff') [G] and *misteriarcha* ('leader of mysteries', hence 'archbishop'), several extremely rare adverbs such as *incunctanter* [G] and *praecluenter*, and some striking words which are probably coinages: *ambrosciatim* ('ambrosially'), *paradisicola* and *pilivertentia* ('versatility'?). So although the surviving records from Glastonbury are few, they witness to the affectation of the hermeneutic style there as well.

Other centres of uncertain identity

In the last quarter of the tenth century the *Chronicon*, a cursory account of English history based on a lost version of the *Anglo-Saxon Chronicle*, was composed by one Æthelweard.[2] If, as seems almost certain, this historian Æthelweard was identical with the ealdorman of Wessex of that name who witnessed charters between 973 and 998, who was a patron of Ælfric, and whose son Æthelmær founded in 987 the monastery of Cerne, then one may infer that the *Chronicon* was written in Wessex. Æthelweard's Latinity is quite distinctive,[3] and one of its most interesting features is its hermeneutic vocabulary. He uses a variety of grecisms: *anax* ('lord') [G], *artemon* ('ship') [G], *chrisma* [G], *dromon* ('small ship'), *fasma* ('speech', as in Frithegod, not 'phantom'), *pancalus* ('all-good'), *phagolidorus* ('swallower of insults') [G], *scarmos* (σκαλμός, 'thole'), *sinclitus* ('summoned council') [G], *stefos* (syncopated from στέφανος probably), *stema* [A, G] and *stomion* ('mouth', 'estuary') [G]. Several of these words are not found in glossaries, and the same is true of two other remarkable grecisms – *moneris* (μονήρης, 'ship') and *suda* (σοῦδα, 'rampart') – which are medieval Greek forms and could conceivably have been learned by Æthelweard from a native Greek speaker. There are no notable archaisms in the *Chronicon*, but occasionally Æthelweard uses an extremely rare Latin word from an earlier writer, such as *nexilitas*. Most

[1] Ed. W. Stubbs, *Memorials*, pp. 399–403.
[2] *Chronicon Æthelweardi*, ed. A. Campbell (London, 1962). See also L. Whitbread, 'Æthelweard and the *Anglo-Saxon Chronicle*', EHR 74 (1959), 577–89.
[3] See Campbell's discussion of Æthelweard's Latinity, *Chronicon*, pp. xlv–lx, as well as the accurate discussion by M. Winterbottom, 'The Style of Æthelweard', MÆ 36 (1967), 109–18.

interesting, however, are Æthelweard's neologisms: the adverbs *animotenus* and *facietenus*; the adjectives *bradifonus* (coined on the analogy of βραδύγλωσσος, 'slow of tongue'), *Iupitereus*, *mausoleatus*, *oneriferus* and *paludensis*; or the ponderous verb *historigraphizare*. All these words are particularly arresting in the Latinity of a layman, and for this reason it would be fascinating to discover where Æthelweard received his education.

Also from an indeterminable centre are the pedagogical works of Ælfric Bata. This Ælfric Bata, or simply Bata, was a student of the more famous Ælfric.[1] Since he is thought to have been living at the time of the Norman Conquest, it is generally assumed that he studied with Ælfric at Eynsham (after 1005) rather than earlier at Cerne.[2] He is known as the author of two sets of colloquies;[3] he also produced a revised version of Ælfric's own *Colloquy*.[4] Because all novitiates at any monastery were expected to converse in Latin, it was necessary to devise some means of providing them with sufficient vocabulary for such conversation. Bata's two sets of colloquies, modelled to some extent on those of his master Ælfric, were written to meet that need by presenting in the first set a series of conversations in elementary language and then in the second set a series of dialogues in which more difficult – or hermeneutic – vocabulary was introduced. The elementary *Colloquia* were clearly not intended by Bata to present lexical difficulties, but it is interesting to note that several very unusual words, particularly adverbs, creep in (e.g. *memoriter*, *mensurate* and *morigeranter*); even the word by which the master is addressed – *papas* (πάππας) – is a somewhat unusual grecism. Bata's set of more difficult colloquies (*Colloquia Difficiliora*) naturally presents more obscure vocabulary, but it should be recalled that they were intended as exercises for students and therefore have none of the difficulties of (say) Frithegod. A few common grecisms are found: *basileus* [Ab, G], *biblos* [A, G], *didascolus* [A, G], *rabbites* ('master') [A], *rema* ('word') [G], *sophia* [A, G], *sophista* [A, G], *sophus* [A, G], *sperma* [G], *uranicus* ('celestial') and *xenia* ('hospitality') [G]. Bata's tendency to use uncommon adverbs is more pro-

---

[1] On Bata see the brief discussion by G. N. Garmonsway, *Ælfric's Colloquy* (London, 1939), pp. 7–8.

[2] Cf. Caroline L. White, *Ælfric*, Yale Stud. in Eng. 2 (New Haven, 1898; repr. Hamden (Connecticut), 1974), p. 122, and Garmonsway, *Ælfric's Colloquy*, p. 7.

[3] Ed. W. H. Stevenson, *Early Scholastic Colloquies* (Oxford, 1929), pp. 27–74.

[4] Ed. Garmonsway, *Ælfric's Colloquy*. In one manuscript of the work (Oxford, St John's College 154, 204r) there is a prefatory remark by Bata: 'Hanc sententiam Latini sermonis olim Ælfricus Abbas composuit qui meus fuit magister; sed tamen ego Ælfric Bata multas postea huic addidi appendices' (Stevenson, *Early Scholastic Colloquies*, p. 75). Unfortunately, there is no way of knowing how much Bata actually added to the work, and therefore no way of knowing which part of it is Ælfric's and which Bata's. I suspect that the *exordium* (ed. Garmonsway, pp. 48–9) is not by Ælfric but by Bata: it contains two of the bizarre multi-syllabic adverbs which Bata preferred (*disciplinabiliter* and *morigerate*) as well as the grecism *mathites* [G] and is thus more in the spirit of Bata's style than that of Ælfric's unadorned Latin prose.

nounced in his difficult colloquies: *affectualiter, celotenus, consilenter, delectabiliter* [A], *medulliter, mentaliter, perniciter* [G], *polotenus* and *uolupe* (an archaism). He also uses several unusual words that are found in other Anglo-Latin authors: *floccipendo* [G], *forniforus* (as in Lantfred; glossed by Bata as *didasculus*) and *inbuenta* ('teaching'), probably a coinage by Bata but very reminiscent of the nouns formed from *imbuo* in the writings of B. It would therefore be interesting to learn where Bata composed his colloquies.

The list of tenth-century Anglo-Latin writings which display a hermeneutic style might be prolonged considerably by the mention of many smaller works which display one or two obscure words, insignificant testimonies in themselves but clearly indicative of the wide-spread stylistic tendency of that time: an anonymous poem in honour of St Dunstan which suddenly lapses into Greek ('emulat adomenon, psallomenon, aulomenonque');[1] an epitaph (probably composed at Canterbury) of Archbishop Ælfric which speaks of his remains as *lypsana* (λείψανα);[2] the bizarre verses by one Euben (Welsh Owain) prefixed to the 'Nennian' recension of the *Historia Brittonum*.[3] But perhaps the most interesting index to the pervasiveness of this style in tenth-century England is in the series of royal charters beginning with the reign of Athelstan which are couched in extremely pompous and hermeneutic language.

The Anglo-Latin royal charters of the tenth century preserve roughly the traditional form of English charters of the pre-Alfredian period. From a literary point of view, that form may be described as tripartite: it consists in (1) a proem or exordium in which God's omnipotence and the universal order is proclaimed (or some such statement); (2) the verbal disposition in which the donation is specified (in the tenth century this disposition is usually accompanied by an explanation in English of the boundary clauses); (3) the anathema, a curse on anyone who might dare to alter the terms of the charter. A list of witnesses, usually the king and the principal lay and ecclesiastical ministers of the realm, is appended.[4] The second part was necessarily of a fixed and simple form (the disposition could admit no ambiguity). In the tenth century, however, particularly from the reign of Athelstan (925–39) onwards, certain stylistic changes are introduced within this tripartite framework, especially in the proem.[5] The proem is henceforth written in an intentionally ostentatious and pompous style, no doubt to

---

[1] Ed. Stubbs, *Memorials*, p. 373.
[2] Ed. M. Förster, *Anglia* 41 (1917), 154.
[3] Ed. D. N. Dumville, ' "Nennius" and the *Historia Brittonum*', *Studia Celtica* 10 (1975), where they are assigned to the mid-eleventh century.
[4] Cf. F. M. Stenton, *The Latin Charters of the Anglo-Saxon Period* (Oxford, 1955), p. 55. See also the general remarks by N. Brooks, 'Anglo-Saxon Charters: the Work of the Last Twenty Years', *ASE* 3 (1974), 211–31.
[5] The principal collections of charters are J. M. Kemble, *Codex Diplomaticus Aevi Saxonici*, 6 vols. (London, 1839–48) and *BCS*.

convey an impression of the majesty of the royal donor and the importance of his donation. The principal means of this ostentation is, not surprisingly, the parade of hermeneutic vocabulary. On the simplest level, this vocabulary is merely borrowed wholesale from Aldhelm; Aldhelmian phrases such as *toto conamine mentis, triquadri orbis latitudo* or *peripsema quisquiliarum*, for example, become clichés in the charters of Edward and Athelstan. But beginning with the latter's reign, and then again in the reigns of Eadwig and Edgar,[1] a number of grecisms are introduced which thereafter become part of conventional charter language: *agius* [G], *alogia* [Ab, G], *antilogium* (ἀντιλογία, 'contradiction') [G], *antropus* ('man') [Ab, G], *archimandrita* [A, G], *archon* [Ab, G], *basileus* [Ab, G], *cataclisma* [A, G], *chrisus* ('gold') [G], *cleronomus* ('heir') [Ab, G], *croma* ('colour, complexion') [G], *eon* [G], *epilempticus* [A, G], *gastrimargia* ('gluttony') [A, G], *holocaustoma* ('burnt-offering') [A, G], *kalo* ('to call') [G], *kyrius* ('lord') [A, G], *olus* ('all') [Ab, G], *onoma* ('name') [A, G], *philargiria* ('love of silver') [A, G], *poliandria* [G], *protogenes* [G], *sinthema* ('agreement') [G], *soma* ('body') [G], *sother* ('saviour') [G], *tauma* ('wonder') [G], *theos* [Ab, G] and *usia* ('substance') [G]. This list is not exhaustive and is intended only to indicate what sort of grecisms were employed to ornament the language of royal charters;[2] detailed comment must await the publication of accurate and critical texts of the charters in question. I have mentioned above that grecisms were particularly prominent in charters from Abingdon and Winchester during the ascendancy of Æthelwold in those two places. But it is noteworthy that much of this hermeneutic vocabulary appears in charters that were written during Athelstan's reign, that is, considerably before the monastic reform movement was fully under way. This would suggest that already in the early tenth century there was a vogue in England for the hermeneutic style. One wonders whether the hermeneutic style of Athelstan's charters owes anything to the reputedly close relationship between that king and Oda of Canterbury.[3] In any case, a detailed study of the vocabulary of Anglo-Latin

[1] The charters of Athelstan's reign are *BCS* 641–746, of Eadwig's *BCS* 917–1009 and 1025–35 and of Edgar's *BCS* 1036–1319. These numbers are very approximate, and are intended simply to indicate where a stylistic study of charters might begin. See also *The Crawford Collection of Early Charters and Documents now in the Bodleian Library*, ed. S. A. Napier and W. H. Stevenson (Oxford, 1895), nos. IV–VI.

[2] Three words in these charters deserve special comment in so far as they are also found in Hisperic texts. *Giboniferus* ('fiery') occurs also in the *Rubisca*, and *tanaliter* ('in a deadly manner'?) in the hymn 'Adelphus adelpha'; both these poems are found in the mid-eleventh-century English manuscript from St Augustine's, Canterbury, ULC Gg. 5. 35, and are printed by F. J. H. Jenkinson, *Hisperica Famina* (Cambridge, 1908). The word *iduma* ('hand') is found both in the A-text of the *Hisperica Famina* and also in the *Lorica* attributed to Laidcenn which is found in several English manuscripts (see M. Herren, 'The Authorship, Date of Composition and Provenance of the So-Called *Lorica Gildae*', *Ériu* 24 (1973), 35–51).

[3] According to Oda's biographer Eadmer at least, Oda and Athelstan were inseparable friends – even to the extent that Oda accompanied Athelstan during the Battle of *Brunanburh* (PL 133, col. 936).

royal charters could give an accurate indication of when certain hermeneutic words first appeared in Anglo-Latinity; it might also indicate that the exclusive occurrence of certain words in several charters would argue for a common centre of origin for them.[1] But a study on this scale is beyond the scope of the present survey.

CONCLUSIONS

Several observations emerge from the above survey of tenth-century Anglo-Latin works which affect the hermeneutic style. Most surprising is the extent of the list. It includes virtually every known tenth-century Latin author or work which has survived. There is, in fact, only one notable exception: Ælfric. It is not simply that Ælfric did not affect the hermeneutic style; he reacted vigorously against it. Thus in the Latin preface to his *Catholic Homilies* he explains that he has written in English rather than Latin so that his meaning will penetrate more directly to the hearts of his readers or listeners: 'ideoque nec obscura posuimus verba, sed simplicem Anglicam'.[2] His reference to *obscura verba* is clearly a rejection of the contemporary stylistic fashion. This rejection is all the more surprising given Ælfric's personal relationship with both Æthelweard and Bata, two of the most eager proponents of the style. Apparently the stylistic movement was so influential that even as industrious a teacher as Ælfric was powerless to retard it. Although it was influential everywhere in tenth-century England, one may remark differing tendencies (or emphases) in the various monastic centres where it was cultivated: a pronounced penchant for neologism at Canterbury, a predilection principally for the grecism at Winchester, and Byrhtferth's fondness for unusual polysyllabic adverbs at Ramsey (a fondness also remarkable in Bata's works, wherever he may have been). Perhaps the most surprising fact to emerge is that many of the most unusual words in tenth-century Anglo-Latinity are not known from either of the three principal sources of hermeneutic vocabulary – Aldhelm, Abbo's third book and the large collection of glossaries published by Goetz. Many of these otherwise unrecorded words are undoubtedly neologisms, particularly in a writer such as Frithegod. But one gets the impression that source-books of such vocabulary, and possibly even texts in Greek, that are unknown to us, may have been available to tenth-century English authors. No accurate statement on this subject can be made until the many glossaries and *glossae collectae* which survive in English manuscripts have been printed.

[1] See the remarks by D. A. Bullough, 'The Educational Tradition in England from Alfred to Ælfric: Teaching *Utriusque Linguae*', *Settimane di Studio del Centro Italiano di Studi sull'Alto Medioevo* 19 (1972), 466–78, and by N. Brooks, 'Anglo-Saxon Charters', *ASE* 3 (1974), 227.

[2] Ed. B. Thorpe, *The Homilies of the Anglo-Saxon Church: the First Part containing the Sermones Catholici or Homilies of Ælfric* (London, 1844–6) I, 1.

In view of the prominence of the hermeneutic style in tenth-century England, the repudiation of it by modern scholars is disappointing. Invariably it is castigated as 'uncouth' or 'barbarous' and its practitioners are dismissed with contempt as the fellows of Dogberry.[1] More disappointing is the suspicion that the general distaste for this style has led to its neglect both by historians of literature and compilers of dictionaries. In the recent and comprehensive *Mittellateinisches Wörterbuch*,[2] for example, I have been unable to locate a large proportion of the more unusual Anglo-Latin neologisms (*Beelzebutinus* and *beliabus*, for example), and even for so common a grecism as *adelphus* no citations from Anglo-Latin sources are given. This neglect is partly due to the fact that many Anglo-Latin works are available only in inaccessible and often execrable editions. Nearly all of the tenth-century Latin works discussed above are in need of re-editing. One hopes that the recently inaugurated *Dictionary of Medieval Latin from British Sources*[3] will, when complete, provide an essential tool for the study of the hermeneutic style in Anglo-Latinity. For, however unpalatable this style might be to modern taste, it was none the less a vital and pervasive aspect of late Anglo-Saxon culture, and it deserves closer and more sympathetic attention than it has previously received.

But beyond its interest as a literary phenomenon, it is probable that more detailed study of the hermeneutic style might provide a useful tool for historical research. An attempt to trace the appearance and movements of the more unusual hermeneutic words might possibly supplement the diplomatic study of Anglo-Latin charters. This is also true of other Anglo-Latin literature. Consider one final example: there exists a saint's life concerning one Rumwold, an infant saint who was the grandson of King Penda of Mercia and who during his brief three-day life preached the gospel with great success. This *Vita S. Rumwoldi*[4] has been printed only once, and it seems to have escaped the notice of students of Anglo-Latin literature. Nothing whatsoever is known about the date or circumstances of its composition. Nothing can be learned from internal evidence, save that the events of Rumwold's life took place in the region of Buckinghamshire (suggesting only that the work is an English rather than continental composition). In the absence of any other dating evidence, the following speculations might be helpful. The prologue of the *Vita S. Rumwoldi* is written in a rather inflated style, and it parades grecisms such as *dedasculus* [A, G] and *thema* [G].

[1] See *inter alia* the remarks of W. M. Lindsay in Stevenson, *Early Scholastic Colloquies* (pp. vi–viii).
[2] Ed. O. Prinz (Munich, 1967–); only vol. I (A–B) and parts of vol. II (to *cognoscibilis*) have so far appeared.
[3] *Dictionary of Medieval Latin from British Sources*, ed. R. E. Latham, fascicule I: A–B (London, 1975).
[4] Ed. *Acta Sanctorum, dies tertia Novembris*, pp. 682–90.

These words might occur in an Anglo-Latin work of any period. But one word in the prologue is more nearly datable: *floccipendo* [G]. I have suggested above that this word first appeared in Anglo-Latin writing in Oda of Canterbury; thereafter it was used by Lantfred and Bata. This affectation of hermeneutic style in the prologue, however, indicates that the work is not a Norman product, for post-Conquest authors strongly avoided the stylistic excesses of pre-Conquest Latinity. This may (very tentatively) suggest that the *Vita S. Rumwoldi* was composed *c.* 950 × 1050,[1] and that it is a literary product of the tenth-century monastic revival in England. But conjectures of this sort must wait until further work has been done on tenth-century Anglo-Latin texts and glossaries.[2]

[1] This date would agree with that of the earliest manuscript of the *Vita S. Rumwoldi* (CCCC 9) which is eleventh-century.

[2] I should like to acknowledge the help of David Dumville and Michael Winterbottom, who read the typescript of this article and made many constructive suggestions, and also that of three scholars who helped me with various problems and who are mentioned in notes throughout: Peter Clemoes, Peter Dronke and Michael Herren.

APPENDIX I

GLOSSARIAL POEMS OF MEDICAL TERMINOLOGY FROM CANTERBURY

Cambridge, University Library, Gg. 5. 35, 422v–3r

(*a*)

422v

Dic duo que faciunt pronomina nomina cunctis;
omnia dic que sunt uerbi, que silliba signet:
quid mininga,[1] cimus,[2] crassis?[3] quid sterea,[4] colis?[5]
quid ris[6] quidue farinx,[7] nistis?[8] quid glossa,[9] geosis?[10]
quid flebs,[11] hota,[12] nefron,[13] cistis,[14] thessis,[15] anathossis?[16]
quid trix,[17] derma,[18] pisis,[19] neutis,[20] hacmen,[21] diliponta,[22]

Glosses in MS

[1]mininga est membranum quo cerebrum continetur. [2]cimus est humor sanguinis: uel flegma uel colera, uel rubea uel nigra. [3]crassis est temperantia que constat calido, sicco humido. [4]sterea est pars in terraneorum omnigena. [5]colis est fel, unde et colera. [6]ris est nares odorum omnium susceptores. [7]farinx est gula per quam spiramus et aerem ducimus et uocem emittimus. [8]nistis est ieiunus intestinus, neurosus, triplex, in sinistra parte positus, in quem multe currunt uene, per quas maxima pars suci emanat. ieiunus: hoc dicitur quia numquam quid stercoris in se continet sed protinus ad inferiora dimittit. [9]glossa est lingua neruosa atque carnosa. [10]geosis est gustus in lingua ministratus. [11]flebs est uena, sanguinis uasculum. [12]hotis est auris neruosa et cartiloginosa, uocum et sonorum receptaculum. [13]nefron est renes per quos aquosa pars sanguinis colatur et ad uesicam fertur. [14]cistis est uesica in qua humor colligitur et per uirgam egeritur. [15]tessis est habitudo corporis. [16]anathosis est adductus sanguinis in uenis. [17]trix est capilli uel pili. [18]derma est pellis uel cutis. [19]pisis est cibi et potus digestio. [20]neutis est puerulus. [21]hacmen est etas iuuenilis. [22]diliponta est cotidiana uel tertiana uel quartana.

auxitis,[23] gemoni,[24] tacui,[25] satrex,[26] cacohesis?[27]
ipsa quidem sed non eadem que te ipsa nec ipsa?[28]
sinon exposueris, indonatus abibis!

[23]auxitis est incrementum corporis longitudine et latitudine constans. [24]gemoni est anime principatus in toto corpore regnans. [25]tacui est auditus/423r/ex spiritu sicciore consistens. [26]satrex dicitur caro; est enim sanguinis coagulatio. [27]cachoesis est egritudo magna et pessima cum fantasia. [28]ipsa est auis foenix.

(b)

423r

Flegmon, apoplexis, reuma, liturgia, spasmus,
coriza, idrofobos, stranguiria, satiriassis,
tisis, emathoicus, nefresis, cacexia, brancus,
tetanus, epaticus, nictalmus, atrophia, ligmus,
angina, idrolion, idgundis, pelagra, sciros,   5
scurria, sintexis, scotomia, scara, scanosis,
scleroma, stiperion, siringia, serpitiones,
parotidas, steatema, tromtis, narcodia, pota,
squibula, bisane, abomaton, adina, anaprosis,
algima, bolimus, agripnia: tricocinare!   10

Notes

flegmon: from φλέγμα (n. sg.; the author perhaps assumed that the -*a* termination was n. pl., as it would be in Latin, whence he arrived at the spurious singular form **φλέγμον): cf. *CGL* III, 601. *apoplexis:* cf. *CGL* III, 596 (apoplexia: subita gelatio sanguinis que similis est paralesis in ictu corporis et anime); from ἀπόπληξις. *reuma:* ῥεῦμα. *liturgia:* a confusion (influenced by λειτουργία, 'liturgy'?), probably for either ληθαργία or perhaps even λιπυρία. *spasmus:* *CGL* III, 606 (spasmus: contractio uel tremor ex parte una quelibet); from σπασμος. *coriza:* κόρυζα. *idrofobos:* *CGL* III, 602 (idrofabus: canis rabidi morsus uel aliarum ferarum); cf. Isidore, *Etym.* IV.6.15; from ὑδροφόβος. *stranguiria:* *CGL* III, 605 (stranguiria: que paruas cum dolore per urinam guttas emittunt); from στραγγουρία. *satiriassis:* *CGL* III, 605 (satiriasis: impetus desiderii circa ueretrum sine mensura cum dolore et pruritu); from σατυρίασις. *tisis:* probably for *tussis*; cf. *CGL* III, 606 (tussis: pectoris grauitudo et toracis constrictio); but cf. φθίσις. *emathoicus:* *CGL* III, 600 (emotoicus qui sanguinem reiciunt). *nefresis:* from νέφρησις; cf. *CGL* III, 603 (nefretice dolor circa renes). *cacexia:* *CGL* III, 599 (catexia: marasmus); from καχεξία. *brancus:* *CGL* III, 598 (brancis: gula); from βράγχος. *tetanus:* *CGL* III, 606 (tetanus: neruorum tensio et dolor ceruicis); from τέτανος. *epacticus:* ἡπατικός. *nictalmus:* perhaps a compound of νύξ and ὀφθαλμός (cf. νυκτάλωψ) or else a confusion of νυσταγμός; cf. *CGL* III, 603 (nectalopas: que per diem uidere non possunt). *atrophia:* ἀτροφία. *ligmus:* *CGL* III, 602 (ligmus: singultus); from λυγμός. *angina:* a well-attested Latin word. *idrolion:* *CGL* III, 600 (idrolio: aqua cum oleo). *idgundis:* *CGL* III, 602 (idgundis: nescia). *pelagra:* *CGL* III, 604 (palagra: pustula rupta in cute). *scirus:* *CGL*

III, 605 (scirus: humor cum calositate fedissima maxime circa muscolorem capitis que est cum sensu curabilis est que uero sine sensu incurabilis).   *scurria: CGL* III, 605 (scuria: per quam in totum denegatur urina).   *sintexis: CGL* III, 605 (simtexis: longa egritudo et color uiridis uel pallidus uel plumbo similis). *scotomia:* cf. *CGL* III, 605 (scotomatice: graece girus dicitur .i. uertigines nigras patiuntur et cadunt).   *scara: CGL* III, 605 (scara: scabies super uulnera). *scanosis: CGL* III, 605 (scanosis: stupor).   *scleroma: CGL* III, 605 (Rome, Vat. reg. lat. 1260 reads 'sclero. duria' and Bernensis 337 reads 'scleroma. durities'. This may suggest that the author of the poem was using the Berne rather than the Vatican manuscript of this medical glossary, or else a copy related to the Berne manuscript); from σκλήρωμα.   *stiperion: CGL* III, 606 (stipterion: agra humida). *siringia: CGL* III, 605 (siringias: cademopia).   *serpitiones: CGL* III, 606 (serpitionis: uulnera cancrena).   *parotidas: CGL* III, 603 (parotidas: similes sunt glandiolis que circa aurem nasci solent hec passio duplex est una curabilis alia fit incurabilis).   *steatema: CGL* III, 605 (steotema: apostema habens in se humorem adipi similem et putredinem cancrenas).   *tromtis: CGL* III, 606 (tromis: tremor). *narcodia: CGL* III, 603 (narcodia: medicamentum somniferum).   *pota: CGL* III, 604 (pota: farcim).   *squibula: CGL* III, 606 (squibula: stercus induratus). *bisane: CGL* III, 598 (bisane: glandolas).   *abomaton: CGL* III, 597 (abomathon: balneum est ex ortigo feruente factum).   *adina:* possibly for *adita* (*CGL* III, 596: adita, ulcera oris uel lingue in colore albo aut rubeo siue nigro maxime infantibus euenit) or a confused form of ἀδήν.   *anaprosis: CGL* III, 597 (anaprosis: torcionis uel rugitus inter cutem et ipiclo).   *algima: CGL* III, 596 (algima: dolor); from ἀλγήμα.   *bolimus: CGL* III, 598 (bolimus: facedicus); from βόλιμος. *agripnia: CGL* III, 597 (agripnia: uigilia nmia [*sic*]); from ἀγρυπνία.   *tricocinare: CGL* III, 606 (tricocinare: sadaciare). DuCange, *Glossarium Mediae et Infimae Latinitatis* gives 'setaciare. cribrare' and 'setatiare. farinam purgare', (i.e. 'to sift flour'); cf. *CGL* VII, 366.

APPENDIX II

GODEMAN OF WINCHESTER,
'ON THE BENEDICTIONAL OF ST ÆTHELWOLD'

BM Add. 49598, 4v–5r

4v

  Presentem biblum iussit perscribere presul
  Uuintoniae Dominus quem fecerat esse patronum
  magnus Aþeluuoldus, uere gnarus bene Christi
  agnos uelligeros ab demonis arte maligna
  conseruare; deo fructum quoque reddere plenum   5
  iconomos clarus, uenerabilis atque benignus
  hic cupit, arbiter ut uenerit qui discutit orbis
  totius factum – quid quilibet egerit – atque
  mercedem reddet qualem tunc forte merentur:
  aeternam iustis uitam iniustis quoque poenam.   10

quendam subiectum monachum circos quoque multos
in hoc precepit fieri libro bene comptos,
completos quoque agalmatibus uariis decoratis
multigenis miniis pulchris necnon simul auro.
craxare hunc sibi prescriptus fecit boanarges   15
idcirco ut soteris populum in biblo potuisset
sanctificare, deoque preces effundere sacras
pro grege commisso, nullum quo perdat ouilis
agniculum paruum, ualeat sed dicere laetus:
'memet ego adsigno ecce tibi pueros quoque quos tu   20
seruandos mihi iam dederas; nullum lupus audax
exillis rapuit lurcon temet faciente.
sed simul adstamus uitam cupimusque manentem
percipere, in caelisque frui cum principe summo
cuius membra sumus, caput est qui iure salusque   25
baptizatorum in patris et natique flaminis almi
nomine clarisono, si non per deuia uergant
sedque fidem teneant factis quoque iussa salutis
perficiant, heresimque omnem de corde repellant;
peccat⟨i⟩que malum semper superare studentes   30
coniuncti domino sint in caelis sine fine.'
hoc cunctis clemens tinctis baptismate sacro
concedat Christus soter est qui rex bonus orbis,
atque patri magno iussit qui scribere librum hunc
aeternum regnum concedat in arce polorum.   35
omnes cernentes biblum hunc semper rogitent hoc
post metam carnis ualeam caelis inherere:
obnixe hoc rogitat scriptor supplex Godemannus.

5r (at line 20)

Note

Translations of this poem are printed by G. F. Warner and H. A. Wilson, *The Benedictional of St Æthelwold*, Roxburghe Club (Oxford, 1910), pp. xii–xiii, and by F. Wormald, *The Benedictional of St Ethelwold* (London, 1959), pp. 7–8.

APPENDIX III

OSWALD OF RAMSEY, 'ON COMPOSING VERSE'

Cambridge, University Library, Gg. 5. 35, 419r–v

419r

Centum concito sic qui nouit condere uersus
nullo crimine commaculatos, ordine gratos,
sensu denique confertos et cursibus aptos –
laudis munera dat dictanti scansio lucens:
Virgilianus hic dicetur maxime uates.   5

ingeniosis ars hec paret nescia mismet:
experientis sensum exercet sepius ipsam,
doctilogorum nam socium dat doctificando.
istos texuit Osuuoldus, qui est nescius artis;
tantum nomine cognoscit hanc nescius actu.   10
ob hoc cernuus omnipotentem deprecor orans
idem quatinus haud omittat criminis ergo
perpetuali infaust*u*m subdi segnitiei.
mentem tangere is dignetur pneumate sancto
prudens utpote prudens dicar nomine statim;   15
concopulari necnon doctis quiuero post hinc.
   lectos cernere qui dignaris, corrige, uersus,
radens noxia uatis, delens crimina noxe:

419v   restituentur perpetualia premia facto!
uatis gloria stat rectori maxima digne.   20
uersa uertice iosum scandens perlege susum.

13 MS infaustam

Translation

He who knows how to compose quickly a hundred lines in this manner, marred by no fault, pleasing in their arrangement, and then full of meaning and suitable in their cadences – (why,) the resplendent scansion confers the bounty of praise on the poet: let this poet by all means be called 'Vergilian'. This unwitting skill of mine obeys the intellectuals: it often taxes the mind of someone experiencing it, for by its intellectualizing it provides a companion for the verbally-learned [8].

Oswold, who is ignorant of the art (of composition) composed these lines; he knows this art by name only and is ignorant of its workings. For that reason, praying as a suppliant, I beseech omnipotent God that he not permit (?) unfortunate me – for the sake of an error – to be subjected to perpetual sluggishness. If he deign to touch my mind with the Holy Ghost, I shall straightway be called wise in the true sense of the word; henceforth I'll also be able to associate with learned men [16].

You who deign to examine my select verses, correct them, stripping off the poet's peccadilloes, deleting the errors of his (metrical) offence: let perpetual rewards be returned for this deed! – the greatest glory of the poet justly accrues to his corrector [20].

Scanning downwards with the top turned down, read upwards (i.e. the poem can be read upside-down or downside-up).

Notes

This poem is accompanied in the manuscript by a number of glosses of no great interest, and I have not thought it necessary to reproduce them.

12   *omittat*. It is difficult to see what Oswald intends by this word, but it seems best to take it in the sense of *permittat*.

Michael Lapidge

APPENDIX IV

TWO POEMS BY DUNSTAN, ABBOT OF GLASTONBURY

(a) Oxford, Bodleian Library, Auct. F. 4. 32 (S.C. 2176), 1r

> Dunstanum memet clemens rogo, Christe, tuere,
> Tenarias me non sinas sorbsisse procellas.

Translation

I ask you, merciful Christ, that you watch over me, Dunstan, that you not allow
the Taenarian storms to swallow me.

(b) Cambridge, Trinity College O. 1. 18 (1042), 112v–13r

112v O PATER OMNIPOTENS, DIGNERIS FERRE DONANTI
     P remia, qui super alta poli quoque regmina, necnoN
     A c terram, pelagi simul atque profunda, per omne iD
     T am meriti angelicos saeclum ciues regis almI,
     E t sancti in tribuas operis me crescere nemreG,   5
     R ite tuum semper ualeam quo psallere nomeN.

  k O tu nate, patris gremio qui congeris actV
     M aterno tectus populos, queo for⟨t⟩e relatuM
     N empe pium formare, deus quia cerneris, astrA,
     I nclite, quod mundo monstrant, mihi prendere post oB   10
     P erfectam throno tribuas caeli rogo palmam aB
     O ccasum munus uitae exiguum atque coruschA.

  k T eque patris nati, rogo, spiritus, alma reclangiT
     E n ubi, sancte, queam cum carmina uoce repentE
     N amque humili conscendere chors dum busta relinquaM,   15
     S anctorum pia uota ferens iam pulueris istuD
     D octiloquo saeclum qui iam spreuere boatV,
     I ntrepidus trino et clarum conclangere carmeN.

113r k G audia quam implores caelesti semine neuiS
     N untius angelico ut me famine, uirgo, salutaT   20
     E xplosis natum es concepto crimina natA
     R egmina qui trinum retinet mihi mystica numeN,
     I ntuitusque pii dignetur cernere uisV
     S oluere tu proprium rogo quo dare longa per ęuuM.

  k F erte precor cęteris distincti cum angelici reX   25
     E lapsisque patres pręsagi qui ordinibus P̄
     R eddere confantes cunctisque duces pia promtE
     R egmina nouenis patriarchae Enoh mihi cumpaR

E t cum uos Habraham uates domino regit almE
D ignetur ut opem tribus Helia in pere soniS   30
O logiam pellax ualeat ne dicere 'puppuP'.

k   N unc priscos misero cuncti patres rogo pro mE
     A uxilium trepido et ⟨t⟩rinus post fundite doneC
     N eofilax sancti mihi cum P⟨e⟩tro principe soluaT
     T etrificumque preces superem noui hostem ut in orbE.   35

     I   ncipit et uersus claudit ceu, Xpicte, rependaS.

8 MS fore

Glosses in MS

25 *above* angelici: s⟨cilicet⟩ o   29 *above* uates: s⟨cilicet⟩ o   34 *above* neofilax: naos .i. templum
naofilax .i. templi custos

Notes

Even a cursory reading of this poem will indicate how fiercely difficult it is. One senses immediately that the difficulty is intentional, and that Dunstan presents the poem to his readers as a deliberate challenge. It would seem that he wrote out each section in prose and then recast the words in hexameters with a defiant disregard of normal Latin syntax. The poem, therefore, is to be approached in the spirit of a crossword puzzle. The scribe has given some small assistance by indicating vocatives in lines 25 and 29, and by writing a small *k* in the left-hand margin to indicate the beginning of each new stanza (I have reproduced these letters). Beyond that, each reader is on his own. The only certainty is that each stanza gets progressively more difficult. I have conjecturally rearranged the words of each stanza below, and then have provided a translation of my rearrangements. Other rearrangements are no doubt possible in each case. I have had the benefit of expert advice from Peter Dronke, Michael Herren and Michael Winterbottom, but if difficulties remain, it is because I myself have been unable to respond sensitively to Dunstan's thousand-year-old challenge.

However the various stanzas are construed, the poem is evidently a series of prayers by Dunstan to God the Father, to Christ, to the Holy Ghost, to the Virgin, to the prophets, and to the church fathers and apostles. This series of invocations in some ways resembles the various *loricae* (particularly that of Laidcenn, ed. Jenkinson, *Hisperica Famina*). The acrostic form of the poem seems to be directly indebted to Aldhelm's acrostic preface to his *Carmen de virginitate*; at several places Dunstan's diction repeats that of Aldhelm (cf. below, my note to line 31).

The other surviving manuscript of the poem (Cambridge, Trinity College B. 14. 3 (289), 65v) is manifestly an incomplete copy of the poem as it is found in Trinity O. 1. 18, and I have therefore not reported any of its readings.

5 *nemreg.* This is *germen* spelled backwards for the sake of the acrostic (what Virgilius Maro Grammaticus would have called *scinderatio fonorum*).

26 P̄: the compendium for *pre*.

30 *pere* appears to be a syncopated form of *perite* 'skilfully' (cf. DuCange, *s.v.*).

Alternatively, *pere* might be combined with *o* of line 31 to form one word: *opere*. As I understand the stanza, the threefold repetition of the syllable 'o' is intended to vanquish the devil's bisyllabic muttering 'puppup'.

31 *logiam*. Possibly from λογία (n. pl. of λογίον), which Dunstan mistakenly assumed to be a feminine singular form with acc. sg. in *-m*. Mistakes of this sort are common when the source of vocabulary is a glossary.

31 *puppup*. Cf. Aldhelm, *Carm. de virg.*, praef. 15–20: 'ne praedo pellax... ualeat sanctos fallere...ne possit rabula raptor / regales uastans caulas bis dicere puppup'.

Syntactical rearrangement

O pater omnipotens, digneris ferre premia donanti – ⟨tu⟩ qui super alta poli quoque regmina, necnon ac terram, pelagi simul atque profunda – per omne id saeclum regis angelicos ciues tam almi meriti; et tribuas crescere in me germen sancti operis, quo semper ualeam rite psallere nomen tuum [6].

O tu, nate, qui, materno gremio tectus, patris actu populos congeris – nempe pium relatum for⟨t⟩e formare queo, quia deus cerneris, quod, inclite, astra coruscha ⟨te⟩ monstrant; atque rogo, post occasum uitae, mihi tribuas ab throno caeli prendere munus exiguum ob perfectam palmam [12].

Te rogo, sancte spiritus patris natique: namque ubi alma chors carmina reclangit, en cum humili uoce queam repente conscendere dum busta relinquam, iam ferens pia uota sanctorum qui iam spreuere istud saeclum pulueris doctiloquo boatu, et intrepidus conclangere carmen clarum trino [18].

Virgo, quam nuntius angelico famine salutat, explosis neuis nata es: rogo ut implores natum – caelesti semine concepto qui trinum numen retinet mystica regmina – crimina mihi soluere, quo longa gaudia dare per proprium ęuum intuitusque pii uisu me cernere dignetur [24].

Ferte, precor, uos patres presagi, patriarchae, uates angelici distincti, duces alme confantes cum domino regmina pia – Habraham, Helia, Enoh cumpar cum cunctis ceteris – ut rex dignetur promte reddere mihi pere opem in tribus sonis 'O', ne pellax, qui regit pre nouenis ordinibus elapsis, ualeat dicere logiam 'puppup' [31].

Nunc rogo priscos patres cum Petro principe pro me misero trepidoque: fundite preces et auxilium ut trinus neofilax cuncti noui sancti post mihi soluat donec superem tetrificum hostem in orbe [35].

Versus incipit et claudit ceu, Christe, rependas [36].

Translation

⟨To the Father⟩: O omnipotent Father, may you deign to bring rewards to the donor – (you) who above the depths and realms of the heaven as well as the earth and at the same time the recesses of the sea – throughout all this world you rule the angelic citizens of such bounteous merit; and may you grant to grow in me the seed of holy labour by which I may always be able to hymn appropriately your name [6].

⟨To the Son⟩: O you, Son, who, concealed in your mother's womb, you gather together peoples by your Father's act – for I perchance am able to compose a holy narrative because you are seen to be God, because, glorious one, the glittering stars show (you) to the world; and I ask, after the close of my life, that you grant to me from the throne of heaven to take a tiny gift because of the honour (I have) attained [12].

⟨To the Holy Spirit⟩: I beseech you, Holy Spirit of the Father and Son: for when the holy throng re-echoes its songs, may I then with humble voice be able to ascend quickly as I leave the grave, bearing then the holy prayers of the saints who already have scorned this present world of dust with their learned outpourings, and may I fearlessly be able to pour out my glorious song to the triune (God) [18].

⟨To the Virgin⟩: Virgin, whom the messenger salutes in angelic speech, you were born without stain: I ask that you implore him – who, born from the conception of celestial seed holds the mysterious command as trinal deity – to forgive me my sins, that he may deign to grant longlasting joys through his own eternity and to look upon me with the sight of his holy vision [24].

⟨To the prophets⟩: Grant, I beseech you, O you prophetic fathers, O you patriarchs, O you prophets of angelic distinction, O you leaders blessedly confessing with the Lord his holy governance – Abraham, Elijah, Enoch his companion, together with all the rest – that the king quickly deign to render skilfully his aid to me in the three sounds of 'O', lest the deceitful one, who rules in the front of the nine fallen orders, be able to say the word 'puppup' [31].

⟨To the apostles and church fathers⟩: Now I beseech the ancient fathers with Peter their leader on behalf of wretched and anxious me: pour out your prayers and aid so that the trinal custodian of each new saint may afterwards forgive me until I may overcome the hideous enemy in this world [35].

The poem begins and ends as, Christ, you grant [36].

A Canterbury classbook of the mid-eleventh century (the 'Cambridge Songs' manuscript)

A. G. RIGG and G. R. WIELAND

Cambridge, University Library, Gg. 5. 35 is known to scholars principally for the contents of fols. 432–41, the lyric anthology known (somewhat misleadingly) as the 'Cambridge Songs'.[1] Important though this group of poems is for the history of the Latin lyric, it has diverted attention from the contents of the manuscript as a whole, which presents a remarkable range of texts, mainly poetic, from the Early Christian, Carolingian and Anglo-Latin periods. Physical description, moreover, has generally been confined to the section containing the 'Cambridge Songs' and consequently the method of compilation of the whole codex has been neglected.[2] The Cambridge University Library catalogue, for instance, gives the impression of forty-four works entered sequentially in the manuscript, and leaves unexplained such curiosities as no. 41 'Prose treatise on medicine' and no. 44 'Certain medical prescriptions', which appear to sandwich between them the 'Cambridge Songs' and another group of 'hymns'.[3] This article describes the compilation as a whole, its physical appearance, its genesis, and its contents in detail.[4]

DESCRIPTION OF THE MANUSCRIPT

Analysis reveals four parts (of which the first was supplemented by the addition of seven quires). These are: I(a) fols. 1–209 and (b) fols. 210–76 (the

---

[1] The standard edition is by Karl Strecker, *Die Cambridger Lieder*, Monumenta Germaniae Historica 40, 2nd ed. (Berlin, 1955); see also *Carmina Cantabrigiensia*, ed. W. Bulst (Heidelberg, 1950). Facsimile and commentary by K. Breul, *The Cambridge Songs: a Goliard's Song Book of the Eleventh Century* (Cambridge, 1915). The 'Songs' have been edited many times; see also Philipp Jaffé, *ZDA* 14, n.F. 2 (1869), 449–95, and Paul Piper, *Nachträge zur älteren deutschen Literatur, von Kürschners deutscher National Literatur* 162 (Stuttgart, n.d.), 206–34.

[2] The whole manuscript was described by Robert Priebsch, *Deutsche Handschriften in England* (Erlangen, 1896) I, 20–7. Priebsch collated the leaves but did not observe the division of parts I, II and III.

[3] *Catalogue of the Manuscripts preserved in the Library of the University of Cambridge* III (Cambridge, 1858), 201ff.

[4] The article has been written in collaboration: the physical description and account of the compilation are mainly by A. G. Rigg and the detailed contents list is mainly by G. R. Wieland. We are extremely grateful to Professor Clemoes and Dr Michael Lapidge for their vigilance and expert advice on the compilation and the bibliography. We would also like to thank Professors Leonard Boyle, O.P., Virginia Brown and Angus Cameron for palaeographical advice and for their helpful reading of the article.

supplementary quires); II fols. 280–369; III fols. 370–431; and IV fols. 432–46. The evidence for this separation of parts rests on collation of gatherings, blanks at the end of parts, changes of hand and of lay-out and similar details. Parts I(*a*), II and III were written by two scribes (A and B) working in close collaboration.[1] The hands and punctuation[2] suggest that the order of writing was I(*a*), III, II. Part IV was written by scribe A. Leaves were left blank at the end of parts III and IV. This compilation, together with two stages of supplementation in part I(*b*) by scribes A and D and the filling of some of the blank leaves at the end of part IV by scribe C, was made in about 1050. Three leaves, now lost, were probably left blank by scribe D at the end of part I(*b*). The blank leaves at the end of part III and the rest of the blank leaves at the end of part IV were filled by scribe E about 1100. Quire signatures, which take into account scribe D's supplementation of part I(*b*), run through parts I(*a*) and (*b*), II and III: they indicate (unless the scribe of the signatures made a mistake) the loss of a quire at the end of part I(*b*). As the last leaf of the first quire of part IV is missing (after fol. 440), we cannot tell whether the signatures once extended into this part as well. (None survives at the end of the second quire of part IV.) In the twelfth century a contents list was provided; this was supplemented early in the fourteenth century, when some notes were added and the manuscript was foliated. In the nineteenth century the manuscript was again foliated. Differences between the two foliations show that several leaves were lost in the meantime, especially towards the end of the book. The nineteenth-century foliation is used throughout this article; when, occasionally, a fourteenth-century number is cited it is prefixed by an asterisk. The sequence of compilation and accretion is represented diagrammatically in fig. 1.

Measurements and lay-out

The manuscript (trimmed) measures 213 × 145 mm; text area 184 × 110 mm. Sheets were pricked before folding; prickmarks are still visible. Drypoint framing and ruling. Parts I(*a*), II and III have thirty-one lines per page, single column, amply spaced to allow for glossing. Part I(*b*) has forty lines per page; the prose writing is across the page, and there are no glosses. Part IV also has forty lines per page, but is initially ruled in two columns; the fill at the end of part IV by scribe E is written across the page (there is no vertical ruling). Writing is above the top line of the frame in all parts.

---

[1] Alternation between the hands is as follows (if no line number is given, the new hand begins at the top of the page): 1r A, 52v30 B, 53r12 A, 56v B, 56v24 A, 58r10 B, 59v A, 63r B, 64r A, 66r B, 66v A, 67r B, 68r A, 70v B, 71v A, 73r B, 73v A, 75v B, 76v A, 78r B, 79r A, 83v22 B, 84r20 A, 84v18 B, 86v A, 88r B, 88v A, 89v B, 90v A, 111r B, 116r12 A, 126v15 B, 144v7 A, 144v19 B, 170r A, 172r B, 173v A, 175r B, 176r A, 184v B, 195r A, 303r B, 303v A, 370r B, 380r A, 380v B and 389v A. B also wrote the inscription on 219v in part I(*b*).

[2] See below.

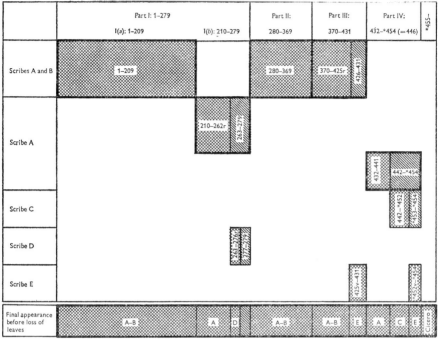

Written areas   Blank leaves   Fourteenth-century folio numbers are prefixed * (see fig. 2)

FIG. I   The compilation of ULC Gg. 5. 35

Hands

The five scribes (A, B, C, D and E) all wrote caroline minuscule. A and B (see pl. I) can be distinguished by their forms of **r** and **g**: A has a short-stemmed, round-shouldered **r** and a wide-looped **g**; B has a longer, more insular **r**, with a long descender and a sharp tick to form the shoulder, and a short-looped **g**. In part IV A uses the Anglo-Saxon wynn rune.

Glosses

Copious Latin glosses (and a few Old English ones) are provided for the texts in parts I(*a*), II and III. These are almost all in hands A and B: each scribe is usually responsible for the glosses to the section of which he had written the main text, but there is some overlapping; letters and words that have been lost in the trimming of the manuscript have sometimes been supplied in a somewhat later hand. There are a few cases of syntactical glossing.[1]

---

[1] See Fred C. Robinson, 'Syntactical Glosses in Latin Manuscripts of Anglo-Saxon Provenance', *Speculum* 48 (1973), 443–75; both alphabetical and dot-sequence systems are used. On the Old English glosses (in the texts of Juvencus, Sedulius, Prudentius, Aldhelm, Milo and others), see A. S. Napier, *Old English Glosses*, Anecdota Oxoniensia, Med. and Mod. Ser. 11 (Oxford, 1900). A full-length study of the glosses in this manuscript is being prepared by G. R. Wieland.

Decoration

In all parts written by scribes A and B new poems, sections within long poems and sections of prose are provided with rubric initials in alternating shades of light red and maroon. The opening initial *M* on 1r is in a zoomorphic interlace style with dragon's head terminals. Chapter headings in the margin and in the body of the text are also often in rubric: they seem usually to have been written by scribes A and B themselves. Display script for titles and incipits is usually in rustic capitals. The text of 211r–25r consists of diagrammatic acrostic poems: the backgrounds for these diagrams are in very vivid colours.

Collation of leaves

Flyleaves: i (modern paper), ii–iii (original parchment), fols. 447–8 (modern paper). Part I(*a*) (fols. 1–209): 1^{10}–17^{10}, 18^{10} (lacks 10 after fol. 179, lost before the fourteenth-century foliation), 19^{10}–21^{10}. The two central leaves in each of quires 2, 3, 5 and 13 are singletons. Part I(*b*) (fols. 210–76): 22^{10}, 23^{10}, 24^{10} (lacks 6 after fol. 234, lost since the fourteenth-century foliation), 25^{10}–27^{10}, 28^{10} (lacks 8–10 after fol. 276, probably blank, lost since the fourteenth-century foliation). The quire signatures indicate that a whole quire is missing at this point; if so, it was lost before the fourteenth-century foliation, but there may have been an error in the quire numbering. Part II (fols. 280–369): 29^{10}–37^{10}. The two central leaves in each of quires 29, 30, 32, 34 and 36 are singletons. Part III (fols. 370–431): 38^{10}–42^{10}, 43^{12}. Leaves 5 and 8 in quire 43 are singletons. Part IV (fols. 432–46): 44^{10} (lacks 10 after fol. 440, lost before the fourteenth-century foliation), 45^{14} (lacks 2–3 after fol. 441, 6–11 after fol. 443, all lost since the fourteenth-century foliation; see fig. 2). The fourteenth-century foliation shows that the missing second and third leaves of quire 45 did not have conjugates in the second half of the quire; they perhaps formed a bifolium.

Signatures

The quire signatures running through parts I(*a*) and (*b*), II and III are placed in each case at the foot of the verso of the last leaf; some of the numbers have been partly lost in the trimming and some are wanting altogether. As already stated, unless there was an error in the numbering, a quire has been lost at the end of part I(*b*) after quire 28. There are no catchwords.

Punctuation

The verse texts of parts I(*a*), II and III, usually in hexameters or elegiacs, are written as verse, with each metrical line given a separate line on the page. Sometimes, as on 83v, the initials of the second half-lines (of a lyric metre)

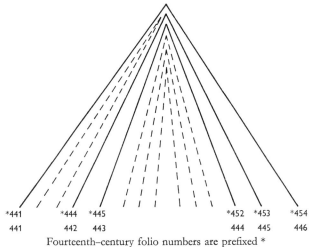

*441   *444   *445   *452 *453   *454
441   442   443   444   445   446
Fourteenth–century folio numbers are prefixed *

FIG. 2   Quire 45 of ULC Gg. 5. 35

are lined up vertically, giving the impression of two columns. In the Boethius (170r–209v) the hexameter and elegiac metra are written as verse; the poems in lyric metres are written across the page as prose, but each verse line is separated by at least a punctum (or greater punctuation if the syntax requires it).

Hands A and B share one system of punctuation (see pl. I), placed after the final letter of the line, not at the margin. This consists of a hierarchy of punctum (.), punctus elevatus (ꬵ), punctus versus (;) and periodus (.,) or doubled periodus (.,.,); the punctus interrogativus (ꝑ) is also used. This system obtains throughout part I(*a*); it is also used in part III up to 389v, where scribe A begins to use a sharper tick in the punctus elevatus (ꞏⸯ) and a quite different style of punctus versus (ꝙ). This new style is found throughout part II, suggesting that II (which was all written by scribe A except for 303r) was written after part III. This style of punctus versus is found in other Canterbury books.[1]

In part IV the narrow columns prevent the verse from being set out line by line, and in any case many of the poems are sequences, which are usually treated as long prose sentences in medieval manuscripts. Stanzas normally begin on a new line and are marked at the end with a punctum; complete poems end with a punctum, a periodus or a double periodus. An attempt is made to make the verse and manuscript line correspond wherever possible.

[1] See T. A. M. Bishop, *English Caroline Minuscule*, Oxford Palaeographical Handbooks (Oxford, 1971), esp. pl. iv(b). Bishop's plates from manuscripts of both St Augustine's and Christ Church, Canterbury, all show a similar hierarchy in the punctuation, but the addition of the periodus (.,) in ULC Gg. 5. 35 adds a further sophistication to the system.

Some of the poems in the manuscript are provided with neums, sometimes in just the first few lines.

Foliation

The foliation in the early-fourteenth-century hand, which is also that of the additions to the contents list (see below), omits the number 79 (i.e. numbers fol. 79 as 80), but the error is cancelled out by the repetition of the number 294. The nineteenth-century foliation omits the numbers 235 and 277–9, presumably because the fourteenth-century foliation showed loss at these points.

Contents lists and notes

On iii^v is a full contents list in a hand of the middle of the twelfth century. This list has been amplified and annotated in the fourteenth-century hand which is also that of the foliation: folio numbers and somewhat more detailed titles were added to the earlier list (see pl. II). There are a few errors; for instance, 'quedam rithmica carmina' (the 'Cambridge Songs') are said to start on fol. 424 instead of fol. 432. The fourteenth-century additions show that part IV once included 'Versus de laude cuculi' on a folio (*450), now lost, between 443 and 444 (see fig. 2).[1] The twelfth-century list has a final item, 'Oraciones ciceronis', to which the fourteenth-century annotator adds the reference 'fo. 455 usque in finem' (i.e. the leaf (*455), now lost, after fol. 446). The *Oraciones* thus began on the first leaf of a now missing quire after quire 45.[2] There are several notes in the body of the manuscript in the fourteenth-century hand (e.g. 126r, 262r and 367r); there are other notes, perhaps of the fifteenth century, on 407r and 423r, indicating that the manuscript was in more or less constant use.

An antiquary's hand provides another contents list on ii^v–iii^r; this list formed the basis of the Cambridge University Library catalogue entry. Notes by the Cambridge librarian, J. M. K[emble], are written on the modern flyleaves at the end of the manuscript.

Origin and provenance

A twelfth-century hand (probably not that of the first contents list) has headed iii^v 'Liber Sancti Augustini Cant.' The main hands are clearly insular and the punctuation system resembles that of other Canterbury books:[3]

---

[1] Probably one of Alcuin's famous poems on the cuckoo (MGH Poetae 1, 270; nos. 57 and 58).

[2] If scribe E completed his medical text on fol. *455, the Cicero must have been written by E or later. It is more likely, however, that the Cicero was in a quite separate booklet, and that, if E finished his text at all, he did so on other blank leaves.

[3] See above, p. 117, n. 1.

there is no reason to doubt that the manuscript was both compiled and kept at St Augustine's, Canterbury.[1]

Date

The last dated entry in the 'Cambridge Songs' section is 1039, the death of the emperor Conrad II.[2] The hand is of the mid-eleventh century; as noted above (on palaeographical grounds), the latest additions to the manuscript, by scribe E, were made before about 1100.

Summary

Three separate but related books, I(*a*), III and II, were prepared by scribes A and B for classroom use. They were ruled with thirty-one lines per page and written with ample space for interlinear and marginal glosses; scribe B took little part in the writing of part II. Scribe A supplemented part I by adding seven quires, I(*b*), ruled for forty lines, to accommodate the text of Rabanus Maurus's *De sancta cruce*. The three parts were brought together in their present order. The 'Cambridge Songs', written by scribe A and perhaps not intended for classroom use, were placed next; this section had two columns of forty lines. Thus far the manuscript was rubricated. Some leaves of the second quire of part IV (only the first leaf of this quire being occupied by the 'Cambridge Songs') were filled by scribe C with miscellaneous poems, but these were not rubricated. Leaves left blank by scribe A in Part I(*b*) were filled by scribe D with a treatise on music. Finally, rather later, scribe E filled in blank leaves at the end of parts III and IV with a medical treatise. In the twelfth century a contents list was made, showing a text of Cicero as the final item. In the fourteenth century the contents list was amplified and the whole manuscript was foliated. Later the text of Cicero was lost together with some other leaves (one from quire 24, three from quire 28 and eight from quire 45).

---

[1] Kemble's conjecture (on 448r) that the manuscript 'must have been written in France' has no basis. Despite the title of his book (see above, p. 113, n. 2), Priebsch did not believe that the manuscript was German; he accepted, as most scholars since have done, that the 'Cambridge Songs' section was copied in England from an exemplar written in the area of the Lower Rhine, as is evident from the contents of the 'Songs'. M. R. James (*Ancient Libraries of Canterbury and Dover* (Cambridge, 1903), pp. lxx, lxxxv and 521) identifies Gg. 5. 35 with no. 1437 in the late-fifteenth-century catalogue of St Augustine's, Canterbury. The entry reads: 'Juuencus poeta infra in colleccionibus cum A. 2° fo. *Illius*. D G .' The description of the contents corresponds to our manuscript, in which Juvencus is the first item and in which the twelfth-century contents list is headed, in another hand, 'Collectiones cum A' (see pl. II), a typical St Augustine's letter-mark. The pressmark of Gg. 5. 35, on iiiᵛ, is 'Di xj Gra ij', that is, Distinctio xi, Gradus ii, the second shelf of the eleventh stack: the pressmark for no. 1437 ('D G ') is unfortunately incomplete. On the other hand, the *secundo folio* reference ('*Illius*') does not match Gg. 5. 35, which has *Visceribus* at this point. The identification is not made by Neil R. Ker, *Medieval Libraries of Great Britain*, 2nd ed. (London, 1964), p. 40. The St Augustine's catalogue entry no. 1438 appears at first sight to be closer to Gg. 5. 35, but in fact can be firmly identified with BM Royal 15. A. xvi. James (pp. 503–4) also prints Leland's description (from *Collectanea* IV.7) of a St Augustine's manuscript clearly identical with Gg. 5. 35.   [2] See no. 33 in Strecker's edition.

A. G. Rigg and G. R. Wieland

CONTENTS

Manuscript headings (printed in small capitals) are given only when they are useful and appropriate; titles in lower case are editorial. Editions cited are generally those available in standard series, not necessarily the most recent. Except where stated, ULC Gg. 5. 35 was not mentioned in these editions. Where possible, items are grouped in subdivisions according to author or theme, but in the anonymous pieces some inconsistency has been inevitable. The following abbreviations are used: CCSL = Corpus Christianorum Series Latina; Chevalier = U. Chevalier, *Repertorium Hymnologicum*, 6 vols. (Louvain, 1892–1921); CSEL = Corpus Scriptorum Ecclesiasticorum Latinorum; MGH Auct. Antiq. = Monumenta Germaniae Historica, Auctores Antiquissimi; MGH Poetae = MGH Poetae Aevi Carolini; PL = Migne, Patrologia Latina.

Part I(a): fols. 1–209

1. Juvencus

1r   a. ARS JUVENCI PRESBITERI . . . DE EVANGELIO DOMINI NOSTRI
Inc. Matheus instituit virtutum tramite mores
Frequent glosses (some Anglo-Saxon). Ed. J. Hümer, CSEL 24.

52v   b. VERSUS EIUSDEM
Inc. Has mea mens fidei vires sanctique timoris
These verses constitute the last eleven lines of the poem and are not usually separated; ed. Hümer.

2. Sedulius (see pl. I)

53r   a. PASCHALE CARMEN SEDULII RETHORIS NOVI ET VETERIS TESTAMENTI
Versus Asterii
Inc. Sume pater meritis veracis dicta poete
(Text)
Inc. Paschales quicumque dapes conviva requiris
Frequent glosses. Ed. J. Hümer, CSEL 10, 14; the *Versus Asterii* are on p. 307.

81v   b. YMNUS SEDULII DE VETERI ET NOVO TESTAMENTO
Inc. Cantemus socii domino cantemus honorem
Glosses. Ed. Hümer, CSEL 10, 155.

83r   c. Alphabetical hymn
Inc. A solis ortus cardine adusque terre limitem
Neums in lines 1–2. Ed. Hümer, CSEL 10, 163. See also A. S. Walpole, *Early Latin Hymns* (Cambridge, 1922; repr. Hildesheim, 1966), no. 31.

84r   d. Acrostic poems
        Inc. Sedulius domini per culta novalia pergens
        Ed. Hümer, CSEL 10, 309.

84r   *Inc.* Sedulius Christi miracula versibus edens
        Ed. Hümer, CSEL 10, 307. In acrostich and telestich the two poems
        form the words SEDULIUS ANTISTES.

3. Arator

84v   a. Prologue addressed to Abbot Florianus
        Inc. Qui meriti florem maturis sensibus ortum
        Ed. A. P. McKinlay, CSEL 72, 1; this MS mentioned but not used.

85r   b. Prologue addressed to Pope Vigilius
        Inc. Moenibus undosis bellorum incendia cernens
        Glosses. Ed. McKinlay, p. 3.

85v   c. HISTORIE APOSTOLICE LIBER ARATORIS SUBDIACONI AECCLESIAE
        ROMAE
        Inc. Ut sceleris iudea sui polluta cruore
        Frequent glosses. Ed. McKinlay, p. 10.

126r   d. VERSUS CUIUSDAM SAPIENTIS DE ARATORE
        Inc. Versibus egregiis decursum clarus arator
        Ed. McKinlay, p. xxix.

126r   e. ITEM VERSUS LAUDATIVI DE ARATORE COMPOSITI ELEGIACO CARMINE
        Inc. Ad iuvenes converte tuam fratercule musam
        Ed. McKinlay, p. xxix, attributed to Johannes Foldensis.

4. Tiro Prosper

126v   a. VERSUS TITULANTIS CUIUSDAM SAPIENTIS IN LIBRUM PROSPERI
        RETHORIS
        Inc. Haec augustini ex sacris epigrammata dictis
        PL 51, col. 51.

126v   b. PREFATIO SANCTI PROSPERI IN EPIGRAMMATA SUA SUPER DICTA
        SANCTI AUGUSTINI
        Inc. Dum sacris mentem placet exercere loquelis
        PL 51, col. 498.

146r   c. TIRONIS PROSPERI EXORTATIO AD UXOREM
        Inc. Age iam precor mearum comes in remota rerum
        Few glosses. PL 51, col. 611.

5. Prudentius

148r a. PSICHOMACHIA PRUDENTII
Inc. Senex fidelis prima credendi via
Copious glosses, two in Old English. Ed. M. Cunningham, CCSL 126, 149.

164r b. EIUSDEM TITULI DE HISTORIIS VETERIS ET NOVI TESTAMENTI PER METRUM QUOD GRAECE DIROCHEUM VEL TETRASTICON VOCATUR
Inc. Aeva columba fuit tunc candida nigra deinde
Ed. Cunningham, p. 390.

6. Lactantius

167r LIBELLUS DE FENICE PARADISI UT FERTUR HABITATRICE
Inc. Est locus in primo felix oriente remotus
Few glosses. Ed. S. Brandt, CSEL 27, 135. After the title (same hand): 'Quidam ferunt lactantium hunc scripsisse libellum.'

7. Boethius

170r ANICII MANLII SEVERINI BOETII...PHILOSOPHIAE CONSOLATIONIS...
Inc. Carmina qui quondam studio florente peregi
Copious glosses. Ed. L. Bieler, CCSL 94. Ends on 209v.

Part I(b): fols. 210–76

8. Rabanus Maurus

209v a. PROLOGUS IN LIBRO MAGNENTII RABANI MAURI DE LAUDE SANCTE CRUCIS
Inc. Hortatur nos lex divina ad deferendum domino dona
PL 107, col. 145. Scribe Λ added seven quires to part I(a) to accommodate the text, but began writing on 209v.

210v b. INTERCESSIO ALBINI PRO MAURO
Inc. Sancte dei praesul meritis in saecula vivens
PL 107, col. 137.

211r c. Coloured diagrams of acrostics etc., depicted in crosses and figures
Inc. Musa cita studio gaudens nunc dicere numen
PL 107, col. 147, where the plates are reproduced in black and white.

225v d. Text
Inc. Mos apud veteres fuit ut gemino stilo
PL 107, col. 265. Text ends on 262r; 262v is blank.

AA. *Addition by scribe D: musical treatise*

263r *Inc.* (A)d musice initiamenta quemlibet ingredi cupientem
Expl. Ego sum via veritas et vita alleluia alleluia
Ed. M. Gerbert, *Scriptores Ecclesiastici de Musica Sacra Potissimum* (San Blasiani, 1784; repr. Milan, 1931), p. 104. Attributed in the edition to 'Ubald seu Hucbald'; the twelfth-century contents list calls it 'Musica Augustini'. Ends on 276r; 276v is blank; fols. 277–9, probably blank, are missing.

Part II: fols. 280–369

9. Aldhelm

280r a. ALTHELMI PRESULIS IN LIBRUM DE VIRGINITATE PROHEMIUM
Inc. Metrica tirones nunc promant carmina castos
Ed. R. Ehwald, MGH Auct. Antiq. 15, 350; this MS was used.

319v b. DE VIRTUTUM PUGNA CUM VITIIS
Inc. Digestis igitur sanctorum laudibus almis
This section constitutes lines 2446–904 of the *De Virginitate*, ed. Ehwald, p. 452.

10. Milo

327r LIBER MILONIS MONACHI DE LAUDE PUDICITIE VEL SOBRIETATIS
Inc. Principibus priscis vatum placuisse camenas
Ed. L. Traube, MGH Poetae 3, 612; this MS was used.

11. Lapidary poem

362r VERSUS DE XII LAPIDIBUS PRETIOSIS
Inc. Cives celestis patrie regi regum concinite
Neums in first line. Ed. A. Lentini, 'Il Ritmo *Cives coelestis patriae*...', *Benedictina* 12 (1958), 15–26, and P. Dronke, 'Tradition and Innovation in Medieval Western Colour-Imagery', *Eranos Jahrbuch* 40 (1972), 50–106 (text, from this MS only, on pp. 76–9). The date of Gg. 5. 35 precludes earlier ascriptions of the poem to Anselm of Laon and Marbod of Rennes and Lentini's proposal of Amato of Monte Cassino.

12. Alphabetical hymn on All Saints

362v *Inc.* Aula superna poli reboet modulamine dulci
Some glosses. Chevalier no. 23275; unpublished.

13. Abbo of St Germain

363v *Inc.* Clerice dypticas lateri ne dempseris umquam
Copious glosses. Ed. P. von Winterfeld, MGH Poetae 4, 116; this MS was used. The poem (unascribed in the MS) is the 'Hisperic' third book of Abbo's *Bella Parisiacae Urbis*.

14. Hymns

365v a. *Inc.* O dee cunctipotens anime dator o dee christe
Chevalier no. 12883 (refers to this MS); unpublished.

366r b. *Inc.* Omnipotens solus regnas qui trinus et unus
Chevalier no. 14100 (refers to this MS); unpublished.

15. Hugbald

367r a. IRRISIO CUIUSDAM SCOLASTICI CONTRA CALVOS
Inc. Stridula musca volans calvum conspexit euntem
Neums in first three lines. Ed. A. Riese, *Anthologia Latina* 1.2 (Leipzig, 1906), 150, from this MS.

367r b. RESPONSIO HUGBALDI DE LAUDE CALVORUM
Inc. Carmina clarisone calvis cantate camenae
The entire poem consists of words beginning with the letter *C*. Ed. P. von Winterfeld, MGH Poetae 4, 267; this MS was used.

16. Nightingale poem

369r VERSUS DE FILOMELA
Inc. Sum noctis socia sum cantus dulcis amica
Ed. A. Riese, *Anthologia Latina* 1.2 (Leipzig, 1906), 130 (no. 130).

17. Verses on the Creation

369v *Inc.* Primus in orbe dies lucis primordia sumpsit
Ed. F. Vollmer, MGH Auct. Antiq. 14, 256: the edition attributes the poem to Eugenius Toletanus.

Part III: fols. 370–431

18. Eusebius

370r ENIGMATA EUSEBII DE DEO
Inc. Cum sim infra cunctos sublimior omnibus adsto
Glosses; solutions in margin. Ed. Fr Glorie, CCSL 133, 210; this MS was used.

19. Tatwine

374v ENIGMATA TAUTUINI
Inc. Stamine metrorum exstructor conserta retexit
Glosses. Ed. Fr Glorie, CCSL 133, 167; this MS was used.

20. Alcuin

378r a. DOGMATA ALBINI AD CAROLUM IMPERATOREM
Inc. Impleat o vestrum domini dilectio pectus
Ed. E. Dümmler, *ZDA* 21 (1877), 68, from this MS; see W. Meyer, *Nachrichten von der königlichen Gesellschaft der Wissenschaften zu Göttingen. Philologisch-historische Klasse* (1907), p. 39, who attributes to Smaragdus.

379v   b. DISTICA EIUSDEM AD EUNDEM REGEM
      Inc. O praesul patriae prudens et rex venerande
      Ed. Dümmler, p. 72; see also Meyer.

21. Scotus quidam

381r   VERSUS CUIUSDAM SCOTI DE ALFABETO
      Inc. Principium vocis veterumque inventio prima
      Ed. Fr Glorie, CCSL 133A, 729; this MS was used.

22. Boniface

382r   a. (BONIFACII AENIGMATA: supplet manus recentior)
      Inc. Aurea iure decem transmisi poma sorori
      Ed. Fr Glorie, CCSL 133, 278; this MS was used. The colophon calls
      the poem DE VIRTUTIBUS, without ascription; gap left for title on 382r.

385r   b. DE ACERBISSIMIS MALIS
      Inc. Cernebam tetrum lustrans per saecula monstrum
      Ed. Glorie, p. 310; this MS was used.

23. Hymn

388v   *Inc.* Sancte sator legis lator suffragator largus dator
      Line left blank for title. Ed. C. Blume, *Analecta Hymnica* 51 (Leipzig,
      1908), 299–300 (no. 229); this MS was used. Also ed. G. Baesecke,
      Das lateinisch-althochdeutsche Reimgebet (*Carmen ad Deum*) (Berlin, 1948),
      pp. 9–24.

24. Epitaph on Alcuin

388v   EPITAPHIUM ALBINI
      Inc. Hic rogo pauxillum veniens subsiste viator
      Ed. E. Dümmler, MGH Poetae 1, 350; cf. no. 20.

25. Simphosius

389r   ENIGMATA SIMPHOSII
      Inc. Hec quoque simposius de carmine lusit inepto
      Glosses. Ed. Fr Glorie, CCSL 133A, 620; this MS was used.

26. Aldhelm

394r   ALTHELMI ENIGMATA MILLE VERSIBUS CURRENTIA
      Inc. Arbiter aethereo iugiter qui regmine sceptra
      Frequent glosses; in acrostich and telestich the prologue spells out
      'Aldhelmus cecinit millenis versibus odas'. Ed. Fr Glorie, CCSL 133,
      377; this MS was used.

27. Cato

407r a. EPISTULA CATONIS
Inc. Cum animadverterem quam plurimos graviter in via
Ed. M. Boas, *Disticha Catonis* (Amsterdam, 1952).

407v b. DISTICHA CATONIS
Inc. Si deus est animus nobis ut carmina dicunt
Ed. Boas, p. 34.

28. Columban

412v VERSUS COLUMBANI ABBATIS DE BONIS MORIBUS OBSERVANDIS
Inc. Haec precepta legat devotus et impleat actu
Ed. E. Dümmler, MGH Poetae 1, 275; this MS was used.

29. Bede

416r a. VERSUS BEDE DE DIE JUDICII
Inc. Inter florigeras fecundi cespitis herbas
Ed. J. Fraipont, CCSL 122, 439.

418v b. Riddles
Inc. Nil herebo melius celo sic peius habetur
Frequent glosses, some of which give solutions to the riddles, which are mainly grammatical puzzles. The ascription to Bede, not in the text, is made by the twelfth-century contents list. Ed. F. Tupper, 'Riddles of the Bede Tradition', *MP* 2 (1904–5), 561–72; text and glosses edited, with notes, from this MS.

30. Oswald

419r *Inc.* Centum concito sic qui novit condere versus
Frequent glosses; internal attribution 'istos tcxuit osuuoldus'. Ed. M. Lapidge, above, pp. 106–7; from this MS only.

31. Hymn

419v *Inc.* Terrigene bene nunc laudent ut condecet almum
Glosses; unpublished.

32. 'Rubisca'

419v *Inc.* Parce domine digna narranti Indigna licet palam peccanti
Frequent glosses; Greek words are intermingled, and the stanzas for X and Y are in Greek. Ed. F. J. H. Jenkinson, *Hisperica Famina* (Cambridge, 1908), p. 55; this MS was used. New edition forthcoming by M. Herren (Pontifical Inst. of Med. Stud., Toronto).

33. Abecedarius

420r   *Inc.* Adelphus adelpha meter alle philus hius tigater
Frequent glosses. Ed. Jenkinson, p. 61; this MS was used. New edition forthcoming by M. Herren (see above, no. 32).

34. Greek alphabet

420v   The names of the letters (in Roman characters) are written above.

35. Greek prayers

420v a. *Inc.* O theos istin boythian mu proskis kyrrie
Glossed 'Deus in adiutorium...' etc.

421r b. *Inc.* Patir imon o en tis uranis
Glossed 'Pater noster qui es in celis...' etc.

36. Metrical versions of the 'Pater noster'

421r a. *Inc.* Sancte pater summa celi qui sedis in aula
Ed. H. Walther, 'Versifizierte *Paternoster* und *Credo*', *Revue du Moyen Âge Latin* 20 (1964), 45–64; this MS was used.

421r b. *Inc.* O genitor nostri celi qui in sede moraris
Ed. Walther, '*Paternoster* und *Credo*'; this MS was used.

37. Liturgical prayers in Greek

421v a. *Inc.* Doxa enipsistis theo ke epis gis (= the *Gloria*)

421v b. *Inc.* Pisteugo is enan theon patiran (= the Creed)
The gloss translates (b) into Latin.

38. Verses on the Creed

422r   *Inc.* Confiteor dominum nunc patrem cunctipotentem
Ed. H. Walther (see no. 36); this MS was used.

39. Medical riddle

422v   *Inc.* Dic duo que faciunt pronomina nomina cunctis
Ed. M. Lapidge, above, pp. 103–4.

40. Medical expressions in verse

423r   *Inc.* Flegmon apoplexis reuma liturgia spasmus
Ed. M. Lapidge, above, pp. 104–5.

41. Verses on the 'Te Deum'

423r   a. *Inc.* Te eternum patrem tellus veneratur et omnis
Unpublished.

423v   b. *Inc.* Omnipotentem semper adorant et benedicunt omne per evum
Ed. E. Dümmler, MGH Poetae 2, 394.

42. Bibliotheca magnifica

423v   BIBLIOTHECA MAGNIFICA DE SAPIENTIA
Inc. Me sine matre pater genuit pariente puellam
A series of riddles on school subjects. Ed. J. A. Giles, *Anecdota Bedae, Lanfranci et Aliorum*, Caxton Soc. (London, 1851; repr. New York, 1967), p. 50, from this MS. Ends on 425r.

BB. Later addition by scribe E: medical treatise

425v   *Inc.* (Q)ui vult potionem solutionis accipere hoc modo id faciat
L. Thorndike and P. Kibre, *Catalogue of Incipits of Medieval Scientific Writings in Latin* (Cambridge, Mass., 1963), col. 1212; unpublished. Runs to end of 431v, and continues on 444v–6v.

Part IV: fols. 432–46

43. The 'Cambridge Songs'

432r

Forty-five pieces, almost all poems. The collection includes love songs, historical poems, fabliaux, macaronic (German–Latin) and German poems, lyrics on philosophical subjects, hymns, extracts from classical poets (mainly *planctus*) and pieces on music. The collection appears to have been copied from an anthology composed in the Lower Rhine area; the last datable entry refers to the death of Conrad II (1039). Some of the erotic poems have been erased. Ed. K. Strecker (Berlin, 1955) and others.[1]

44. Miscellaneous poems by scribe C[2]

442ra a. *Inc.* Turgens in terra lucifer ille
The fall of man and the redemption; although there is no major initial or title, the round number of lines (one hundred) suggests that the poem is complete. Unpublished.

442vb b. *Inc.* Alme facture sator et nutritor
Hymn in twelve sapphic stanzas; unpublished.

[1] See above, p. 113, n. 1.
[2] A brief notice of some of these poems is given by Priebsch (*Handschriften*, p. 24).

443ra c. *Inc.* Criste mearum lux tenebrarum
    Chevalier no. 36103. Ed. L. Traube, MGH Poetae 3, 737; this MS was used.

443ra d. *Inc.* Conditor almus christus olimpi
    Ed. Traube, p. 737; this MS was used.

443rb e. *Inc.* David regem inclita proles
    Unpublished.

443va f. *Inc.* David vates dei filius isai
    Unpublished.

443vb g. *Inc.* Virgo dei genitrix eia obsecro
    Incomplete (the next six leaves are missing); unpublished.

444r (*top*) 'ut pro nostris depreceris dominum nostris delictis'.

45. Pseudo-Vergil

444r   *Inc.* Ut belli sonuere tube violenta peremit
    Written across the page; neums in all eight lines; no ascription in this MS. Ed. A. Riese, *Anthologia Latina* 1.1 (Leipzig, 1894), 306 (no. 392). The rest of 444r is blank.

BB. *Later addition by scribe E continued*

444v   See above, 425v; the text breaks off in mid-sentence at the foot of 446v. It may have finished on the next leaf, where, according to the twelfth-century list of contents, a now missing final item, 'Oraciones ciceronis', began; more probably it was continued on other blank leaves at the end of the Cicero.

Conclusions

The manuscript consisted initially of a group of three classbooks. They were probably planned to form a complete collection, as the most elaborate initial is the M on 1r, which surpasses the simple coloured initials at the beginning of parts II and III. The three books appear to have been graded according to difficulty and educational value. The first (I(a)) contains relatively straightforward material, itself graded in order of difficulty: Juvencus, Sedulius, Arator, Prosper, Prudentius, Lactantius and Boethius. The second in order of composition (III) comprises principally riddle collections and difficult poems: Eusebius, Tatwine, Alcuin, Boniface, Simphosius, Aldhelm, Cato, Columbanus, Bede and anonymous poems and prayers, some in Greek. The third (II) is less organized, but presents much the same level of difficulty as part III: Aldhelm, Milo, Hugbald and various difficult poems. The pedagogic purpose of the compilation is quite clear: the glosses themselves are frequently instructive, sometimes giving lists of synonyms and paradigms as well as clarifying the meaning. Apart from their grammatical utility, the texts themselves (especially in part I(*a*)) provide a fundamental literary programme in Christian Latin poetry. The educational value of the collection was enhanced by the addition by scribe A of Rabanus Maurus's *De laude Sancte Crucis* to form part I(*b*) and also by scribe D's musical treatise at the end of I(*b*). The 'Cambridge Songs', copied from a German exemplar, were attached either because of their interest as a lyric collection or simply because they were written by scribe A. The classbook illustrates the kinds of texts studied in school, the way in which they were taught and the care with which textbooks were prepared. It offers a remarkable insight into educational practice in the late Anglo-Saxon period.

An unknown English Benedictine gradual of the eleventh century

K. D. HARTZELL

The most famous manuscripts with music of the early Middle Ages in England are the Winchester 'Tropers' at Oxford and Cambridge. More has been written about them than about all the lesser known sources put together, and it is right that this should have been so, for the troper at Cambridge preserves one of the oldest repertories of polyphonic music while the other, the so-called 'Æthelred troper', has provided generations of scholars with the task of establishing its relationship to the other manuscript. This activity has resulted in a high degree of clarification,[1] but the Winchester 'Tropers' are not the whole of early English medieval music – even though a study of their combined trope repertories would be a welcome contribution – and we must begin to turn our attention to other sources of the period.[2]

Within the past few decades a number of manuscripts have come to light and the somewhat latent interest in the monophonic music of the medieval period shows signs of revival. Two manuscripts in the British Museum have been well served by Mr D. H. Turner.[3] Most of the substantial sources from early medieval times have been known to students through the publications of Frere and Hughes, and Heinrich Husmann has recently listed some of

---

[1] A. Holschneider, *Die Organa von Winchester* (Hildesheim, 1968) with complete bibliography; and T. A. M. Bishop, *English Caroline Minuscule* (Oxford, 1971), p. xi, n. 1 and item 27.

[2] There is a pressing need for a full length study of the first portion of BM Cotton Caligula A. xiv, involving the cooperative efforts of scholars in art history, medieval Latin poetry, palaeography and music. I offer a small point as a possible incentive for such a study. The first miniature in the manuscript, that of St Stephen on 3v, is an addition. It is the only painting to have a gold border and the only one to have the writing around the outside border set on a rather dark piece of vellum. It is almost as though the artist responsible for obliterating the original writing (and/or another miniature?) was unable to execute the task successfully.

[3] BM Egerton 3759 (s. xiii[1]) (see D. H. Turner, 'The Crowland Gradual: an English Benedictine Manuscript', *Ephemerides Liturgicae* 74 (1960), 168–74); BM Add. 52359 (s. xiv in.) (see D. H. Turner, 'The Penwortham Breviary', *Brit. Museum Quarterly* 28 (1964), 85–8); New York, Pierpont Morgan Library, M. 926 (s. xi, containing the earliest recension of the Office of St Alban and a practically complete portion of the music for an Office of St Birinus) (see K. D. Hartzell, 'A St Albans Miscellany in New York', *Mittellateinisches Jahrbuch* 10 (1975), 20–61). C. Hohler, 'The Durham Services in Honour of St Cuthbert', *The Relics of Saint Cuthbert*, ed. C. F. Battiscombe (Durham, 1956), pp. 155–91, is a seminal paper for many areas.

them in his volume for the *Répertoire International des Sources Musicales*.[1] In addition to these there are a number of early service books with music, some musical additions to non-liturgical books, and some significant fragments which with few exceptions have not been examined by persons interested primarily in music.[2] The purpose of this article is to draw attention to the major importance of one of these neglected sources.

On p. 47 of *Durham Cathedral Manuscripts*,[3] nestled in a large paragraph and overwhelmed by the format of the rest of the volume, there is the following brief description of a manuscript in Bishop Cosin's Library at the University Library, Durham: 'an exquisite small Hymnal with musical notation of the late XIth century or early XIIth, which contains hymns to St Oswald and St Cuthbert'. In fact what Sir Roger Mynors was describing is not a hymnal but a small gradual, and the so-called 'hymns to St Oswald and St Cuthbert' are actually proses, or what are commonly called sequences, added at the beginning and end of the book to adapt it for Durham.

The Cosin Library, named after John Cosin, bishop of Durham in the mid-seventeenth century, was catalogued anonymously in the eighteenth century by the Revd Thomas Rud, Librarian to the Dean and Chapter of the Cathedral. Rud called the manuscript a book of hymns with musical notation and he identified it as one of the books given to the library by the Revd George Davenport, the first keeper of Bishop Cosin's Library.[4] The credit for identifying it and postulating its probable origin belongs to Professor Helmut Gneuss of the English Seminar at Munich whose brief description, jotted down in 1955, is on file at the University Library in Durham.[5] Dom Anselm Hughes recently referred to it in his Jarrow Lecture,

---

[1] *The Winchester Troper*, ed. W. H. Frere, Henry Bradshaw Soc. 8 (London, 1894); W. H. Frere, *Bibliotheca Musico-Liturgica*, Plainsong and Med. Music Soc., 4 fascicles in 2 vols. (London, 1894–1932; repr. Hildesheim, 1967); Anselm Hughes, *Anglo-French Sequelae Edited from the Papers of the Late Henry Marriott Bannister* (Burnham and London, 1934); and H. Husmann, *Tropen- und Sequenzenhandschriften* (Munich, 1964).

[2] An exception is Holschneider, *Die Organa von Winchester*. L. Gjerløw has published the English missal fragment in Oslo and a few facsimiles in *Adoratio Crucis* (Oslo, 1961). Sotheby's sale catalogue of 12 July 1971 contains a plate of a noted folio of the recently discovered 'Anderson' Pontifical, now BM Add. 57337. This important manuscript is inventoried in J. Brückmann, 'Latin Manuscript Pontificals and Benedictionals in England and Wales', *Traditio* 29 (1973), 391–458, a valuable bibliographical survey, which, unaccountably and incredibly, does not state which of the sources contain music. No comprehensive listing of service books with music other than Frere's exists, but such a list can be initiated by consulting the publications of the Henry Bradshaw Society.

[3] R. A. B. Mynors, *Durham Cathedral Manuscripts to the End of the Twelfth Century* (Durham, 1939).

[4] Rud's catalogue was printed by J. Raine (*Catalogi Veteres Librorum Ecclesiae Cathedralis Dunelmensis*, Surtees Soc. 1 (London, 1838), 139–91). The description of the Cosin Gradual is on p. 179.

[5] Professor Gneuss has kindly informed me that he has referred to the manuscript three times in print: see his review of N. R. Ker, *English Manuscripts in the Century after the Norman Conquest*, *Anglia* 78 (1960), 493f.; *Hymnar und Hymnen im englischen Mittelalter* (Tübingen, 1968), p. 245; and 'Latin Hymns in Medieval England: Future Research', *Chaucer and Middle English Studies in Honour of Rossell Hope Robbins*, ed. B. Rowland (London, 1974), p. 424, n. 41.

'The Music of Aldwyn's House at Jarrow and the Early Twelfth Century Music of Durham Priory'.[1]

How Davenport obtained the manuscript is not known, but it may be surmised that it came to him from a John Heath whose name is at the top of 2r. The present Keeper of Rare Books at Durham University Library, Dr A. I. Doyle, has informed me that there were several John Heaths in a local family and that he is not certain which of them might be the one concerned. Other names sprinkled through the manuscript suggest the doodling of schoolboys.

The manuscript remained unknown for so long not only because of mis-description over the years (one is tempted to say centuries) but primarily because the Revd Walter Howard Frere, one of the distinguished liturgical scholars of his day, did not examine the Cosin collection during his excursions gathering material for his *Bibliotheca Musico-Liturgica*, a 'descriptive handlist of the musical and Latin-liturgical manuscripts of the Middle Ages preserved in the libraries of Great Britain and Ireland'. Incidently, Frere did not intend his handlist to be comprehensive and many small collections, including the Cosin Library, were not investigated. Had he found it, Frere would have recognized Cosin V. V. 6, to give the manuscript its correct identification, as one of the most important sources for the history of music in England in the Middle Ages, and, we may safely add, the most important source of its kind to be found in the last half century.

Cosin V. V. 6 consists of viii + 115 + vi folios of elegantly prepared vellum, a total of 129 leaves. The folios measure 162 mm × 105 mm and have sixteen lines of music and text to the page. The writing space occupies 114 mm × 64 mm within singly ruled guidelines. It is bound in a nineteenth-century binding of dark brown leather which is secured at the leading edge by a metal clasp. The spine is gently rounded and the words *LIBER | HYMNO-RUM | M.S.* are stamped approximately one third of the way down from the top. At the foot of the spine are the letters *V. V. | 6.* The bookplate of Bishop Cosin's Library is pasted on the inside front cover. Unfortunately, although there are few lacunae within sections, it is impossible to give even an approximate collation, for the folios appear to be irregularly sewn and in some cases glued. To provide a collation that would be enlightening, the manuscript would need to be unbound.

The contents are as follows:

1. 2r–8v. Eleven proses which are additions to the main manuscript.[2]

---

[1] Published by the rector of Jarrow, Jarrow on Tyne, 1972.

[2] The proses are as follows (*RH* = U. Chevalier, *Repertorium Hymnologicum*, 6 vols. (Louvain, 1892–1921), and *AH* = G. M. Dreves, C. Blume and H. M. Bannister, *Analecta Hymnica Medii Aevi*, 55 vols. (Leipzig, 1886–1922)):

No two seem to have been written by the same hand. The date of writing is the late eleventh century and the twelfth, although the music for the last proses dates from the late Middle Ages.

2. 9r–19r. A Kyriale, beginning imperfectly with part of the prosula to the *Kyrie eleison* entitled *Clemens rector*. Very little of the prosula is written at the top of 9r and the Kyriale is probably missing only one leaf.[1] This section includes a full complement of *Gloria in excelsis* and the number of Kyries is also extensive.[2] The hand is that of the main manuscript and can be dated in the last quarter of the eleventh century. All the sections are in this hand

		RH	AH
Alme concrepent	Aidan	—	
Christo regi cantica	Nicholas	3170	VIII, 194
O alma trinitas	Cuthbert	12646?	VII, 239
Precelsa seclis	Vincent	15220	LIII, 359
Sollemnitas sancti Pauli	Paul	19168	LIII, 330
Regis Oswaldi	Oswald	17229	X, 280
Post partum virgo	B.V.M.	15178	LIII, 190
Ave preclara maris stella	B.V.M.	2045	L, 313
Ave Maria gratia plena	B.V.M.	1879	LIV, 337
Laudes crucis attollamus	Exaltatio Crucis	10360	LIV, 188
Verbi dei parens	B.V.M.	21325	X, 108.

[1] The first three prosulae are those found in the series in Worcester, Cathedral Library, F. 160, printed in *The Winchester Troper*, ed. Frere, pp. 125ff. For the term 'prosula', cf. P. Evans, *The Early Trope Repertory of Saint Martial de Limoges* (Princeton, 1970), pp. 9–15.

[2] The Kyries and Glorias with textual addition are as follows (*WT* = *The Winchester Troper*, ed. Frere, a *WT* page number in triple figures signifying a trope which is not in either of the Winchester manuscripts; numbers from *RH* are given where thought necessary):

	RH	AH XLVII	WT
[Clemens rector]		6	50
Cunctipotens genitor		4	48
Pater creator omnium		14	49
Kyrie fons bonitatis	6429	5	—
Rex magne genitor	17470	116	132
O pater excelse		17	51
Conditor kyrie		16	51
Kyrie deus sempiterne	4508	13	125
Lux et origo		12a	51
Qui deus et rector		182	60
Laudemus dominum	10299	190	134
Qui de morte	16400	183	134
Quem vere pia laus		185	56
O laudabilis rex		177	59
Ave deus summe trinitas	1770	—	55
Quem decet	32294	192	135
Quem dominum rerum		171	56
Quem iugi voce	16294	—	136
O gloria sanctorum		172 + 223	59
Deus invisibilis	4450	—	61
Angelica iam pater	1047	—	58
Ut possimus consequi	21027	—	57

except where noted.[1] A number of Kyries do not have prosulae. Fols. 15 and 16 should be interchanged.

3. 19v–21r. The Frankish acclamations entitled *Laudes regiae*, beginning with the words *Christus vincit*.[2] A thirteenth-century hand has added a *Sanctus* after the conclusion of the *Laudes* on 21r, and on the verso, which was originally blank, a number of boys have scribbled some doggerel.

4. 22r–99v (for 40r see pl. III*a*). The Temporale, beginning imperfectly with part of the Offertory for the first Sunday in Advent. The first leaf is again probably all that is missing. Part of the music for the Veneration of the Cross on Good Friday until the middle of the Friday in Easter week is also missing. The Temporale concludes (93v–9v) with Masses for the Holy Trinity and for the Dedication of a Church, and various Votive antiphons. The original notation has been erased in a number of places especially during Advent and Eastertide. Occasionally a sixteenth-century truant has filled in these deletions with scrawl on a three-line staff. Two alleluias have been added to 99v by scribes working in the twelfth century.

5. 100r–9v. A fragment of the Sanctorale, beginning in the Introit for the Vigil of John the Baptist (23 June) and concluding in the Mass for the Octave of the Assumption of the Blessed Virgin Mary (22 August). No *Commune Sanctorum* has been preserved, but the manuscript must have originally included one.

6. 110r–13r. The remainder of the Kyriale, containing settings of *Sanctus* and *Agnus dei*.[3] This part also begins imperfectly. A *Sanctus* written in the early twelfth century has been added to 111r. 113v is blank.

---

[1] I should like to thank Mr T. A. M. Bishop for confirming this. He is inclined to date the scribe possibly very late-eleventh-century or early-twelfth. Dr N. R. Ker has also informed me that he believes it to date from s. xi/xii.

[2] E. Kantorowicz, *Laudes regiae* (Berkeley, 1946) and B. Opfermann, *Die liturgischen Herrsche-rakklamationen des Mittelalters* (Weimar, 1953).

[3] The *Sanctus* and *Agnus* settings with textual addition are as follows:

	RH	AH XLVII	WT
[Deus pater ingenitus]	25435	—	65
Ante secula deus pater	23039	—	66
Perpetuo numine	31616	286	128
Ex quo sunt omnia	26279	289	138
Omnipotens pater ingenitus	—	—	—
Laudes deo ore	38615	340	127
Quem Iohannes in deserto	32307	—	67
Quem Iohannes in Iordane	16292	385	129
Spes mundi laus	19281	394	139
Omnipotens eterna		385	67
Qui patris in solio		386	67
Deus deorum	4434	419	129
Lux lucis		387	68
Qui sedes in throno	32444	—	68
Omnipotens verbum	—	—	—
Qui deus es verus	32393	414	129

7. 114r–19v. Antiphons and other music for processional use. There are lacunae during the music for the Palm Sunday procession and at the end of this section.

8. 120r–3r. A modest Tonale, beginning *Primum querite regnum dei*.[1] With the *Laudes regiae* this is the only part of the manuscript to be complete.

9. 123v–9v. Additions in different hands, consisting of processional antiphons and proses which date in the twelfth century.[2] On 128v, and undoubtedly out cf place, are ordos of various votive Masses in the hand of the main scribe.

The corpus of proses which were added in the late eleventh century and the twelfth at the beginning and end of the book and which emphasize saints venerated at Durham – Aidan, Cuthbert and Oswald – makes it certain that the manuscript was at Durham when they were written. But it is equally clear that the main manuscript was not written there. It contains features which show its origin to have been Christ Church, Canterbury, the seat of the archbishop. The first is the *Laudes regiae*. In the famous Worcester Anti-phoner of the thirteenth century the sequence of acclamations proceeds according to a customary formula: pope, king, queen, archbishop, bishop, military heroes (or princes).[3] In the Cosin Gradual the archbishop is honoured before the queen, and there is no mention of a bishop, which, for the cathedral priory of the archbishop, would have been redundant. More specifically, in the series of invocations following the heading *N. archiepiscopum*, the name *Dunstane* is the only one for which capitals are used. The second feature is the proper prose of the *Dedicatio ecclesiae* (97r–8v), *Virginis matris annua*, which points to a church dedicated to Christ and the Virgin – Christ Church, Canterbury.[4] The third comprises the two decorated initials which the gradual preserves, one a capital *P*, the initial of *Puer* for the Introit at Christ-mas, *Puer natus est nobis*, and the second, the capital *S* of *Spiritus*, the first word of the Introit for Pentecost, *Spiritus domini*.[5] The style of these initials

[1] M. Huglo, *Les Tonaires* (Paris, 1971).
[2] The proses are as follows:

		RH	AH
Mane prima sabbati	Easter	11064	LIV, 214
Splendor christi sacerdos	Cuthbert	41019	XLII, 190
Ave mundi spes Maria	B.V.M.	1974	LIV, 340
Regis Oswaldi	Oswald	17229	X, 280

[3] See above, p. 135, n. 2. The *Laudes* are on pls. 201 and 202.
[4] I owe this point to Professor Gneuss.
[5] The manuscript may have originally contained at least three other decorated initials. The Kyriale opens imperfectly but may have only one leaf missing. The Temporale may also have only one leaf missing. A hypothetical lay-out of the pages preceding each imperfect beginning con-firms these points. The R of *Resurrexi*, the first word of the Introit for Easter, almost certainly would have been elaborately decorated, thus making at least three other initials to add to the two now existing. I do not include the clumsy *G* which introduces the settings of *Gloria in excelsis* in this list of initials.

is distinctive and is similar to that in manuscripts produced at Christ Church from approximately 1070 to 1100.[1]

A little more can be said about the contents of the manuscript. In order to do so, reference must be made to a herculean project in the editing of Gregorian chant manuscripts which has been under way at the Benedictine abbey of Solesmes for more than thirty years. In 1957 the first volume of a critical edition of the Roman Gradual was issued by the Solesmes monks.[2] It listed most of the manuscript graduals and noted missals found in the libraries of the world, from the earliest – the Gradual of Monza of the early eighth century – to a few significant sources of the sixteenth century. The next volume, which appeared three years later, presented two gigantic collations of musical variants, the first involving 197 manuscripts, the second the oldest and most important sources.[3] From the manner in which the raw data was presented in this volume, it was clear that with some help from an experienced computer programmer its data could be transferred to punched cards and the variants in Cosin V. V. 6 compared with those in the 197 sources used for the initial collation. There seemed little point in attempting a comparison with the oldest sources, for we were more interested in fitting the Cosin Gradual into the families of chant manuscripts established by the first collation than we were in fitting it into the much more limited and complicated collation of 310 variants used for the oldest sources. The project was duly undertaken[4] and established conclusively that a strong relationship exists between the Cosin Gradual and four important graduals, of which two are English, Oxford, Bodleian Library, Rawlinson C. 892 (s. xii/xiii) and Worcester, Cathedral Library, F. 160 (s. xiii med.), and two are French, Paris, BN lat. 18010 (s. xi ex.) and Paris, Bibliothèque Mazarine, 384 (s. xi). These manuscripts come from Downpatrick (Ireland), Worcester, Corbie and St Denis respectively. The Downpatrick book is based on an earlier one from Winchester.[5] The Worcester Gradual of the thirteenth century is bound in with the famous antiphoner of that cathedral which has been printed in facsimile in *Paléographie Musicale* 12. Since Corbie supplied monks to Abingdon in the mid-tenth century as part of the monastic reform movement, and from Abingdon monks went to many important English

[1] C. R. Dodwell kindly confirmed this a few years ago. See Dodwell, *The Canterbury School of Illumination 1066–1200* (Cambridge, 1954). The colouring in Cosin V. V. 6 is not so strong as that found in some of the 'Lanfranc' books such as Cambridge, Trinity College B. 5. 28 or Cambridge, University Library, Ff. 3. 9.

[2] Abbaye Saint-Pierre de Solesmes, *Le Graduel Romain, Édition Critique par les Moines de Solesmes*, pt II, *Les Sources* (Solesmes, 1957).

[3] *Le Graduel Romain*, pt IV, *Le Texte Neumatique*, 1: *Le Groupement des Manuscrits* (Solesmes, 1960).

[4] I hope to publish a detailed explanation of this project in the near future.

[5] *The Missal of the New Minster, Winchester*, ed. D. H. Turner, Henry Bradshaw Soc. 93 (London, 1962), App., p. 3.

monasteries, and since St Dunstan, during his exile in Europe, spent a few years at a monastery which had received strong influence from St Denis, the royal abbey near Paris, it is generally acknowledged that the affinity of these four graduals to each other reflects the carrying over after the Conquest of the Corbie St Denis tradition of chanting cemented strongly in the mid-tenth-century Benedictine revival.[1]

There are several possible explanations for the close relationship of Cosin V. V. 6 to these particular graduals. One is that it reflects, as they do, a pre-1066 state of affairs. This hypothesis suffers, of course, from the disadvantage of treating the Anglo-Saxon church as a homogeneity, when we know that it was nothing of the kind. Further, no service book of Christ Church earlier than the Cosin Gradual survives, so that we are unable to say positively what type of chant was used there prior to the Conquest. The influence of Bec was especially strong at Christ Church and at places using the Lanfranc Constitutions such as St Albans and Durham. Alas, no chant books of Bec survive from the eleventh century, so that it is impossible to tell whether Bec used a Corbie–St Denis type of gradual during its formative period, and none seems to survive from its foundations in this period. The later books of Bec and its sphere, Paris, BN lat. 1105 (s. xiii) and Leningrad, Public Library, O. v. I. 6 (s. xii), present variants which differ considerably from those in Cosin V.V.6 and its related group.[2] It is not impossible, though the possibility is remote, that an early gradual of Bec is reflected in Cosin V. V. 6, since Bec was not founded from another house and in learning was *sui generis*. It is also possible that the Cosin Gradual was the result of fusing a Bec book and an English book, whether from Canterbury or Winchester. This is certainly an attractive hypothesis, since we know there was Bec influence in liturgical matters at Christ Church. The list of alleluia verses for the Sundays after Pentecost in the Bec Missal is basically that found in the Cosin Gradual and in quite a few other manuscripts from post-Conquest England, but does not to my knowledge appear in pre-Conquest books.[3] However, the similarity of alleluia lists is generally taken

---

[1] Worcester, F. 160 and Rawlinson C. 892 are closer to each other than to any of the other sources. This is not surprising when we recall that Worcester is known to have derived some of its pre-Conquest liturgical books from Winchester. Worcester, F. 173, a substantial fragment of an early-eleventh-century noted missal, was written at Winchester. F. E. Warren, 'An Anglo-Saxon Missal at Worcester', *The Academy*, 12 December 1885, pp. 394–5. For more on the Corbie–St Denis–Worcester–Ireland 'cocoon', see *Le Groupement des Manuscrits*, p. 245.

[2] See below, Appendix.

[3] M. Huglo, 'Les Listes Alléluiatiques dans les Témoins du Graduel Grégorien', *Speculum Musicae Artis. Festschrift Heinrich Husmann zum 60. Geburtstag* (Munich, 1969), pp. 219–27. *The Bec Missal*, ed. A. Hughes, Henry Bradshaw Soc. 94 (London, 1963), xi–xiii, the work of D. H. Turner. Leningrad O. v. I. 6 and Cosin V. V. 6 should be added to his list. For the Leningrad manuscript, see *Consuetudines Beccenses*, ed. M. P. Dickson, Corpus Consuetudinum Monasticarum 4 (Siegburg, 1967), xii, n. 19.

to indicate liturgical affinity, not necessarily affinity in chanting. To extract the Bec elements of musical importance appears not to be possible. We also have to remember that the computer study has been confined to a comparison of musical variants in the proper chants of the Mass in Cosin V. V. 6 with those in 197 other sources. Proses are not part of this study, nor are processional antiphons, the *Laudes regiae*, the many settings of the Ordinary, and the Tonale. Extended studies of each of these areas may result in findings which indicate a different source or sources than the strong pre-Conquest Corbie–St Denis tradition. A rudimentary glance at the repertory of proses in the Temporale, for instance, reveals divergences from the Winchester 'Tropers'. But we need not expect this type of work to disturb tentative conclusions regarding the basic book reached on other grounds. The hypothesis that seems to me at present most likely is that the Cosin Gradual is in the main an English book preserving the type of chant used in the pre-Conquest church – more specifically, on the strength of its place of origin, the chant used at Canterbury before the Normans came.

Why was the manuscript sent to Durham and at what time is that likely to have happened? In order to promote a liturgical order based on the 'customs of those monasteries which in [his] day had the greatest prestige in the monastic order', Lanfranc drew up a set of constitutions for his cathedral priory of Christ Church. A date as early as 1073–4 has been proposed for their adoption at Canterbury. Dom David Knowles knew them 'to have been applied, at least in great part, at a dozen or so of the principal cathedrals and abbeys of England'.[1] One of the most important of the extant copies of the Constitutions, and the one on which Knowles's own edition of them is based, is Durham, Cathedral Library, B. IV. 24, and it is described in full by Mynors in *Durham Cathedral Manuscripts*. 'The text of Lanfranc's Constitutions, according to Professor Mynors, is "written in a late-eleventh-century Christ Church, Canterbury, hand", and probably formed part of the gift of books from Canterbury to the bishop.'[2] There would have been no better time for the Cosin Gradual to have been sent to Durham than when Durham became monastic after William of St Calais became bishop in 1081 – probably when the Constitutions were sent – and no better reason for it to

---

[1] *The Monastic Constitutions of Lanfranc*, ed. D. Knowles (London, 1951), p. xxii.

[2] Knowles, *ibid.* p. xxiii, quoting Mynors, *Durham Cathedral Manuscripts*, p. 45. Durham B. II. 10, letters of St Jerome, came to Durham from Christ Church in this period: 'in a hand characteristic of Christ Church, Canterbury' (Mynors, *ibid.* p. 37); 'was, I believe, brought from Christ Church' (Dodwell, *Canterbury School of Illumination*, p. 116, n. 2). The beginning of the passage *DORMIENTEM TE ET MULTO iam tempore* shown by Mynors's pl. 26 exhibits the same type of structure in the passage in capitals as that in the passage in Cosin V. V. 6 *PUER NATUS est nobis* (30r), i.e., some letters are made to fit inside others if space is lacking on the line but not to protrude outside the horizontal guidelines. Another such passage in V. V. 6 is the beginning of the settings of *Gloria in excelsis* on 13r. Many of the Carilef books have no such crowding of letters. They are simply strung out in common style.

have been sent than to assure adherence on the part of Durham Priory to the traditions in singing practised at Canterbury.

These circumstances would certainly account for the physical character of the manuscript – aside from the lacunae which plague its contents. It is perhaps the most beautiful manuscript of its type that I have seen. The scribes carried out their task with great pains. There are only a few places where a later scribe, perhaps the precentor at Durham, was required to change a few notes. This of course means that the manuscript was used and that the chant followed the guidelines set by this book soon after it was received. The exact hand of the text has not been identified.[1] Liturgical hands in this period are hard to pin down, for they infrequently have recourse to the common abbreviation conventions found in other types of Latin books.[2] The notation has been entered with the same care as the text. The scribe was probably Norman (for a facsimile of 40r, see pl. III*a*), for the notation is Norman and not that found in Anglo-Saxon manuscripts before the Conquest. It is certainly the case that, if the manuscript was a gift to William of St Calais around 1083 when the first monks were professed at Durham, it is written in a script and a notation that would have been familiar to the new bishop and to a Norman precentor. Still another reason for considering it a gift is the range of its contents. As shown by the list above, pp. 133–6, they are of a scope which would have been expected only of a book intended to be a reference tool, one to be consulted in every situation. It is not far-fetched to think that it might have included a complete antiphoner which has been unfortunately lost.

As mentioned above, the repertory of alleluia verses during the crucial seasons of the liturgical year – the Sundays after Easter and those after Pentecost – is usually an accurate guide to liturgical affinity: the Cosin Gradual has exactly the same series as that in BM Harley 5289, a fourteenth-century missal of Durham Priory.[3] There is thus every likelihood that the manuscript remained at Durham throughout the Middle Ages, even though it does not appear in any of the medieval *catalogi veteres* printed by James Raine for the Surtees Society in the early nineteenth century.[4] It is quite possible that the book was kept in the choir and would not have been inventoried with those in the library. Because of its size it may have been part of the equipment of the succentor or even the schoolmaster.

To sum up, Cosin, V. V. 6, a small gradual, was produced at Christ

[1] So T. A. M. Bishop.

[2] For English and Norman writing in the late eleventh century, see N. R. Ker, *English Manuscripts in the Century after the Norman Conquest* (Oxford, 1960), ch. v, pp. 22–32.

[3] The listing of post-Pentecost alleluias in *Missale ad Usum Ecclesiae Westmonasteriensis* (ed. J. Wickham Legg, 3 vols., Henry Bradshaw Soc. 1, 5 and 12 (London, 1891–7), III, 1487–501) does not faithfully include all of those mentioned in the Harley Missal.

[4] See above, p. 132, n. 4.

Church, Canterbury, in the last quarter of the eleventh century, probably around 1080. It contains music for the Mass which is similar to that undoubtedly sung in a number of readily identifiable places in England before the Norman Conquest. It was probably sent to Durham around 1083 in order to assure musical and liturgical uniformity with Canterbury in the new monastic foundation. It is written in a script and a notation that would have been familiar to the new bishop. It is likely to have remained at Durham ever since.

Very few musical sources are known from this period. Of these the celebrated Winchester 'Tropers' and the Troper in BM Cotton Caligula A. xiv preserve music which can be dated earlier, but in some ways the Cosin Gradual is more interesting, for it contains a great deal of music these books do not, music earlier in date than that preserved in any other extant English manuscript. It is in fact the earliest relatively complete gradual that we possess. The importance of this find – a new source for the music of the Mass as it was sung in the cathedral priories of Canterbury and Durham in the eleventh century – can hardly be over-emphasized.[1]

APPENDIX

VARIANTS 51–150 IN 'LE GROUPEMENT DES MANUSCRITS'
COMPARED IN COSIN V. V. 6 AND OTHER MANUSCRIPTS FROM
ENGLAND, NORTHERN FRANCE AND NORMANDY

Cos Cosin V. V. 6
Iri Oxford, Bodleian Library, Rawlinson C. 892
Vor1 Worcester, Cathedral Library, F. 160
Den1 Paris, Bibliothèque Mazarine, 384 (St Denis)
Den4 Paris, BN lat. 9436 (St Denis)
Cor Paris, BN lat. 18010 (Corbie)
Bec Paris, BN lat. 1105 (Bec)
Rop Leningrad, Public Library, O.v.I.6 (St Nicaise de Meulan (use of Bec))
Evr3 Paris, BN n.a. lat. 1773 (Évreux)
Pro1 Provins, Bibliothèque Municipale, 12 (St Père de Chartres)
Rog2 Rouen, Bibliothèque Municipale, 277 (Rouen cathedral)
Rog3 Paris, BN n.a. lat. 541 (Rouen cathedral)
Sic Madrid, BN Vᵃ 20–4 (St Ouen de Rouen brought to Sicily)
Evr1 Rouen, Bibliothèque Municipale, 305 (Montaure, in the diocese of Évreux)

[1] An earlier version of this paper was read at the Eighth Conference on Medieval Studies at Western Michigan University. I would like to thank the Research Foundation of the State University of New York for generous support in 1971 and 1972 in the form of Faculty Research Fellowships. I would also like to thank Messrs Bishop, Doyle, Gneuss, Hohler and Ker for reading this paper and for making comments, many of which I have tried to follow. I am especially grateful to Christopher Hohler for discussing the implications of the computer study at great length.

For the meaning of A, B and C in each variant see *Le Groupement des Manuscrits*.
D = a lacuna, a second hand, an illegible entry etc.

	Cos	Iri	Vor1	Den1	Den4	Cor	Bec	Rop	Evr3	Pro1	Rog2	Rog3	Sic	Evr1
51	C	C	C	C	C	C	D	C	C	D	A	A	C	C
52	A	A	A	B	B	A	D	A	A	A	B	A	B	B
53	B	A	A	A	A	A	D	B	B	B	B	B	B	B
54	B	B	B	B	B	B	D	B	B	D	B	B	B	B
55	B	B	B	B	B	B	D	B	B	B	B	B	B	A
56	A	A	A	A	A	A	D	B	B	B	A	B	B	B
57	A	A	A	D	A	A	D	B	B	B	B	B	B	A
58	A	A	B	D	B	A	D	B	B	B	B	B	B	B
59	A	A	A	A	A	A	B	B	D	D	B	B	B	D
60	B	B	B	B	B	B	A	A	A	D	A	A	A	B
61	A	A	A	A	A	A	B	B	B	B	A	A	B	B
62	A	A	A	A	A	A	A	A	A	B	B	B	D	A
63	B	B	B	B	B	B	A	A	A	A	B	B	B	B
64	A	A	A	A	A	A	A	A	A	A	B	B	A	A
65	A	A	A	A	A	A	A	A	A	A	B	A	A	B
66	B	B	B	B	B	D	B	B	B	B	B	B	B	A
67	B	B	B	B	B	B	B	B	B	B	B	B	B	B
68	D¹	C	C	C	C	C	A	A	A	A	B	B	A	B
69	B	B	B	B	B	B	B	B	B	B	B	B	B	B
70	A	A	A	A	A	A	A	A	B	A	B	B	B	A
71	B	B	B	B	B	B	B	B	B	B	B	B	B	D
72	B	B	B	B	B	D	D	A	A	A	B	B	A	B
73	B	B	B	B	B	B	A	A	A	A	B	B	A	B
74	B	B	B	B	B	B	A	A	D	B	B	B	A	B
75	B	B	B	A	A	B	D	A	A	A	B	B	A	A
76	A	A	A	A	A	A	A	A	A	A	B	D	A	A
77	A	A	A	A	A	A	B	B	B	B	B	B	B	A
78	A	A	A	A	A	A	B	B	B	B	B	B	A	A
79	B	A	B	A	A	B	B	B	B	B	B	B	B	B
80	C	C	C	D	C	C	C	C	C	A	C	A	A	C
81	B	A	B	B	B	B	A	B	B	B	B	B	B	B
82	A	A	A	A	A	A	A	A	A	A	A	A	A	A
83	D²	C	C	C	C	C	C	C	C	A	C	D	C	C
84	D³	B	B	B	B	B	B	A	B	A	B	D	B	A
85	D⁴	A	A	A	D	B	B	B	B	A	B	D	B	A
86	A	A	A	A	A	A	A	A	A	A	A	D	A	A
87	B	B	B	B	B	B	A	A	A	A	D	A	A	A
88	A	A	A	D	B	A	B	B	A	A	B	D	B	A
89	B	B	B	D	B	B	A	A	A	A	B	D	B	B
90	B	B	B	B	B	B	C	C	B	C	B	D	B	B
91	B	B	B	B	B	B	B	B	B	B	B	D	B	B
92	A	B	B	B	B	A	B	B	B	B	B	B	B	B

¹ The original reading was C. It was altered to B very soon after writing. At the third appearance of the motive, the reading, unaltered, is C.

² A later hand has entered C. As far as I can tell, that is what the original read. The first neum began below the bottom line of the three-line staff and the repeated *os* are all faintly visible between the bottom two lines. The passage is at present noted on a three-line staff.

³ A later hand has entered B. As far as I can tell, that is what the original read. This case was difficult to decide. The passage is at present noted on a three-line staff.

⁴ A later hand has entered B. As far as I can tell, that is what the original read. The passage is at present noted on a three-line staff.

	Cos	Iri	Vor1	Den1	Den4	Cor	Bec	Rop	Evr3	Pro1	Rog2	Rog3	Sic	Evr1
93	B	B	B	B	B	B	B	B	B	D	B	B	B	D
94	A	D	A	B	B	D	D	A	B	B	B	B	D	B
95	B	B	B	B	B	B	B	B	B	A	B	B	B	B
96	A	A	A	A	A	D	A	A	A	A	A	A	A	C
97	B	B	B	B	B	D	A	A	B	A	A	A	D	B
98	A	A	A	A	A	D	A	A	B	A	A	A	B	B
99	B	B	B	B	B	D	B	B	B	A	B	B	B	B
100	D	B	B	B	B	D	A	B	A	A	B	B	A	D
101	D	A	A	D	A	A	D	A	A	B	A	A	A	B
102	D¹	B	B	D	B	B	D	B	B	B	A	B	B	B
103	D²	A	D	D	A	A	D	B	B	B	B	B	B	B
104	D³	A	A	D	A	A	D	B	B	B	A	A	B	B
105	A	A	A	A	B	A	D	A	A	A	B	B	A	B
106	A	A	A	A	A	A	D	A	A	A	A	A	A	D
107	B	B	B	B	B	A	D	B	B	B	B	B	B	B
108	B	B	B	B	B	B	D	A	A	A	B	B	A	A
109	D	A	D	A	A	A	B	A	B	B	B	B	B	B
110	B.	B	B	B	B	B	B	B	B	B	B	B	B	B
111	A	A	A	A	A	A	B	B	B	B	A	A	B	B
112	D	B	B	B	B	A	B	B	B	B	B	B	B	B
113	C	C	C	C	C	C	B	B	C	B	C	C	C	C
114	A	A	A	A	A	A	A	A	A	B	B	B	B	D
115	B	B	B	B	B	B	B	B	B	A	B	B	A	B
116	A	A	A	A	A	A	B	B	B	B	B	B	B	B
117	B	B	B	B	B	B	B	B	B	B	B	B	B	B
118	A	A	A	A	A	B	B	B	B	B	B	B	B	B
119	B	B	B	B	B	B	B	B	A	B	B	B	B	B
120	B	C	C	C	C	B	A	A	A	D	A	A	A	B
121	A	A	A	B	B	A	A	A	A	A	B	D	B	D
122	B	B	B	B	B	B	A	A	B	A	A	A	A	A
123	B	B	B	B	B	B	B	B	B	B	B	B	B	B
124	A	A	A	A	A	A	A	A	A	B	A	B	B	B
125	B	B	B	B	B	B	A	A	A	A	B	B	B	B
126	B	B	B	B	B	B	B	D	B	A	B	B	B	B
127	A	A	A	A	A	A	B	B	B	B	B	B	B	B
128	B	A	B	A	A	B	A	A	B	B	B	B	B	B
129	B	B	B	B	B	B	A	A	A	A	A	A	A	B
130	B	B	B	B	B	B	B	B	B	B	B	A	A	A
131	D	A	A	A	A	A	A	A	A	A	A	A	A	B
132	D	A	A	A	A	A	A	A	A	A	A	D	A	B
133	D	A	A	A	A	A	B	B	B	A	B	B	B	A
134	D⁴	A	A	A	A	A	A	A	A	B	D	A	D
135	B	B	B	D	D	B	B	B	B	B	B	D	B	B
136	D	B	D	B	B	A	A	A	A	B	B	B	B	A
137	D	A	D	A	B	A	B	B	A	A	B	A	A	A
138	B	B	D	B	B	A	B	B	B	B	B	B	B	B
139	D	B	B	B	B	A	B	B	B	B	B	B	B	B
140	A	B	B	B	B	A	B	B	B	B	B	B	B	B

¹ Taking the reading in the *Graduale Romanum* as a guide, 102 seems to be B. I argue from the manner in which the parchment has been disturbed. Part of the neum on '*fa*-ciet' is still visible.

² This appears to be A, but it is very hard to read.

³ This also appears to be A, but again it is very hard to read. My decision is based on the neums before it and on the location of the erasures.

⁴ A later hand has entered A. As far as I can tell, that is what the original read. The passage is at present noted on a three-line staff.

	Cos	Iri	Vor1	Den1	Den4	Cor	Bec	Rop	Evr3	Pro1	Rog2	Rog3	Sic	Evr1
141	D	B	D	B	B	A	A	A	D	A	B	B	B	D
142	D	B	D	B	B	A	B	B	D	B	B	B	B	D
143	D	A	D	A	A	A	B	B	B	B	B	D	B	A
144	D	B	B	B	B	A	B	B	B	B	B	B	B	B
145	D	B	D	B	B	A	A	A	A	B	B	D	B	D
146	A	A	A	A	A	A	A	A	A	A	B	B	A	A
147	C	C	C	C	C	C	A	A	C	A	C	C	C	C
148	B	B	B	B	B	B	A	A	A	A	B	B	A	B
149	B	B	B	B	B	B	B	B	B	B	B	B	B	B
150	A	A	A	A	A	A	A	A	A	A	A	B	B	A

Some aesthetic principles in the use of colour in Anglo-Saxon art

J. J. G. ALEXANDER

In a paper in *Anglo-Saxon England* 3 N. F. Barley has drawn attention to the richness of Anglo-Saxon colour vocabulary, which, he suggests, emphasized the light–dark axis of colour perception to a greater degree than does our own, in which hue is differentiated and then qualified adjectivally, pale, dark, etc.[1] It is interesting to examine actual Anglo-Saxon artifacts with his observations in mind. The main sources for our knowledge of the Anglo-Saxons' use of colour are the illuminated manuscripts of which the earliest surviving are of the seventh century. We have only one small fragment of wall-painting, the recently discovered mural at Winchester datable to *c.* 900.[2] There is a considerable amount of metal-work and jewellery, of which the Sutton Hoo find, a seventh-century burial hoard, is the most spectacular,[3] and there are some embroideries of the early tenth century found in the tomb of St Cuthbert, now at Durham.[4] There are also literary descriptions of works of art, especially church furnishings.[5] The paucity of surviving material and the lack of descriptions of identifiable objects are obvious disadvantages. In addition there has to be considered the extent to which the use of colour changed and developed over the period *c.* 650–1050. In this paper some examples of manuscript illumination will be discussed.

The earlier period from *c.* 650 to the later ninth century, the 'insular' period as it is convenient to call it, saw the northern peoples in Ireland and England translating the illusionistic figural art of the classical Mediterranean world into their own language of non-figural, abstract pattern, a tendency that can be seen even in Mediterranean art from at least the fourth century.[6] One consequence was the disappearance of three-dimensional spatial repre-

[1] Nigel F. Barley, 'Old English Colour Classification: Where do Matters Stand?', *ASE* 3 (1974), 15–28.

[2] M. Biddle, 'Excavations at Winchester, 1966. Fifth Interim Report', *AntJ* 47 (1967), 277–9, pls. xxiii and liv(*a*).

[3] R. L. S. Bruce-Mitford, *The Sutton Hoo Ship-Burial* (London, 1968).

[4] R. Freyhan, 'The Place of the Stole and Maniples in Anglo-Saxon Art of the Tenth Century', *The Relics of St Cuthbert*, ed. C. F. Battiscombe (Oxford, 1956), pp. 409–32.

[5] O. Lehmann-Brockhaus, *Lateinische Schriftquellen zur Kunst in England, Wales und Schottland vom Jahre 901 bis zum Jahre 1307* (Munich, 1956).

[6] E. Kitzinger, *Early Medieval Art in the British Museum*, 2nd ed. (London, 1955), p. 7.

sentation, which has received much attention, partly as concomitant to the importance attached to its recovery at the Renaissance.[1] But changes in the use of colour are an equally important aspect of this rejection of the principles of classical art.[2]

An illusionistic use of colour requires accuracy of observation in two respects. First, objects must be represented in the colours by which we recognize them every day, their actual or 'surface' colour as Katz calls it. Consistency is an important factor here. For example, if the same person is represented in consecutive scenes the colour of his hair or of his clothes should remain the same. Secondly – and this will sometimes contradict the first point – the effects of light must be taken into account. Since they affect our perception, shadows, textures, reflections and proximity to other colours must be observed and utilized by any artist aiming at illusion ('representational' colour). In the high Middle Ages in the west the effect of light came to be ignored almost altogether. Regarding the first point, consistency was certainly not considered an overriding factor and it was not even a binding rule that natural colours should be retained so that objects should be recognizable, although on the whole this was the practice.

The development in the insular period cannot be better demonstrated than by comparing the well-known Ezra portrait in the Codex Amiatinus of the early eighth century[3] and the Matthew portrait in the Lindisfarne Gospel of *c.* 698.[4] In the former the artist working at Wearmouth/Jarrow has retained the Late Antique illusionistic palette of his sixth-century model, so that, for instance, the interior of the book cupboard is darker, because in shadow, and the panels of the doors are also modelled in dark and light.

[1] Cf. S. Y. Egerton Jr, 'Alberti's Colour Theory', *Jnl of the Warburg and Courtauld Insts.* 32 (1969), 109.

[2] A useful introductory account of colour perception is G. M. Murch, *Visual and Auditory Perception* (Indianapolis, 1973). See also David Katz, *The World of Colour* (London, 1935). For medieval and later use of colour in art see F. Haeberlein, 'Grundzüge einer nachantiken Farbenikonographie', *Römisches Jahrbuch für Kunstgeschichte* 3 (1939), 75–126 (I am grateful to Mr John Mitchell for this reference); H. Jantzen, 'Über Prinzipien der Farbengebung in der Malerei', repr. *Über den gotischen Kirchenraum und andere Aufsätze* (Berlin, 1951), p. 61; W. Schöne, *Über das Licht in der Malerei* (Berlin, 1954); and E. Gombrich, 'Light, Form and Texture in XVth Century Painting', *Jnl of the R. Soc. of Arts* (October 1964), 826–49. The account devoted specifically to colour in manuscript painting by J. J. Tikkanen, *Farbengebung in der mittelalterlichen Buchmalerei*, Societas Scientiarum Fennica. Commentationes Humanarum Litterarum 5.1 (Helsingfors, 1933) does not consider later Anglo-Saxon illumination. It is discussed, however, by H. Roosen-Runge, *Farbgebung und Technik frühmittelalterlicher Buchmalerei*, Kunstwissenschaftliche Studien 38, 2 vols. (Munich, 1967), with information also on the pigments used and technical treatises.

[3] Florence, Biblioteca Laurenziana, Amiatinus 1. See R. L. S. Bruce-Mitford, 'The Art of the Codex Amiatinus', *JBAA* 32 (1969), 1–25; for a colour plate see C. Nordenfalk, 'Book Illumination', *Early Mediaeval Painting* (Geneva, 1957), p. 119.

[4] BM Cotton Nero D. iv; Nordenfalk, 'Book Illumination', colour pl., p. 117. For the relationship of the two miniatures and the lost Cassiodoran model see R. L. S. Bruce-Mitford in *Evangeliorum quattuor Codex Lindisfarnensis*, ed. T. D. Kendrick, text vol. (Lausanne, 1966).

The colour range is sombre and fairly restricted and this to some extent suggests an interior with limited light. In the Lindisfarne Matthew portrait, by contrast, the illusionistic colour is abandoned, just as the spatial setting disappears. For example, the books held by the angel and the inspiring figure are no longer reddish brown, as if covered in leather (the same colour as the still surviving binding of the Stonyhurst Gospel[1]), but a bright green. This colour is chosen simply to contrast with the contiguous colours and to balance the saint's mantle. The use of abstract colour and the absence of illusionistic modelling do not mean that the range of hues in insular art is limited or that differences of tone are ignored. The range of colours in the Lindisfarne Gospels is considerable and it is used with great subtlety in the cross carpet pages, for example. But the colours are juxtaposed as in a floor mosaic,[2] and one has only to see how relatively dead the pages look in a black and white reproduction to realize that the distinction is one of hue. Indeed the tonal values are purposely kept the same so that the ambiguous interplay of background and foreground shapes, one of the essential elements of the pattern making, is preserved. Technical factors are obviously important in the overall effect – for instance, the range of pigments available to the artist or whether he has the technical skill to apply and burnish gold leaf. The essential thing, however, is not what colours are used but the *way* they are used, as is clear from the comparison of the Ezra and the Matthew, almost contemporary works by artists living in centres not far distant.

In the later period, following the re-establishment of contact with the continent under Alfred the Great (d. 899) and particularly his grandson Athelstan (d. 939), artists in England returned to a figural art of a more naturalistic kind.[3] The main stimulus was ninth-century Carolingian art, which had in turn copied Late Antique and Early Christian models with varying degrees of faithfulness. The result was to re-establish naturalistic colour, at least as compared with such far-fetched examples of non-naturalistic colour as the Macregol Gospels made in Ireland in the early ninth century;[4] in that book the stripes of green and orange on the evangelist's robes are without representational significance and barely distinguishable from the intricate frames of the borders. Nevertheless the result is certainly not

---

[1] *The Stonyhurst Gospel of St John*, ed. T. J. Brown (Oxford, 1969).

[2] T. D. Kendrick (*Anglo-Saxon Art to A.D. 900* (London, 1938; repr. 1972)) compares the carpet pages to Roman mosaics.

[3] F. Wormald, 'The Winchester School Before St Æthelwold', *England before the Conquest: Studies in Primary Sources Presented to Dorothy Whitelock*, ed. Peter Clemoes and Kathleen Hughes (Cambridge, 1971), and R. Deshman, 'Anglo-Saxon Art after Alfred', *Art Bull.* 56 (1974), 176–200.

[4] Oxford, Bodleian Library, Auct. D. 2. 19; O. Pächt and J. J. G. Alexander, *Illuminated Manuscripts in the Bodleian Library, Oxford* III: *British, Irish and Icelandic Schools* (Oxford, 1973), no. 1269. On the whole, Irish miniatures tend to greater abstraction both in form and in colour than Anglo-Saxon ones. However, mutual influence was, of course, extensive.

a completely naturalistic colour, even in a manuscript as influenced by Carolingian art as the Benedictional of St Æthelwold of *c*. 975–80. In this manuscript's miniature of the baptism (25r), for example, there is a bright pink background behind the figures with narrower bands of blue and grey above.[1] The origin of such a background can be traced to the atmospheric sky effects of Late Antique painting, as seen for example in the Vatican Vergil of *c*. 400.[2] In Carolingian manuscripts, such as the Bible of Charles the Bald of *c*. 870,[3] the colours begin to be more differentiated in bands running from blue to orange as opposed to a gradual soft merging into each other. In the Benedictional the naturalistic effect has been completely lost. So too with the modelling of round forms, such as thighs or arms, in light and dark. Here again an illusionistic device is quickly turned to pattern. The point is that in the later period too, though within a different artistic language, there is a clear tendency to an abstract, as opposed to a naturalistic, use of colour, even if it does not go so far as in the insular period.[4]

Two ways in which later Anglo-Saxon artists made new and notable colour experiments deserve comment. The first is in the use of precious metals. Gold is surprisingly uncommon in insular manuscripts.[5] The first manuscript of the later period in which it is extensively used is the Benedictional of St Æthelwold, where the scribe Godeman mentions in his poem at the beginning of the manuscript that the bishop commanded the book to be painted in gold and colours.[6] In the figure of St Æthelthryth (90v), for instance, the entire mantle and veil of the saint is highly burnished gold.[7] Even more spectacular in effect is the miniature of St John in a gospels written at Christ Church, Canterbury, by the scribe Eadwig *c*. 1020 (see pl. V).[8] The figure's overmantle is again brilliantly burnished gold, and gold is used not only for the frame and the arch under which he sits but also for many details in the miniature. Gold used in this way is entirely non-naturalistic, first because it will vary as to whether it registers as dark or light according to how the light falls on the page, and secondly because it emphasizes the unity of decorative and figural motifs. On this page the rectangular frame,

[1] BM Add. 49598; F. Wormald, *The Benedictional of St Ethelwold* (London, 1959), and Nordenfalk, 'Book Illumination', colour pl. p. 180.

[2] Vatican, Vat. Lat. 3225; Nordenfalk, 'Book Illumination', colour pl. p. 94.

[3] Rome, San Paolo fuori le Mura; Nordenfalk, 'Book Illumination', colour pl. p. 153.

[4] Deshman ('Anglo-Saxon Art after Alfred', p. 199) speaks of colour compartmentalizing the composition in the Benedictional. He also stresses the continuation of the decorative principles of Hiberno-Saxon art.

[5] H. Roosen-Runge, 'The Pictorial Technique of the Lindisfarne Gospels', in *Evangeliorum quattuor codex Lindisfarnensis*, ed. T. D. Kendrick (Lausanne, 1966).

[6] Wormald, *Benedictional of St Ethelwold*, p. 7; for the Latin text see Michael Lapidge, 'The Hermeneutic Style in Tenth-Century Anglo-Latin Literature', App. II, above, pp. 105–6.

[7] Wormald, *Benedictional of St Ethelwold*, pl. 6.

[8] Hanover, Kestner Museum. Exhibited, *English Illuminated Manuscripts 700–1500* (Brussels, 1973), no. 10, colour pl.

the corner rosettes, the large central area of the robe and the smaller blobs of the inkwell, scroll end, knife and throne all balance and complement each other in an abstract design. Gold was not the only metal employed. In another gospels partly written by Eadwig, the so-called Grimbald Gospels, silver has been extensively used.[1] Unfortunately it has tarnished and stained the page, so that the original effect is lost. Contemporary and later accounts make it clear how highly gold was admired in works of art both on account of its intrinsic value and for its brilliance.

The second innovatory technique is that of coloured ink drawings. Carl Nordenfalk has observed that this use of a multiplicity of colours links the drawings with the titles and initials of the text, which were written in similar inks.[2] This observation may explain the origin of a practice for which there seems to have been no precedent.[3] Certainly in the illustrations in the calendarial material in the Leofric Missal, probably the earliest surviving example of this technique, most of the drawings have the function of diagrams and are closely connected with the text which is partly written in and around them.[4] Precisely the same colours – orange, green and blue – are used for the script as for the drawings. Once such figures in diagrams had been coloured, artists seem to have realized the possibility of using this technique for other illustrations which were physically and thematically closely linked with the text. They could give their illustrations vivacity and interest without sacrificing the unity of the page. This would explain the fact that this technique is commonest where drawings are inserted in the columns of script, as in the Prudentius at Cambridge, the Junius 'Cædmon' manuscript in Oxford and the Harley Psalter.[5]

One of the most outstanding Anglo-Saxon manuscripts of the later period in its use of colour is the sacramentary given by Robert of Jumièges to his old monastery after he had been expelled from the see of Canterbury in 1052.[6] Here the colour is applied in fluid swirling washes which intensify the drama of the action. They have in fact something of the expressionistic quality of

---

[1] BM Add. 34890; Nordenfalk, 'Book Illumination', colour pl. p. 181. For Eadwig as the scribe, see T. A. M. Bishop, *English Caroline Minuscule* (Oxford, 1971), p. 22.

[2] Nordenfalk, 'Book Illumination', p. 187.

[3] The only earlier coloured ink drawing I know is in Vatican Pal. Lat. 834, a ninth-century Bede from Lorsch, where one of the three persons of the Trinity is in blue ink and the other two are in brown.

[4] Oxford, Bodleian Library, Bodley 579; Pächt and Alexander, *Illuminated Manuscripts*, no. 25. See A. Heimann, 'Three Illustrations from the Bury St Edmunds Psalter and their Prototypes', *Jnl of the Warburg and Courtauld Insts.* 29 (1966), 39–43.

[5] Cambridge, Corpus Christi College 23; Oxford, Bodleian Library, Junius 11; and BM Harley 603 (F. Wormald, *English Drawings of the Tenth and Eleventh Centuries* (London, 1952), nos. 4, 50 and 34). Probably all are Canterbury manuscripts.

[6] Rouen, Bibliothèque Municipale, Y. 6 (274); *The Missal of Robert of Jumièges*, ed. H. A. Wilson, Henry Bradshaw Soc. 11 (1896). See E. C. Hohler, 'Les Saints Insulaires dans le Missel de l'Archevêque Robert', *Jumièges, Congrès Scientifique du XIIIᵉ Centenaire* (Paris, 1955) I, 293–303.

a painting by Munch. It seems to me that the colour also has a thematic significance and emphasizes connections between different scenes. For example, at the nativity (32v) a brilliant yellow sky suggests the break of day, the glorious dawn of the redemption, and we see this still as the Magi ride towards Bethlehem (36v; see pl. VI) and at the Epiphany (37r). Herod and the Jewish priests, however, are shown above on the former page (36v) against a dark and threatening blue background. For the scene of the betrayal (71r) bands of dark blue and of orange are used as if to show an angry sunset. The later scene of the angel addressing the three women after the resurrection (72v; see pl. VII) is framed with an identical pointed arch, no doubt intentionally to suggest a parallel between the two scenes, one showing the messenger of death and the other the messenger of life. The parallel is emphasized by the use of the same horizontal bands of blue and orange, but there is a subtle difference, for, whereas in the betrayal the lower band is a dark brown, in the three Marys scene it is a light pink. Surely this is an intentional device to distinguish the early morning, with its dawn of hope after the women's anguish, from the night scene with its evil protagonist. In the crucifixion (71v) and the deposition (72r) a yellow central band again denotes the morning and poignantly recalls the beginning of the cycle, the redemption, which is here completed. In the deposition there is also a darker band perhaps suggesting the darkness at midday, whilst the frantic zigzags on the lower levels of both miniatures may suggest the upheaval of the cosmos described in the gospels.

The use of colour and the artist's sources in the illustrations of this great book remain to be investigated. Some scenes derive in iconography from the Benedictional of St Æthelwold, but there appear to be new sources too, and the same is true of the style. The discovery of some fragments of an illustrated manuscript at Damme seem to me of importance in this respect.[1] They contain passages from St Matthew written in Anglo-Saxon caroline minuscule and three miniatures, the miracle of the possessed men and the Gadarene swine (see pl. VIII), the story of St Peter recovering the tribute money from a fish (see pl. IVd) and a third scene of doubtful meaning.[2]

[1] Damme, Musée van Maerlant; A. Boutemy, 'Les Feuillets de Damme', *Scriptorium* 20 (1966), 60–5 and pls. 7b and 8–10. Exhibited, *English Illuminated Manuscripts 700–1500* (Brussels, 1973), no. 7. I am particularly grateful to the Conservateur, M. C. Neuhuys, for his courteous help in providing me with colour and black and white photographs of the leaves.

[2] The small piece of text on one side of the first leaf contains Matthew VIII.23–8 marked for two lections with the rubric 'In illo tempore' (before verses 23 and 28). However, there appear to be textual difficulties in assuming that the fragments are from a gospel lectionary in that these passages do not normally follow each other in a lectionary. These also affect the interpretation of the third scene in which Christ sits on a mount with three figures on each side. Boutemy thinks this is the transfiguration but apart from the textual difficulty that the transfiguration reading (Matthew XVII.1–9) does not come at the same point as the tribute money (Matthew XVII.24ff.) there should be five figures, not six, and the normal representation is quite different.

u ersib: ut nostris diuinae gloria legis
O rnamenta libens caperet terrestria linguae,
h ec mihi pax tribuit xpi. pax hec mihi saecli.,
Q uam fouet indulgens terrae regnator apte
C onstantinus adest cun gloria diua merenti
Q ui solus regum sacri sibi nominis horret
I mponi pondus: quo iustis dignior actis
A eternam capiat diuina insaecula uitam.
p er dominu lucis xpm. qui insaecula regnat, dñ.,

INCIPIT PASCHALE CARMEN SEDULII RE
  THORIS NOUI ET VETERIS TESTAMENTI :
S ume pater meras ueracis dicta poete.   VersAsteri
Q ue sine figmenti condita sunt uitio,
Q uo caret alma fides quo sci gra xpi.
P er qua iustus at talia sedulius.
A steriiq: tui semp meminisse iubeto.
C uius ope & cura edita sunt populis.
Q ue quamuis summi celebrent pscta fa stus.
P lus tam admeritum est si uig& ore tuo.

P ASCHALES QVI CVMQ:
  dapes conuiua requiris.
  Dignat nris accubitare thoris.
  Pone supciliu si te cognoscis amicum.,
  Nec queras opus hic codicis artificis.
  Sed modice content adi sollempnia mensae.
  Plusq: libens animo quam satiare cibo.,
  At si magnaru capis dulcedine reru.
  Diuitiisq: magis deliciosus amas
  Nobilium nitidis doctoru uescere cenis
  Quoy multiplices nec numerant opes.,

Collices · cu · A ·
Liber sca̅ Augustini ...

In hoc uolumine continentur ista.
Iuuenalis. de q̅ ... fol̅. i.
Sedulius. de ... fo̅ ...
Arator subdiacon̅g fo̅ 29 ...
Epigmata p̅spi · ...
Prudencia de sichomachia · ... fo̅ 168 ·
Theukon p̅deuci de ueri ꝫ nouo testam̅to · y fo̅ 164 H
Boeci̅ de philosophica consolatione · fo̅ 191 ·
Rabani̅ de laude sce̅ crucis · fo̅ 210 ·
musica augustini · fo̅ 268 ·
Aldelm̅ s̅ laude uirginu̅ · Item ei̅sde de ꝟtub; pugna cu̅ ... to̅ 319 ·
aulo de laude pudicicie ul' sobrietat̅s · fo̅ 324 ·
versus cui̅sda̅ s̅ xii lapidib; · 393
hriflo cui̅sda̅ scolastica q̅ caluos · fo̅ 367 ·
enigmata eusebii · fo̅ 370 ·
Enigmata tautunui · fo̅ 318 · dicta ei̅s ad ... fo̅ 319 ·
Enigmata albini · a caple ... fo̅ 318 ·
Distica ei̅s · fo̅ 319 ·
versus cui̅sda̅ scoti s̅ alfabeto · fo̅ 381 ·
Ide̅ de miñs ꝫ uirtutib; · fo̅ 382 ·
Enigmata simphosii · fo̅ 399 ·
Enigmata aldelmi · fo̅ 362 ·
Liber catonis · fo̅ 60A H
Beda s̅ die iudicii · ... fo̅ 212 ·
Enigmata ei̅s · ... fo̅ 221 ·
l̅s de libalib; artib; · ... fo̅ 322 ·
Queda̅ phisica expimenta — fo̅ 322 ...
Queda̅ rithmica carmina fo̅ 324 ·
Qe̅tus ciceronis — fo̅ 344 ... u̅sꝫ ... fin̅o
... de laude cuculi · fo̅ 345 ·

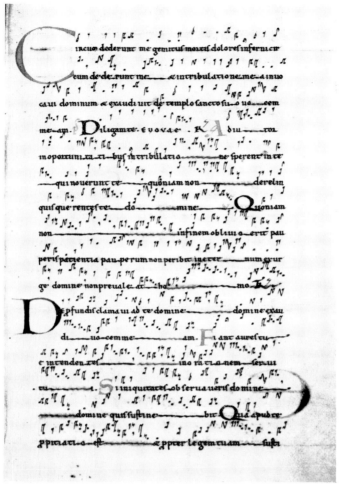

IIIa Durham, University Library, Cosin V. V. 6, 40r (actual size)

IIIb and c Florence, Biblioteca Laurenziana, VI. 23. *Photos: G. Sansoni*
    b 16v: Christ heals the possessed men at Gerasa
    c 36r: St Peter fishing for the tribute money

IV*b* Liverpool City Museum, Ivory (M. 8062): St Peter fishing for the tribute money

IV*a* Aachen Domschatz, Gospels of Otto III, 88v: Christ heals the possessed man at Gerasa. *Photo: Bildarchiv Foto, Marburg*

IV*c* Düsseldorf, Landes- und Stadtbibliothek, B. 113, 5r: Christ heals the leper. *Photo: Rheinisches Bildarchiv, Cologne*

IV*d* Damme, Musée van Maerlant, fragments of a gospel book (?): St Peter fishing for the tribute money

V Hanover, Kestner Museum, Eadwig Gospels (page size 224 × 164 mm), 147v:
St John the Evangelist

VI   Rouen, Bibliothèque Municipale, Y. 6 (274) (page size 322 × 225 mm), 36v:
Herod and the chief priests; the Magi ride towards Bethlehem. *Photo: Lauros–Giraudon*

VII   Rouen, Bibliothèque Municipale, Y. 6 (274) (page size 332 × 225 mm), 72v:
the three Marys at the grave. *Photo: Lauros–Giraudon*

VIII Damme, Musée van Maerlant, fragments of a gospel book (?)
(page size 315 × 183 mm): Christ heals the possessed men at Gerasa

The iconography of these scenes suggests eastern sources. The Christ is bearded and the two scenes of the Gadarene swine and St Peter fishing are found in Middle Byzantine gospel books (see pls. III*b* and *c*).[1] Both are also found in Ottonian works: the first is in a series of gospel books and gospel lectionaries (see pl. IV*a*) and in one of the wall-paintings at Reichenau Oberzell,[2] the second, much the rarer, is on an ivory plaque now at Liverpool, which perhaps originally formed part of the antependium of Magdeburg Cathedral (see pl. IV*b*).[3] These Ottonian works are themselves thought to depend on Middle Byzantine sources. Recent studies have suggested that Anglo-Saxon artists may have had access to Middle Byzantine illuminated manuscripts.[4] From the point of view of the style this seems a more likely source of influence than an Ottonian work in the case of the Damme fragments. Most of the Ottonian manuscripts have already moved farther from a Late Antique style in the use of gold backgrounds, flattened architectural features and planar space.[5] The dense crowd of apostles behind the Christ in the miracle of the possessed does not suggest an Ottonian model. This miniature in particular clearly indicates an ultimate dependence on Late

The text leaf contains the Ammonian sections in the margin (incorrectly, Mark should be xlvii not lxvi). I do not know whether or how often they are included in lectionaries, but it seems to me more likely that we have a fragment of a gospels marked with the lections. The mysterious scene might then represent Christ teaching his apostles on the analogy of the gospels, Florence, Biblioteca Laurenziana, VI. 23 (see below, n. 1).

[1] Paris, BN grec. 74, 16r, 72v and 125r, late-eleventh-century, and Florence, Laur. VI. 23, 16v, 70v and 121r, eleventh-to-twelfth-century, illustrating the accounts in Matthew, Mark and Luke of the Gadarene swine. Laur. VI. 23, 36r shows the episode of St Peter fishing for the tribute money. See H. Omont, *Évangiles avec Peintures Byzantines du XI*[e] *Siècle* (Paris, 1908), and T. Velmans, *La Tétraévangile de la Laurentienne*, Bibliothèque des Cahiers Archéologiques 6 (Paris, 1971).

[2] A. Boeckler, *Ikonographische Studien zu den Wunderszenen in der ottonischen Malerei der Reichenau*, Bayerische Akademie der Wissenschaften. Phil. Hist. Klasse Abh. n.F. 52. (Munich, 1961); H. Buchthal, 'Byzantium and Reichenau', *Byzantine Art – an European Art. Lectures*, ed. M. Chatzidakis (Athens, 1966); and G. Schiller, *Iconography of Christian Art* (London, 1971) I, 173. The scene was represented in Canterbury manuscripts of the twelfth century with two possessed, but in a very abbreviated form: BM Add. 37472, 1v (see C. R. Dodwell, *The Canterbury School of Illumination* (Cambridge, 1954), pl. 66), and Paris, BN lat. 8846, 3v (see H. Omont, *Psautier Illustré (XIII*[e] *Siècle)* (Paris, n.d.), pl. 7).

[3] A. Goldschmidt, *Die Elfenbeinskulpturen aus der Zeit der karolingischen und sächsichen Kaiser VIII–XI. Jahrhundert* (Berlin, 1918; repr. 1970) II, no. 11; Schiller, *Iconography of Christian Art* I, 157. St Peter is shown kneeling, not standing as on the Damme page. He kneels in Florence, Laur. VI. 23 and also in the Syrian gospels written in 586 by the monk Rabbula, Florence, Biblioteca Laurenziana, I. 56, 9r; see the facsimile ed. C. Cecchelli, G. Furlani and M. Salmi, *The Rabbula Gospels* (Olten and Lausanne, 1956). I am grateful to Dr Elizabeth Temple for bringing this to my attention.

[4] R. Deshman, 'The Iconography of the Full-Page Miniatures of the Benedictional of St Æthelwold', Ph.D. dissertation, Princeton, 1970, and 'Anglo-Saxon Art after Alfred', and D. Talbot Rice, 'Britain and the Byzantine World in the Middle Ages', *Byzantine Art – an European Art*, ed. Chatzidakis.

[5] The few miniatures in the *Codex Egberti* which are by the Master of the *Registrum Gregorii* preserve much more of Late Antique illusionism but the short bulky figures are not like those on our leaves.

Antique painting. The lake into whose grey-green water the swine rush is illusionistically painted and the wispy plants on its upper margin are a survival of a naturalistic landscape setting. The little town above is represented in a convention familiar from Late Antique and Early Christian manuscripts.

If the Anglo-Saxon artist copied a Middle Byzantine source preserving such illusionistic details, probably this was a full-page miniature: in other words he is unlikely himself to have adapted the strip composition found in the eleventh-to-twelfth-century Byzantine gospel books. Such a full-page composition, though none actually survives in Byzantine examples, is thought to lie behind the Ottonian copies.[1] It should be pointed out, however, that there are certain divergencies in the iconography of the Damme leaf from that transmitted in the Ottonian copies. First, the latter all show one possessed man according to the accounts in Mark and Luke, not two, as here, according to St Matthew. Second, there are no devils here, either fleeing from the possessed's mouth or riding on the backs of the swine. Third, the poses of the two possessed are different from those of the possessed in the Byzantine or Ottonian examples, the former bending down (see pl. III*b*), the latter with arms chained behind their backs (see pl. IV*a*). Fourth, the tombs mentioned in the text and shown in the Byzantine examples and in some of the Ottonian ones are not represented. We seem to have a closely related but nevertheless divergent tradition.[2]

One other small difference is the running position of the messengers above. This may be a contribution of the Anglo-Saxon artist, but even here the way the figures turn in space suggests a good model. Their vivacious activity calls to mind the Carolingian Rheims school and raises another possibility for the model of the leaves.[3] A fragment of a gospel book in Düsseldorf contains two drawings in the style of the Utrecht Psalter made at Rheims *c.* 820–30.[4] The first shows Christ healing the leper (see pl. IV*c*), the second, perhaps, the Christ child disputing in the temple. This fragment seems to show that a Carolingian gospel book illustrated with miracle scenes once existed and came from precisely that school which so influenced Anglo-Saxon artists. The possibility must at least be considered that the Damme artist was copying not Byzantine but Carolingian miniatures of the Rheims

[1] Buchthal, 'Byzantium and Reichenau', pp. 51 and 55–6.
[2] The Early Christian tradition as represented in an ivory in the Louvre or at Sant'Apollinare Nuovo, Ravenna, is also different; see Schiller, *Iconography of Christian Art* I, figs. 524 and 436. The fishing episode is also differently shown; see above, p. 151, n. 3.
[3] I have not come across any directly comparable running figures, though in the Utrecht Psalter two figures stand with one leg raised; E. T. De Wald, *The Illustrations of the Utrecht Psalter* (Princeton, 1933), pls. xlviii (28r) and li (31v).
[4] Düsseldorf, Landes- und Stadtbibliothek B. 113; V. H. Elbern, 'Das Essener Evangelistarfragment', *Das Erste Jahrtausend. Textband II*, ed. V. H. Elbern (Düsseldorf, 1964), 992–1006, Abb. 1–2.

school. These would have been paintings, however, rather than drawings, in the style of, for example, the Hincmar Gospels.[1] The iconography of their scenes might still be eastern in origin, of course, but lacking some of the picturesque details which we find in the Middle Byzantine representations.[2]

A small detail in the Damme leaf suggests that its place of origin might be Canterbury. On the right the artist has turned a bush or plant into an arabesque scroll with leaf forms which can be paralleled in Canterbury manuscripts.[3] The figure style also bears comparison with that of the 'Cædmon' manuscript, probably from Canterbury, in which there occurs the same sort of architectural canopy as that in the St Peter miniature.[4] Stylistic similarities with the Arundel Psalter made at Canterbury *c*. 1012–23[5] suggest that this was where the Sacramentary of Robert of Jumièges was made too. If so, our hypothetical painted Carolingian (or alternatively Byzantine) model might also have been the source for the experiments in colour made in the Sacramentary. Those experiments would still be new and highly original but would rest on an earlier model preserving an atmospheric illusionistic colouring deriving from Late Antique, possibly eastern sources. Though there are many gaps in our evidence the concept of a highly creative and productive scriptorium at Canterbury in the early eleventh century, stimulated above all by Carolingian Rheims school painting and drawing, would seem to me to make sense.

In both the early and the later period of Anglo-Saxon art we have seen a tendency to use colour in an abstract, even expressionistic, manner. In both periods colour is used in a rich variety of hues but the different colours tend to be distributed over the page, linking different figures and objects to each other in a pattern and even uniting the subject of the miniature and the border around it. In this way the eye is led from point to point and the effect tends always to be restless and excitable. On the whole the tones are kept fairly uniform and fairly light, colours with an admixture of white being prominent, especially in the later period. Darker colours are less frequent and in some cases may have a sinister or threatening import. In both periods the colours are light in tone if compared to the Ottonian or the Romanesque

---

[1] Rheims, Bibliothèque Municipale, 7; J. Hubert, J. Porcher and W. F. Volbach, *Carolingian Art* (London, 1970), pl. 105.

[2] This scene is found in the Ottonian works where the stooping leper carries a similar horn over his shoulder, but neither Boeckler nor Buchthal discusses the Düsseldorf fragment. Buchthal ('Byzantium and Reichenau', p. 56) observes that there must have been other, western models besides the Middle Byzantine one for the Ottonian representations. Eastern elements in the iconography of the Utrecht Psalter are, of course, well known; see G. R. Benson and D. Tselos, 'New Light on the Origin of the Utrecht Psalter', *Art Bull.* 13 (1931), 13ff.

[3] E.g. the Bosworth Psalter, BM Add. 37517.

[4] Bodleian Junius 11, 10r and 58r; *The Cædmon Manuscript*, ed. I. Gollancz (Oxford, 1927).

[5] BM Arundel 155; Wormald, *English Drawings*, no. 26.

palette. These pale colours and in the later period the use of blobs of white and zigzag outlines for garments are characteristic of many of the miniatures and give a brilliant and vivid effect. The same is true of the coloured ink drawings. It may be that this is an aesthetic preference which is connected both with poetic conventions of light and dark as good and evil and also, perhaps, with the Old English colour vocabulary.

Corrections to Hildebrand's corpus of Anglo-Saxon moneyers: from Cnut to Edward the Confessor

VERONICA SMART

For a long time now students of early personal names have taken evidence from the many coins whose reverse legends preserve the names of Anglo-Saxon moneyers. Lists have been made which are more or less accurate and comprehensive, often with name forms normalized for convenience. Thus Searle cited, with misgivings,[1] his published sources which included Ruding,[2] Hildebrand and the British Museum Catalogue.[3] The latter in its turn included in its lists many names taken from other collections, often from coins that the compilers had not seen. In fact many of the printed lists of moneyers contain names repeated from earlier lists. To a great extent these derive ultimately from that immense treasury of Viking Age coins, B. E. Hildebrand's systematic arrangement from the Anglo-Saxon content of the Swedish coin hoards.[4] So large were Hildebrand's resources for the reigns of Æthelred and Cnut that his catalogue, published almost a hundred years ago, still comes close to being exhaustive, so that even the recently published Danish national collection adds relatively few coins – or at least legends – that are not registered there, and complements it only in the later reigns when the Scandinavian material becomes more sparse. If Hildebrand's catalogue is to be used as a reference system for the publication of other coins, as is commonly the case particularly in Scandinavia, and if philological use is to be made of Hildebrand's transcriptions, his source material, the coins themselves, must be subject to a new scrutiny.

As the basis for his publication Hildebrand formed a systematic collection of coins out of the much larger body of the Swedish hoards, his intention being to include only one example of each combination of dies. Those coins

---

[1] W. G. Searle, *Onomasticon Anglo-Saxonicum* (Cambridge, 1897), p. x ('many such names, however, seem to require further investigation, being very unintelligible as printed').

[2] R. Ruding, *Annals of the Coinage of Great Britain* (London, 1840).

[3] H. A. Grueber and C. F. Keary, *A Catalogue of English Coins in the British Museum, Anglo-Saxon Series* II (London, 1893).

[4] *Anglosachsiska Mynt i Svenska Kongliga Myntkabinettet funna i Sveriges Jord*, 2nd ed. (Stockholm, 1881).

which he believed, sometimes erroneously, to be duplicates of this selection were left unpublished. Further, since Hildebrand's work was completed new coin hoards have been discovered in Sweden, and a few years ago work was begun on preparing all this material for publication, whereupon a number of errors in Hildebrand's attributions and readings came to light. Several short notes appeared in numismatic journals, and in 1960 Miss G. van der Meer published a paper that was both a résumé of already published corrections and a first publication of many more.[1] Since then a few more corrections have been published, and these are incorporated into this article. A systematic checking of the Hildebrand material was completed in the autumn of 1973, and it is the results of this work since the publication of Miss van der Meer's paper which are presented here.

For the most part there is nothing numismatically esoteric in the methods used to obtain correct readings. Since each die was hand-cut, the variation between dies of the same type, mint and moneyer can be considerable and it is not usually difficult to tell even with the naked eye which coins are struck from the same die. Thus in a very large body of material it is possible to obtain a more accurate reading by comparing several specimens sharing one or both dies than by simply transcribing what is visible on an individual coin, since that may be worn or badly struck. At its simplest this method may be used within one mint to correct a misread moneyer's name or the form of a name. Errors naturally occur most readily in prolific, multi-moneyer mints, but even smaller mints have proved not to be free from a proliferation of mythical moneyers. Corrections have different degrees of significance. Thus, amending Cnut 2135 EADMVND to GODMAN or Cnut 2279 EDꝔERD to ÆLꝔERD affects only the accurate cataloguing of these particular coins and not the evidence for when and where Eadmund and Edwerd were working since they are well attested by other dies. On the other hand names such as Cnut 2119 BRYNIA and Cnut 3600 ÆSCꝔINE exist only as misreadings of BRVNMAN and EADꝔINE, for they are not otherwise recorded as moneyers' names in this period.

Throughout the checking of Hildebrand's collection particular attention has been paid to those cases in which his transcriptions have supplied the sole evidence for a moneyer's name or name form at a particular mint, and this has very often resulted in the reattribution of a coin from one mint to another. The mint signature, being often subject to very curt abbreviation, has naturally more chance of being misread than the moneyer's name, which is rendered in full. In cases where the mint signature is not wholly legible

[1] 'Some Corrections to and Comments on B. E. Hildebrand's Catalogue of the Anglo-Saxon Coins in the Swedish Royal Coin Cabinet', *Anglo-Saxon Coins, Studies presented to F. M. Stenton*, ed. R. H. M. Dolley (London, 1960), pp. 169–87.

a search can be made for other coins from the same dies at mints where there is good evidence for a moneyer of that name. Most satisfactorily a clearer example of the coin reverse will be found. Thus of the three coins of a Harold I moneyer LEOFNOÐ, which Hildebrand's reading assigns to Chester, only one in fact has a Chester mint signature. The first (341) can be shown by the die-comparison method to read not ON LE but ON CE for Canterbury; by the same method the next in order should be given to Gloucester, whilst the third remains the sole evidence for this Leofnoth at Chester. Again, removing Harold I 86 from Derby to Thetford (ON ÐEO not ON DEO) destroys the evidence for an Ælfwine as a Derby moneyer.

In other cases there may be no other extant example of the reverse, but the mint where the obverse die was used may help to clarify a doubtful attribution. Harold I 730, which Hildebrand reads as having only L for its mint signature and consequently gives to London, can equally be read as GL. There is no example of this reverse die showing an unequivocal GL, but the obverse of the problematical coin appears with another reverse showing the same moneyer's name and a clear Gloucester mint signature. Although inter-mint obverse die links are not unknown, even for mints not immediately adjacent, there must be a strong presumption that the Gloucester attribution is the correct one in this case.

When a coin is reattributed from one mint to another the moneyer's name is not invalidated as the form of a personal name recorded at the time of the currency of its type, but its geographical association is altered and this can be significant, especially where the distribution of non-Old English names is concerned. In rare cases a reconsideration of the mint signature may remove an erroneous form of the mint name from the record. Hildebrand records the nonce-form CANTOR amongst his Canterbury coins of Cnut Type I (*recte* Harthacnut) which is no more than a misreading of the more acceptable STANFOR for Stamford.

Ideally it is hoped that there will eventually be a new edition of *Anglo-sachsiska Mynt*, incorporating, as well as corrections of errors in the 1881 edition, such additional details as are now required by numismatic publication, weights, die axes, stylistic grouping and division of legends, and possibly more extensive illustration. The purpose of this paper is simply to correct Hildebrand's register of moneyers' names and the mints at which they appear, in order that the onomastic evidence from his enormous collection may be used with greater confidence. Every coin in the collection has been examined, so that where no correction has been noted it can be assumed that what Hildebrand printed is on the coin. Where a correction has already appeared in print (since Miss van der Meer's paper) only the conclusions are given, with a reference to the publication. For those published here for the first time the evidence on which they are based is set out in detail, but all the corrections have been placed in one sequence to facilitate the use of the list in conjunction with *Anglosachsiska Mynt*. The list begins with the reign of Cnut, since the checking had already proceeded as far as the end of the Æthelred material in time for its results to be incorporated in Miss van der Meer's paper.

My thanks are offered herewith to Först Antikvarie fil. dr. Brita Malmer Mand the staff of Kungliga Myntkabinettet, Statens Historiska Museum, Stockholm, where Hildebrand's collection is housed, to the Swedish Humanistic Research Fund who have financed this work in association with the forthcoming publication of the Swedish hoards, and to Mr R. H. M. Dolley for all his assistance.

The following abbreviations are used:

BEH	B. E. Hildebrand, *Anglosachsiska Mynt* (see above, p. 155, n. 4)
BMC	*British Museum Catalogue* (see above, p. 155, n. 3)
Commentationes 1	*Commentationes de Nummis Saeculorum IX–XI in Suecia Repertis, Pars Prima*, ed. N. L. Rasmusson and L. O. Lagerqvist (Lund, 1961)
Dolley *BNJ* 31	R. H. M. Dolley, 'Two Anglo-Saxon Notes', *BNJ* 31 (1962), 53–6
Dolley *BNJ* 33	R. H. M. Dolley, 'Some Mis-attributed *Fleur-de-Lis* coins of Harold I', *BNJ* 33 (1964), 45–7
Dolley *NC*	R. H. M. Dolley, 'Two Mythical Moneyers of Exeter and of Lincoln', *Numismatic Circular* 71 (1963), 248
Hauberg	P. C. Hauberg, *Myntforhold og Udmyntninger i Danmark indtil 1146* (Copenhagen, 1900)
Hildebrand	See above, BEH
Lyon *et al.*	C. S. S. Lyon, G. van der Meer and R. H. M. Dolley, 'Some Scandinavian Coins in the Names of Æthelræd, Cnut, and Harthacnut Attributed by Hildebrand to English Mints', *BNJ* 30 (1961), 235–51
Mossop	H. R. Mossop *et al.*, *The Lincoln Mint* c. *890–1279* (Newcastle upon Tyne, 1970)
SCBI	Sylloge of Coins of the Brit. Isles (London, 1958–), esp. 5 *Coins of the Chester Mint*; 8 *Hiberno-Norse Coins in the British Museum*; 13–15 *Royal Collection Copenhagen, Cnut*; 18 *Royal Collection Copenhagen, Harold I – Stephen*; and 19 *Bristol and Gloucester Museums*
Seaby	P. Seaby, 'The Sequence of Anglo-Saxon Coin Types 1030–50', *BNJ* 28 (1955), 111–46
Smart	Veronica Smart, 'Cnut's York Moneyers', *Otium et Negotium, Studies in Onomatology and Library Science presented to Olof von Feilitzen*, ed. F. Sandgren (Stockholm, 1973), pp. 221–31
van der Meer	'Some Corrections' (see above, p. 156, n. 1)

CNUT

All coins of types A–D, Ee–Eh, Ek–El and F are Scandinavian issues.

59   The mint is Thetford (ON ÐE) not Bedford (BEH ON BE). The coin is a die duplicate of 3509.

130 BEH + BRIHRED ON CANT but the coin is a die duplicate of 178 and the moneyer is ᚹINRÆD. Thus the evidence for Brihtred as a Canterbury moneyer is for Cnut's last type only.

141 The mint is Stamford (ON STANFOR) not Canterbury (BEH ON CANTOR), as is confirmed by a reverse die link with 3267.

142 BEH + GODSVNV ON CENT. Godsunu seems unknown as a Canterbury moneyer except by this coin. The second letter of the mint signature is not clear and could be read as R, giving GRNT for Cambridge where a Godsunu is known in the same type.

403 The mint is shown to be Oxford (OCX) not Exeter (BEH ECX) by a reverse die link with 3038. Lifinc should be deleted as an Exeter moneyer.

500 The mint is probably Nottingham: *Commentationes* I, 222.

525 BEH + COLGRIM ON EOFE but the moneyer is in fact GODMAN and the mint signature reads ON EORC: Smart, p. 223.

632 The coin is of a transitional type belonging to the beginning of Edward the Confessor's reign: Seaby, p. 134.

665 The coin reads + HILDRED ON CR and not, as BEH gives it, ON EO. The reverse die is the same as 252 which BEH gives to Cricklade, but 252 links into a die chain of Scandinavian imitations and therefore 665 is probably also Scandinavian, especially in view of its barbarous obverse. Hildred's other two coins read EO and the fabric is consonant with English work, but the style of the obverses is anomalous and of neither of the two styles employed consistently on York coins. Searle's only instance of the name *Hildred* or *Hildered* is the Cnut moneyer, and his reference to *BMC* must point to these three Hildebrand coins, as *BMC* lists the moneyer in italics to indicate that the name is added from supplementary sources and not from a coin in the British Museum. In view of the anomalies surrounding the only two dies to bear this name, a moneyer Hildred at York should be regarded with caution.

692 BEH + OSBARN MO O EOFRᚹ but the obverse has characteristics associated with East Anglia and the Five Boroughs. Osbarn is not otherwise recorded as a York moneyer but an Osbern is known at Derby in Cnut's first type. It is possible to read the legend as

... MO DEORBY, but no clear example of the die has been found, nor any confirmatory obverse die link.

720-1 These two coins are duplicates reading OVÐG:RM. The form OVÐGIRM transcribed by BEH does not exist and SCBI 13 789, which perpetuates the error, is from the same reverse die again.

965 BEH +GODIC M [..] GLE would suppose the old *monetarius* contraction in place of the locative preposition, which is not found at Gloucester in this reign. The moneyer's name in fact reads GODƷINE.

1042 A cut-halfpenny on which only the second element of the moneyer's name is certain, the coin is placed by BEH with coins of Leofsig. The reverse die is the same as 1072 which supplies the missing element as ƷVLF- and gives the complete reading +ƷVLFSIG ON GRN.

1061 BEH ORIST can equally be read as ORNST with the line of the reverse cross supplying the second vertical of the N as is frequently found.

1075-6 These are duplicates reading +ƷVLMÆR ON GRAN.

1109 BEH +BRIHTNOÐ ON HÆ, but the mint is Malmesbury not Hastings. The coin is from the same reverse as 2891-2, which are themselves duplicates though Hildebrand reads them severally as ME and MEA. The mint signature is ME followed by a wedge over a pellet. Since the only other supposed coin of Brihtnoth at Hastings has previously been reattributed to Winchester (van der Meer, p. 178), this moneyer's name should be deleted from this mint.

1158 BEH ON EOREF should be read as O HEORET followed by three pellets.

1245 BEH +GODELEOF ON HVN is a London coin of this moneyer reading +GODELEOF ON LVND.

1253 BEH +STANER MO HV I read as STANMER with N and M ligatured.

1286 BEH +LIOFSI ON LÆƷEEI is the only evidence adduced for a moneyer Liofsi or Leofsige at Lewes, but in fact this is a coin of Bedford where the name is known. The obverse is from the same die as 64. I read the reverse as +LIOFSI ON BEDEŁI.

1502-5 BEH records 1504-5 as the Ec type, Quatrefoil with sceptred portrait, but 1502-3 are also of this type.

1536 BEH +COLGRIM ON LINC but a very worn coin and almost illegible, especially from a photograph. It appears in Mossop as no. 1 on pl. lxiv, but in fact the mint is ƷINC for Winchester and the moneyer is GODƷINE. The coin is from the same dies as 3752.

1553 The by-name may be read sƷOT, as in BEH, or SPOT.

1565 BEH + GODꝼINE ON LIN has already been reattributed by implication since it does not appear in Mossop. The correct mint is Rochester (+ GODꝼINE ON ROF) and it is a die duplicate of 3077.

1593 Hildebrand omits to record that this coin is of the variety of Pointed Helmet with right-facing bust, type Ga.

1595–8 This Leodmær group is not included in Mossop and provides another example of the confusion that can arise between the mint signatures of Lincoln and Winchester. 1595 is a duplicate of 3774 + LEODMÆR ON ꝼINC and 1596–7 are from the same reverse die on which BEH reads the mint name LIINC, but the initial LI is almost certainly a misreading of ꝼ. The fact that the obverse die of 1597 is found again amongst the dies of Leodmær at Winchester confirms the reattribution. 1598 is a difficult coin in that it appears to read + LEODNÆR ON LINC, but in view of the rarity of Old English names in *Leod-* amongst moneyers and the elimination of the rest of the Lincoln evidence for the name, I am not happy about a straightforward Lincoln attribution. Moreover, since the obverse is so badly blundered that BEH does not attempt to classify it even as an 'irregular' form, some sort of irregular die cutting, whether unofficial English or Scandinavian imitation, is indicated. Thus there is no certain evidence for a Leodmær amongst Lincoln moneyers.

1650 This coin appears in Mossop as no. 2 on pl. xlvi. The clearest letters of the mint signature are the final CO, which, along with the well attested Lincoln moneyer's name MANA, seems to make the Lincoln attribution likely. However, examination of the coin itself shows the legend to be + MANA ONRÐꝼICO, which suggests the mint of Norwich. There haplography is frequent, since the initial of the mint repeats the N of ON. Mana or Manna is a Norwich moneyer, and the obverse die of the problematical coin is the same as that used by Manna at Norwich for striking BEH 2958. The final O is curious but may be an attempt to restore its earlier omission.

1658 The coin is of the Ga variety.

1775 This coin is a fabrication. Made up of two (unjoined) cut-half-pennies, which fit fairly neatly together since they share a die axis. The only difficulty is that read together they give the awkward obverse legend + CNVC RCX. Mossop wisely refused to consider Thurulf a Lincoln moneyer on the evidence of this supposed penny and succeeded in die-linking the mint-only half with SCBI 14, 1839 + SꝼAFVA ON LINCOL, and as such the halfpenny appears at

Mossop pl. lxv, no. 8. The moneyer half can be identified with Thurulf the Stamford moneyer. Cnut Type I, to which BEH assigns this halfpenny along with its supposed complement, is really a Harthacnut type differing from Harthacnut's Arm and Sceptre type (BEH Harthacnut B) only in styling the king Cnut instead of giving the full name Harthacnut. The National Museum in Copenhagen has a coin of Harthacnut of this type (SCBI 18 707) which is from the same dies as the Thurulf cut-halfpenny and supplies the full legend as + ÐVRVLF ON STANF.

1849   BEH + ÆADRIC ON LVNDE.

1853   BEH + ÆEDRIC ON LVNDE.

1898   BEH + ÆLFRIC ON LVNDE.

1900   BEH + ÆLFRIC ON LVNDE.

These four coins, variously read and catalogued, are all from the same reverse die. The clearest legend appears on yet another example from the die, added to the trays of Hildebrand's collection adjacent to 1853 after the publication of BEH. This coin shows that the correct reading is ÆEDRIC. After that penny was struck the die seems to have been used in deteriorating condition, so that the other coins are difficult to read individually.

1910   BEH + ÆLFSTAN ON LVDEN is *recte* + LIFSTAN ON LVDEN, the coin being a duplicate of 2629.

2017   BEH BRHITNOÐ gives an erroneous form of the name. The coin is a duplicate of 2053 BRIHTNOÐ.

2019–20 Probably struck in Scandinavia but possibly from English dies: Lyon *et al.*, p. 244.

2021   The mint is Canterbury, ON CEN, not BEH ON LVN, and the coin is a duplicate of 129.

2119   BEH + BRYNIA M LVND presents a non-existent name. The legend should be read as + BRVNMAN LVND; cf. 2030 and 2046 for omission of the preposition.

2135   The moneyer is GODMAN, not BEH EADMVND.

2147   The moneyer is EALDRED, not BEH EADRED, who now disappears as a moneyer of Cnut's Quatrefoil type.

2275   BEH + EDƷERD N LNND, *recte* + LEƷERD N LNND, is a duplicate of 2613. The evidence for a London moneyer Lewerd or Leofweard depends on this die and, in the form LIOFƷERD, on 2654 which Hauberg (p. 113) claimed for the Danish mint of Lund on account of the mint signature LVDI. The portrait on 2275 and 2613 is executed in none of the styles found on Cnut's English Quatrefoil coins but is very similar to that of the rare Hiberno-Norse pennies which take Quatrefoil for their prototype, either issued in the name of Sihtric or reproducing the CNVT of the original. A further criterion of Hiberno-Norse die cutting is the upright cross + instead of the X in REX which BEH classifies as 'irreg. 54' on 2613 but has failed to notice on 2275. In the absence of a die link one can note the similarity between these coins and the Hiberno-Norse pennies in the British Museum illustrated in SCBI 8 60–1. The recognition as imitations of certain coins previously accepted as English puts the interpretation of this legend in question. Clearly it means that the statement of mint is false as far as that coin is concerned. What is more doubtful is whether the personal name can still be accepted as denoting a moneyer who was working at the mint named during the currency of the prototype – in fact whether the whole legend is a copy from a non-surviving official coin or whether it is a random, though often correct and literate, composition of elements from more than one coin. Clearly legends of this type cannot be given the same authority as those from official English dies, and linguistic deductions can seldom be safely made on the basis of the forms they exhibit.

2279   Although the deterioration of the die makes identification difficult, this coin and probably 2278 should be read as +ÆLꝠERD, not BEH EDꝠERD, and 2279 is a duplicate of 1985.

2320   BEH EDꝠNE should read EDꝠIIG, as correctly recorded for its reverse die duplicate 2229.

2342   The moneyer's name should read EALGAR, for this is a duplicate of 2217. Thus the BEH name FALGAR need not be considered.

2476   BEH reads +GODꝠINE LV, but the first letter of the mint signature is uncertain. The portrait is in the style associated with Lincoln. Miss van der Meer in a manuscript note on the ticket suggests SV = Sudbury.

2568   The coin is from the same reverse die as 2537; both should read LEOFSAN.

2740–1   These are from the same reverse die, and die link into a chain of Scandinavian imitations. The only other coin of this moneyer ÐORED is 2732, which is of the Scandinavian type BEH Cnut B: Lyon *et al.*, p. 245.

2745,   Scandinavian, probably from the mint of Lund: Hauberg, pp. 112–
2748   13, and Lyon *et al.*, p. 249.

2882   Not BEH +CEOLNOÐ ON MÆLD but +LEOFNOÐ ON CENT, a die duplicate of 152 (Canterbury). Delete Ceolnoth as a Maldon moneyer in Cnut's last type.

3036   Edward the Confessor's rare transitional Arm and Sceptre type from the beginning of his reign. The obverses of this type are frequently blundered and Seaby (p. 114) reads this as EDCC and not as an attempt at CNVT.

3140   BEH +GODƿINE ON SER but in fact the same moneyer ON SCR, i.e. Shrewsbury not Salisbury. The same dies are found on a coin correctly assigned to Shrewsbury at 3168.

3368   BEH +ƿVLFSIGE M O STA, but the last quarter of the legend is holed and the only certain letter of the mint is the final A. Wulfsige is not otherwise known as a Stamford moneyer in this reign but is known at Cambridge from a great many dies, and the reading GRA is certainly possible. There is no confirmatory die link and the style is acceptable at either mint.

3418   BEH +SƿEGNN ON SVÐG, but I read it as +ÆÐELƿIN ON SVÐG, which is the same reading, and I think the same die, as SCBI 15 3712. Against the coin in the Sylloge volume is the note that the moneyer is not known for either Southwark or Sudbury under Cnut, but in fact the derived form ÆGELƿINE appears on BEH 3375 in the last type of the reign.

3518   Probably Scandinavian: Lyon *et al.*, p. 245.

3600   BEH +ÆSCƿINE ON ƿELIN is the only recorded instance of this name being borne by a moneyer. The name is rare and documentary instances of it are uncertain or early. Its appearance on a coin however is illusory. The coin is a duplicate of 3609 and bears the common name EADƿINE. 3608, for which BEH gives the irregular reading EADƿIDE, almost certainly reads EADƿINE also. There is some evidence of the coin slipping during striking and receiving a blurred impression of the die.

3696   BEH +ÆÐELRD ON ƿINCS postulates a Winchester moneyer Æthel-red, which is not supported by any other coin. The following coin, 3697, is a duplicate which supplies the correct reading +ÆÐELRIC ON ƿINCS.

3745   BEH +GODRIC ONI ƿINCE is in reality a coin of London and the moneyer is not Godric but Godinc, as appears from its reverse die duplicate 2409 +GODINC ON LVNDE.

HAROLD I

13   BEH +LEOFƿINE ON BED (Bedford) is really ON ÐEO for Thetford. The obverse is the same die as 956 and a die duplicate is to be found at SCBI 15 563. Thus Leofwine as a Bedford moneyer in this reign is mythical.

58   BEH +SVNDEID ON C can belong only to the curious group of reverse dies 455–9 SVMREID, SVNRDDE, SVOIIREID, progessively blundered forms of the Lincoln moneyer's name *Sumerleda*. All these coins attempt the Lincoln mint signature (LIC, LNC, IIC), and presumably the C of 58 is an error for L or a mistaken placing of the C of the mint signature. There is no die link between 58 and 455–9 but they share an unusual style. In view of the similarities an unsupported attribution to Canterbury cannot be sustained; yet the attribution persists and a reverse die duplicate in Copenhagen, SCBI 18 23, is given to Canterbury. Hildebrand may have connected this form with the Canterbury moneyer Winedæig and overlooked the Lincoln parallels. Whether this whole blundered group should be attributed to Lincoln or regarded as Scandinavian is uncertain, since a coin in Copenhagen reading +SVMREID ON LIC (SCBI 18 257 and Mossop, pl. lxii no. 20) belongs to a variety of the type (designated as Bc by Hildebrand) which is probably not English: van der Meer, p. 184.

64–6   Hildebrand reads 64 as +ꝑVLNON ON CEN. The mint signature is illegible towards the end but begins with L, not C, probably LI or LE. It is a reverse die duplicate of SCBI 18 197 which unfortunately does not have a more legible mint signature though it is attributed there to Leicester. The Sylloge coin is catalogued with the name as ꝑVLNON, but there is an editorial emendation to ꝑVLNOÐ which applies equally to its Stockholm counterpart. Although there is no obverse die link that would tie the coins to Leicester, the Sylloge attribution is more likely than Hildebrand's, especially as the only supporting evidence for Wulfnoth at Canterbury is 65, BEH +ꝑVLNOÐ ON CEN, which is from the same obverse die as the Leicester coin 365. The mint signature of 65 should be read LEH instead of CEN, and both 64 and 65 be removed to the Leicester mint. Similarly 66, which appears in BEH as +ꝑVLSTAN ON CEN, is a duplicate of 371 and should be read as +ꝑVLSTAN ON LEH.

74   The mint is York: Dolley *BNJ* 33.

86   The mint is Thetford: Dolley *BNJ* 33.

134   BEH LEOFꝑINE ON E could equally be read ON B (Bedford, Bristol) or ON H (Northampton). Leofwine is an Exeter moneyer for Cnut and Harthacnut but is not otherwise known for Harold.

148   BEH +ÆLFꝑINE ON EOF I read as ON O+ and an Oxford attribution is supported by an obverse die link with 794.

171–2 Both are cut-halfpennies. The mint signature should be completed in both cases as DOFR, not BEH EOFR, as their Dover die duplicates 112 and 114 demonstrate. The moneyer in both cases is EDƿINE.

180   The mint is Hertford: Dolley *BNJ* 33.

266   The mint is Bristol: Dolley *BNJ* 33.

287   Possibly +ÆLFƿINE (not BEH LEFƿINE) ON HAM.

306   The mint is Wareham and the moneyer SIIDEMAN: Dolley *BNJ* 33.

336   The mint is Canterbury: Dolley *BNJ* 33.

420   The moneyer is HVNNA and the mint Malmesbury: Dolley *NC*.

501   Possibly +ÆLFRED ON SER (Salisbury) rather than BEH ON LVN.

502   BEH ÆLFRED ON LVN is a die duplicate of 714 and should be read as LIFRED ON LVN. The legend has no initial cross. If the reattribution of the preceding coin is correct Ælfred can no longer be regarded as a *Fleur-de-Lis* type moneyer at London.

513   BEH +ÆÐELƿINE ON L is a duplicate of 178 +ÆÐELƿINE ON which Hildebrand rightly attributes to York. The variety with three pellets in place of the *fleur-de-lis* on the reverse is not known at Exeter, which would otherwise be an alternative mint.

574   BEH gives the irregular form EDHIE for the moneyer's name but in fact it reads EDƿIIE.

695   This coin is a duplicate of a Northampton penny 289 and reads +LEOFƿINE O HAM, not BEH ON LV. Leofwine at London is well attested in Harold's first type but is not otherwise recorded there in *Fleur-de-Lis*.

718   The obverse die is shared by the two subsequent coins, which belong to a non-English type, and by 653, which Hauberg (p. 114) claims as Danish.

730   BEH +ƿVLFƿERD ON L, but his single letter of the mint signature may equally be read as GL. Wulfwerd is a Gloucester moneyer but not otherwise recorded for London in this reign. There is no useful reverse die link. The Copenhagen coin SCBI 18 433 is equally ambiguous and Hildebrand's attribution has been followed, but the obverse die was used for the Gloucester coins BEH 254 and SCBI 18 140.

739   BEH +ƿVLSIE ON LVND and 740–1 +ƿVLSTN ON LVND are all from the same reverse die. The correct reading is the latter, which removes Wulsie from the roll of London moneyers in this reign.

742–3   BEH +ƿVLƿII ONN VN should be read ON HVN and the coin removed from London to Huntingdon. This is confirmed by the indisputable Huntingdon coin 312 which uses the same obverse die.

832   A cut-halfpenny. All that is visible of the moneyer's name is LE and Hildebrand interprets the final letters OBE as part of the Shrewsbury

mint signature, with the moneyer having one of the mint's *Leof-* names. As such an extended form of the mint signature in this divided-legend type would require a monothematic, or at least a very short, moneyer's name, the attribution needs to be re-examined. That OBE should be treated as O BE and the moneyer's name supplied as LEOFÐEGN is shown by a comparison with the Bedford coin 12, +LEOFÐEGN O BE, which proves to be from the same reverse die.

838   A cut-halfpenny which belongs to the Shrewsbury mint and whose legend can be completed +LEOFƿIINE ON SCROB from a duplicate, SCBI 18 482.

839   BEH +ÆLFRED ON ZE. The straight, and particularly the retrograde straight, s in coin inscriptions would be an anachronism in this reign. The mint signature is really CÆ for Canterbury and the coin is from the same obverse as 39.

866   BEH +ÆLFƿNE ON STA, but I read +LEF- or +LIFƿNE ON STA though I can find no die link to support this reading. A Leofwine is known as a Stamford moneyer in Cnut's last type and midway through Edward the Confessor's reign but I know of no other example of an Ælfwine at that mint.

870   BEH ARCYL is an illusory form of this name, the Y being simply I with a crack in the die. The reading is ARCIL as on 867–9, the first of which is a duplicate of 870.

875   BEH +CASVLF ON STAN, which is a duplicate of SCBI 18 510 but read there as CASGRI, with a note that the moneyer is not known in BEH. CASGRI seems to be the better reading but is even more of an onomastic problem than CASVLF, unless it is a triple-error attempt at the prolific Stamford moneyer Fargrim.

895   BEH +GODƿNE ON STA is a duplicate of 889 +GODRIIC ON STA, which is the correct reading.

983   The mint is Derby: Dolley *BNJ* 33.

995   BEH +GOLSIIG ON ƿIL but from the same dies as SCBI 18 581, which is correctly read as +GOLSAN ON ƿIL. Another coin in Copenhagen, but not in BEH, is a penny which shows GOLDSTAN as a Wilton moneyer in the previous type, Harold A, and so provides a context not only for GOLSAN but also for the name on BEH 994, GODAN, which is more likely to be another blundering of this than an inflected form of *Goda*, a name not recorded for Wilton. There is thus no Wilton moneyer Gol(d)sig.

1025–7, 1031–2   All these coins are from the Worcester mint: Dolley *BNJ* 33.

1029   BEH + LIIFINC ONN ꝺINC I read as + LIIFINC ONN HÆ for Hastings, but I have not been able to die-link it to that mint.

1034–7   There is no reason to read SꝺILEMAN and SꝺRACVLF, as in BEH, rather than SPILEMAN and SPRACVLF.

1049   BEH 'uncertain mint' is probably from the same obverse die as the Nottingham coin SCBI 18 497, where Blacaman, the moneyer postulated by Hildebrand, is known.

HARTHACNUT

6   A cut-halfpenny, BEH 'probably Æthelwine', but from the same reverse die as SCBI 18 612, where the complete coin reads + ÆÐESTAN ON BRYCS.

11, 82   These two coins are reattributed to Langport: Dolley *BNJ* 31.

83   Dolley *BNJ* 31 infers from prosopography that the missing first element of the moneyer's name on this cut-halfpenny is not *Ægel-* but some form of *Leof-*. This is confirmed by a coin in Oslo published in Mossop as pl. lxiv, no. 15, which was struck from the same reverse die and supplies the legend + LEFꝺINE ON LINCO.

87–8,   Scandinavian: Lyon *et al.*, p. 249. Thus of the coins listed under
140–1   Harthacnut for London by Hildebrand only 111–32 and 146–7 are English. The rest are probably from the Danish mint of Lund.

EDWARD THE CONFESSOR

The material belonging to this reign is very different from that belonging to the times of Æthelred and Cnut. There are no longer vast quantities of coins from Scandinavian hoards for comparison. Hildebrand records only 800 coins of Edward as against 3869 from the shorter reign of Cnut and this scarcity is paralleled in published and unpublished Scandinavian hoards. Each coin is now far more likely to be unique, and if a reading appears uncertain there is less opportunity either to change or to confirm it. Some transcriptions could well be challenged by the discovery of new material. It is important that doubtful legends should be put on record even when their true attribution has not been solved, as one coin in such an incomplete situation can greatly distort the evidence.

25   BEH SNEꝺINE, but more likely SMEꝺINE; cf. SCBI 19 xxx.

35   BEII EANꝺERD, but in fact EADꝺERD, a die duplicate of *BMC* 54.

47   BEH LEOISTAN, but the coin is a duplicate of 45 and reads LEOFSTAN.

80   BEH ꝺVLꝺII, but the first letter is not ꝺ but could be C, in which case it might be read CYLꝺII; cf. *BMC* 175 and 183 CILꝺI.

85   BEH +GODƿINE ON DOR. In the absence of other evidence for Godwine at Dorchester in this reign an alternative reading ON IIOR (= NOR for Norwich) should be considered.

173   BEH +ÆLFƿINE ON GICLST is a Chichester, not an Ilchester, penny, as it is claimed to be in BEH. The reverse is the same as *BMC* 106 and the mint signature is CICEST.

175   This coin may also be from Chichester. Although part of the mint signature is broken away it seems to end in CES rather than BEH EL.

214   I read this coin as CILƿINE rather than BEH ÆLFƿINE.

235   ERNƿI rather than BEH ERMƿI. A flaw on the die is responsible for the apparent M.

264   A die duplicate, SCBI 5 282, completes the legend of the Stockholm fragment as +COLÐEGN ON LEI and not *Colbrand* as BEH implies.

314   Almost certainly GVÐFERÐ, not BEH CVÐFERÐ.

347   BEH +LADMER ON LINC, but correctly +LADMER ON ƿINC for Winchester.

419   A completing example, placed with this coin in the tray but not appearing in BEH, shows that BEH's irregular form ÆLFƿOND is illusory and that the correct reading is ÆLFƿOLD.

442   BEH BRVNMAN, but the coin is from the same reverse die as 434, correctly read as BRVHMGN.

451   EALGAR, not BEH EADGAR; cf. SCBI 18 1857 for the moneyer, though not the same die.

481   EDRIC, not BEH EDƿNE.

491   Probably ON LIN, not BEH ON LVN, but I know of no Lincoln die link.

509   Not Edward Type A. The bust is like that of Harold Bc and the legend is illegible. Possibly Scandinavian.

557   Probably VHITRED, as *BMC* 889.

699   This fragment is from the same dies as is a coin from the Stora Bjers find, Stenkyrka parish, Gotland, which reads +ÐVRTILF ON STA, and the obverse is found again on SCBI 18 1196 with a reverse reading ÐVRVLF, for which this is presumably an error.

700   BEH records this coin as partly illegible and gives the legible portion as +ƿI[ ]C STAN, reconstructing the legend as *Wileric* at Stamford. STAN, however, is not the mint but the second element of the moneyer's name ÆLFSTAN and the letters ƿI indicate the mint. The reverse die is the same as 758 which is correctly read as +ÆLFSTAN O ƿI. It is attributed to Wilton by coins of the same

moneyer and type which have the fuller legends ᚹIL and ᚹILTV, while the moneyer is not recorded at Winchester in the type.

768   BEH read ÆSTANR, but the final letter is uncertain; it may be a second N.

Late Anglo-Saxon metal-work: an assessment

DAVID A. HINTON

It is a decade since the British Museum published its catalogue of late Anglo-Saxon metal-work[1] – 'late' in this context meaning between the eighth century and the eleventh – and the only museum with a comparable collection has now produced an equivalent volume.[2] Probably there will not be any more such catalogues, for no other museum has enough metal-work to make a separate publication worthwhile, although composite catalogues, like the numismatists' sylloges, could be produced; for example, Cambridge, Ipswich, King's Lynn and Norwich would make a substantial East Anglian contribution. Except for catalogues, it seems unlikely that there will ever be books devoted exclusively to the metal-work of post-pagan England, since this is not a subject that can be isolated from its archaeological and art-historical contexts. If there is a distinction between archaeology and art history, metal-work, since it is relevant to both, provides a bridge between them, although often a minor one.

A limiting factor is the small size of the corpus of late Saxon metal-work: the British Museum's catalogue contains 153 objects, the Ashmolean's thirty-nine and a possible forgery. Both museums have increased their collections since the catalogues were completed, and other museums have also made acquisitions from chance finds or planned excavations, but the number of objects will always be small in comparison with the quantities of pagan burial jewellery, and with the countless medieval bronze trinkets. To talk of style-changes and schools, of production centres and patronage, may be over-ambitious when the student hardly needs a card-index, let alone a computer, to recall most of the data.

The essential preliminary is of course to date the data within satisfactory limits. Professor D. M. Wilson stated the rigid principle of working from the known to the unknown and demonstrated the pitifully disproportionate ratio between the two,[3] which has not improved in the last few years. No further coin-dated hoard has been recovered, nor any object that can be

---

[1] D. M. Wilson, *Anglo-Saxon Ornamental Metalwork 700–1100 in the British Museum* (London, 1964).
[2] D. A. Hinton, *Anglo-Saxon Ornamental Metalwork 700–1100 in the Department of Antiquities, Ashmolean Museum* (Oxford, 1974).
[3] D. M. Wilson and C. E. Blunt, 'The Trewhiddle Hoard', *Archaeologia* 98 (1961), 106–8.

David A. Hinton

linked by an inscription to a known historical figure. Even the name on a recently discovered finger-ring cannot be read with certainty.[1] Scientific tests do not yet help with the nicer points of chronology, although some useful work of authentication has been done: for example, the justification of the Fuller brooch by its niello content has restored confidence in an outstanding ninth-century object that must be prominent in any discussion of its period.[2] The spectacular demonstration that seventh-century gold objects underwent a steady debasement almost decade by decade, in line with the composition and increasing scarcity of gold coins,[3] is probably not applicable to later centuries. With gold available on a much more random basis than from the melting-down of coins, the metal content of an object would vary according to what the smith happened to have for the melting-pot. Silver objects may be expected to follow the native currency more closely, but fluctuations in the alloys of the tenth- and eleventh-century coinage do not follow a steady line, although at least the minor element zinc follows a recognizable curve.[4] But zinc fluctuates only between three and six per cent, hardly enough to allow analysis to resolve all doubts about the date of an object. What hope is there for bronze? The isolation of an additive that is specific to a certain place at a certain time is a metallurgist's pipe-dream.

Likewise hopes that more precise epigraphy would lead to more accurate dating of inscribed objects have been dashed. There is now greater precision – in a work of scholarship and erudition by Dr E. Okasha[5] – but the sad fact is that letter forms can be no more closely dated by style than can art forms.[6] None of the inscribed pieces has had a narrower date range imposed on it by Dr Okasha's work.

It is still not possible therefore to assign more than broad dating limits to most metal objects. The excavator who finds, for example, a Trewhiddle style strap-end may be glad to have something that he can display to the public, but he may not make much use of it in his discussion of the site. As an isolated object it can safely be dismissed as intrusive if it does not fit the expected chronology. Even if its chronology is acceptable it is still less

[1] E. Okasha and L. Webster, 'An Anglo-Saxon Ring from Bodsham, Kent', *AntJ* 50 (1970), 102–4.
[2] R. L. S. Bruce-Mitford, 'Late Saxon Disc-Brooches', *Dark Age Britain*, ed. D. B. Harden (London, 1956), pp. 178–80.
[3] P. D. C. Brown and F. Schweizer, 'X-Ray Fluorescent Analysis of Anglo-Saxon Jewellery', *Archaeometry* 15. 2 (1973), 175–92.
[4] H. McKerrell and R. B. K. Stephenson, 'Some Analyses of Anglo-Saxon and Associated Oriental Silver Coinage', *Methods of Chemical and Metallurgical Investigation of Ancient Coinage*, ed. E. T. Hall and D. M. Metcalf (London, 1972), pp. 195–209.
[5] *Hand-List of Anglo-Saxon Non-Runic Inscriptions* (Cambridge, 1971).
[6] E. Okasha, 'The Non-Runic Scripts of Anglo-Saxon Inscriptions', *Trans. of the Cambridge Bibliographical Soc.* 4 (1964–8), 331 and 336–7.

useful for absolute dating purposes than is a coin, and many excavators might prefer to rely on their pottery sequences. Coins and pots may be expected to have had a brief life-cycle; a gold ring could already have been an antiquity when lost. Wilson has reminded archaeologists that there is a cautionary tale for them in the sword of King Offa, an antique weapon when owned by the Ætheling Athelstan early in the eleventh century.[1] Similarly in the middle of the previous century a certain Wynflæd bequeathed an 'old filigree brooch' which was nevertheless still worth six mancuses.[2] At best the excavator can be told the probable century of manufacture of the object that he has found, but he must decide for himself how long it is likely to have been in use.

A few late Saxon metal-work objects can claim to have more than passing interest for archaeologists. A small quatrefoil bronze piece that has foliage of late-tenth- or early-eleventh-century type is still one of our few positive indications of pre-Conquest activity on the site of the modern Southampton.[3] A fragment of a silver strap-end from St Sampson's churchyard, Cricklade, probably of the late ninth century or the early tenth,[4] is at least as good evidence for the date of the settlement of the burh as are the 'few pieces of middle Saxon pottery'[5] from the defences. Finds from such sites as Whitby[6] show metal-working in monastic establishments. Light industrial activity at *Hamwih*[7] or York[8] is useful evidence about early urban crafts, presumably by specialist workers.

Ornaments are rediscovered in much the same way as are contemporary coins: a few come from controlled excavations, some are found at random in fields or builders' trenches and some have no reliable provenance. Recent work on the distribution of early English coinage has helped to elucidate likely mint sources, circulation areas and trade centres.[9] Fig. 3 is an attempt to correlate this information with the gold and silver objects of the same period. To Dr D. M. Metcalf's plotting of late-seventh- and eighth-century sceattas and Offa's silver pennies[10] (shown as circles and squares respectively)

[1] Wilson and Blunt, 'Trewhiddle', p. 107, n. 1.
[2] *Anglo-Saxon Wills*, ed. D. Whitelock (Cambridge, 1930), p. 13.
[3] Report by D. M. Wilson, in P. V. Addyman and D. H. Hill, 'Saxon Southampton: a Review of the Evidence. Part II', *Proc. of the Hampshire Field Club* 26 (1969), 71.
[4] Hinton, *Ashmolean Catalogue*, no. 7.
[5] C. A. R. Radford, 'Excavations at Cricklade', *Wiltshire Archaeol. Mag.* 67 (1972), 96.
[6] C. R. Peers and C. A. R. Radford, 'The Saxon Monastery of Whitby', *Archaeologia* 89 (1943), 27–88. [7] Addyman and Hill, 'Southampton', pp. 66–72.
[8] D. M. Waterman, 'Late Saxon, Viking and Early Medieval Finds from York', *Archaeologia* 92 (1959), 59–105.
[9] D. M. Metcalf, 'The Prosperity of North-Western Europe in the Eighth and Ninth Centuries', *EconHR* 2nd ser. 20 (1967), 344–57, and 'The "Bird and Branch" Sceattas in the Light of a Find from Abingdon', *Oxoniensia* 38 (1972), 51–65.
[10] 'Prosperity', p. 346 and 'Sceattas', p. 54. I am very grateful to Dr Metcalf for allowing me to use his maps and lending me his notes and for many discussions.

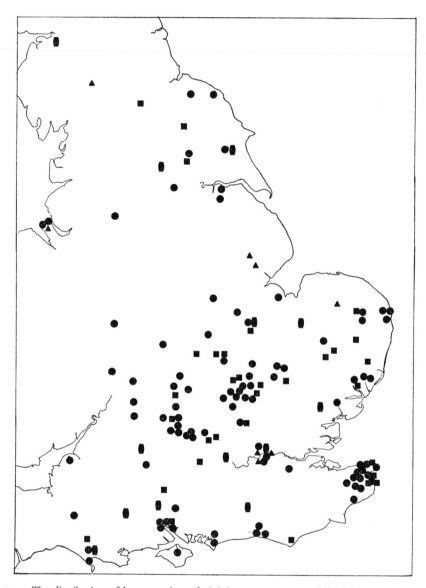

FIG. 3   The distribution of late-seventh- and eighth-century sceattas, Offa's silver pennies and eighth-century gold and silver objects. The sceattas are represented by circles, the pennies by squares and the gold and silver objects by barrels and triangles respectively

have been added the known find-spots of eighth-century rings, sword-hilts etc. in gold and silver (barrels and triangles respectively). Obviously opinions would differ about which objects should be included on such a map and the selection is inevitably in some respects arbitrary; for instance, all the Trewhiddle style objects have been excluded on the assumption that at least most of them were of ninth-century and not eighth-century manufacture. As a consequence there are not very many barrels and triangles. But what is immediately obvious is that they overlap the circles and squares in only a few places.

This failure of the objects in precious metal to synchronize with the coins may reflect only their more haphazard use and loss. Nevertheless the antithesis is striking: there is nothing at all from the coin-rich Midlands or from Kent. The concentration in the north may be distorted by Viking raiders. On the other hand, the cluster of four gold rings from Dorset, Wiltshire and west Hampshire may be a genuine reflection of the kind of 'basic regional prosperity'[1] that helps to explain the commercial activity of *Ham-wih*, for which this area was presumably the sheep-rich hinterland. It also points to the particular wealth of Wessex in the pre-Viking period, wealth that was to be of fundamental importance in the kingdom's successful defence. It is worth noting that one of the rings is from Dorchester, Dorset,[2] where coins have also been recovered. These are signs of activity in that town at a time when Winchester was largely 'open and undeveloped',[3] its commercial life slight.

The emergence of Wessex as the dominant kingdom in the ninth century, and of Winchester in the tenth as one of the great centres of European art, is hardly observable in the metal-work. The Trewhiddle style is not geographically confined[4] and no new styles evolved. Attempts to attribute the Alfred Jewel, the Fuller brooch and the Abingdon sword to a Winchester workshop active in King Alfred's reign, on the grounds of their symbolism and use of a particular form of leaf,[5] are not borne out by what has been found in the recent excavations,[6] which have provided only a single strap-end as a stylistic parallel.[7] The characteristics of objects like the pair of ninth-

---

[1] D. M. Metcalf, 'Monetary Expansion and Recession', *Coins and the Archaeologist*, ed. J. Casey and R. Reece (Oxford, 1974), p. 216.

[2] Hinton, *Ashmolean Catalogue*, no. 8.

[3] M. Biddle, 'Winchester: the Development of an Early Capital', *Vor- und Frühformen der europäischen Stadt im Mittelalter*, ed. H. Jankuhn, W. Schlesinger and H. Steuer (Göttingen, 1974), p. 245.

[4] Wilson, *British Museum Catalogue*, pp. 34–5.

[5] D. A. Hinton, 'Two Late Saxon Swords', *Oxoniensia* 35 (1970), 3–4.

[6] Directed by Mr M. Biddle, who has very kindly allowed me to see the metal objects and to refer to them here.

[7] Report by V. I. Evison, in M. Biddle and R. N. Quirk, 'Excavations near Winchester Cathedral, 1961', *ArchJ* 119 (1961), 186.

century garter-tags from a grave[1] are not distinctive enough to be attributed to any specific place of manufacture. Conversely tags from the near-by burh at Portchester have patterns similar to that on the reverse of the Alfred Jewel[2] but are no reason for regarding Portchester as an international art centre! It had close links with Winchester, both geographically and through its ownership, for it was held by the bishop until 904 and then by the crown: the maker of the tags might well have had a Winchester training. On the other hand another Portchester tag has an exact parallel at Glastonbury,[3] which illustrates the difficulty of defining the range of influence of any one centre. Although Winchester can be seen as a formative centre for manuscript painting and textiles from the late ninth century,[4] the evidence that it was also one for metal-work is frustratingly slight. Studies of the Alfred Jewel, however, continue to support its connection with King Alfred; Mr D. R. Howlett has argued that its iconography can be closely linked to the king's philosophical writings.[5]

This jewel, of the last decades of the ninth century, is one of the few objects that can be given a reasonably close date.[6] If it was used as an *æstel*, an aid in reading and copying manuscripts in a religious establishment, not only is it our latest object in the tradition of a king as a 'generous giver of gold' but also it introduces a new emphasis on ecclesiastical rather than personal treasure. Mr M. Dolley has recently shown that the tenth century saw a very marked change in secular ornaments.[7] He notes that only two of the tenth- and eleventh-century Saxon objects in the British Museum are of precious metal, the rest being in bronze or pewter, and suggests that this resulted from a shortage of privately owned bullion caused at least in part by over-valuation of the silver coinage after Edgar's reform of *c*. 973–5, so that individuals could not afford to wear gold and silver. He also lists the eight surviving coin-imitation brooches of the tenth and eleventh centuries, using them to show that, since only three were made of silver after 973, there was a move away from precious metals. In fact this figure can be reduced to two, as superficial tests on an Ashmolean brooch have subsequently shown that it too is of base metal, not silver.[8]

[1] Report by D. M. Wilson, in M. Biddle, 'Excavations at Winchester 1964', *AntJ* 45 (1965), 263–4.
[2] Report by D. A. Hinton, in B. W. Cunliffe, *Portchester Castle Excavations*, forthcoming.
[3] P. Rahtz and S. Hirst, *Beckery Chapel, Glastonbury, 1967–8* (Glastonbury, 1974), fig. 23, no. 14.
[4] F. Wormald, 'The "Winchester School" before St Æthelwold', *England Before the Conquest: Studies in Primary Sources presented to Dorothy Whitelock*, ed. Peter Clemoes and Kathleen Hughes (Cambridge, 1971), 305–13.
[5] 'The Iconography of the Alfred Jewel', *Oxoniensia* 39 (1974), 44–52.
[6] Hinton, *Ashmolean Catalogue*, no. 23.
[7] 'The Nummular Brooch from Sulgrave', *England before the Conquest*, ed. Clemoes and Hughes, p. 346.
[8] Hinton, *Ashmolean Catalogue*, no. 39; item (*b*) in Dolley's list ('Nummular Brooch', p. 346).

Sword-hilts tell much the same story. Gold is not found on them after the early tenth century and they have much less silver. Base metals were increasingly used instead, even to the extent of a cast brass pommel and guards on the Mileham sword[1] and the cast bronze guard of the Exeter hilt,[2] both ascribed to the eleventh century. Although an exact number of known English swords of the eighth to eleventh centuries cannot be given because opinions about origins differ, enough have survived to suggest that they are representative. Representative also is the absence of tenth- and eleventh-century finger-rings matching in quality those of earlier days. Since knowledge of the earlier rings comes almost entirely from chance finds, not from the specialized circumstances of deposited hoards, it is reasonable to assume that their later absence is not merely the result of unrepresentative collection but a true indication that they were not produced.

Brooches, sword-hilts and finger-rings were not the only ornaments in the period, for tenth- and eleventh-century wills contain references to arm-lets. In *c.* 950 Wynflæd gave her 'gold-adorned wooden cup' to Edwold so that he might use the gold 'to enlarge his armlet'.[3] The armlet seems from this to have been not so much a work of art as a piece of bullion indicating a man's wealth and status, to be enlarged by fusing more gold to it – and presumably to be reduced in times of adversity. If the armlets were little more than weights of bullion, surviving examples would not be easy to ascribe to any particular area or date, being without significant ornamental features. The Ashmolean Museum has two objects that probably date from this period and might be armlets. These are circles of plaited metal rods, one from Long Wittenham, Berkshire, in silver,[4] the other from Brightlingsea, Essex, in gold.[5] Similar twisted rods are suggested by the drawing of a warrior's gear in an eleventh-century manuscript.[6] There is no mention of an armlet of gold after the second decade of the eleventh century, nor indeed of any personal ornament, in the wills.

Documentary evidence therefore, like the archaeological, indicates that there was much less gold and silver jewellery in the eleventh century than before. Nor does literary evidence necessarily give a different impression. The 'decorated' and 'golden-hilted' sword which, according to the poem (161b and 166b), was carried by Byrhtnoth at the Battle of Maldon in 991 may either have been an old weapon[7] or represent traditional literary con-

---

[1] D. M. Wilson, 'Some Neglected Late Anglo-Saxon Swords', *MA* 9 (1965), 39–40.

[2] V. I. Evison, 'A Sword from the Thames at Wallingford Bridge', *ArchJ* 124 (1967), 171–2.

[3] Whitelock, *Wills*, p. 13. See also Bruce-Mitford, 'Disc-Brooches', p. 171.

[4] Acc. no. 1957.61; *Oxoniensia* 23 (1958), 133, fig. 40.   [5] Acc. no. 1927.6639.

[6] BM Cotton Tiberius C. vi, 10v; Evison 'Sword', p. 184, fig. 9c, and *Walpole Soc.* 38 (1960–2), pl. 9.

[7] Byrhtnoth ironically offers the Vikings the tribute of 'old swords' (47b). I am indebted to Pro-fessor Clemoes for drawing my attention to this and other points about the *Maldon* poem.

vention. The presence of such convention in the poem may be inferred from the personification attributed to armour: *seo byrne sang | gryreleoða sum* ('the corslet sang a terrible song', 284b–5a). M. D. Cherniss has demonstrated that it was characteristic of heroic literary tradition thus to personify weapons, as in *Beowulf, Waldere* and other poems.[1] Again, is *The Battle of Maldon* conventional when it speaks of Byrhtnoth as *sincgifa* ('treasure giver', 278a) and *beahgifa* ('ring giver', 290b), seeing that no ring of this time has survived that is worthy of presentation to a warrior? At any rate it is worth noticing that the direct speech of Ælfwine, Offa, Leofsunu and the rest contains no reference to gifts, and the narrator specifies only presents of horses. And was the *Maldon* poet being conventional too when ascribing the traditional booty motive to one of Byrhtnoth's attackers (*he wolde þæs beornes beagas gefeccan, | reaf and hringas and gerenod swurd* ('he wanted to take the warrior's valuables, clothing and rings and decorated sword'), 160–1)? It is by no means certain that such references need to be taken at their face value.

It may be that, as Mr Dolley contends, the Edgar coinage reform made a real difference and within a generation precious objects had disappeared as a side-effect of the over-valuation of silver, or we may have to do with changing demand rather than changing supply. The clause in Æthelred's code of *c.* 1009 directing that 'every man is to come barefoot to church without gold and ornaments'[2] might be a sumptuary law or a piece of rhetoric in a codified penitential or a reflection of changing attitudes. The last is possibly suggested by the mocking treatment of the smith in Ælfric's *Colloquy*.[3] So too the speeches of Byrhtnoth's followers might indicate a new society tied to its lord by bookland and not by treasure. Both the surviving finger-rings that are most likely to have been royal gifts, those inscribed with the names of Æthelswith[4] and Æthelwulf,[5] are ninth-century. They have no successors. In Ireland also, not directly affected by the dealings of the English royal mints, there may have been a change in taste, for Mlle Françoise Henry does not consider that any of the Irish penannular brooches need be later than the tenth century.[6]

Even some of the English swords of the later tenth century and the eleventh that do have decoration tend to show 'lack of foresight in planning

---

[1] 'The Cross as Christ's Weapon: the Influence of Heroic Literary Tradition on *The Dream of the Rood*', *ASE* 2 (1973), 244–50, following N. D. Isaacs, 'The Convention of Personification in *Beowulf*', *Old English Poetry: Fifteen Essays*, ed. R. P. Creed (Providence, Rhode Island, 1967), pp. 215–48.

[2] *English Historical Documents* c. *500–1042*, ed. D. Whitelock (London, 1955), p. 409.

[3] *Ælfric's Colloquy*, ed. G. N. Garmonsway (London, 1939), p. 40; see H. R. Loyn, *Anglo-Saxon England and the Norman Conquest* (London, 1962), pp. 103–6. I owe this suggestion and reference to Mr Patrick Wormald.

[4] Wilson, *British Museum Catalogue*, no. 1.

[5] *Ibid.* no. 31.

[6] *Irish Art in the Romanesque Period, 1020–1170* (London, 1970), pp. 74–5.

the lay-out'.[1] The discovery of an ownership inscription, *Æþel...mec ah* ('Æthel... owns me'), incised into the horn handle of one of these later swords,[2] shows that the concept of personification continued to exist, but perhaps as no more than a conventional formula, since the inscription is irregularly cut, although properly serifed. Not only did elaborate decoration disappear from the hilts of swords but also the technique of pattern-welding died out during the tenth and eleventh centuries.[3] This is usually ascribed to the use of better iron ores for the blades, but it may also reflect a trend to plainer weapons.

Both the ninth-century royal rings have Christian symbolism, the Lamb of God and the Early Christian peacocks. The ninth century has other examples of symbolism on jewellery, one of which is the Alfred Jewel, also a product of court patronage. The other two objects bearing clearly established symbolic imagery, the Abingdon sword with its representation of the four evangelists[4] and the Fuller brooch depicting the five senses,[5] are outstanding and must have been owned by men of high status. All are the work of no more than two or three generations of craftsmen, whose successors were to produce nothing comparable. The thegn of King Alfred or Edward the Elder whose sword was fortified with Christian symbolism as he went into battle against the pagan Danes was clearly a man of wealth, whose heirs were not to patronize the heirs of his silversmith. For them the Christian battle had been fought and won and their faith needed no buttressing from their jewellery. The symbol-bearing objects show a sophistication of understanding amongst the ninth-century aristocracy. Was it the counterpart for their successors no longer to vaunt their wealth in the old barbaric tradition by rich display on their swords, their rings and their brooches? It may be significant that the two latest silver disc-brooches are the worst in quality; the coarse wires of the Canterbury brooch[6] and the crudely incised decoration on the Sutton brooch[7] may show that their owners were not members of the higher aristocracy, who would hardly have tolerated such low standards.

The metal-work may therefore reflect not the poverty of the aristocracy in the tenth and eleventh centuries but their increasing sophistication. In this more pious age, when a thegn like Godwine had the Last Judgement carved

[1] Evison, 'Sword', p. 174.
[2] From Wareham, Dorset, now in the Dorset County Museum, Dorchester. The inscription was revealed after recent restoration by Mr Rodney Alcock. It will be more fully discussed in the report of recent excavations at Wareham by R. Hodges and myself.
[3] Evison, 'Sword', p. 181.
[4] Hinton, *Ashmolean Catalogue*, no. 1.
[5] Bruce-Mitford, 'Disc-Brooches', pp. 183–90.
[6] Hinton, *Ashmolean Catalogue*, no. 6.
[7] Wilson, *British Museum Catalogue*, no. 83.

on his personal seal,[1] gold and silver were lavished on the church instead. The spoil-carts of William the Conqueror laden with the treasures of Ely were not bearing a base burden. England was a rich country,[2] which presumably argues for a balance of trade leading to a favourable inflow of silver that must have found its way to the landowning producers, if only as coin. To show that the years 973–5 were really a watershed it is necessary to prove that there was a shortage of silver in private hands thereafter, not just that no silver objects were produced. The evidence of the surviving wills suggests large holdings at least in coin, although the frequently used word 'pounds' perhaps implies bullion, as does the phrase 'an ore's weight'.[3] There are bequests of marks of gold in the eleventh century, but this does not necessarily mean that gold was to be handed down, for the figures may be no more than assessment values. The cumulative impression however is of substantial private holdings of coin and possibly also of bullion, despite the Danegeld levies. It seems that the melting-pot to turn coin and bullion into ornaments was available to the landowners had they wished to use it, but that they chose not to. The changes in the metal-work may indicate changing tastes that in turn reflect changing social attitudes. It may well be that for late Anglo-Saxon England, at least in its higher ranks, the barbaric world of the Germanic past was dead.

Late Anglo-Saxon metal-work is usually difficult to date closely, difficult to ascribe to a place of manufacture and difficult to attribute to a particular social rank of ownership. Yet these objects are not of just antiquarian or art-historical interest and it is to be hoped that further work will show that they should be given due consideration in social and economic studies. A man's sword is a direct record of the man himself.

[1] Okasha, *Hand-List*, no. 117. Dr Okasha translates 'minister' as 'priest', but the *Medieval Latin Word-List* does not give this meaning until 1166, and it appears that in the charters priests are careful to sign as 'sacerdos' or 'presbyter'. See also the review in *Jnl of the Eng. Place-Name Soc.* 4 (1972).

[2] P. H. Sawyer, 'The Wealth of England in the Eleventh Century', *TRHS* 15 (1965), 145–64.

[3] Whitelock, *Wills*, no. XXVII.

The Vikings in England: a review

GILLIAN FELLOWS JENSEN

In the preface to F. M. Stenton's collected papers Lady Stenton notes that the publication of *Anglo-Saxon England* in 1943 marked the culmination of a life-time spent largely preparing for and writing a book in which 'place-names, coins and charters, wills and pleas, archaeology and the laws of the Anglo-Saxons were all for the first time adequately used to produce a balanced narrative, supported by Domesday Book and the twelfth-century charters which made it easier to understand the earlier material'.[1] Indeed, with the exception of archaeology, Sir Frank had been actively engaged in all these fields of research, as is revealed by the list of his published works, and it seemed unlikely at the time that it would ever be necessary to make major adjustments to the view of the Scandinavian settlements that he presented. Only twelve years had passed, however, when voices of dissent began to arise and the first of three papers that were to herald two decades of controversy about the Vikings in England was published. The present review examines the most significant contributions to the ensuing debate and considers whether it has, in fact, been necessary to depart substantially from the views held by Stenton.

The first scholar to enter the arena was the historian R. H. C. Davis in 1955.[2] His expressed aim was to consider whether or not there had been a systematic settlement of East Anglia by the rank-and-file of the Danish armies in the ninth century. He deals with the various types of evidence that had been relied upon by earlier scholars, namely the narrative of the *Anglo-Saxon Chronicle*, the terminology in thirteenth-century deeds, the personal names borne by the free peasants of East Anglia in the eleventh and early twelfth centuries, the Scandinavian element in East Anglian place-names and the fact that Scandinavian place-names and free peasantry are both particularly numerous in the Norfolk Broadland. He shows that the words of the *Chronicle* may mean merely that East Anglia was divided by the Danes into administrative districts, that the terminology of the deeds does not necessarily reflect a Scandinavian system of land-sharing, that not every man with a Scandinavian name was of Scandinavian descent, that a Scandinavian

[1] *Preparatory to 'Anglo-Saxon England', being the Collected Papers of Frank Merry Stenton*, ed. D. M. Stenton (Oxford, 1970).
[2] 'East Anglia and the Danelaw', *TRHS* 5th ser. 5 (1955), 23–39.

place-name does not necessarily reflect a settlement established by the Danish army or inhabited by its members, and finally that there had been an English free peasantry in East Anglia before the Viking settlements. Davis concludes that the Danish settlement of East Anglia was less intense than that of the northern Danelaw and that the weight of the evidence is against the theory of a settlement there by the Danish soldiers of the rank-and-file.

In 1956 Davis's paper was joined by one by the philologist A. L. Binns.[1] He considers that the style of the sculptured stone crosses at Middleton in Yorkshire contains Irish, Scandinavian and Anglian elements and he investigates the cultural background that would have been necessary for the development of such a style. He observes that place-names are not an accurate guide to the composition of those levels of society able to erect monuments. In Middleton and its neighbourhood, for example, the place-names are predominantly Anglian, but Binns notes that the personal names borne by the local tenants in Domesday Book are mainly Scandinavian and that the stone sculpture was obviously designed to please Viking taste. From these facts he concludes that the Vikings often took over Anglian villages as going concerns. This conclusion now seems perfectly reasonable, even obvious, but no one had ever stated it so clearly before. Not only Stenton[2] but also the great Swedish place-name scholar Eilert Ekwall[3] had been content to note that Scandinavian immigration had to be very considerable before it left any marked trace on the local nomenclature in areas where there already was a large English population. Binns assumes that, although the Scandinavian settlement in Northumbria was predominantly Danish, the settlement of the Middleton area was rather connected with the Norse kingdom in York. He thinks that the crosses were probably erected between 919, when the Norwegian Ragnvald became established in York, and 954, when the last Scandinavian ruler was finally expelled from the city. Later Christian peasants of Anglo-Scandinavian stock would not have been likely to set up crosses with the half-defiant harking back to paganism that Binns considers characterizes Middleton B.

The third and most controversial paper appeared in 1958. This was the historian P. H. Sawyer's devastating assault on beliefs concerning the size of the Viking armies and the density of the Danish settlement.[4] His attack is directed against Stenton's assessment of the settlement as 'a migration' and

---

[1] 'Tenth Century Carvings from Yorkshire and the Jellinge Style', *Universitet i Bergen Årbok 1956*, Historisk-antikvarisk rekke 2 (1956), 1–29.

[2] See, e.g., *Anglo-Saxon England*, 2nd ed. (Oxford, 1947), p. 517.

[3] 'The Scandinavian Settlement', *Introduction to the Survey of English Place-Names* (Cambridge, 1924), pp. 55–92, esp. 80–6, and 'The Scandinavian Settlement', *An Historical Geography of England before A.D. 1800*, ed. H. C. Darby (Cambridge, 1936), pp. 133–64, esp. 160–3.

[4] 'The Density of the Danish Settlement in England', *Univ. of Birmingham Hist. Jnl* 6 (1958), 1–17.

Ekwall's opinion that in an area such as Lincolnshire 'the number of new settlers was about equal to, or even greater than, that of the native population'. He examines the evidence of the *Anglo-Saxon Chronicle* with a critical eye. He considers that the figures quoted for the size of the Viking fleets and armies are exaggerated. The survival of the Scandinavian language in England and its influence on English can be explained partly by the similarity of the two languages to each other and partly by the fact that in the areas of settlement positions of power would normally be held by men of Scandinavian descent and the Scandinavian language would confer prestige on its speakers. It is merely this Scandinavian influence on the English language that is reflected in the numerous place-names of Scandinavian origin, and a map showing all the Scandinavian and Scandinavianized place-names in England will include many names not formed or transformed until after the Norman Conquest. Such names are irrelevant for the study of the original Scandinavian settlements. Sawyer acknowledges that the rate of expansion of settlement cannot be determined but ventures to suggest that of the approximately 220 Lincolnshire place-names in *bý*, no more than perhaps twenty were formed in the ninth century. A man with a Scandinavian personal name is not necessarily of Scandinavian descent and a place-name consisting of a Scandinavian personal name plus the English element *tūn* should be left out of account in any assessment of the evidence for Scandinavian settlement. Sawyer's general conclusions are that the largest Danish armies in the ninth century hardly numbered more than two or three hundred men. Many of their members settled in England and were probably joined there by other Danes. They did not displace or overwhelm the English but settled where they could, often on unoccupied land.

I have dealt with the papers of Davis, Binns and Sawyer in some detail partly because it was these which sparked off the still-continuing discussion of the problems of the Scandinavian settlement and partly because they touch upon most of the types of evidence which have been drawn upon in subsequent contributions to the debate. I go on to consider briefly the various arguments that have been put forward by scholars from all the relevant fields of research. My own work for the past thirteen years has been mainly concerned with the personal names and place-names of the Danelaw. The place-name scholar of today, however, no longer looks upon his work as a purely linguistic problem but acknowledges that co-operation with historians, archaeologists, numismatists, geographers, geologists and others is essential. The present review will, I hope, reveal some of the fruits of this co-operation. Little attention will be paid to the political history of the period or to conditions in the Scandinavian homelands; for these and other aspects of the Viking problem there are two excellent review articles by the Scandinavian historians Per Sveaas Andersen and Inge Skovgaard-Petersen.[1]

The first edition of P. H. Sawyer's *The Age of the Vikings* appeared in 1962.[2] In this book Sawyer deals with the problem of Scandinavian settlement in greater detail than had been possible in the provocative article of 1958. He argues convincingly that the *Anglo-Saxon Chronicle* was a work of propaganda, extolling the rôle played by the West Saxons in the struggle against the invaders and hence tending to exaggerate the importance of Viking activity. Most of the other contemporary sources were written by churchmen, who looked upon the Scandinavian settlements merely as bases for further depredations and stressed the destructive nature of their activity. With the exception of the scaldic verses embedded in them, the Icelandic sagas have little worth as historical sources for the Viking period. Sawyer's assessment of the written sources has been generally accepted and most later scholars have been content to refer to his conclusions. D. M. Wilson, however, considers that the outright condemnation of the sagas needs moderating[3] and Sven Ulric Palme notes that Sawyer might have paid more attention to the correspondence of such men as Einhard of Seligenstaedt, Lupus of Ferrières and Hincmar of Rheims.[4] Alistair Campbell has made a detailed study of the historical accuracy of some scaldic verses dealing with the exploits of the Vikings in England.[5] The verses seem to be contemporary with the events to which they refer but the amount of factual evidence that can be drawn from them is small.

There has been less agreement about Sawyer's argument as to the motive behind the raids and settlements. Sawyer emphasizes that to contemporaries the word 'Viking' meant a pirate but notes that not all the Scandinavians who came to England were pirates. Some were traders and others settlers in search of land. In Sawyer's opinion these latter looked upon the raids as a way of accumulating capital with which to settle. He builds this argument partly on the fact that the earliest payments of money to the Danes never reached Scandinavia[6] and partly on an interpretation of the word *feohlease* in the *Chronicle* for 896 as 'without money'. Sawyer assumes that it was only those Vikings who were moneyless who did not settle in England but had to continue their search across the sea. He suggests that land-hunger was

---

[1] Per Sveaas Andersen, *Vikingetid og Rikssamling* (Oslo, 1969), esp. 'Vikingetidens Ekspansjon: England og Irland', pp. 26–9, and Inge Skovgaard-Petersen, 'Vikingerne i den nyere Forskning', *Historisk Tidsskrift* 12. række 5 (Copenhagen, 1971), 651–721.

[2] *The Age of the Vikings*, 1st ed. (London, 1962), 2nd ed. (1971).

[3] *SBVS* 16 (1962), 104.

[4] 'Vikingatågen i Väst – Deras Förutsättningar och samhälleliga Följder', *Nordisk Tidskrift för Vetenskap, Konst och Industri* (Stockholm, 1962), pp. 223–39, esp. 226–7.

[5] *Skaldic Verse and Anglo-Saxon History* (London, 1971); cf. Sawyer, *The Age of the Vikings*, 1st ed., pp. 38–41. [6] See below, pp. 189–90.

the main motive behind the raids in the ninth century and that the reason that the Danish raids on England began much later than the Norwegian ones may have been that pressure on the available resources of land became serious at a later date in Denmark than in Norway. Sven Ulric Palme, however, considers that the evidence for a population explosion in Scandinavia in the Viking age that can be drawn from onomastic and archaeological evidence is ambiguous.[1] Niels Lund argues that the actions of the Danish armies in eastern and northern England do not suggest that they were prompted by land-hunger.[2] On the contrary, they travelled from town to town forcing the inhabitants to buy peace. Niels Lund and Aksel E. Christensen both argue that the term *feohlease* means 'property-less' and refers to those Vikings who were not already associated with the existing settlements.[3] Lucien Musset also disagrees with Sawyer about the motives for the raids.[4] He considers that colonization was merely a by-product of the raids, and notes that in the lower Seine area the Vikings continued in the 'Danegeld phase' for two generations from 845 to 911, as opposed to only one generation in England, 845–76. It seems that the Vikings resorted to colonization only when other means of exploiting the land had been exhausted. In the second edition of *The Age of the Vikings* Sawyer acknowledges that land-hunger can hardly have been the main driving force behind the Danish Vikings.[5] They are rather to be considered as pirates whose field of activity had been extended to England. The Norwegians, on the other hand, were chiefly on the look out for new land.

Sawyer agrees with Davis that sokemen are not to be taken as evidence for the number of Scandinavian settlers in an area and finds it most likely that the sokemen were English peasants whose social, legal and economic status may have been altered as a result of the Danish conquests.[6] H. R. Loyn, however, considers that although the sokemen may not have been descendants of the Danish settlers, it is reasonable to explain their presence as the result, direct and indirect, of a large-scale Scandinavian immigration.[7] Niels Lund argues that there is no reason to believe that the sokemen were descended from Danish settlers but that the Viking attacks may have hastened consolidation into manorial estates in 'English' England, whereas in the Danelaw itself the Danes simply took over the administration as they

---

[1] 'Vikingatågen', p. 232.
[2] 'The Secondary Migration', *Med. Scandinavia* 2 (1969), 196–201, esp. 198.
[3] Niels Lund, *De danske Vikinger i England. Røvere og Bønder* (Copenhagen, 1967), pp. 40–2, and Aksel E. Christensen, *Vikingetidens Danmark* (Copenhagen, 1969), pp. 170–2 and 203–6.
[4] 'Les Deux Âges des Vikings: Réflexions et Observations d'un Historien Normand', *Med. Scandinavia* 2 (1969), 187–93, esp. 188–9.
[5] Pp. 206–9.
[6] *The Age of the Vikings*, 1st ed., pp. 163–4.
[7] *Anglo-Saxon England and the Norman Conquest* (London, 1962), pp. 54–5.

found it.[1] Sawyer, however, has noted that the compilers of Domesday Book left out large numbers of rent-paying tenants from the accounts of some counties and that these were precisely the people who were counted as freemen or sokemen in other counties.[2] This variation of treatment from county to county means that the contrast in Domesday Book between the Danelaw with its free peasantry and the rest of the country is more apparent than real. It should also be noted that G. W. S. Barrow has recently demonstrated that the organization of the land into sokes seems to have been common and of great antiquity in both England and Scotland.[3]

It has sometimes been argued that Scandinavian influence is reflected in the administrative and legal terminology and practice current in England in later centuries. Sawyer, however, has shown that the supposedly Scandinavian duodecimal system of assessment was found also in the non-Scandinavian areas of England and A. Tomkinson notes its use in Oxfordshire.[4] Sawyer has also drawn attention to the fact that duodecimal and decimal systems of assessment exist side by side in Normandy but that here the decimal system is considered to be of Scandinavian origin and the duodecimal system to be Frankish. Lady Stenton has contended that ancient Scandinavian elements may have survived as complicating factors in thirteenth-century criminal procedure, without coming to the notice of the justices,[5] but J. M. Kaye has noted that the existence of the office of *sacrabar* appears to be the only specific piece of evidence advanced in support of this contention.[6] He thinks it likely that the word *sacrabar* itself represents the full extent of the borrowing from Scandinavia.

A good deal of attention has been paid during the past fifteen years to the archaeological evidence in Scandinavia and the British Isles for the Viking raids and settlements. Bertil Almgren has stressed the importance of Viking ships and horses for the success of the raids.[7] The rather surprising ease with which this success was achieved must have been in large part due to the fact that the shallow draught of the Viking ships gave them several advantages. They were fast-sailing, they could use oars as a complement to sails and they

[1] *De danske Vikinger*, pp. 84–7.
[2] 'The Two Viking Ages of Britain: a Discussion', *Med. Scandinavia* 2 (1969), 163–76 and 203–7, esp. 170.
[3] *The Kingdom of the Scots* (London, 1973), pp. 7–28.
[4] Sawyer, *The Age of the Vikings*, 2nd ed., p. 172, and A. Tomkinson, 'The Carucage of 1220 in an Oxfordshire Hundred', *Bull. of the Inst. of Hist. Research* 41 (1968), 212–16.
[5] Doris M. Stenton, *English Justice between the Norman Conquest and the Great Charter 1066–1215* (London, 1965), pp. 55–6.
[6] 'The Sacrabar', *EHR* 83 (1968), 744–58.
[7] 'Vital Factors in the Success of the Vikings', *Proc. of the Sixth Viking Congress*, ed. Peter Foote and Dag Strömbäck (Uppsala, 1971), pp. 33–7, summarizing the arguments of the author's 'Vikingatåg och Vikingaskepp', *Tor* 8 (1962), 186–200, and 'Vikingatågens Höjdpunkt och Slut', *Tor* 9 (1963), 215–50.

made it possible for the Vikings to use islets in shallow estuaries as landing-places and winter strongholds, since the ships of the English drew too much water for them to be able to land there. A further advantage of the Viking ships was that it was comparatively easy to land horses from them and this was important for the later raids on England, when the Danes landed with a well-trained, heavily armed professional cavalry that was capable of over-running the boroughs which the English had fortified against Viking attack. Sawyer had earlier argued that the Viking ships could not have been very large since it would have been necessary to construct the keel out of one piece of wood,[1] but D. M. Wilson has noted that long ships with scarphed keels were built in Scandinavia in the thirteenth century and that there seems no reason to deny the possibility that they could also have been constructed in the Viking period.[2] In the second edition of his book Sawyer still seems to think that the size of the ships was to some extent limited by the length of timber available, but Else Roesdahl has noted that in accepting that Æthelred's England was conquered by fair-sized armies transported in large ships, possibly with crews of more than sixty men, Sawyer is implicitly crediting the shipbuilders of Swein and Cnut with the skill to make a stable composite keel.[3]

There has been much discussion of the Trelleborg-type camps in Denmark and full agreement has not yet been reached as to the date of their construction and the function for which they were designed. In 1962 Sawyer was unwilling to date them more closely than 950–1050 and he did not consider that there was any good reason for associating them with Cnut.[4] By 1971, however, he was willing to accept Olaf Olsen's dating of the camps to 970–1020 and treats them as good evidence for the size and organization of the Danish armies under Swein Forkbeard in the reign of Æthelred.[5] A dissenting voice has been raised by Tage E. Christiansen.[6] He does not agree that the forts were training-camps and barracks for Swein's armies but considers that the claim of navigable access to Trelleborg from the Great Belt rests upon irresponsible use of some limited trial investigations. He thinks it most likely that they were garrison-forts, erected by the Danish king in about 1000 to strengthen his control over the surrounding areas. Ole Klindt-Jensen has recently argued that the forts may have had a function as places of refuge and protection for the local population rather than as either barracks or garrisons.[7] Else Roesdahl notes that the forts could not have

---

[1] 'Density', p. 4. [2] *SBVS* 16 (1962), 105–6.
[3] Sawyer, *The Age of the Vikings*, 2nd ed., pp. 81 and 132, and Else Roesdahl, *SBVS* 18 (1973), 408.
[4] *The Age of the Vikings*, 1st ed., pp. 132–3. [5] *Ibid.* 2nd ed., pp. 136–7.
[6] 'Træningslejr eller Tvangsborg', *Kuml* (1970), 43–63.
[7] 'The Problem of Evaluating Archaeological Sources in Early Historical Time', *Actes du VIIIᵉ Congrès International des Sciences Préhistoriques et Protohistoriques. Beograd 9–15 Septembre 1971* III (Belgrade, 1973), 346–52.

held 5,000 men as stated by Sawyer.[1] P. G. Foote and D. M. Wilson have suggested tentatively that the Trelleborg-type camps might have been a Danish invention, based on long experience of building temporary structures in England and elsewhere, although their form may have been inspired by the circular fortifications long known on the Baltic islands.[2]

In fact, it seems that such fortifications as the Vikings built in England were mainly of a temporary nature, for there is hardly any trace of them left today. Sawyer takes this comparative lack of evidence to support his theory that the ninth-century Danish armies must have been small.[3] Rosemary Cramp, however, notes that the Viking invaders taught the English the value of fortified towns, and records that some vestiges of a Viking fortification have been excavated at York.[4]

Sawyer has noted that there is a vast number of stones with runic inscriptions in Scandinavia, some of which provide information about Viking expeditions to England and elsewhere.[5] Sven B. F. Jansson has examined the Swedish rune stones and notes that all the inscriptions which mention Swedish voyages to England belong to the first half of the eleventh century, the period to which the great majority of the Anglo-Saxon silver coins that have been found in Sweden also belong.[6] These Swedish inscriptions are particularly significant, since there is little other evidence for Swedish participation in raids on the west.

Sawyer notes that comparatively few pagan Danish graves have been found in England and both he and D. M. Wilson suggest that this is probably because the Danes were quick to adopt Christian forms of burial or at least to bury their dead in Christian churchyards, where the graves would be disturbed and removed with the passage of time.[7] Most of the pagan grave-finds probably belong to the earliest phase of settlement. Some of them have been found in Christian churchyards and these would represent the kind of harking back to paganism that Binns reads into the sculpture on the Middleton B cross. Wilson has argued that some of the stone crosses in Northumbria were erected within a generation of Halfdan's settlement.[8] He looks upon the Middleton cross as the work of an English craftsman struggling

[1] 'The Viking Fortress of Fyrkat', *Château Gaillard* 6 (1972), 195–202, and *SBVS* 18 (1973), 408.
[2] *The Viking Achievement* (London, 1970), p. 272.
[3] *The Age of the Vikings*, 1st ed., pp. 126–8.
[4] *Anglian and Viking York*, Borthwick Papers 33 (York, 1967), 14.
[5] *The Age of the Vikings*, 1st ed., pp. 41–4.
[6] *Swedish Vikings in England. The Evidence of the Rune Stones* (London, 1966).
[7] Sawyer, *The Age of the Vikings*, 1st ed., pp. 63–4 and 227, n. 34, recording the suggestion to this effect by P. S. Gelling; D. M. Wilson, 'The Vikings' Relationship with Christianity in Northern England', *JBAA* 3rd ser. 30 (1967), 37–46, and 'Archaeological Evidence for the Viking Settlements and Raids in England', *Frühmittelalterliche Studien* 2 (1968), 291–304; and Foote and Wilson, *Viking Achievement*, p. 413.
'Vikings' Relationship', p. 45.

to attain the new style brought over by his Viking masters from Scandinavia.[1] That he was an insular craftsman is demonstrated by the fact that he executed the Anglo-Saxon interlace patterns more competently than the other ornamental motifs. Recently James T. Lang has argued that, while Binns was correct in assigning the Middleton crosses to the tenth century, his generally accepted suggestion that Middleton B represents a heathen Viking's grave must be rejected.[2] The carving actually represents a local aristocrat seated on a chair. Pagan overtones may, however, be reflected in the fact that this superficially Christian monument seems to be concerned more with the prestige of the warrior than with his salvation.

Wilson has noted that there is no settlement site of uniquely Viking character in England.[3] Rosemany Cramp, however, shows how archaeological material has thrown light on the expansion of the town of York after the Viking settlement and the consequent wider trading contacts.[4] The finds from York can be paralleled from Viking trading sites such as Birka and Kaupang. P. S. Gelling has examined the medieval shielings on Man.[5] There is very little evidence for dating them, but such as there is would fit in well with the suggestion that the practice of transhumance in the island owed its main development to the Vikings.

The numismatic evidence for the Viking raids and settlements is derived from coin hoards in Scandinavia and the British Isles. Aksel E. Christensen and Sven Ulric Palme are inclined to see the coin hoards in Scandinavia in the context of trade.[6] Philip Grierson, however, points out that the reputation of the Vikings as traders depends very largely on ambiguous archaeological evidence or on the misinterpretation of the written sources.[7] He considers that the alternative channels by which goods passed from hand to hand, namely 'theft' and 'gift', were more important than trade in the Viking period. Sawyer notes that there is a scarcity of ninth-century western European coins in the Scandinavian hoards in spite of the fact that large sums of tribute must have been paid to Viking raiders in this century.[8] He assumes that the coins had been used by the raiders as a sort of capital with which to settle.[9] Some English coins were imported into Scandinavia before the reign of Æthelred but the main stream began with the renewal of Viking raids on England at the end of the tenth century. Among the causes for the renewed

---

[1] David M. Wilson and Ole Klindt-Jensen, *Viking Art* (London, 1966), pp. 104–14.
[2] 'Some Late Pre-Conquest Crosses in Ryedale, Yorkshire: a Reappraisal', *JBAA* 3rd ser. 36 (1973), 16–25.
[3] 'Archaeological Evidence', p. 302.   [4] *Anglian and Viking York*, p. 17.
[5] 'Medieval Shielings in the Isle of Man', *MA* 6–7 (1962–3), 156–72.
[6] Christensen, *Vikingetidens*, p. 194, and Palme, 'Vikingåtagen', p. 237.
[7] 'Commerce in the Dark Ages', *TRHS* 5th ser. 9 (1959), 123–40, esp. 127 and 131.
[8] *The Age of the Vikings*, 1st ed., pp. 83–116.
[9] Cf. his explanation of *feohlease*, discussed above, p. 184.

Viking attacks on England at this time Sawyer reckons the need to compensate for the failing supply of Kufic silver and the presence of large amounts of silver in England, perhaps as a result of the growing trade in wool.[1] A very large number of the English coins found in Scandinavia were minted after 1023, that is after the last recorded payment of tribute to Danish raiders in 1018. This continuing stream of English coins probably reflects the payments made by Cnut and his sons to their mercenaries with the aid of the tax known as *heregeld*, a tax which continued to be levied by Edward the Confessor until the last of the Scandinavian mercenaries were sent home in 1051. With the ending of the *heregeld* the number of English coins in Scandinavian hoards was reduced to a mere trickle. Ole Klindt-Jensen has urged caution in dealing with the evidence of coins.[2] There was no rich production of coins in western Europe in the ninth century and this alone makes it unreasonable to expect to find many western coins in the Scandinavian hoards. Nor should it be forgotten that in the early Viking period it was hardly worth-while bringing west European coins to Scandinavia, where they would only have the value of the silver, whereas in their places of issue they might have a higher nominal value.[3] C. S. S. Lyon considers that insufficient attention has hitherto been paid to relating the composition of the Scandinavian hoards to the recorded circumstances in which England was harried by the Vikings and large tributes were paid.[4]

In his book on the Hiberno-Norse coins in the British Museum R. H. M. Dolley has a very important chapter in which he discusses the historical background to the Viking raids on the British Isles as illustrated by the chronological and geographical distribution of 210 hoards from Great Britain and Ireland.[5] D. M. Wilson has plotted graphically the coin hoards recorded by Dolley.[6] He notes a significant rise in depositions between 869 and 878, at the very period when the Vikings were most active in their settlement of England, and a small peak in the graph in the 920s, when Wessex and Mercia were trying to straighten out the political situation in the north. In connection with a description of a small hoard from Ireland Dolley has noted that almost forty-five per cent of the early-tenth-century coins from England found in Irish hoards derive from eastern England, the region which is most remote from Ireland.[7] For the period *c.* 925–*c.* 975, on the

---

[1] 'The Wealth of England in the Eleventh Century', *TRHS* 5th ser. 15 (1965), 145–64.

[2] 'Scandinavians in the British Isles', *Med. Scandinavia* 2 (1969), 193–5.

[3] Noted by Roesdahl, *SBVS* 18 (1973), 406, referring to S. Bolin, 'Mohammed, Charlemagne and Ruric', *Scandinavian Economic Hist. Rev.* 1 (1953).

[4] 'Historical Problems of Anglo-Saxon Coinage. (4) The Viking Age', *BNJ* 39 (1970), 193–204, esp. 199.

[5] *The Hiberno-Norse Coins in the British Museum* (London, 1966); cf. his *Viking Coins of the Danelaw and of Dublin* (London, 1965).   [6] Wilson, 'Archaeological Evidence', pp. 296–9.

[7] 'The *c.* 1843 Leggagh (Nobber) Coin-Hoard Reconsidered', *Riocht Na Midhe* 5.2 (1972), 14–21.

other hand, the Irish finds are dominated by coins from the Chester area. Dolley suggests that the finds of early-tenth-century coins may be connected with the removal to Ireland of the more militant among the Danes of East Anglia at a time when the remaining colonists preferred to submit to Edward the Elder. There is a comparative scarcity of early-eleventh-century coin hoards in England, but Dolley is disinclined to think that this scarcity reflects a marked reduction in devastation.[1] He suggests that by the second half of the reign of Æthelred England was probably suffering from gross over-taxation and that hoarding would also have been discouraged by fluctuations in the weight of the coinage, which would deter men from being caught with large sums of money in their possession.

Dolley has drawn attention to the fact that in Northumbria the Viking settlers in 867 overthrew a culture which had already dispensed with coinage and argues that for almost thirty years the settlers appear to have felt no need to remedy the deficiency.[2] Most numismatists are, in fact, agreed that the year 895 should be taken as an absolute *terminus post quem* for the inception of the Viking silver coinage of Northumbria, but Georg Galster has argued that the solitary coin of Halfdan in the Cuerdale hoard is probably one of the oldest and that it may have been struck in London during the years 874–7.[3] Dolley, arguing that the Viking coinage did not begin until about 895, notes that, in spite of a fifty-year break in mint activity north of the Humber, there were men available in York with the skill and the bullion to strike a very large silver coinage which compares favourably with that of Alfred himself.[4] As working hypotheses he suggests that the moneyers may have come from Canterbury, where there is a hiatus in the coinage, or from Carolingian territory. It seems clear, at any rate, that the men who struck the first Viking coinage were neither Northumbrians nor Viking craftsmen. P. H. Sawyer suggests that the silver used in these issues had been won in the Viking raids.[5] The occupation of York by Edmund in 944 seems to have brought little change to the mint there. Of the twelve moneyers who struck for the Viking kings between 939 and 944 at least seven and very probably nine also struck for the English king between 944 and 947.[6]

Coins are an important source of evidence for the study of personal

---

[1] ' "The Two Viking Ages of Britain" – an Irish Comment', *Med. Scandinavia* 2 (1969), 179–85, esp. 183.

[2] 'The Post-*Brunanburh* Viking Coinage of York', *Nordisk Numismatisk Årsskrift* (1957–8), 13–88.

[3] 'Cuerdale-Fundet og de danske Vikingekonger i det 9. Århundrede', *Aarbøger for nordisk Oldkyndighed og Historie* (1962), 1–36, esp. 16–20.

[4] 'Post-*Brunanburh*', pp. 37–9; cf. C. S. S. Lyon and B. H. I. H. Stewart, 'The Northumbrian Viking Coins in the Cuerdale Hoard', *Anglo-Saxon Coins*, ed. R. H. M. Dolley (London, 1961), pp. 96–121.

[5] 'The Vikings and the Irish Sea', *The Irish Sea Province in Archaeology and History*, ed. Donald Moore (Cardiff, 1970), pp. 86–92, esp. 91.

[6] Dolley, 'Post-*Brunanburh*', p. 81.

names. It is particularly interesting to see how the balance between English, Scandinavian and continental Germanic names varies from mint to mint and from issue to issue. Of the sixteen named moneyers striking the York Viking coinage, for example, seven have English names, four Scandinavian ones and two continental Germanic ones and three have names whose origin is doubtful. This is an interesting reflection of the cosmopolitan community at York which Dolley has deduced from other features of the coinage. In recent years there have been several detailed treatments of the names of moneyers. Some of these studies throw light on the Scandinavian settlement and its consequences. Olof von Feilitzen has examined the personal names in the coinage of Edgar (959–75).[1] He notes thirty-four Scandinavian names, but their local distribution cannot be determined because the majority of the coins bear no mint signature. After the reform of the coinage at the end of Edgar's reign the mint signature always appears on the coins and in her examination of the moneyers between 973 and 1016 Veronica Smart has been able to divide the country into regions.[2] She reveals that Scandinavian influence was still very marked at York in this period. Chester and Lincoln also show a fairly large proportion of Scandinavian names, but these are comparatively rare in East Anglia and the rest of the southern Danelaw. Mrs Smart returns to the York mint in a paper on Cnut's moneyers there.[3] The names of the moneyers are still overwhelmingly Scandinavian and there has not been any proportional decline since the reign of Æthelred, in spite of the lapse of time since the borough was formally incorporated into the English kingdom. Finally, Veronica Smart has dealt with the names of the moneyers of the Lincoln mint between *c.* 890 and 1279.[4] She shows how in the early period Scandinavian names equal or even outnumber all others, while towards the end of Æthelred's reign Scandinavian names account for no more than a third of the total. Rather surprisingly there is no recovery of the Scandinavian preponderance in the reigns of Cnut and his sons. Mrs Smart notes that, compared with the predominantly English mint at Winchester and the predominantly Norse one at York, Lincoln occupies a middle position.

This pattern of distribution of Scandinavian personal names is reflected in other sources than the English coinage. The necessity for collecting and

---

[1] Olof von Feilitzen and Christopher Blunt, 'Personal Names on the Coinage of Edgar', *England before the Conquest: Studies in Primary Sources presented to Dorothy Whitelock*, ed. Peter Clemoes and Kathleen Hughes (Cambridge, 1971), pp. 183–214, esp. 208.

[2] 'Moneyers of the Late Anglo-Saxon Coinage 973–1016', *Commentationes de Nummis Saeculorum IX–XI in Suecia Repertis* II, Kungl. Vitterhets Historie och Antikvitets Akademiens Handlingar Antikvariska Serien 19 (Stockholm, 1968), 191–276.

[3] 'Cnut's York Moneyers', *Otium et Negotium. Studies in Onomatology and Library Science presented to Olof von Feilitzen*, ed. Folke Sandgren (Stockholm, 1973), pp. 221–31.

[4] 'A Note on the Moneyers of the Mint of Lincoln', H. R. Mossop *et al.*, *The Lincoln Mint c. 890–1279* (Newcastle upon Tyne, 1970), pp. 20–7.

analysing the entire stock of personal names in specific parts of the Danelaw has been argued by Olof von Feilitzen.[1] I have examined the Scandinavian personal names that were in use in Lincolnshire and Yorkshire from the time of the first settlements until the beginning of the thirteenth century.[2] I acknowledge that Scandinavian personal names may well have been borne by men of English descent but argue that this is no reason for refusing to accept the many Scandinavian personal names in England as evidence for the presence there of men and women of Scandinavian origin. The Scandinavian names are not only numerous but also varied in type, and the vitality of the Scandinavian nomenclature must reflect the name-giving customs of a Scandinavian-speaking community of some considerable size and not merely the influence of a trend-setting aristocratic minority. I have also examined Lincolnshire names from about 1225.[3] I note the same swift decline in the popularity of Scandinavian and English names in the first quarter of the thirteenth century as has been recorded in other areas of England.[4]

D. M. Wilson has noted that on the Viking crosses from the Isle of Man Scandinavian and Celtic names are found side by side.[5] This can be compared with the way in which Yorkshire and Lincolnshire men with Scandinavian names gave their children non-Scandinavian ones and vice versa, and how some children of a family might have Scandinavian names while others had English ones.[6]

One of the problems connected with the use of personal names as evidence for Scandinavian settlement in England is that it is only comparatively rarely possible to determine in what village or even in which wapentake or hundred a man originated.[7] This is one of the reasons why place-names, which can almost always be located, are so much better evidence. Many recent books and papers have been devoted to the treatment of place-names as evidence for the Scandinavian settlement. It seems most satisfactory to deal first with the contributions devoted to the names in restricted areas. I take them in topographical order, starting in the north-west and moving anti-clockwise round the coast. After this systematic examination I note some of the general problems of interpretation involved.

W. F. H. Nicolaisen has examined the distribution of some Scandinavian

---

[1] 'Notes on some Scandinavian Personal Names in English Twelfth-Century Records', *Person-namnsstudier 1964. Tillägnade minnet av Ivar Modéer (1904–1960)* (Stockholm, 1965), pp. 52–68.

[2] *Scandinavian Personal Names in Lincolnshire and Yorkshire*, Navnestudier 7 (Copenhagen, 1968).

[3] 'The Names of the Lincolnshire Tenants of the Bishop of Lincoln *c.* 1225', *Otium et Negotium*, ed. Sandgren, pp. 86–95.

[4] *Ibid.* p. 95, n. 10.

[5] 'Vikings' Relationship', pp. 40–1, and 'Archaeological Evidence', p. 303.

[6] Fellows Jensen, *Scandinavian Personal Names*, pp. lxiii–lxiv.

[7] *Ibid.* p. xxvi.

elements in south-west Scotland and shows that there is a close relationship to the area south of the border, particularly Cumberland, Westmorland, Lancashire and the North Riding of Yorkshire.[1] W. H. Pearsall has studied the distribution of place-names in Cumberland in relation to the geology, flora and fauna.[2] The places with Anglian names tend to be found where there was good plough-land, whereas the Vikings seem to have penetrated into areas more suited for pastoral activity.

A. H. Smith has noted that to judge from the place-names the Danish occupation of Yorkshire and the East Midlands in the last quarter of the ninth century left Westmorland practically untouched.[3] He suggests that the capture of York by the Vikings in 915 and the subsequent close relations of that city with Dublin could have exposed Westmorland to Irish-Norwegian influence. He is inclined to think that older English place-names may lie behind several of the Scandinavian names in Westmorland. Assar Janzén considers that Smith tends to under-estimate the Scandinavian element,[4] but in fact Smith points out that the Scandinavian settlement in the county must have been extensive.

Margaret Gelling has examined the Scandinavian place-names in the Isle of Man and shown that they are not confined to settlements or to prominent coastal features.[5] Only two of the Celtic names on Man can be shown to be pre-Viking (Douglas and Rushen) and the predominance of Scandinavian names in the twelfth- and thirteenth-century records cannot merely be due to the fact that Norse was the language of the ruling class or of the scribes. The rate of survival of Scandinavian names shows that they were in general currency. The linguistic evidence of the runic inscriptions agrees with that of the place-names in pointing to a relatively slight Gaelic linguistic survival during the period of Viking rule. Norse seems to have been the predominant language from *c*. 900 to *c*. 1300 and did not fully die out on the island until the fifteenth century. The Manx names in *eary* ('shieling') are considered by Mrs Gelling to be post-Norse Gaelic formations. She assumes that Scandinavian terms were applied to the shielings in the Norse period and were replaced later by *eary*. This explanation is rather unsatisfactory, however, for, although the word *eary* is probably of Scottish Gaelic origin, it seems to have been known and used by the Vikings, who must have brought it with them to Yorkshire and the Faroes from Man or the Atlantic islands.

Nora Chadwick notes that Viking settlements were apparently of vital

---

[1] 'Norse Place-Names in South-West Scotland', *Scottish Stud.* 4 (1960), 49–70.
[2] 'Place-Names as Clues in the Pursuit of Ecological History', *Namn och Bygd* 49 (1961), 72–89.
[3] *The Place-Names of Westmorland*, Eng. Place-Name Soc. 42–3 (Cambridge, 1967), esp. 42, xxxix–xlv.
[4] *Namn och Bygd* 55 (1967), 191–3.
[5] 'The Place-Names of the Isle of Man', *Jnl of the Manx Museum* 7 (1970–1), 130–9 and 168–75.

importance to the political economy of the Lancashire coast-lands.[1] There
is a twelve-mile broad coastal belt of flat, black fields that seems to have
been reclaimed from marshes by farmers of Norwegian stock. Settlements
with Scandinavian names only give way to settlements with English names
on the higher ground to the east. This Scandinavian colonization is probably
to be connected with the expulsion of many Scandinavians from Ireland
when Dublin was recaptured by the Irish in 902. It would be the growing
threat from the Irish–Norwegian settlers in Lancashire and Cheshire that
led Æthelflæd to build her line of forts from north Wales to Manchester in
the first quarter of the tenth century.[2]

J. McN. Dodgson has published the first four of the projected five
volumes of *The Place-Names of Cheshire*.[3] Until volume five appears, however,
the best guides for the Scandinavian settlement in the county remain
Geoffrey Barnes's paper from 1956 and Dodgson's from 1967.[4] Both Barnes
and Dodgson assume that the element *hulm* is a Danish test-word, but I have
shown that the spellings in *hulm* in English place-names reflect either a
scribal convention or a West Midland dialect form.[5] This will necessitate
a reassessment of the onomastic evidence for the part played by the Danes
in the settlement of north-west England. Scandinavian settlement names in
Cheshire are most frequent in the Wirral peninsula. The settlers there seem
to have been Norwegians from Ireland, whereas in east Cheshire the
Scandinavian place-names probably mark the western limits of the settlements which resulted from the Danish conquest of Mercia. Dodgson notes
that the Scandinavian immigrants into Cheshire found a firm English establishment in control of the territory but that there are many minor names of
Scandinavian origin which are evidence for the infiltration of English territory by Scandinavian settlers.[6] Dodgson has also examined the evidence for
the location of the Battle of *Brunanburh*.[7] He notes that there was a recognized
Norse colony in Wirral throughout the tenth and eleventh centuries and that
presumably a Norse expedition passing up the Mersey estuary would be
able to rely upon its sympathy at the very least. Dodgson considers that
Bromborough in Wirral is the most eligible site for the battle. Finally
Dodgson has devoted a paper to the names in the city of Chester, in which

[1] 'The Vikings and the Western World', *Proc. of the International Congress of Celtic Stud.* (Dublin,
1962), pp. 13–42, esp. 29–31, building on F. T. Wainwright, 'The Scandinavians in Lancashire',
Trans. of the Lancashire and Cheshire Ant. Soc. 58 (1945–6), 71–116.
[2] F. T. Wainwright, 'Æthelflæd Lady of the Mercians', *The Anglo-Saxons: Studies in some Aspects
of their History and Culture presented to Bruce Dickins*, ed. Peter Clemoes (London, 1959), pp. 53–69.
[3] Eng. Place-Name Soc. 44–7 (Cambridge, 1970–2).
[4] Geoffrey Barnes, 'The Evidence of Place-Names for the Scandinavian Settlements in Cheshire',
Trans. of the Lancashire and Cheshire Ant. Soc. 63 (1952–3), 131–55, and J. McN. Dodgson, 'The
English Arrival in Cheshire', *Trans. of the Hist. Soc. of Lancashire and Cheshire* 119 (1967), 1–37.
[5] *SBVS* 18 (1970–1), 201–6.   [6] 'English Arrival', pp. 2–7.
[7] 'The Background of *Brunanburh*', *SBVS* 14 (1956–7), 303–16.

he takes the existence there of the parish church of St Olave by 1119 at the latest as evidence for the presence of a distinctively Scandinavian community in Chester in the eleventh century.[1]

Melville Richards has examined the Scandinavian place-names in Wales.[2] He notes that there were Norse trading stations along the coast of south Wales in the twelfth century and that a group of Scandinavian names in Flintshire probably points to penetration from the Scandinavian settlements in Cheshire. Most of the Scandinavian place-names in Wales, however, are names of significant coastal landmarks such as promontories, rocks and islands. They have no phonological or semantic relations whatsoever with the Welsh names which they have in some cases supplanted and this reveals that the Vikings and the native Welsh were not on speaking terms when the Scandinavian names were coined. This is in contrast with many of the earlier English or Anglicized place-names in Wales, which can be shown to be adaptations or semi-translations of already existing Welsh names, and also with many of the Scandinavianized place-names in England.

A brief account of Norfolk place-names has been provided by O. K. Schram.[3] He notes that the only area in which Scandinavian names predominate is to the north of Yarmouth, the hundreds of East and West Flegg, where there is a concentration of *bȳs*. The comparative rareness of Scandinavian place-names in Norfolk is rather surprising in the light of the recorded settlements of Vikings in the area. It is possible that further research into the minor names of East Anglia will reveal a considerable infiltration of Scandinavians into areas already colonized by the English. This is suggested by a short paper by Karl Inge Sandred.[4] He has examined some Fenland place-names and notes that there are numerous field- and minor names there which contain Scandinavian elements and personal names although Scandinavian major names are almost entirely absent.

The Scandinavian element in Derbyshire place-names has been treated by Kenneth Cameron.[5] He shows that the settlement was heaviest in the north-east and south-east and that there is some evidence in the north-west for settlement at a later period by people of Scandinavian descent coming from Cheshire and Lancashire.

[1] 'Place-Names and Street-Names at Chester', *Jnl of the Chester Archaeol. Soc.* (1970), 29–61, esp. 52–6.

[2] 'Norse Place-Names in Wales', *Proc. of the International Congress of Celtic Stud.* (Dublin, 1962), pp. 51–60.

[3] 'Place-Names', *Norwich and its Region*, Brit. Assoc. for the Advancement of Science (1961), pp. 141–9.

[4] 'Ortnamns- och ordstudier i Englands Fenland', *Ortnamnssällskapets I Uppsala Årsskrift* 1972, 41–52.

[5] 'The Scandinavians in Derbyshire: the Place-Name Evidence', *Nottingham Med. Stud.* 2 (1958), 86–118, and *The Place-Names of Derbyshire*, Eng. Place-Name Soc. 27–9 (Cambridge, 1959), esp. **27**, xxx–xxxviii.

Three scholars have dealt with field-names in the East Midlands. I have examined the names recorded in a mid-fourteenth-century survey.[1] The distribution of the names which contain one or more Scandinavian elements reveals that Scandinavian influence is most marked in Lincolnshire, Nottinghamshire, Leicestershire and Rutland, less so in Bedfordshire, Huntingdonshire and Northamptonshire, and almost non-existent in Oxfordshire and Buckinghamshire. This confirms the evidence of the major names, but I argue that it would be dangerous to read more into the evidence of the field-names than that the Danish settlers had introduced into the vocabulary and nomenclature of the East Midlands a wealth of loan-words connected with farming and topography. Kenneth Cameron has examined some twelfth-century field-names from the Lincolnshire village of Dunholme.[2] He considers that these demonstrate strikingly the influence which the Danish language had on the local vocabulary. The same conclusion is reached by F. T. Wainwright in his study of the field names of the Leicestershire village of Hoby in 1322.[3]

Kenneth Cameron has written three papers in direct opposition to Sawyer's denigration of place-names as evidence for Scandinavian settlement.[4] He asserts that, although Sawyer is probably correct in assuming that the ninth-century Viking armies were small, there was a considerable Scandinavian immigration into the East Midlands and to explain this he postulates a secondary immigration along the Humber and the Wash in the course of the first two generations after the original settlement. He bases his conclusions on a study of the topographical situation of villages with English and Scandinavian names, the quality of the land itself, the availability of fresh water and the nearness to rivers, roads and trackways. He also calculates the proportion of villages with the various types of name which have become parish villages or which have been lost since the time of Domesday Book, and he examines the nature of the first elements that are combined with *bý* and *thorp* and notes the significance of the large number of simplex names in *thorp*. He comes to the conclusion that many of the hybrids in *tūn* represent old-established English villages whose names had merely been partly Scandinavianized by the Vikings, that the names in *bý* represent colonization

---

[1] 'English Field-Names and the Danish Settlement', *Festskrift til Kristian Hald*, Navnestudier 13 (Copenhagen, 1974), 45–55.

[2] 'Early Field-Names in an English-Named Lincolnshire Village', *Otium et Negotium*, ed. Sandgren, pp. 38–43.

[3] *Archaeology and Place-Names and History* (London, 1962), pp. 86–8.

[4] *Scandinavian Settlement in the Territory of the Five Boroughs: the Place-Name Evidence*, Inaugural lecture (Nottingham, 1965); 'Scandinavian Settlement in the Territory of the Five Boroughs: the Place-Name Evidence Part II, Place-Names in *Thorp*', *Med. Scandinavia* 3 (1970), 35–49; and 'Scandinavian Settlement in the Territory of the Five Boroughs: the Place-Name Evidence Part III, the Grimston-Hybrids', *England before the Conquest*, ed. Clemoes and Hughes, pp. 147–63.

in the strict sense, and that the *thorp*s probably result in the main from secondary colonization.

A. H. Smith has noted that Scandinavian influence is not as marked in the West Riding as in the other two Ridings of Yorkshire and that within the Riding itself the concentration of Scandinavian elements varies greatly, being strongest in the extreme north-west and weakest in the south and west and centre.[1] Some of the wooded and marshy areas remained undeveloped in Viking times but the Vikings seem to have occupied and developed some areas which had been neglected by the English. Smith assumes that many of the hybrid place-names were the creation not of Viking settlers but of Englishmen of a later age whose vocabulary contained many words of Scandinavian origin. Grimston hybrids, however, probably represent older Anglian villages that were taken over by the Vikings. Bertil Hedevind has examined the place-names and minor names of Dentdale and shown that their evidence corroborates the theory of a chiefly Norwegian colonization in this part of the West Riding.[2] Assar Janzén has written an important paper on the evidence for Irish-Norwegian influence on Yorkshire place-names in which he argues convincingly that there are no certain instances of inversion compounds in Yorkshire.[3] He has also argued that the element *ergh* (*ærgi*), 'shieling', is more likely to have been brought from Ireland to York, whence it spread rapidly throughout the surrounding countryside, than by Norwegians coming from Westmorland over the Pennines.[4] This element, however, does not seem to have been current in Ireland and is more likely to have spread to England from Man or the Atlantic islands. P. H. Sawyer has noted that field-names recorded in thirteenth-century documents from Baldersby in the North Riding reveal that the local speech of the area had remained English but an English showing strong Scandinavian influence.[5]

I have applied the methods used by Cameron to the place-names of Yorkshire.[6] My survey reveals that villages with hybrid or Scandinavianized names are often older English settlements that had been taken over by the Vikings, that the *bý*s mark the colonization by the Danes of the best available

---

[1] *The Place-Names of the West Riding of Yorkshire*, Eng. Place-Name Soc. 30–7 (Cambridge, 1961–3) esp. 36, 44–66.

[2] 'Scandinavian Elements in the Dialect and Place-Names of Dent in the West Riding of Yorkshire', *Trans. of the Yorkshire Dialect Soc.* 10 (1958), 26–35, and *The Dialect of Dentdale in the West Riding of Yorkshire*, Acta Universitatis Upsaliensis, Studia Anglistica Upsaliensia 5 (Uppsala, 1967).

[3] 'Are There So-Called Inversion Compounds in Yorkshire Place-Names?', *Namn och Bygd* 48 (1960), 43–81.

[4] 'The Viking Colonization of England in the Light of Place-Names', *Names* 20 (1972), 1–25, esp. 23.

[5] 'Baldersby, Borup and Bruges: the Rise of Northern Europe', *Univ. of Leeds Rev.* 16 (1973), 75–96.

[6] *Scandinavian Settlement Names in Yorkshire*, Navnestudier 11 (Copenhagen, 1972).

vacant land, and that the *thorps* mark the subsequent exploitation of land less immediately favourable for agriculture. There is also evidence that when the Vikings settled in English villages they sometimes did not change the name at all and sometimes substituted a Scandinavian name for an original English one.[1] Confirmation of the place-name evidence can be drawn from an examination of the Domesday assessments of vills with different kinds of names.

Glanville R. J. Jones has attempted to resolve the controversy about the density of the Danish settlement in Yorkshire by looking at it against the background of pre-existing territorial organization.[2] He sees the settlement not as an occupation of virgin land but rather as an adaptation of a pre-existing, and in large measure surviving, organization. Discrete estates were characteristic of Yorkshire in 1086 but surprisingly few of their *foci* bear Scandinavian names. The majority of the Scandinavian place-names in Yorkshire are borne by appendant hamlets of discrete estates or by unitary manors. Jones assumes that Scandinavian noblemen took over the estate *foci*, while a relatively small number of their followers were endowed with intermediate rights over appendant hamlets. He is undoubtedly correct in assuming that the Danes tended simply to take over pre-existing territorial arrangements and that they often settled in vills with English names, but probably he underestimates the amount of new colonization and hence the density of the Danish settlement.

The last county whose Scandinavian names have been examined recently is Durham. V. E. Watts notes that the majority of the Scandinavian names in the county are to be found in the only Durham wapentake, that of Sadberge.[3] He assumes that these names arose in conjunction with the Scandinavian settlement in north Yorkshire, probably as a result of secondary colonization from there. There may also have been, however, some Irish-Norwegian settlers who penetrated into the county from Cumberland.

After this survey of the treatment of the Scandinavian place-names in individual areas I turn to some of the more general conclusions that have been reached. Several scholars have emphasized that the Viking settlers often occupied old established villages, sometimes without making any attempt to alter the existing English name. Sven Ulric Palme has noted that Sawyer's early view of Danish colonization on inferior land was indebted to the old view of the Frankish colonization of the land between the Rhine and the Loire 500 years before.[4] Sawyer, however, was not careful to draw

---

[1] *Ibid.* pp. 218–20, and Wilson, 'Archaeological Evidence', p. 292, quoting W. G. Collingwood, *Yorkshire Archaeol. Jnl* 23 (1915), 297.
[2] 'Early Territorial Organization in Northern England and its Bearing on the Scandinavian Settlement', *The Fourth Viking Congress*, ed. Alan Small (Edinburgh, 1965), pp. 67–84.
[3] 'Place-Names', *Durham County and City with Teesside* (Durham, 1970), pp. 251–65, esp. 257–61.
[4] Palme, 'Vikingatågen', p. 228.

the necessary distinction between new colonization in the strict sense and farms which had merely received new owners or tenants.

That the *bý*s belong to an early stage of the Scandinavian settlement has been argued by F. T. Wainwright on the basis of the presence of archaic Scandinavian personal names as first elements of the names in *bý*.[1] By archaic names he means those that became obsolete in England at an early date, but Sawyer has pointed out that many more Scandinavian personal names must have remained in use in England than happen to be recorded in Domesday Book and other eleventh- and twelfth-century sources, and the figures which I have derived from place-names in Lincolnshire and Yorkshire can hardly be used to support Wainwright's argument.[2] Kristian Hald suggests that a good indication of the relative age of a place-name can be given if it contains a personal name which can be shown to have been either archaic or a young formation in the Scandinavian homelands.[3]

Wainwright has also argued that linguistic influence is not necessarily a sure guide to density of population.[4] In a thinly populated area a mere dozen or so Scandinavians might produce an overwhelming linguistic superiority, whereas several hundreds might make far less impression on the place-names of an area that was already thickly populated by Englishmen. It is probably this fact that can answer a question raised by Niels Lund.[5] Lund argues that if the Danish armies had had anything to do with a peasant settlement, Danish place-names should have been found clustering round the boroughs and he considers that the distribution of Danish place-names is evidence of a secondary migration independent of the armies in the boroughs. The lack of Scandinavian place-names round the boroughs, however, may simply reflect the density of the earlier English settlement in these areas.

Sawyer has argued that the spread of Scandinavian place-names into the areas of secondary settlement was due neither to conquest nor to secondary migration but to internal colonization in the tenth and eleventh centuries.[6] The names given to these new settlements simply reflect the Scandinavian influence on English speech. Sawyer suggests that the comparative lack of Scandinavian place-names in Cambridgeshire and Northamptonshire may be due to the fact that the extension of the settled areas in these counties was later, when Scandinavian speech was no longer so influential. Cameron, however, has noted that there is no evidence that the extension of the settled

---

[1] *Archaeology and Place-Names and History*, pp. 78–81.
[2] Sawyer, *The Age of the Vikings*, 1st ed., p. 162, and Fellows Jensen, *Scandinavian Personal Names*, p. xxxiii, n. 5.
[3] 'A Reply to Peter Sawyer on "The Two Viking Ages of Britain"', *Med. Scandinavia* 2 (1969), 185–7, and *Personnavne i Danmark, Oldtiden* (Copenhagen, 1971), pp. 50 and 115.
[4] *Archaeology and Place-Names and History*, pp. 76–7.
[5] 'Secondary Migration', p. 199.
[6] 'The Two Viking Ages', pp. 171–2.

area in these two counties occurred later than in the territory of the Five Boroughs[1] and John Steane has recently argued that not only had the basic settlement pattern in Northamptonshire been laid down by the middle of the eleventh century but also in large parts of the county the cultivated area had reached its maximum extent by then.[2] Approximately eighty-nine per cent of Northamptonshire settlement names are recorded in Domesday Book. This high figure is similar to those quoted by Sawyer for the East and North Ridings of Yorkshire, where Scandinavian settlement names are numerous.[3] I have argued that the Scandinavian place-names in Yorkshire can hardly be the result of a gradual extension of the settled area by internal colonization.[4] The semantic content and linguistic form of the names and the comparative lack of hybrid formations among the names in *bý* and *thorp* indicate that most of the Scandinavian place-names were coined by Viking settlers when they still used their own language in Yorkshire.

Largely as a result of the work on place-names, Sawyer had radically revised his view on the Scandinavian settlement in the second edition of *The Age of the Vikings*.[5] He was now willing to accept both the hybrid names and the *thorp*s as evidence of Scandinavian settlement and wrote, 'The hybrid names...seem to represent an earlier stage of the conquest and colonization than the names in *bý*, which are generally not on such good land, and the names in *bý* are themselves earlier, as a group, than the names in *thorp*.' He still, however, looked upon the extension of the Scandinavian settlements in England as 'the beginning of that process of internal colonization that was to reach its greatest extent in the thirteenth century'. Since then Sawyer's views seem to have changed again and he has recently argued that 'between the coming of the English and the Norman Conquest there was neither a steady and prolonged expansion of the cultivated area nor a general increase in the number of settlements'. He suggests the possibility that many Scandinavian place-names 'mark not so much an extension of settlement as its reorganization under new lords'.[6]

Any study of the Scandinavian place-names in England is complicated by uncertainty as to the degree of mutual intelligibility of Scandinavian and English and as to how long the Scandinavian language survived in use in England. I consider that it is hardly likely that the ninth-century Northumbrians, speaking a West Germanic language, would easily be able to understand Danes and Norwegians speaking a North Germanic one.[7] This is not,

[1] 'Linguistic and Place-Name Evidence', *Med. Scandinavia* 2 (1969), 176–9.
[2] *The Northamptonshire Landscape* (London, 1974), pp. 89–91.
[3] 'Baldersby', pp. 86–7.
[4] *Scandinavian Settlement Names*, pp. 237–45.
[5] Pp. 163 and 174.　　　　　　　　　　[6] 'Baldersby', pp. 92 and 90.
[7] 'The Attitude of the Vikings to English Place-Names in Yorkshire', *Årsberetning for Selskab for nordisk Filologi 1971–73* (Copenhagen, 1975), 5–12.

however, to say that communication would have been impossible without the acquisition of bilingualism. R. I. Page considers it unlikely that the Scandinavian inscriptions found in England represent a continuity of usage from pre-Conquest and Viking times.[1] They are more likely to reflect a new influx of Scandinavian speakers in the tenth and eleventh centuries from areas such as Man, where the language persisted much longer. They stand in marked contrast to other vernacular inscriptions from northern and eastern England in the Viking period. These show a clear continuity of English used in formal style from the eighth century to the eleventh. The contrast with the Isle of Man, where Scandinavian inscriptions are plentiful, is as yet unexplained. Aslak Liestøl has argued that the majority of Viking-Age Scandinavians of any social standing were able to read and write,[2] but the literacy of the Vikings is hardly confirmed by the absence of Scandinavian inscriptions in north-east England.[3] Almost all the written evidence suggests that the Danes very soon adopted English, liberally sprinkled with Scandinavian loan-words, as their normal means of communication. That the Scandinavian language may have survived longer as a spoken tongue is suggested by some scattered evidence. I have noted that post-Domesday Book scribes sometimes Scandinavianized English place-names in both Lincolnshire and Yorkshire.[4] Dietrich Hofmann sees the pronominal form *hanvm* on the Aldbrough sundial as evidence of just how far the blending of the two languages could go in daily life.[5]

The many Scandinavian loan-words in English have been generally accepted as an indication that there was a comparatively large number of Scandinavians resident in England. P. H. Sawyer, however, has referred to Uriel Weinreich's statement that, even for extensive word transferring, large numbers of bilingual speakers need not be involved and the relative size of the groups is not necessarily a factor.[6] It should not be forgotten, however, that, while a small Danish aristocracy could well have imposed its own words for various types of ships and its legal terminology on a numerically superior English population, it is hardly likely that a few aristocratic Danes could have been responsible for the vast number of loan-words which replaced perfectly adequate English words for familiar objects and con-

[1] 'How Long did the Scandinavian Language Survive in England? The Epigraphical Evidence', *England before the Conquest*, ed. Clemoes and Hughes, pp. 165–81, and *An Introduction to English Runes* (London, 1973), esp. ch. 14, 'Anglo-Saxon and Viking', pp. 190–9.

[2] 'The Literate Vikings', *Sixth Viking Congress*, ed. Foote and Strömbäck, pp. 69–78.

[3] Fellows Jensen, 'The Attitude of the Vikings', pp. 7 and 11.

[4] 'The Scribe of the Lindsey Survey', *Namn och Bygd* 57 (1969), 58–74, and *Scandinavian Settlement Names*, pp. 137–9.

[5] *Nordisch-englische Lehnbeziehungen der Wikingerzeit*, Bibliotheca Arnamagnæana 14 (Copenhagen, 1955), §409.

[6] Uriel Weinreich, *Languages in Contact: Findings and Problems* (New York, 1953), p. 92, quoted by Sawyer, *The Age of the Vikings*, 2nd ed., p. 171.

cepts.[1] An interesting side-light on the transmission of loan-words has been cast by Lucien Musset.[2] He has examined a number of terms of English or Anglo-Scandinavian origin which are found in field-names in Normandy. He suggests as a working hypothesis that the Viking chiefs who settled in Normandy in about 930 brought with them a following of peasants, perhaps slaves, that had been recruited in the Danelaw. This onomastic evidence for comings-and-goings between England and Normandy has recently been confirmed by a small coin hoard from Mont-Saint-Michel that can be dated to *c.* 935–*c.* 945.[3]

Standard English contains many Scandinavian loan-words but even more are found in the northern dialects and it might be thought that the dialects would be able to provide supplementary evidence about the distribution and density of the Scandinavian settlements in England. Christian Matras has examined what he calls 'Atlantic vocabulary', that is a number of words which are characteristic of the areas where the Norwegians settled in the Viking period, namely Ireland, Man, parts of Scotland and north England, the Hebrides, the Orkneys and the Shetlands, the Faroes and Iceland.[4] Eduard Kolb has used the distribution of dialect words to show that the northern boundary of the area of intense Scandinavian settlement was approximately from the Solway-Wear to the Tees.[5] The dialect boundaries have remained comparatively stable here. The southern boundary, however, runs from the Lune to the Humber and certainly does not correspond with the southern boundary of the Danelaw, for it excludes the East Midlands and East Anglia, where place-names and historical sources both confirm the presence of Danish settlers. Martyn Wakelin considers that all the Scandinavian dialect words originally had a much wider distribution in a southerly direction.[6] These words have tended to recede northwards with the passage of time and the increasing prestige of Standard English. Many of them have receded as far as the Humber–Ribble boundary, which is the oldest and most stable dialect boundary in England, going back to the time before the Viking invasions. The Humber, of course, was not only a dialect boundary but also a traditional political frontier. In discussing the difference between the York Viking kingdom and the rest of the Danelaw A. L. Binns notes that southern monarchs would have been more sensitive to

[1] Fellows Jensen, 'The Attitude of the Vikings', pp. 9–10.

[2] 'Pour l'Étude des Relations entre les Colonies Scandinaves d'Angleterre et de Normandie', *Mélanges de Linguistique et de Philologie Fernand Mossé in Memoriam* (Paris, 1959), pp. 330–9.

[3] Michael Dolley and Jacques Yvon, 'A Group of Tenth-Century Coins Found at Mont-Saint-Michel', *BNJ* 40 (1971), 1–16.

[4] 'Atlantssiðir – Atlantsorð', *Fróðskaparrit* 7 (Tórshavn, 1958), 73–101.

[5] 'Skandinavisches in den nordenglischen Dialekten', *Anglia* 83 (1965), 127–53.

[6] *English Dialects: an Introduction* (London, 1972), esp. 'The Scandinavian Element', pp. 130–8.

any alien independence south of it than north of it.[1] It would also have been fraught with more danger and difficulty to face the Vikings north of the Humber. Even after the English kings had recovered Northumbria, they still seem to have regarded it as a threat to their security. Dorothy Whitelock has examined their policy and noted how very frequently they appointed as archbishop of York and as earl of Northumbria men who had connections with the eastern Danelaw.[2] Such men would be familiar with the Anglo-Danish language and customs and yet unlikely to work for Northumbrian independence.

The attitude of the Vikings to Christianity has already been touched on in the discussion of the stone sculpture and that of the Christians to the Vikings in the discussion of the written sources. There are, however, other sources of information about the contact of heathenism with Christianity. Excavations of monastery sites have confirmed that the chronicles are correct in stating that the first contacts of the Vikings with Christianity were violent.[3] Ninth-century Viking graves from Norway contain loot from England, including objects of Christian significance taken from churches or abbeys. The Vikings could also have a less directly detrimental influence on Christianity. Nora Chadwick has noted that in Ireland there was a change in the economic status of the scholar and scribe during the Viking age and this resulted in the migration of scholars with their books to the continent, not to hide from the Vikings but in search of an atmosphere of security and a wealthy lay patronage.[4]

After the early raids the Vikings do not seem to have been aggressively antagonistic to Christianity. R. I. Page has pointed out that the dispossessed community of St Cuthbert could wander at will throughout the Viking area before finally settling at Chester-le-Street.[5] Kathleen Hughes has noted that contact between the churches in England and Ireland continued into the tenth century in spite of Viking raids, which might be expected to have made the voyages difficult and dangerous.[6] The heathen Viking religion was without any firm central organization and its generally pantheistic nature probably made it easy for its adherents to accept the Christian God, particularly since Anglo-Saxon writers endowed Christ with such markedly heroic attributes.[7] The church in its turn may have accepted some of the Norse

---

[1] *The Viking Century in East Yorkshire*, East Yorkshire Local Hist. Ser. 15 (1963), 24.
[2] 'The Dealings of the Kings of England with Northumbria in the Tenth and Eleventh Centuries', *The Anglo-Saxons*, ed. Clemoes, pp. 70–88.
[3] Wilson, 'Vikings' Relationship', pp. 37–8, and 'Archaeological Evidence', p. 302.
[4] 'The Vikings and the Western World', p. 42.
[5] Noted by Wilson, 'Vikings' Relationship', pp. 45–6.
[6] 'Evidence for Contacts between the Churches of the Irish and English from the Synod of Whitby to the Viking Age', *England before the Conquest*, ed. Clemoes and Hughes, pp. 49–67, esp. 65–7.
[7] Wilson, 'Vikings' Relationship', p. 46.

religious legends and used them to illustrate the fall of the pagan gods and Christ's defeat of the devil. From passive acceptance of Christianity the Viking settlers and their descendants progressed fairly quickly to a more active participation in the Christian life. In the Isle of Man, for example, the Scandinavian settlers became at least formally Christian by the middle of the tenth century, when the first memorial crosses and cross-slabs appear.[1] Memorial crosses were also raised in northern England and the Scandinavian settlers even began to build churches. Churches dedicated to St Olave were founded in Chester, York, Exeter, Southwark, Chichester, Grimsby and London.[2] On the site of St Mary Castlegate in York have been found the remnants of a tenth- or eleventh-century dedication slab of a church whose founders bear Viking names.[3] Orm Gamalsson, whose name suggests Viking parentage, bought and restored the church of St Gregory in Kirkdale, Yorkshire, between 1055 and 1065.[4]

It has even been argued that the Christianized Danes of the Danelaw were influential in the conversion of the Danish homeland.[5] Olaf Olsen points out that the English and Danish churches share several features which distinguish them from the church on the continent.[6] Several of these features may have been introduced into Denmark by Cnut and his Anglo-Saxon bishops and priests, however, and it is difficult to determine whether English influence had been marked in the earlier period. Olsen argues that many of the English loan-words in Danish ecclesiastical language were borrowed at a very early date, for they denote liturgical objects in daily use and some of the most essential theological concepts. Peter Skautrup has pointed out, however, that it is often difficult to be sure whether a word is of English or Saxon origin and even some of the clearly English words may have been introduced at second-hand by the Saxons.[7]

Although some of the problems presented by the various kinds of evidence for the Viking raids and settlement have remained unsolved, general agreement has been reached on a number of points. It seems that the motive force behind the Danish Vikings was not land-hunger but plunder. The partition of England and the settlements there did not take place until other forms of exploitation had been exhausted. The fleets and armies in the early period were comparatively small but those of Swein and Cnut were probably larger and more highly organized. Sawyer still thinks that the number of settlers

[1] David M. Wilson, 'Manx Memorial Stones of the Viking Period', *SBVS* 18 (1970–1), 1–18.
[2] Dodgson, 'Place-Names and Street-Names', p. 52.
[3] Cramp, *Anglian and Viking York*, p. 21, and E. Okasha, *Hand-List of Anglo-Saxon Non-Runic Inscriptions* (Cambridge, 1971), p. 131.
[4] Okasha, *Hand-List*, pp. 87–8.
[5] Gwyn Jones, *A History of the Vikings* (London, 1968), pp. 126 and 424.
[6] 'Die alte Gesellschaft und die neue Kirche', *Acta Visbyensia* 3 (1967), 43–54.
[7] *Det danske Sprogs Historie* I (Copenhagen, 1944), 168–73.

has been greatly exaggerated and that they were hardly more than a dominant minority. While acknowledging that the distribution of sokemen in eleventh-century England cannot be used as an indication of the settlement of the rank-and-file of the Danish army, most other scholars are agreed that the number of settlers was considerable. On the whole it seems that the most satisfactory explanation for the numerous Scandinavian place-names is Cameron's theory of a secondary migration from Denmark. The original armies can hardly have been responsible alone for all the villages with Scandinavian names, particularly since the Vikings also settled in old established English villages.

The present review has revealed that not all the points made by Stenton in favour of a dense Scandinavian settlement have survived the scholarly assaults of the past twenty years. His picture of the social, administrative, legal and economic effects of the Viking invasions and settlement has been radically revised, but his general thesis that there was a large number of settlers has been confirmed by the evidence of place- and personal names. A number of questions still remain to be answered, but there is every hope that further research and continuing co-operation between historians, archaeologists, numismatists and philologists in Scandinavia and the British Isles will lead to their solution.[1]

[1] For advice, assistance and encouragement in the preparation of this review I am indebted to Michael Dolley, Jørgen Steen Jensen, R. I. Page, Else Roesdahl, P. H. Sawyer and J. A. B. Townsend.

Short titles of Old English texts

BRUCE MITCHELL, CHRISTOPHER BALL
and ANGUS CAMERON

This is the list referred to by Helmut Gneuss in his 'Guide to the Editing and Preparation of Texts for the Dictionary of Old English', *A Plan for the Dictionary of Old English*, ed. R. Frank and A. Cameron (Toronto, 1973), pp. 9–23.[1] The list has been prepared for use in *The Dictionary of Old English* and in *Old English Syntax* now in preparation by Bruce Mitchell, and will (the compilers dare to hope) replace previous systems, including F. P. Magoun Jr's 'Abbreviated Titles for the Poems of the Anglo-Saxon Poetic Corpus'.[2] It will be used in *Anglo-Saxon England* where appropriate.

THE CONVENTIONS

References to texts

Three ways of making the initial reference to a particular text presented themselves – by manuscript (following the numbers in N. R. Ker, *Catalogue of Manuscripts Containing Anglo-Saxon* (Oxford, 1957)), by the name of the editor(s) of the standard edition or by the name of the text. The last was felt to be more convenient than the manuscript and more lasting than the name of the editor(s). But it was recognized that provision had to be made for reference to a particular manuscript or edition.[3]

This system worked without difficulty for the books of the bible and for verse texts. But when we turned to other prose texts, to glosses and to inscriptions it became clear that any list of abbreviations which attempted to distinguish by name each passage of Old English down to the shortest would be intolerably cumbersome and that for many less familiar items reference would have to be made to 'A List of Old English Texts' by Angus Cameron (*Plan*, pp. 25–306), which – with the necessary amendments – will

---

[1] Hereafter referred to as *Plan*.

[2] *Études Anglaises* 8 (1955), 138–46. This list has won little acceptance, probably because Magoun sacrificed too many familiar abbreviations. The device of a uniformly three-letter abbreviation lost its attractiveness because it could not be carried out effectively for the prose and glosses. But the article still offers a useful system of cross-reference between the Bibliothek der angelsächsischen Poesie and The Anglo-Saxon Poetic Records.

[3] See below.

form part of the apparatus of the *Dictionary*. So the short titles for these texts are followed by the appropriate Cameron reference number.

Widely accepted abbreviations for individual texts, such as *Bede* and *Or*, have of course been retained. To reduce the number of abbreviations, to make them as short as possible and to facilitate comparison of like with like, blanket short titles have been adopted for series of texts. Thus *HomS* 1–50 stands for Cameron B3.2.1–3.2.50 'Homilies for Specified Occasions' and *Scrib* 1–3.41 for Cameron B27.1–27.3.41 'Directions to Readers; Scribbles'. The more obvious short title will be adopted for texts which are double listed under separate headings by Cameron (*Plan*, p. 27) – thus Cambridge, Corpus Christi College 41, listed in *Plan* as B3.2.29 and B8.5.3, will be cited as *Nic(D)* rather than *HomS* 29 – and for texts which, though in a series, have been given their own short titles – thus for Cameron B12.7 *The Benedictine Office LitBen* will be preferred to *Lit* 7.

Readers will find that many familiar abbreviations have gone – thus *VP(s)* (the Vespasian Psalter) becomes *Ps(A)* – and that (abbreviations for) the names of editors appear only in the special circumstances outlined below. The first draft of this list was criticized on both these counts. On the first, the compilers felt that the preferences of established scholars were of less account than the three objectives enunciated in the preceding paragraph. On the second, they can only say that they tried a system which incorporated references to the names of editors, but the resulting list contained considerably more abbreviations than the present one and many of them were intolerably long. The whole basis of the proposed system is that reference to Cameron's 'List' – which, as already noted, will form part of the first fascicle of the *Dictionary* – is inevitable for everything except the poetry and a few well-known prose texts.

In the case of texts already edited, the edition to which reference is to be made will be specified in the final form of Cameron's 'List', but normally the short title will not contain (an abbreviation for) the name of the editor. When a passage is quoted from these texts, the appropriate reference (by page and line number *or* by item and line number; see below) will follow. Thus *HomU* 21.5.11 will refer the reader to page 5 line 11 of Napier's *Wulfstan...Homilien* (Cameron B3.4.21) and *ÆHom* 3.89 will refer him to line 89 of homily III in Pope's *Homilies of Ælfric* (Cameron 1.4.3). When there is a conflict between the Cameron number of an item and that in the specified edition, the former will prevail. Thus *HomS* 22.101 refers to line 101 of Assmann's homily XIII (Cameron B3.2.22).

When a later publication supplements an earlier standard edition (an obvious abbreviation for) the name of the editor of the later work may be added to the short title. Thus in the case of Cameron B1.8.6 'Ælfric's Letter to Wulfgeat', *ÆLet* 6 will refer the reader to Assmann's text and *ÆLet Pope* 6 to that of Pope. The addition of (an abbreviation for) the editor's name will be obligatory when there is no complete edition of a particular text. Thus Cameron B9.7 'Alcuin, *De Virtutibus et Vitiis*' will be referred to as *AlcAss*, *Alcförst*, or *AlcWarn*, as appropriate.

Texts for which new editions are in progress will be cited from the edition(s) specified in the 'List' until there is a better one. Texts at present unedited have been given short titles. So Cameron B3.2.37 'Homily for Tuesday in Rogationtide' (Ker 331 art. 55) is *HomS* 37. In some cases reference to the manuscript by title and folio number may be necessary in the early fascicles of the *Dictionary*. When a new or revised edition of a text is published, some distinguishing mark will be added to the existing short title. This will usually take the form of (an abbreviation for) the name of the new editor or of the reviser. If the original editor is responsible, the edition number will be denoted by an arabic numeral in round brackets after the existing title.[1]

Any changes made while the *Dictionary* is in production will be noted in the appropriate fascicle and will be consolidated in a final 'List of Short Titles' when the *Dictionary* is complete.

References to different versions and/or manuscripts

Capital letters without brackets after an abbreviation indicate separate items which are always distinguished, e.g. *GenA* and *GenB*.

When an abbreviation is followed by a capital letter (either alone or with other letters) inside round brackets, a particular manuscript of the text in question is being designated. The symbols for the manuscripts are those used by the editor of the edition to which reference is made, apart from the psalms and gospels, on which, see below. The degree of difference between versions of the same text varies widely and the editors of the *Dictionary* are at the moment unable to decide in every case whether or not a variant version needs to be concorded and quoted separately. So a flexible system has been adopted. When *Brun* appears alone, the reference is to the text of *The Battle of Brunanburh* printed in volume 6 of The Anglo-Saxon Poetic Records. But if necessary a reference can be made to a particular manuscript by the addition of the letter *(A)*, *(B)*, *(C)* or *(D)*, as appropriate. *Mutatis mutandis* the same system applies throughout. Thus in the case of *CP* (*Cura Pastoralis*), where Sweet prints two versions, the Cotton and the Hatton manuscripts can be distinguished as *CP(C)* and *CP(H)*, although normally

---

[1] It is desirable that future editors give marginal references to the edition which they (hope to) supersede; see Bruce Mitchell's comments on this point in *Computers and Old English Concordances*, ed. Angus Cameron, Roberta Frank and John Leyerle (Toronto, 1970), p. 86.

the page reference will suffice. *Bede* will refer to the text of Bede's *Ecclesiastical History* printed by Miller; *Bede(T)*, *Bede(C)*, *Bede(B)*, *Bede(O)* and *Bede(Ca)* designate the various manuscripts. In texts such as Gregory's *Dialogues*, where MSS *C* and *H* appear on the same page when both are extant, they and MS *O* can be distinguished when necessary, but page and line reference will suffice when the extant manuscripts agree on the point in question.

References to editions

Roman numerals – I, II or i, ii, according to the choice of the publisher concerned – refer to volume numbers except in the abbreviations for the titles of those poems whose title includes a roman numeral. Arabic numerals are used for sequences of separate texts, such as the charters, homilies, riddles and psalms.

For continuous prose texts references are by page and line. When a prose text consists of a number of separated items numbered continuously from beginning to end, the reference is given by piece and line number; an example is Pope's *Homilies of Ælfric* (EETS 259 and 260). When this is not possible – as in Napier's *Wulfstan*, where the line numbers begin afresh on each page, and in Morris's *Blickling Homilies*, where no line numbers are given – page and line number are used.

For the bible, references are by chapter and verse. For runic inscriptions, non-runic inscriptions and charters, the reference will be to the item number in R. I. Page's projected edition of the runes, E. Okasha's *Hand-List of Anglo-Saxon Non-Runic Inscriptions* (Cambridge, 1971) and P. H. Sawyer's *Anglo-Saxon Charters* (London, 1968) respectively. Legal references follow the system used by F. Liebermann in *Die Gesetze der Angelsachsen* (Halle, 1903–16).

The charters present a special problem because there is no one complete edition. For short charters the Sawyer numbers will suffice, but something more may be needed for longer ones. Where this is so, an editorial designation will be added after the charter number according to the following system.

B	*Cartularium Saxonicum*, ed. W. de Gray Birch
BMFacs	*Facsimiles of Ancient Charters in the British Museum*, ed. E. A. Bond
H	*Select English Historical Documents of the Ninth and Tenth Centuries*, ed. F. E. Harmer
Ha	*Anglo-Saxon Writs*, ed. F. E. Harmer
K	*Codex Diplomaticus Ævi Saxonici*, ed. J. M. Kemble
N	*The Crawford Collection of Early Charters and Documents*, ed. A. S. Napier and W. H. Stevenson
OSFacs	*Facsimiles of Anglo-Saxon Manuscripts*, ed. W. B. Sanders

R   *Anglo-Saxon Charters*, ed. A. J. Robertson
W   *Anglo-Saxon Wills*, ed. D. Whitelock

and so on, as necessary. References such as *Ch* 1188 *H* 2.11 (page 2 line 11 of Harmer's *Select Documents*) and *Ch* 1428 *Ha* 113.40 (line 40 of charter 113 in Harmer's *Writs*) will then be possible.

The poems are cited according to the lineation of The Anglo-Saxon Poetic Records or, in the case of the few poems not found there, according to the lineation of the editions specified in the list. With the charms, *Metres* and riddles, the item number precedes the line number. In the Paris Psalter, of course, the reference is by psalm and verse.

In the last four sections of the list the name of the editor from whose edition the work is quoted is given where possible. An asterisk against a particular text indicates that it is as yet unedited. Where there is more than one edition of a text or when the short title refers to a series of texts, the abbreviation 'ed' is used to signify 'editor(s) or (in the case of unedited texts) manuscript(s) listed in the *Plan*'.

THE LIST

The list aims at covering all known sources of Old English, but it would be more than surprising if there were no errors, omissions, inconsistencies or practical difficulties in the list as it stands. Criticisms or suggestions will be gratefully received by any one of the three signatories.

For ease of initial presentation and absorption, and for the convenience of those using only one type of text, the abbreviations are presented in seven separate sections. These lists will, of course, be conflated for ease of reference before publication of the works in which they are to be used.

Short titles may be italicized or not, according to the practice of the publisher concerned. No full stops will be used.

General abbreviations

Æ   Ælfric (to precede all his works)[1]
Ca   Canticle
Ch   Charter
Cr   Cross
Ep   Epilogue
Fr   Fragment
Gl   Gloss/Glossary

---

[1] For the attribution, see P. A. M. Clemoes, 'The Chronology of Ælfric's Works', *The Anglo-Saxons: Studies in some Aspects of their History and Culture presented to Bruce Dickins*, ed. Peter Clemoes (London, 1959).

Hom	Homily/Homiletic
Hy	Hymn
Lit	Liturgy/Liturgical
LS	Life/Lives of Saint(s)
M	(when used initially) Metrical
Pr	Prayer
Pref	Preface
Prov	Proverb
Ps	Psalm/Psalter
R	Rule
Rid	Riddle
W	Wulfstan (to precede all his works)[1]

These general abbreviations may be combined to form such references as *PsCa(J)* for Cameron C11.4 'Canticles in the Arundel Psalter'.

Books of the bible[2]

Gen[3]	*Deut*	*Matt/Mt*
Exod	*Josh*[3]	*Mark/Mk*
Lev	*Judg*[3]	*Luke/Lk*
Num[3]	*Ps*	*John/Jn*

The final choice of the abbreviations for the four gospels will depend on the publisher concerned.

For the Heptateuch, reference to the manuscripts will be by means of the abbreviations set out by S. J. Crawford, *The Old English Version of the Heptateuch*, EETS 160, 1, and by C. and K. Sisam, *The Salisbury Psalter*, EETS 242, ix–x. So *Ps(A)* = the Vespasian Psalter, *Ps(F)* = the Stowe Psalter, and *Ps(P)* = the prose psalms of the Paris Psalter.

For the gospels the following system will obtain:

Li	Lindisfarne Gospels
Ru1	Rushworth Gospels (Mercian)
Ru2	Rushworth Gospels (Northumbrian)
WS	West Saxon Gospels
WSA	Cambridge, University Library, Ii. 2. 11
WSB	Oxford, Bodleian Library, Bodley 441
WSC	BM Cotton Otho C. i
WSCp	Cambridge, Corpus Christi College 140
WSH	Oxford, Bodleian Library, Hatton 38
WSR	BM Royal 1. A. xiv

[1] For the attribution, see *The Homilies of Wulfstan*, ed. Dorothy Bethurum (Oxford, 1957).
[2] Details of those portions extant in Old English will be found in B8 'Biblical Translations', *Plan*, pp. 116–18.
[3] For details of the portions attributed to Ælfric, see *Plan*, p. 84.

Thus *Matt(Li)* or *Mt(Li)* means the Lindisfarne version of St Matthew and *Mark(WSH)* or *Mk(WSH)* the West Saxon version of St Mark in Hatton 38.

Verse texts

References consisting of a roman numeral followed by an arabic one are to volume and page number in The Anglo-Saxon Poetic Records

Aldhelm	Aldhelm (VI. 97)
Alms	Alms-Giving (III. 223)
And	Andreas (II. 3)
Az	Azarias (III. 88)
BDS	Bede's Death Song (VI. 107)
Beo	Beowulf (IV. 3)
Brun	Battle of Brunanburh (VI. 16)
BrussCr	Brussels Cross (VI. 115)
Cæd	Cædmon's Hymn (VI. 105)
Capt	Capture of the Five Boroughs (VI. 20)
CEdg	Coronation of Edgar (VI. 21)
ChristA	Christ (III. 3), lines 1–439
ChristB	Christ (III. 15), lines 440–866
ChristC	Christ (III. 27), lines 867–1664
Cnut	Cnut's Song (*Liber Eliensis*, ed. E. O. Blake, R. Hist. Soc., Camden Soc. 3rd ser. 92 (London, 1962), 153)
CPEp	The Metrical Epilogue to the Pastoral Care (VI. 111)
CPPref	The Metrical Preface to the Pastoral Care (VI. 110)
Creed	Creed (VI. 78)
DAlf	Death of Alfred (VI. 24)
Dan	Daniel (I. 111)
DEdg	Death of Edgar (VI. 22)
DEdw	Death of Edward (VI. 25)
Deor	Deor (III. 178)
Dream	Dream of the Rood (II. 61)
Dur	Durham (VI. 27)
El	Elene (II. 66)
Exhort	Exhortation to Christian Living (VI. 67)
Exo	Exodus (I. 91)
Fates	Fates of the Apostles (II. 51)
Finn	Battle of Finnsburh (VI. 3)
Fort	Fortunes of Men (III. 154)
FrCask	The Franks Casket (VI. 116)

GDPref	Metrical Preface to Gregory's Dialogues (VI. 112)
GenA	Genesis (I. 1), lines 1–234 and 852–2936
GenB	Genesis (I. 9), lines 235–851
Gifts	Gifts of Men (III. 137)
Glor I	Gloria I (VI. 74)
Glor II	Gloria II (VI. 94)
Godric	Godric's Prayer (*EStn* 11 (1888), 423)
Grave	The Grave (*Erlanger Beiträge zur englischen Philologie* 2 (1890), 11)
GuthA	Guthlac (III. 49), lines 1–818
GuthB	Guthlac (III. 72), lines 819–1379
Hell	Descent into Hell (III. 219)
HomFr I	Homiletic Fragment I (II. 59)
HomFr II	Homiletic Fragment II (III. 224)
Husb	Husband's Message (III. 225)
Instr	Instructions for Christians (*Anglia* 82 (1964), 4)
JDay I	Judgement Day I (III. 212)
JDay II	Judgement Day II (VI. 58)
Jud	Judith (IV. 99)
Jul	Juliana (III. 113)
Kenelm	Distich on Kenelm (N. R. Ker, *Catalogue of Manuscripts Containing Anglo-Saxon* (Oxford, 1957), p. 124)
KtHy	Kentish Hymn (VI. 87)
KtPs	Psalm 50 (VI. 88)
LEProv	Latin–English Proverbs (VI. 109)
Loth	Distich on the Sons of Lothebrok (N. R. Ker, *Catalogue of Manuscripts Containing Anglo-Saxon* (Oxford, 1957), p. 124)
LPr I	Lord's Prayer I (III. 223)
LPr II	Lord's Prayer II (VI. 70)
LPr III	Lord's Prayer III (VI. 77)
LRid	Leiden Riddle (VI. 109)
Mald	Battle of Maldon (VI. 7)
Max I	Maxims I (III. 156)
Max II	Maxims II (VI. 55)
MCharm	Metrical Charms (VI. 116)
Men	Menologium (VI. 49)
MEp	Metrical Epilogue to MS 41 (VI. 113)
Met	Metres of Boethius (V. 153)

MRune	Rune Poem (VI. 28)
MSol	Solomon and Saturn (VI. 31)
OrW	Order of the World (III. 163)
Pan	Panther (III. 169)
Part	Partridge (III. 174)
Pha	Pharaoh (III. 223)
Phoen	Phoenix (III. 94)
PPs	Metrical Psalms of the Paris Psalter (V. 3)
Pr	A Prayer (VI. 94)
Prec	Precepts (III. 140)
PsFr	Fragments of Psalms (VI. 80)
Res	Resignation (III. 215)
Rid	Riddles (III. 180, 224, 225 and 229)
Rim	Riming Poem (III. 166)
Ruin	Ruin (III. 227)
RuthCr	Ruthwell Cross (VI. 115)
Sat	Christ and Satan (I. 135)
Sea	Seafarer (III. 143)
Seasons	Seasons for Fasting (VI. 98)
Soul I	Soul and Body I (II. 54)
Soul II	Soul and Body II (III. 174)
Summons	A Summons to Prayer (VI. 69)
Thureth	Thureth (VI. 97)
Vain	Vainglory (III. 147)
Wald	Waldere (VI. 4)
Wan	Wanderer (III. 134)
Whale	Whale (III. 171)
Wid	Widsith (III. 149)
Wife	Wife's Lament (III. 210)
Winfrid	A Proverb from Winfrid's Time (VI. 57)
Wulf	Wulf and Eadwacer (III. 179)

Prose texts

Reference, in this and subsequent sections, is by page and line unless otherwise specified

Short title	Reference number	Identifying title	Reference to edition by
Ad	B5.2	Adrian and Ritheus	Kemble
ÆAbus	B1.6.2	De duodecim abusivis	Morris
ÆAdmon 1–3	B1.9.3, 1.9.6, 1.9.7	Admonitions	ed
ÆCHom I, II	B1.1, 1.2	Catholic Homilies	Thorpe (by homily and line)
ÆCreat	B1.6.4	De creatore et creatura	*
ÆEtat	B1.6.5	De sex etatibus mundi	*
ÆGl	B1.9.2	Glossary	ed
ÆGram	B1.9.1	Grammar	Zupitza
ÆHex	B1.5.13	Hexameron	Crawford
ÆHom 1–31	B1.4.1–31	Homilies of Ælfric	Pope (by homily and line)
ÆHomM 1–12, 14, 15	B1.5.1–12, 14, 15	Miscellaneous homilies by Ælfric	ed (where possible, by homily and line)
ÆIntSig	B1.6.1	Interrogationes Sigewulfi in Genesin	MacLean
ÆLet 1–3	B1.8.1–1.8.3	Letters	Fehr (by letter and sentence)
ÆLet 4	B1.8.4	Letter	Crawford (by line)
ÆLet 5–7	B1.8.5–1.8.7	Letters	ed
ÆLS	B1.3	Lives of Saints	Skeat (by life and line)
ÆSpir	B1.6.3	De septiformi spiritu	Napier
ÆTemp	B1.9.4	De temporibus anni	Henel
Alc	B9.7	Alcuin, De virtutibus et vitiis	ed
Alex	B22.1	Alexander's Letter to Aristotle	Rypins
ApT	B4.1	Apollonius of Tyre	Goolden
Aug	B9.8	Augustine	Warner
Bede	B9.6	Bede, History of the English Church and Nation	Miller

Short title	Reference number	Identifying title	Reference to edition by
BenR	B10.3.1	Benedictine Rule	Schröer
BenRW	B10.3.4	Benedictine Rule, Winteney version	Schröer
BlHom	B3.1.1	The Blickling Homilies	Morris
Bo	B9.3	Boethius, The Consolation of Philosophy	Sedgefield
ByrM	B20.20.1	Byrhtferth's Manual	Crawford
Cb	B15	Charters in English	Sawyer (by charter number)
Charm 1–18	B23.1.1–23.1.18	Prose charms and charm headings	ed
ChrodR	B10.4	Chrodegang, Regula canonicorum	Napier
Chron	B17	Chronicles and historical texts	Earle and Plummer (by letter, page and line, annal, e.g. ChronA 94.1 (905))
Comp 1.1–19	B20.1.1–20.19	Computus	ed
Conf 1.1–11	B11.1.1–11.1.11	Confessional and penitential texts	ed
ConR	B10.7	Rules of confraternity	Birch
CP	B9.1	Gregory the Great, The Pastoral Care	Sweet
Crypt 1, 2	B26.1, 26.2	Cryptograms	Förster
Days 1–6	B23.2.1–23.2.6	Tables of lucky and unlucky days	ed
Eluc	B9.9	Honorius of Autun, Elucidarium	Warner
GD	B9.5	Gregory the Great, Dialogues	Hecht
HomM 1–15	B3.5.1–3.5.15	Miscellaneous homilies	ed (where possible, by homily and line)
HomS 1–50	B3.2.1–3.2.50	Homilies for specified occasions	ed (where possible, by homily and line)
HomU 1–57	B3.4.1–3.4.57	Homilies for unspecified occasions	ed (where possible, by homily and line)
KSB 1–11	B18.1–18.11	Lists of kings, saints and bishops	ed
KtLS	B17.10	Kentish royal saints	Förster

Short title	Reference number	Identifying title	Reference to edition by
Lap	B22.3	Lapidary	Evans and Serjeantson
Law	B14	Laws of England	Liebermann (by his system, e.g. *Law* II *Cn* 19.2)
LawF	B14.56	Ymb æbricas	Flower
Lcb I, II, III	B21 et al.	Medical and other texts in Cockayne	Cockayne
Leof	B4.2	Vision of Leofric	Napier
Lett 1-3	B6.1-6.3	Letters	ed
Lit 1.1-11	B12.1.1-12.11	Liturgical texts, creeds and prayers	ed
LitBen	B12.7	Benedictine Office	Ure
LS 1-35	B3.3.1-3.3.35	Sanctorale	ed (where possible, by life and line)
Mart 1-6	B19.1-19.6	Martyrology	ed
Marv	B22.2	The Marvels of the East	Rypins
Med 1.1-5.9	B21.1.1-21.5.9	Medical texts	ed
MsRune 1.1-4.4	B25.1.1-25.4.4	Runic texts	ed
Name 1.1-7	B28.1.1-28.7	Colophons, inscriptions and names	ed
Nic		The Gospel of Nicodemus	
Nic(A)	B8.5.2	Cambridge, University Library, Ii. 2. 11	Hulme
Nic(B)	B8.5.2	BM Cotton Vitellius A. xv	Hulme
Nic(C)	B8.5.3	BM Cotton Vespasian D. xiv	Hulme
Nic(D)	B3.2.29	Cambridge, Corpus Christi College 41	Hulme
Nic(E)	B3.2.29	Cambridge, Corpus Christi College 303	Hulme
Notes 1-26.3	B24.1-24.26.3	Notes and commonplaces	ed
Or	B9.2	Orosius, History of the World	Sweet
PrBl	B23.4	Prohibition against blood-letting	Henel
Prog 1-6	B23.3.1-23.3.6	Prognostics	ed
Prov 1-4	B7.1-7.4	Proverbs	ed

Short title	Reference number	Identifying title	Reference to edition by
Rec 1–26.3	B16.1–16.26.3	Records	ed
RegC 1, 2	B10.5.1, 10.5.2	Regularis concordia	Zupitza, Schröer
Scrib 1–3.41	B27.1–27.3.41	Directions to readers; Scribbles	ed
Sol	B5.1	Solomon and Saturn	Kemble
Solil	B9.4	St Augustine, Soliloquies	Endter
StWulf	B17.12	Wulfstan II of Worcester	Thorpe
TbCap 1, **2**	B10.6.1, 10.6.2	Theodulf of Orleans, Capitula	ed
VercHom 1–8	B3.1.2	The Vercelli Homilies	Förster (by homily and line)
VercHom 9–23	B3.1.2	The Vercelli Homilies	*
VSal	B8.5.4	Vindicta salvatoris	ed
WCan 1.1, 2	B.13.1.1, 13.1.2	Canons of Edgar	Fowler, *
WHom	B2.1–2.4	Wulfstan's Homilies	Bethurum (by homily and line)
WPol	B13.2–13.6	Institutes of Polity	Jost

Continuous interlinear and occasional glosses

Short title	Reference number	Identifying title	Reference to edition by
Abbo 1, 2	C1.1, 1.2	Abbo of St Germain, Bella Parisiacae urbis	ed
AldÆ 1–5	C33.1–33.5	Aldhelm, Ænigmata	ed
AldMV 1–6	C32.1–32.6	Aldhelm, De laude virginum (verse)	ed
AldV 1–14	C31.1–31.14	Aldhelm, De laude virginitatis (prose) and Epistola ad Ehfridum	ed
ArPrGl 1–3	C23.1–23.3	Prayers	ed
BenRGl	C4	Benedictine Rule	ed
BenRGl 1–3	C48.1–48.3	Benedictine Rule	Logeman
BoGl	C9	Boethius, De consolatione philosophiae	ed
BonGl	C10	Boniface IV, Letter	ed
ChrodRGl	C57	Rule of Chrodegang of Metz	Rosier
Coll	C3	Ælfric, Colloquy	Meritt / Garmonsway

Short title	Reference number	Identifying title	Reference to edition by
ConfGl	C14	Form of confession	Förster
CuthGl 1-7	C47.1-47.7	Bede, Vita S. Cuthberhti (verse)	ed
DProv	C25	Proverbs	Arngart
FulGl	C17	Fulgentius, Injunction	*
GuthGl 1-4	C66.1-66.4	Felix, Vita S. Guthlaci	ed
HyGl 1-4	C18.1-18.4	Hymns	ed
IsGl	C19	Isidore, De miraculis Christi	Napier
LibSc	C6, 15, 20	Defensor, Liber scintillarum	Rhodes
LorGl 1, 2	C22, 83	Lorica of Gildas	ed
Mem	C5	Benedict of Aniane, Memoriale	Napier
MonCa	C12	Monastic canticles	*
OccGl 28-98.2	C28-98.2	Occasional glosses	ed
ProgGl	C16	Prognostics	ed
ProspGl	C24	Prosper, Epigrammata and Versus ad coniugem	Wright-Wülcker
PrudGl 1-9	C94.1-94.9	Prudentius, Psychomachia	ed
PrudT	C26	Prudentius, Psychomachia titles	Zupitza
PsCa	C11	Canticles of the psalter	ed
RegCGl	C27	Regularis concordia	Logeman
RitGl	C2, 13, 21	Rituale ecclesiae Dunelmensis	Thompson and Lindelöf (by page and line, OE and Latin counting as one)
SedGl 1-5	C97.1-97.5	Sedulius, Carmen paschale	ed
		Collected Latin–Old English glosses	
ÆGl	B1.9.2, D10	Ælfric's glossary	Zupitza, *
AntGl	D1	Antwerp glossary	ed
BrGl	D2	Brussels glossary	ed

220

Short title	Reference number	Identifying title	Reference to edition by
CIGl	D8	Cleopatra glossary	ed
CollGl 1–59	D1–59	Latin–Old English glossaries	ed
CorpGl	D4	Corpus glossary	ed
DurGl	D6	Durham glossary	ed
EpGl	D7	Epinal glossary	ed
ErfGl	D36	Erfurt glossary	ed
HlGl	D16.1–16.3	Harley glossary	ed
LdGl	D41	Leiden glossary	ed

Inscriptions

NRune 1–60	F1–60	Vernacular inscriptions in the Latin alphabet	Okasha (by number)
Rune 1–53	E1–53	Runic inscriptions	Page (by number)

Bibliography for 1974

MARTIN BIDDLE, ALAN BROWN, T. J. BROWN,
PETER A. CLAYTON and PETER HUNTER BLAIR

This bibliography is meant to include all books, articles and significant reviews published in any branch of Anglo-Saxon studies during 1974. It excludes reprints unless they contain new material. It will be continued annually. Addenda to the previous bibliographies are included at the appropriate places; one that concerns a book or article is preceded by an asterisk and specifies the year of publication. A.B. has been mainly responsible for sections 2, 3 and 4, T.J.B. for section 5, P.H.B. for section 6, P.A.C. for section 7 and M.B. for section 8. Peter Clemoes has been coordinating editor.

The following abbreviations are used where relevant (not only in the bibliography but also throughout the volume):

AB	*Analecta Bollandiana*
ABR	*American Benedictine Review*
AHR	*American Historical Review*
AntJ	*Antiquaries Journal*
ArchJ	*Archaeological Journal*
ASE	*Anglo-Saxon England*
ASNSL	*Archiv für das Studium der neueren Sprachen und Literaturen*
BGDSL	*Beiträge zur Geschichte der deutschen Sprache und Literatur*
BNJ	*British Numismatic Journal*
BROB	*Berichten van de Rijksdienst voor het Oudheidkundig Bodemonderzoek*
CA	*Current Archaeology*
CCM	*Cahiers de Civilisation Médiévale*
CHR	*Catholic History Review*
DUJ	*Durham University Journal*
E&S	*Essays and Studies by Members of the English Association*
EC	*Essays in Criticism*
EconHR	*Economic History Review*
EEMF	Early English Manuscripts in Facsimile
EHR	*English Historical Review*
ELN	*English Language Notes*
EStn	*Englische Studien*
ESts	*English Studies*
IAF	*Issledovanija po Anglijskoj Filologii*
IF	*Indogermanische Forschungen*

JBAA	*Journal of the British Archaeological Association*
JEGP	*Journal of English and Germanic Philology*
JEH	*Journal of Ecclesiastical History*
JL	Janua Linguarum
JTS	*Journal of Theological Studies*
MA	*Medieval Archaeology*
MÆ	*Medium Ævum*
MLN	*Modern Language Notes*
MLQ	*Modern Language Quarterly*
MLR	*Modern Language Review*
MP	*Modern Philology*
MS	*Mediaeval Studies*
N&Q	*Notes and Queries*
NC	*Numismatic Chronicle*
NM	*Neuphilologische Mitteilungen*
PMLA	*Publications of the Modern Language Association of America*
PQ	*Philological Quarterly*
RB	*Revue Bénédictine*
RES	*Review of English Studies*
SAP	*Studia Anglica Posnaniensia*
SBVS	*Saga-Book of the Viking Society for Northern Research*
SN	*Studia Neophilologica*
SP	*Studies in Philology*
TLS	*Times Literary Supplement*
TPS	*Transactions of the Philological Society*
TRHS	*Transactions of the Royal Historical Society*
YES	*Yearbook of English Studies*
ZAA	*Zeitschrift für Anglistik und Amerikanistik*
ZDA	*Zeitschrift für deutsches Altertum und deutsche Literatur*
ZVS	*Zeitschrift für vergleichende Sprachforschung*

1. GENERAL AND MISCELLANEOUS

Allen, D. F., 'Christopher Blunt: an Appreciation', *BNJ* 42, 1–9

Barley, Nigel F., 'Two Anglo-Saxon Sign Systems Compared', *Semiotica* 12, 227–37

Borroff, Marie, 'John Collins Pope: a Bibliography', Robert B. Burlin and Edward B. Irving, Jr, ed., *Old English Studies in Honour of John C. Pope* (Toronto), pp. 327–30

Brown, Alan K., 'Old English Research in Progress, 1973–1974', *NM* 75, 472–80
'Old English Bibliography 1973', *OE Newsletter* 7.2, 92–116

Campbell, Jackson J., 'Some Aspects of Meaning in Anglo-Saxon Art and Literature', *Annuale Mediaevale* 15, 5–45

Clemoes, Peter, *et al.*, ed., 'Bibliography for 1973', *ASE* 3, 233–70

Dickins, Bruce, '*Two Kembles': John and Henry* (Cambridge)

Doak, Robert, 'Color and Light Imagery: an Annotated Bibliography', *Style* 8.1 Supplement, 208–59 [three entries in index under 'Old English Period', two under 'Beowulf Poet']

*Dodwell, C. R., 'Losses of Anglo-Saxon Art in the Middle Ages', *Bull. of the John Rylands Univ. Lib. of Manchester* 56 (1973), 74–92

Dumézil, Georges, *Gods of the Ancient Northmen*, ed. Einar Haugen, introduction by C. Scott Littleton and Udo Strutynski (Berkeley and Los Angeles)

*Gough, Michael, *The Origins of Christian Art* (London, 1973; New York, 1974) ['Christian Art in Britain', pp. 186–200]

Gruber, Loren C., and Dean Loganbill, ed., *In Geardagum: Essays on Old English Language and Literature* (Denver)

*Holzapfel, Otto, 'Stabilität und Variabilität einer Formel: Zur Interpretation der Bildformel "Figur zwischen wilden Tieren" mit besonderer Berücksichtigung skandinavischer Beispiele', *Med. Scandinavia* 6 (1973), 7–38

Hunter, Michael, 'Germanic and Roman Antiquity and the Sense of the Past in Anglo-Saxon England', *ASE* 3, 29–50

Kabell, Aa., 'Wieland', *Beiträge zur Namenforschung* 9, 102–14

*Kenyon, Christine, 'The Study of Old and Middle English in the Universities of the United Kingdom: an Historical Survey', *Bull. des Anglicistes Médiévistes* 1 (1972), 4–17

Larès, Micheline-Maurice, *Bible et Civilisation Anglaise: Naissance d'une Tradition (Ancien Testament)* (Paris)

Loganbill, Dean, 'Older Literatures and Modern Students', *In Geardargum: Essays on Old English Language and Literature*, ed. Loren C. Gruber and Dean Loganbill (Denver), pp. 38–41

Myers, W. A., 'A Prolegomenon to the Study of Older Literatures', *In Geardagum: Essays on Old English Language and Literature*, ed. Loren C. Gruber and Dean Loganbill (Denver), pp. 1–7

Neumann, Eduard, and Helmut Voigt, 'Germanische Mythologie', *Wörterbuch der Mythologie*, ed. Hans Wilhelm Haussig II: *Götter und Mythen im alten Europa* (Stuttgart)

*Ordnance Survey, [*Maps of*] *Britain before the Norman Conquest* (Southampton, 1973) [871–1066; north sheet and south sheet]

Phillips, C. W., 'The English Place-Name Society', *Antiquity* 48, 7–15

Rubin, Stanley, *Medieval English Medicine* (Newton Abbot and New York)

*Warnicke, Retha M., *William Lambarde: Elizabethan Antiquary, 1536–1601* (Chichester, 1973)

Watson, George, ed., *The New Cambridge Bibliography of English Literature. I: 600–1660* (Cambridge)

*Whitelock, Dorothy, 'The English Place-Name Society 1923–1973', *Jnl of the Eng. Place-Name Soc.* 5 (1972–3), 6–14

2. OLD ENGLISH LANGUAGE

*d'Alquen, Richard, 'The Germanic Sound Shift and Verner's Law: a Synthesis', *General Ling.* 13 (1973), 79–89

*Althaus, Hans Peter, Helmut Henne and Herbert Ernst Wiegand, *Lexikon der germanistischen Linguistik*, Studienausgabe, 1–3 (Tübingen, 1973)

Balaišis, Vytautas, 'Semantische Parallelen (althochdeutsch *weralt*/litauisch *amžius*)', *Wissenschaftliche Zeitschrift der Ernst-Moritz-Arndt Universität Greifswald* 23, 57–9

*Bammesberger, Alfred, 'Altenglisch *gethyngu*', *Münchener Studien zur Sprachwissenschaft* 31 (1973), 5–9

'Altenglisch *brosnian* und *molsnian*', *Münchener Studien zur Sprachwissenschaft* 31 (1973), 11–13

Bammesberger, Alfred, 'Einige versteckte Weiterbildungen von altenglisch *ǣwisc(e)*', *Die Sprache* 20, 130–2

'Altenglisch *gedræg* und *gedreag*', *ZVS* 88, 139–46

Barley, Nigel F., 'Old English Colour Classification: Where do Matters Stand?', *ASE* 3, 15–28

'Perspectives on Anglo-Saxon Names', *Semiotica* 11, 1–31

Baron, Naomi S., 'The Structure of English Causatives', *Lingua* 33, 299–342

*Bauer, Gero, 'Die altenglische Palataldiphthongicrung', *Festschrift Prof. Dr Herbert Koziol zum siebzigsten Geburtstag*, ed. Gero Bauer, Franz K. Stanzel and Franz Zaic, Wiener Beiträge zur englischen Philologie 75 (Vienna and Stuttgart, 1973), 7–21

Bierbaumer, Peter, 'Ae. *fornetes folm*: eine Orchideenart', *Anglia* 92, 172–6

Birkhan, H., 'Niederrheinisch-Friesisches in Schottland und das Alter des germanischen *a*-Umlautes von *u*', *Antiquitates Indogermanicae: Studien zur indogermanischen Altertumskunde und zur Sprach- und Kulturgeschichte der indogermanischen Völker; Gedenkschrift für Hermann Güntert*, ed. M. Mayrhofer, W. Meid, B. Schlerath and R. Schmitt, Innsbrucker Beiträge zur Sprachwissenschaft 12, 427–41

*Bolton, W. F., *A Short History of Literary English*, 2nd ed. (Totowa, New Jersey, 1973)

*Cox, Barrie H., see sect. 6

Cross, J. E., see sect. 3*biii*

Derolez, R., 'Cross-Channel Language Ties', *ASE* 3, 1–14

Dietz, Klaus, 'Zur Phonologie der mittelenglischen Tektalspiranten: die südmittelenglischen Reflexe von ae. *ē(o)g/h*', *Studien zur englischen und amerikanischen Sprache und Literatur: Festschrift für Helmut Papajewski*, ed. Paul G. Buchloh, Inge Leimberg and Herbert Rauter, Kieler Beiträge zur Anglistik und Amerikanistik 10 (Neumünster), 11–36

Dobson, E. J., 'Two Notes on Early Middle English Texts', *N&Q* 21, 124–6 [*wēol, *wēolig*]

Dodgson, J. McN., see sect. 6

Edwards, K. J., see sect. 6

*Eichman, Thomas Lee, 'The Development of Gmc. *kann-'*, *Amsterdamer Beiträge zur älteren Germanistik* 5 (1973), 1–10

Erdmann, P., 'Die Ableitung der altenglischen Substantivparadigmen', *Linguistics* 130, 5–53

*Esau, Helmut, 'The Germanic Consonant Shift: Substratum as an Explanation for the First Sound Shift', *Orbis* 22 (1973), 454–73

Fullerton, G. Lee, 'The Development of Obstruents in Four Germanic Endings', *Linguistics* 130, 71–82

*Gelling, Margaret, see sect. 6

Gelling, Margaret, see sect. 6 (four entries)

Gessman, Albert M., 'Grimm's Law: Fact or Myth?', *Univ. of South Florida Lang. Quarterly* 13, 21–9

Goossens, Jan, *Historische Phonologie des Niederländischen* (Tübingen)

Goossens, Louis, ed., *The Old English Glosses of MS Brussels, Royal Library, 1650 (Aldhelm's 'De Laudibus Virginitatis')* (Brussels)

*Gough, J. V., 'Old English *cuman* and *niman'*, *ESts* 54 (1973), 521–5

Gough, J. V., 'Some Old English Glosses', *Anglia* 92, 273–90

Grant, Raymond J. S., see sect. 5

Gruber, Loren C., and Dean Loganbill, see sect. 1

*Gusmani, Roberto, 'Anglosassone *myltestre* "meretrix"', *Studi Germanici* 26 (1972), 157–67

*Hamp, Eric P., '*Doom* and *do'*, *Lingua Posnaniensis* 16 (1972), 87–90

'Once Again Iranian *ādu-'*, *TPS* 1973, 137

Hamp, Eric P., 'Two Germanic Verb Inventions', *Lingua* 34, 229–34 [*findan; tredan, trod*]

'*Rattus*', *Rheinisches Museum für Philologie* 117, 192

Harbert, Bruce, see sect. 3*c*

Howlett, D. R., see sect. 3*biii*

Jungandreas, Wolfgang, 'Nord-, Ost- und West-germanen im 1. Jahrhundert nach Chr. Geb.', *Leuvense Bijdragen* 63, 197–213

Kirby, I. J., 'Old English *ferð'*, *N&Q* 21, 443

*Köbler, Gerhard, *Lateinisches Register zu den frühmittelalterlichen germanischen Übersetzungsgleichungen*, Göttinger Studien zur Rechtsgeschichte 20 (Göttingen, Zürich and Frankfurt, 1973)

see sect. 3*biii*

*Koziol, Herbert, see sect. 3*bi*

*Kristensson, Gillis, 'Two Berkshire River-Names', *Namn och Bygd* 61 (1973), 49–54

Lass, Roger, 'Strategic Design as the Motivation for a Sound Shift: the Rationale of Grimm's Law', *Acta Linguistica Hafniensia* 15, 51–66

*Lockwood, W. B., 'More English Etymologies', *ZAA* 21 (1973), 414–23 [*ganot, stearn*]

Maak, Hans-Georg, 'Germ. *dall-/*dill-/*dull-'*, *NM* 75, 377–85 [ModE *dally*]

Mayard, Helen, see sect. 6

McClure, Peter, 'Three Plant Names in ME Place-Names and Surnames: "Breme", "Rounce", "Bilbery"', *N&Q* 21, 42–4 [*brēme*]

*Miedema, H. T. J., 'De oudengelse muntnaam *sceat* en het oudfriese diminutivum *skeisen* "duit"', *Naamkunde* 4 (1972), 320–2

Miedema, H. T. J., 'Dialect en Runen van Britsum en de Oudste Anglofriese Runeninscripties', *Taal en Tongval* 26, 101–28

Nevanlinna, Saara, 'Background and History of the Parenthetic *As Who Say/Saith* in Old and Middle English Literature', *NM* 75, 568–601

*Pak, T. y., 'Ross on the Order of Sentence Constituents', *Lingua* 32 (1973), 325–32

Peeters, Christian, 'The Word for "tree" in the Germanic Languages and the Reconstruction of Proto-Germanic', *ZVS* 88, 129–33
'Germanic *kwō(z) "cow"', *ZVS* 88, 134–6
'On the Infinitive Ending in Proto-Germanic', *ZVS* 88, 137–8

Pheifer, J. D., ed., *Old English Glosses in the Épinal–Erfurt Glossary* (Oxford)

Phillips, C. W., see sect. 1

Pisani, Vittore, 'Zum Personalpronomen in einigen idg. Sprachen', *ZVS* 88, 113–16

Rasmussen, Jens Elmegård, 'Haeretica Indogermanica...iii. Gothic *nam:nēmum* and the Indo-European Reduplicaton', *Danske Videnskabernes Selskab*, historisk-filosofiske Meddelelser 43.3, 33–40

*Reszkiewicz, Alfred, *A Diachronic Grammar of Old English* 1 (Warsaw, 1973)

*Rhee, F. van der, 'Vokalalternanzen im germanischen starken Verbum', *Amsterdamer Beiträge zur älteren Germanistik* 5 (1973), 11–31

Robinson, F. C., see sect. 3c

Ross, Alan S. C., 'Anglo-Saxon *e* to *i* before *u*', *N&Q* 21, 123
'Old English *secgan*', *N&Q* 21, 284

Sandred, Karl Inge, 'Two Dialect Words in the Fenland: ModE *haff* and *stow*', *Namn och Bygd* 62, 82–91
see under Seltén, Bo, sect. 9

Schabram, Hans, 'Ae. *wlanc* und Ableitungen: Vorarbeiten zu einer wortgeschichtlichen Studie', *Studien zur englischen und amerikanischen Sprache und Literatur: Festschrift für Helmut Papajewski*, ed. Paul G. Buchloh, Inge Leimberg and Herbert Rauter, Kieler Beiträge zur Anglistik und Amerikanistik 10 (Neumünster), 70–88

*Schibsbye, Knud, *Origin and Development of the English Language. I: Phonology* (Copenhagen, 1972)

Schnall, Uwe, 'Bergung. I. Sprachliches', *Reallexikon der germanischen Altertumskunde*, ed. Johannes Hoops, 2nd ed. II.2–3, 277–9

Scragg, D. G., *A History of English Spelling* (Manchester and New York)

Seebold, Elmar, 'Die ae. Entsprechungen von lat. *Sapiens* und *Prudens*: eine Untersuchung über die mundartliche Gliederung der ae. Literatur', *Anglia* 92, 291–333

*Sen, Subhadra Kumar, 'Gothic *mik*: Reconstruction', *Indian Ling.* 34 (1973), 216–19

Stracke, J. Richard, 'Eight Lambeth Psalter-Glosses', *PQ* 53, 121–8

*Strang, Barbara M. H., and John Fellowe, 'English Language', *The Year's Work in Eng. Stud.* 52 (1973), 34–64

Strauss, Jürgen, *Eine Komponentenanalyse im verbal- und situationskontextuellen Bereich: die Bezeichnungen für 'Herr' und 'Gebieter' in der altenglischen Poesie*, Anglistische Forschungen (Heidelberg) 103

*Szenci, Miklós, Tibor Szobotka and Anna Katona, *Az angol irodalom története* [History of the English Language] (Budapest, 1972)

Törnqvist, Nils, 'Gibt es tatsächlich eine westgermanische Spracheinheit?', *NM* 75, 386–401

Voyles, Joseph B., 'West Germanic Inflection, Derivation and Compounding', JL Ser. Practica 145 (The Hague)

Wakelin, Martyn F., 'New Light on IE r/n Stems in Germanic?', *Studia Linguistica* 28, 109–11 [ModE *udder*]

Watson, George, see sect. 1

*Whitelock, Dorothy, see sect. 1

Zadorožny, B., 'Zur Frage der Bedeutung und des Gebrauchs der Partizipien im Altgermanischen', *BGDSL* (Halle) 94, 52–76

3. OLD ENGLISH LITERATURE

a. General

Campbell, Jackson J., see sect. 1

Clemoes, Peter A. M., 'De quelques Articulations entre Présent et Passé dans la Technique Narrative Vieil-Anglaise', *Actes du Colloque de l'Association des Médiévistes Anglicistes de l'Enseignement Supérieur sur les Techniques Narratives au Moyen Âge*, ed. André Crépin (Amiens), pp. 5–21

Day, Virginia, 'The Influence of the Catechetical *Narratio* on Old English and some other Medieval Literature', *ASE* 3, 51–61

Grant, Raymond J. S., see sect. 5

Gruber, Loren C., and Dean Loganbill, see sect. 1

Hunter, Michael, see sect. 1

Murdoch, Brian O., *The Recapitulated Fall: a Comparative Study in Mediaeval Literature*, Amsterdamer Publikationen zur Sprache und Literatur 11

*Opland, Jeff, 'African Phenomena Relevant to a Study of the European Middle Ages: Oral Tradition', *Eng. Stud. in Africa* 16 (1973), 86–90

*Reszkiewicz, Alfred, *An Old English Reader* (Warsaw, 1973)

*Scragg, D. G., 'Old English Literature', *The Year's Work in Eng. Stud.* 52 (1973), 65–79

Seebold, Elmar, see sect. 2

*Smith, Eric, *Some Versions of the Fall: the Myth of the Fall of Man in English Literature*, with a foreword by J. I. M. Stewart (London and Pittsburgh, 1973)

Watson, George, see sect. 1

Bibliography for 1974

b. Poetry

i. General

*Anderson, Earl R., '*Sæmearh* and Like Compounds: a Theme in Old English Poetry', *Comitatus* 3 (1972), 3–10

Bessinger, J. B., Jr, 'Homage to Caedmon and Others: a Beowulfian Praise Song', *Old English Studies in Honour of John C. Pope*, ed. Robert B. Burlin and Edward B. Irving, Jr (Toronto), pp. 91–106

Burchfield, R. W., 'The Prosodic Terminology of Anglo-Saxon Scholars', *Old English Studies in Honour of John C. Pope*, ed. Robert B. Burlin and Edward B. Irving, Jr (Toronto), pp. 171–202

Hieatt, Constance B., 'Alliterative Patterns in the Hypermetric Lines of Old English Verse', *MP* 71, 237–42

Hume, Kathryn, 'The Concept of the Hall in Old English Poetry', *ASE* 3, 63–74

Johnson, William C., Jr, '"Deep Structure" and Old English Poetry: Notes toward a Critical Model', *In Geardagum: Essays on Old English Language and Literature*, ed. Loren C. Gruber and Dean Loganbill (Denver), pp. 12–18

Kintgen, Eugene R., 'Echoic Repetition in Old English Poetry, Especially *The Dream of the Rood*', *NM* 75, 202–23

*Koziol, Herbert, *Zahlen in englischen Versdichtungen*, Österreichische Akademie der Wissenschaften, phil.-hist. Klasse, Sitzungsberichte 291.5 (1973)

Rarick, Louise, 'Ten-Syllable Lines in English Poetry', *NM* 75, 66–73

Strauss, Jürgen, see sect. 2

Szarmach, Paul, see sect. 3*c*

ii. 'Beowulf'

Anderson, Earl R., '*Beowulf* 2216b–2217: a Restoration', *ELN* 12, 1–5

Berger, Harry, Jr, and H. Marshall Leicester, Jr, 'Social Structure as Doom: the Limits of Heroism in *Beowulf*', *Old English Studies in Honour of John C. Pope*, ed. Robert B. Burlin and Edward B. Irving, Jr (Toronto), pp. 37–79

Bolton, W. F., 'The Conybeare Copy of Thorkelin', *ESts* 55, 97–107

Brown, George Hardin, '*Beowulf* 1278b: *sunu þeod wrecan*', *MP* 72, 172–4

Buckalew, Ronald E., '*Beowulf*, lines 1766–1767: *oððe* for *seoððan*?', *NM* 75, 224–8

Burlin, Robert B., 'Inner Weather and Interlace: a Note on the Semantic Value of Structure in *Beowulf*', *Old English Studies in Honour of John C. Pope*, ed. Robert B. Burlin and Edward B. Irving, Jr (Toronto), pp. 81–9

Cable, Thomas, *The Meter and Melody of 'Beowulf'*, Illinois Stud. in Lang. and Lit. 64 (Urbana etc.)

*Callahan, Patrick J., 'Tolkien, *Beowulf*, and the Barrow-Wights', *Notre Dame Eng. Jnl* 7 (1972), 4–13

Campbell, A. P., 'The Death of Beowulf: Please Indicate Church Affiliation', *Revue de l'Université d'Ottawa* 44, 539–42

Clipsham, David, '*Beowulf* 168–169', *In Geardagum: Essays on Old English Language and Literature*, ed. Loren C. Gruber and Dean Loganbill (Denver), pp. 19–24

Cramp, R. J., '*Beowulf*: §15. *Beowulf* and Archaeology', *Reallexikon der germanischen Altertumskunde*, ed. Johannes Hoops, 2nd ed. 11.2–3, 244

Crook, Eugene J., 'Pagan Gold in *Beowulf*', *ABR* 25, 218–34

Doak, Robert, see sect. 1

Farrell, R. T., '*Beowulf*: B. The Scandinavian Backgrounds of *B[eowulf]*', *Reallexikon der germanischen Altertumskunde*, ed. Johannes Hoops, 2nd ed. 11.2–3, 241–4

Finkenstaedt, Th., '*Beowulf*: A. Das altenglische Epos', *Reallexikon der germanischen Altertumskunde*, ed. Johannes Hoops, 2nd ed. 11.2–3, 237–41

Goldsmith, Margaret E., 'Le Mode Narratif de *Beowulf*', *Actes du Colloque de l'Association des Médiévistes Anglicistes de l'Enseignement Supérieur sur les Techniques Narratives au Moyen Âge*, ed. André Crépin (Amiens), pp. 23–38

Greenfield, Stanley B., '"Gifstol" and Goldhoard in *Beowulf*', *Old English Studies in Honour of John C. Pope*, ed. Robert B. Burlin and Edward B. Irving, Jr (Toronto), pp. 107–17

Gruber, Loren C., 'Motion, Perception, and *oþþaet* in *Beowulf*', *In Geardagum: Essays on Old English Language and Literature*, ed. Loren C. Gruber and Dean Loganbill (Denver), pp. 31–7

Hanning, Robert W., '*Beowulf* as Heroic History', *Medievalia et Humanistica* 5, 77–102

John, Eric, see sect. 6

Kabell, Aa., see sect. 1

*Lupack, Alan C., 'The Beginning of the End: an Inset in *Beowulf*', *Massachusetts Stud. in Eng.* 4 (1973), 15–22

Osborn, Marijane, 'Translations of *Beowulf* (and *The Fight at Finnsburg*): an Updated Bibliography', Chauncey B. Tinker, *The Translations of 'Beowulf': a Critical Bibliography*, ed. Marijane Osborn, with a new foreword by Fred C. Robinson (Hamden, Connecticut), pp. 153–80

Payne, F. Anne, 'Three Aspects of Wyrd in *Beowulf*', *Old English Studies in Honour of John C. Pope*, ed. Robert B. Burlin and Edward B. Irving, Jr (Toronto), pp. 15–35

Renoir, Alain, 'The Terror of the Dark Waters: a Note on Virgilian and Beowulfian Techniques', *Harvard Eng. Stud.* 5, 147–60

Robinson, Fred C., 'Elements of the Marvellous in the Characterization of Beowulf: a Reconsideration of the Textual Evidence', *Old English Studies in Honour of John C. Pope*, ed. Robert B. Burlin and Edward B. Irving, Jr (Toronto), pp. 119–37

'Foreword', Chauncey B. Tinker, *The Translations of 'Beowulf': a Critical Bibliography*, ed. Marijane Osborn (Hamden, Connecticut)

Rosier, James L., 'What Grendel Found: *heardran hæle*', *NM* 75, 40–9

Sandars, N. K., see under Alexander, Michael, sect. 9

Schramm, Gottfried, see under Schmitt, Rüdiger, sect. 9

Stanley, E. G., 'Some Observations on the A3 Lines in *Beowulf*', *Old English Studies in Honour of John C. Pope*, ed. Robert B. Burlin and Edward B. Irving, Jr (Toronto), pp. 139–64

Storms, G., 'The Author of *Beowulf*', *NM* 75, 11–39

*Thundyil, Zacharias P., 'The Doctrinal Influence of the *Jus Diaboli* on *Beowulf*', *Christian Scholar's Rev.* 111 (1973), 150–69

Tripp, Raymond P., Jr, 'A New Look at Grendel's Attack: *Beowulf* 804a–815a', *In Geardagum: Essays on Old English Language and Literature*, ed. Loren C. Gruber and Dean Loganbill (Denver), pp. 8–11

Vickrey, John F., '*Egesan ne gymeð* and the Crime of Heremod', *MP* 71, 295–300

Whitbread, L. G., see sect. 4

Zweig, Paul, *The Adventurer: the Fate of Adventure in the Western World* (New York)

iii. Other poems

Anderson, Earl R., 'Cynewulf's *Elene*: Manuscript Divisions and Structural Symmetry', *MP* 72, 111–22

Anderson, James E., 'Die Deutungsmöglichkeiten des altenglischen Gedichtes *The Husband's Message*', *NM* 75, 402–7

Andersson, Theodore M., 'The Cædmon Fiction in the *Heliand* Preface', *PMLA* 89, 278–84

Barley, Nigel F., 'Structural Aspects of the Anglo-Saxon Riddle', *Semiotica* 10, 143–75

Beck, Heinrich, 'Zur literaturgeschichtlichen Stellung des althochdeutschen Ludwigsliedes und einiger verwandter Zeitgedichte', *ZDA* 103, 37–51 [*Maldon*]

Berkhout, Carl T., '*Feld dennade* – Again', *ELN* 11, 161–2

'The Problem of OE *holmwudu*', *MS* 36, 429–33

'The Speaker in *Resignation*: a Biblical Note', *N&Q* 21, 122–3

Bolton, W. F., 'A Further Echo of the Old English *Genesis* in Milton's *Paradise Lost*', *RES* 25, 58–61

Breuer, Rolf, 'Vermittelte Unmittelbarkeit: Zur Struktur des altenglischen *Wanderer*', *NM* 75, 552–67

Brockman, Bennett A., '"Heroic" and "Christian" in *Genesis A*: the Evidence of the Cain and Abel Episode', *MLQ* 35, 115–28

Brown, George Hardin, 'The Descent–Ascent Motif in *Christ II* of Cynewulf', *JEGP* 73, 1–12

Casteen, John, '*Andreas*: Mermedonian Cannibalism and Figural Narrative', *NM* 75, 74–8

Catalini, Claire, 'An Old English Poem: Further Conjecture', *Hurrahing in Harvest: Saggi in Onore di Carlo Izzo*, Quaderni dell'Istituto di Filologia Germanica [Bologna] (Imola), pp. 107–14 [*Wulf and Eadwacer*]

Chase, Colin, 'God's Presence through Grace as the Theme of Cynewulf's *Christ II* and the Relationship of this Theme to *Christ I* and *Christ III*', *ASE* 3, 87–101

Clausen, Christopher, 'A Suggested Emendation in *Genesis B*', *ELN* 11, 249–50

Cross, J. E., 'Mainly on Philology and the Interpretative Criticism of *Maldon*', *Old English Studies in Honour of John C. Pope*, ed. Robert B. Burlin and Edward B. Irving, Jr (Toronto), pp. 235–53

Daniels, Richard J., 'Bibliographical Notes on the Old English Poem *Judgment Day I*', *Papers of the Bibliographical Soc. of Amer.* 68, 412–13

Eliason, Norman E., 'On *Wulf and Eadwacer*', *Old English Studies in Honour of J. C. Pope*, ed. Robert B. Burlin and Edward B. Irving, Jr (Toronto), pp. 225–34

*Empric, Julienne H., '*The Seafarer*: an Experience in Displacement', *Notre Dame Eng. Jnl* 7 (1972), 23–33

Farrell, R. T., ed., '*Daniel*' and '*Azarias*', Methuen's Old Eng. Lib. (London)

Finnegan, Robert Emmett, 'Three Notes on the Junius XI *Christ and Satan*: lines 78–79; lines 236–42; lines 435–38', *MP* 72, 175–81

Fritz, Donald W., 'Caedmon: a Monastic Exegete', *ABR* 25, 351–63

Fry, Donald K., ed., *Finnsburgh: Fragment and Episode*, Methuen's Old Eng. Lib. (London)

'*Finnsburgh*: a New Interpretation', *Chaucer Rev.* 9, 1–14 [+abstract]

'Caedmon as a Formulaic Poet', *Forum for Mod. Lang. Stud.* 10, 227–47

Grinda, Klaus, see under Schwab, Ute, sect. 9

Hieatt, Constance B., '*The Fates of the Apostles*: Imagery, Structure, and Meaning', *Papers in Lang. and Lit.* 10, 115–25

Hill, Thomas D., 'The *Fyrst ferhðbana*: Old English *Exodus*, 399', *N&Q* 21, 204–5

*Hofmann, Dietrich, 'Die altsächsische Bibelepik: ein Ableger der ags. geistlichen Epik?', *Der Heliand* (Darmstadt, 1973), pp. 315–43

Howlett, D. R., 'Three Forms in the Ruthwell Text of *The Dream of the Rood*', *ESts* 55, 1–5

Irving, Edward B., Jr, '*Exodus* Retraced', *Old English Studies in Honour of John C. Pope*, ed. Robert B. Burlin and Edward B. Irving, Jr (Toronto), pp. 203–23

Joyce, John H., 'Natural Process in *Exeter Book* Riddle 29: "Sun and Moon"', *Annuale Mediaevale* 14, 5–8

Keenan, Hugh T., 'Satan Speaks in Sparks: *Christ and Satan* 78–79a, 161b–162b, and the *Life of St Anthony*', *N&Q* 21, 283–4

Kintgen, Eugene R., see sect. 3*bi* [*Dream of the Rood*]

Kirby, I. J., see sect. 2 [*Wanderer, Seafarer*]

*Köbler, Gerhard, *Verzeichnis der Übersetzungsgleichungen von Heliand und Genesis*, Göttinger Studien zur Rechtsgeschichte 13 (Göttingen, Zürich and Frankfurt, 1972)

*Lendinara, Patrizia, 'Un'Allusione ai Giganti: Versi Gnomici Exoniensi 192–200', *Annali, Sezione Germanica* 15 (Naples, 1973), 85–98 [+abstract]

*Luiselli, Bruno, see sect. 4 [Cædmon's *Hymn*]

Malone, Kemp, 'The Rhythm of *Deor*', *Old English Studies in Honour of John C. Pope*, ed. Robert B. Burlin and Edward B. Irving, Jr (Toronto), pp. 165–9

*Metcalf, Allan A., *Poetic Diction in the Old English 'Meters of Boethius'*, JL Series Practica 50 (The Hague and Paris, 1973)

Mitchell, Bruce, 'The *fuglas scyne* of *The Phoenix*, line 591', *Old English Studies in Honour of John C. Pope*, ed. Robert B. Burlin and Edward B. Irving, Jr (Toronto), pp. 255–61

Nelson, Marie, 'The Rhetoric of the Exeter Book Riddles', *Speculum* 49, 421–40

Osborn, Marijane, 'The Vanishing Seabirds in *The Wanderer*', *Folklore* 85, 122–7

'The Picture-Poem on the Front of the Franks Casket', *NM* 75, 50–65

Pope, John C., 'Second Thoughts on the Interpretation of *The Seafarer*', *ASE* 3, 75–86

'An Unsuspected Lacuna in the Exeter Book: Divorce Proceedings for an Ill-Matched Couple in the Old English Riddles', *Speculum* 49, 615–22

Ramat, Paolo, 'Per una Tipologia degli Incantesimi Germanici', *Strumenti Critici* 24, 179–97

*Schubel, Friedrich, 'Der ags. "klagende" Kuckuck', *Festschrift Prof. Dr Herbert Koziol zum siebzigsten Geburtstag*, ed. Gero Bauer, Franz K. Stanzel and Franz Zaic, Wiener Beiträge zur englischen Philologie 75 (Vienna and Stuttgart, 1973), 280–96

*Serio, John N., 'Thematic Unity in *The Seafarer*', *Gypsy Scholar* 1 (1973), 16–21

Shook, Lawrence K., 'Riddles Relating to the Anglo-Saxon Scriptorium', *Essays in Honour of Anton Charles Pegis*, ed. J. Reginald O'Donnell (Toronto), pp. 215–36

Short, Douglas D., 'The Old English *Gifts of Men*, line 13', *MP* 71, 388–9

Taylor, P. B., 'Text and Texture of *The Dream of the Rood*', *NM* 75, 193–201

Turville-Petre, G., see under See, Klaus von, sect. 9 [*Wanderer*]

Unrue, John C., '*Andreas*: an Internal Perspective', *In Geardagum: Essays on Old English Language and Literature*, ed. Loren C. Gruber and Dean Loganbill (Denver), pp. 25–30

Weimann, K., 'Battle of Brunanburh', *Reallexikon der germanischen Altertumskunde*, ed. Johannes Hoops, 2nd ed. II. 1, 92–3

'Battle of Maldon', *Reallexikon der germanischen Altertumskunde*, ed. Johannes Hoops, 2nd ed. II. 1, 93–5

c. Prose

Anderson, Earl R., see sect. 4

Aronstam, Robin Ann, see sect. 6 [Wulfstan]

Bakhuizen van den Brink, J. N., *Ratramnus: 'De corpore et sanguine Domini'*, Verhandelingen der Koninklijke Nederlandse Akademie van Wetenschappen, afd. Letterkunde n.r. 87 ['Ratramne en Angleterre' (Ælfric), pp. 108–31]

Collins, Rowland L., and Peter Clemoes, 'The Common Origin of Ælfric Fragments at New Haven, Oxford, Cambridge, and Bloomington', *Old English Studies in Honour of John C. Pope*, ed. Robert B. Burlin and Edward B. Irving, Jr (Toronto), pp. 285–326

Dodwell, C. R., and Peter Clemoes, see sect. 5

*Donner, Morton, 'Prudery in Old English Fiction', *Comitatus* 3 (1972), 91–6

Godden, Malcolm R., 'Supplementary Classified Bibliography', repr. of Caroline Louisa White, *Ælfric: a New Study of his Life and Writings* (Hamden, Connecticut), pp. 199–237

Grant, Raymond J. S., see sect. 5 [the Old English Bede]

Gretsch, Mechthild, 'Æthelwold's Translation of the *Regula Sancti Benedicti* and its Latin Exemplar', *ASE* 3, 125–51

Handley, Rima, see sect. 5
Harbert, Bruce, 'King Alfred's *æstel*', *ASE* 3, 103–10
Kotzor, G., 'St Patrick in the Old English *Martyrology*: On a Lost Leaf of MS CCCC 196', *N&Q* 21, 86–7
*Kuhn, Sherman M., 'Was Ælfric a Poet?', *PQ* 52 (1973), 643–62
*Luiselli Fadda, Anna Maria, ed., '*De descensu Christi ad inferos*: una Inedita Omelia Anglosassone', *Studi Medievali* 13 (1972), 989–1011
Robinson, Fred C., ed., *Word-Indices to Old English Non-Poetic Texts* (Hamden, Connecticut) [repr. of Yale Stud. in Eng. 6, 24 and 35: Durham Hymnal glosses, West Saxon gospels, Wulfstan's homilies]
Solari, R., 'Studi sulle Glosse di Lindisfarne al Vangelo di San Luca (Revisione dell'Edizione dello Skeat)', Istituto Lombardo (Milan), Accademia di Scienze e Lettere, *Rendiconti*, Classe di Lettere e Scienze Morali e Storiche 108.2, 551–74
Swanton, Michael, ed., *Anglo-Saxon Prose* (London and Totowa, New Jersey)
Szarmach, Paul, 'Anglo-Saxon Letters in the Eleventh Century', *Acta* 1, 1–4
'Revisions for Vercelli Homily xx', *MS* 36, 493–4
Tiefenbach, Heinrich, see under Holthausen, Ferdinand, sect. 9
*Trahern, Joseph B., Jr, ed., 'Amalarius *Be Becnum*: a Fragment of the *Liber Officialis* in Old English', *Anglia* 91 (1973), 475–8
Tristram, Hildegard L. C., 'Die *leohtfæt*-Metapher in den altenglischen anonymen Bittagspredigten', *NM* 75, 229–49
Wagner, Norbert, 'Die Wolfsinseln bei Jordanes: eine Station auf einer Pelzhandelsroute des frühen 6. Jahrhunderts?', *ZDA* 103, 73–80 [the Old English Orosius]
Waterhouse, Ruth, 'The Hæsten Episode in 894 *Anglo-Saxon Chronicle*', *SN* 46, 136–41
Whitelock, Dorothy, 'The List of Chapter-Headings in the Old English Bede', *Old English Studies in Honour of John C. Pope*, ed. Robert B. Burlin and Edward B. Irving, Jr (Toronto), pp. 263–84

4. ANGLO-LATIN, LITURGY AND OTHER LATIN ECCLESIASTICAL TEXTS

Alcock, Leslie, see sect. 8*e* [Bede, *De Templo*]
Anderson, Earl R., 'Social Idealism in Ælfric's *Colloquy*', *ASE* 3, 153–62
*Bonner, Gerald, 'Anglo-Saxon Culture and Spirituality', *Sobornost* 6 (1973), 533–50
*Boussard, Jacques, see sect. 6
*Bullough, Donald, see sect. 6
Day, Virginia, see sect. 3*a*
Eckenrode, Thomas R., 'Venerable Bede's Theory of Ocean Tides', *ABR* 25, 56–74
*Gamber, Klaus, 'Fragmente zweier Lektionare aus dem 8/9. Jh. in angelsächsische Schrift', *RB* 83 (1973), 432–6
'Fragmenta Liturgica V [36. Fragmente eines vorhadrianischen Gregorianum aus Schäftlarn]', *Sacris Erudiri* 21 (1972–3), 258–64

'Der fränkische Anhang zum Gregorianum im Licht eines Fragments aus dem Anfang des 9. Jh.', *Sacris Erudiri* 21 (1972–3), 267–89

Gneuss, Helmut, 'Latin Hymns in Medieval England: Future Research', *Chaucer and Middle English Studies in Honour of Rossell Hope Robbins*, ed. Beryl Rowland (London), pp. 407–24

Gretsch, Mechthild, see sect. 3*c*

Herren, Michael, 'Some Conjectures on the Origins and Tradition of the Hisperic Poem *Rubisca*', *Ériu* 25, 70–87

'Hisperic Latin: "Luxuriant Culture-Fungus of Decay"', *Traditio* 30, 411–19

Jäschke, Kurt-Ulrich, see sect. 6

*Kottje, Raymund, 'Ein bisher unbekanntes Fragment der *Historia ecclesiastica gentis Anglorum* Bedas', *RB* 83 (1973), 429–32

Loyn, H. R., 'Beda venerabilis', *Reallexikon der germanischen Altertumskunde*, ed. Johannes Hoops, 2nd ed., II. 2–3, 129–32

*Luiselli, Bruno, 'Beda e l'Inno di Cædmon', *Studi Medievali* 14 (1973), 1013–36

Martin, Kevin M., see sect. 6

McGurk, P., '*Computus Helperici*: its Transmission in England in the Eleventh and Twelfth Centuries', *MÆ* 43, 1–5

*McRoberts, D., 'A Continuatio Bedae from Whithorn?', *Innes Rev.* 24 (1973), 69–71

*Schaller, Dieter, 'Der verleumdete David: Zum Schlusskapitel von Bedas *Epistola ad Pleguinum*', *Literatur und Sprache im europäischen Mittelalter: Festschrift für Karl Langosch zum 70. Geburtstag*, ed. Alf Önnerfors, Johannes Rathofer and Fritz Wagner (Darmstadt, 1973), pp. 39–43

Szarmach, Paul, see sect. 3*c*

Taylor, H. M., see sect. 8*e*

Thomas, Charles, see sect. 8*e*

*Triacca, Achille M., 'In Margine al "Sacramento Gregoriano" Recentemente Edito', *Ephemerides Liturgicae* 87 (1973), 415–32 [a reply by Jean Deshusses, pp. 432–4]

*Verey, C. D., 'Some Observations on the Texts of Durham Cathedral Manuscripts A. II. 10 and A. II. 17', *Studia Evangelica* 6, ed. E. A. Livingstone, Texte und Untersuchungen zur Geschichte der altchristlichen Literatur 112 (Berlin, 1973), 575–9

Watson, George, see sect. 1

Whitbread, L. G., 'The *Liber Monstrorum* and *Beowulf*', *MS* 36, 434–71

5. PALAEOGRAPHY, DIPLOMATIC AND ILLUMINATION

Bonner, Gerald, *Wearmouth, Bede and Christian Culture* [catalogue of an exhibition at the Central Museum and Art Gallery, Sunderland, from 6 April to 30 June 1974]

Brooks, Nicholas, 'Anglo-Saxon Charters: the Work of the Last Twenty Years', *ASE* 3, 211–31

Brown, Julian, 'The Distribution and Significance of Membrane Prepared in the Insular Manner', *La Paléographie Hébraïque Médiévale*, Colloques Internationaux du Centre National de la Recherche Scientifique (Paris) 547, 127–35

Cameron, Angus, F., 'Middle English in Old English Manuscripts', *Chaucer and Middle English Studies in Honour of Rossell Hope Robbins*, ed. Beryl Rowland (London), pp. 218–29

Campbell, Jackson J., see sect. 1

Collins, Rowland L., and Peter Clemoes, see sect. 3*c*

Deshman, Robert, 'Anglo-Saxon Art after Alfred', *Art Bull.* 56, 176–200

*Dodwell, C. R., see sect. 1

Dodwell, C. R., and Peter Clemoes, ed., *The Old English Illustrated Hexateuch, BM Cotton Claudius B. iv*, EEMF 18 (Copenhagen)

*Ferrari, Mirella, 'Spigolature Bobbiesi', *Italia Medievale e Humanistica* 16 (1973), 1–41 [esp. 1–14, 'In Margine ai *Codices Latini Antiquiores*']

Friedman, John Block, 'The Architect's Compass in Creation Miniatures of the Later Middle Ages', *Traditio* 30, 419–29 [includes Anglo-Saxon representations]

*Gamber, Klaus, see sect. 4 (three entries)

*Gough, Michael, see sect. 1

Grant, Raymond J. S., 'Laurence Nowell's Transcript of BM Cotton Otho B. xi', *ASE* 3, 111–24

Handley, Rima, 'British Museum Cotton Vespasian D. xiv', *N&Q* 21, 243–50

[Henry, Françoise] *The Book of Kells* (London) [reproductions in colour with a study of the manuscript by Françoise Henry]

*Holzapfel, Otto, see sect. 1

*Kottje, Raymund, see sect. 4

Lewine, Carol F., '*Vulpes fossa habent* or the Miracle of the Bent Woman in the Gospels of St Augustine, Corpus Christi College, Cambridge, MS 286', *Art Bull.* 56, 488–504

*McRoberts, D., see sect. 4

Nordenfalk, Carl, 'Corbie and Cassiodorus, a Pattern Page Bearing on the Early History of Bookbinding', *Pantheon* 32, 225–31

Pope, John C., see sect. 3*biii*

*Thérel, M.-L., 'Remarques sur une Illustration du Livre de la Genèse dans la Bible de Montalcino', *Revue d'Histoire des Textes* 2 (1972), 231–8

Watson, George, see sect. 1

Whitelock, Dorothy, see sect. 3*c*

*Wright, C. E., *Fontes Harleiani: a Study of the Sources of the Harleian Collection of Manuscripts Preserved in the Department of Manuscripts in the British Museum* (London, 1972)

6. HISTORY

*Addleshaw, G. W. O., *The Pastoral Structure of the Celtic Church in Northern Britain*, Borthwick Papers 43 (York, 1973)

Anderson, Earl R., see sect. 4

Bibliography for 1974

Aronstam, Robin Ann, 'Pope Leo IX and England: an Unknown Letter', *Speculum* 49, 535–41

*Baetke, Walter, *Kleine Schriften: Geschichte, Recht und Religion in germanischem Schrifttum*, ed. Kurt Rudolph and Ernst Walter (Weimar, 1973)

*Baker, Alan R. H., and Robin A. Butlin, see sect. 8*c*

*Barrow, G. W. S., *The Kingdom of the Scots* (London, 1973)

*Birkeli, Fridtjov, *Norske steinkors i tidlig middelalder, et bidrag til belysning av overgangen fra norrøn religion til kristendom*, Norske Videnskaps-Akademi i Oslo, Skrifter, hist.-filos. Klasse n.s. 10 (1973)

Birkeli, Fridtjov, 'Norske steinkors i tidlig middelalder', *Historisk Tidsskrift* (Oslo) 1974, 183–4

Blake, D. W., 'Bishop Leofric [of Exeter]', *Report and Trans. of the Devonshire Assoc.* 106, 47–57

*Boussard, Jacques, 'Les Influences Anglaises sur l'École Carolingienne des VIIIᵉ et IXᵉ Siècles', *Settimane di Studio del Centro Italiano di Studi sull' Alto Medioevo* 19 (Spoleto, 1972), 417–52

Brooks, Nicholas, see sect. 5

Brown, Elizabeth A. R., 'The Tyranny of a Construct: Feudalism and Historians of Medieval Europe', *AHR* 79, 1063–88

*Brown, R. Allen, *Origins of English Feudalism* (London and New York, 1973)

Bruder, R., *Die germanische Frau im Lichte der Runeninschriften und der antiken Historiographie* (Berlin and New York)

*Bullough, Donald, 'Alcuino e la Tradizione Culturale Insulare', *Settimane di Studio del Centro Italiano di Studi sull' Alto Medioevo* 20 (Spoleto, 1973), 571–600

*Cox, Barrie H., 'The Significance of the Distribution of English Place-Names in *hām* in the Midlands and East Anglia', *Jnl of the Eng. Place-Name Soc.* 5 (1972–3), 15–73

Cramp, Rosemary, 'The Anglo-Saxons and Rome', *Trans. of the Architectural and Archaeol. Soc. of Durham and Northumberland* n.s. 3, 27–37

Davies, Wendy, 'The Consecration of the Bishops of Llandaff in the Tenth and Eleventh Centuries', *Bull. of the Board of Celtic Stud.* 26, 53–73

Davies, Wendy, and Hayo Vierck, 'The Contexts of Tribal Hidage: Social Aggregates and Settlement Patterns', *Frühmittelalterliche Studien* 8, 223–93

Dodgson, J. McN., 'Addenda and Corrigenda to The Survey of English Place-Names', *Jnl of the Eng. Place-Name Soc.* 6 (1973–4), 35–52

Dumville, David N., 'The Corpus Christi "Nennius"', *Bull. of the Board of Celtic Stud.* 25, 369–80

'Some Aspects of the Chronology of the *Historia Brittonum*', *Bull. of the Board of Celtic Stud.* 25, 439–45

Dymond, D. P., see sect. 8*a*

Edwards, K. J., 'Recent Developments in the Study of Place-Names and the Anglo-Saxon Settlement', *Archaeologia Cantiana* 88, 81–5

Farmer, D. H., 'Saint Wilfrid', *Saint Wilfrid at Hexham*, ed. D. P. Kirby (Newcastle upon Tyne), pp. 35–59

Faull, Margaret L., see sect. 8*c*

Fell, Christine, 'The Icelandic Saga of Edward the Confessor: its Version of the Anglo-Saxon Emigration to Byzantium', *ASE* 3, 179–96

Finberg, H. P. R., *The Formation of England 550–1042* (London)

Fleuriot, L., 'Old Breton Genealogies and Early British Traditions', *Bull. of the Board of Celtic Stud.* 26, 1–6

Freeman, E. A., *The History of the Norman Conquest of England*, abridged ed., intro. by J. W. Burrow (Chicago)

*Gelling, Margaret, *The Place Names of Berkshire* I, Eng. Place-Name Soc. 49 (Cambridge, 1973)

Gelling, Margaret, *The Place-Names of Berkshire* II, Eng. Place-Name Soc. 50 (Cambridge)

'The Chronology of English Place-Names', *Anglo-Saxon Settlement and Landscape*, ed. Trevor Rowley, Brit. Archaeol. Reports 6, 93–101

'Recent Work on English Place-Names', *The Local Historian* 11, 3–7

'Some Notes on Warwickshire Place-Names', *Trans. of the Birmingham and Warwickshire Archaeol. Soc.* 86, 59–79

Godfrey, John, 'The Double Monastery in Early English History', *Ampleforth Jnl* (Summer), pp. 19–32

see sect. 8*e*

Godfrey, John, and Jane Bonner, 'The Bedan Conference', *Ampleforth Jnl* (Summer), pp. 4–18

Gransden, Antonia, *Historical Writing in England* c. *550–*c. *1307* (London)

*Harding, Alan, *The Law Courts of Medieval England* (New York, 1973)

Hart, Cyril, *The Hidation of Cambridgeshire* (Leicester)

Historical Association, *Annual Bulletin of Historical Literature* 57: *Publications of the Year 1971* (London) [Sect. 4, The Earlier Middle Ages, 500–1200, is relevant]

Hunter, Michael, see sect. 1

Imber, Donald, see sect. 8*a*

Jäschke, Kurt-Ulrich, 'Frühes Christentum in Britannien', *Archiv für Kulturgeschichte* 56, 91–123

John, Eric, '*Beowulf* and the Margins of Literacy', *Bull. of the John Rylands Univ. Lib. of Manchester* 56, 388–422

Jones, George Fenwick, 'The *Celtica Lingua* Spoken in the *Saxonicis Oris*: Concerning *Waltharius* vv. 756–780', *Germanic Rev.* 49, 17–22

Kirby, D. P., ed., *Saint Wilfrid at Hexham* (Newcastle upon Tyne)

'Northumbria in the Time of Wilfrid', *Saint Wilfrid at Hexham*, ed. D. P. Kirby (Newcastle upon Tyne), pp. 1–34

see sect. 8*c*

*Kottje, R., see sect. 4

Llewellyn, P. A. B., 'The Roman Church in the Seventh Century: the Legacy of Gregory I', *JEH* 25, 363–80

Loyn, H. R., 'Kinship in Anglo-Saxon England', *ASE* 3, 197–209

'The Hundred in England in the Tenth and Early Eleventh Centuries', *British*

Government and Administration, ed H. Hearder and H. R. Loyn (Cardiff), pp. 1–15

'Bamburgh', *Reallexikon der germanischen Altertumskunde*, ed. Johannes Hoops, 2nd ed. II.1, 27–8

'Beandun', *Reallexikon der germanischen Altertumskunde*, ed. Johannes Hoops, 2nd ed. II.1, 126

'Bedcanford', *Reallexikon der germanischen Altertumskunde*, ed. Johannes Hoops, 2nd ed. II.2–3, 132

'Beranbyrig', *Reallexikon der germanischen Altertumskunde*, ed. Johannes Hoops, 2nd ed. II.2–3, 245

see sect. 4

Martin, Kevin M., 'The *aduentus Saxonum*', *Latomus* 33, 608–39

Mayard, Helen, 'The Use of the Place-Name Elements *mōr* and *mersc* in the Avon Valley', *Trans. of the Birmingham and Warwickshire Archaeol. Soc.* 86, 80–4

McGurk, P., see sect. 4

McNeill, John T., *The Celtic Churches: a History, AD 200 to 1200* (Chicago)

*McRoberts, D., see sect. 4

Musset, Lucien, 'Rouen et l'Angleterre vers l'An Mil', *Annales de Normandie* 24, 287–90

Nichols, W. H., 'Where was Clofeshoh?', *Kent Archaeol. Rev.* 36, 171–2

*Ordnance Survey, see sect. 1

Orlandi, G., see under Morton, Catherine, and Hope Muntz, sect. 9

Phillips, C. W., see sect. 1

Radford, C. A. Ralegh, see sect. 8*e*

Rigold, S. E., see sect. 8*e*

Roper, Michael, 'Wilfrid's Landholdings in Northumbria', *Saint Wilfrid at Hexham*, ed. D. P. Kirby (Newcastle upon Tyne), pp. 61–79

*Rosenthal, Joel T., *Angles, Angels and Conquerors, 400–1154* (New York, 1973)

Sawyer, Peter, see sect. 8*c*

Scammell, Jean, 'Freedom and Marriage in Medieval England', *EconHR* 27, 523–37

Schäferdiek, K., 'Bekehrung und Bekehrungsgeschichte, iii: England und Schottland', *Reallexikon der germanischen Altertumskunde*, ed. Johannes Hoops, 2nd ed. II.2–3, 188–93

Smalley, Beryl, *Historians in the Middle Ages* (London)

Thomas, Charles, see sect. 8*e*

*Thorpe, Lewis, ed., *The Bayeux Tapestry and the Norman Invasion* (London, 1973)

Walker, T. E. C., 'Esher: the Fullinga Dic', *Surrey Archaeol. Collections* 69, 193

Waterhouse, Ruth, see sect. 3*c*

Watson, George, see sect. 1

Weimann, K., see sect. 3*biii* (two entries)

Welldon Finn, R., *Domesday Book: a Guide* (Chichester)

*Whitelock, Dorothy, see sect. 1

Bibliography for 1974

7. NUMISMATICS

[Anon.] 'Sir Francis Hill's Coin Collection', *Seaby's Coin and Medal Bull.* 1974, 123–4 [1,400 coins, about 1,000 minted in Lincoln, most of the rest in Stamford, presented to city of Lincoln, 2 January 1974; mainly late Anglo-Saxon and Norman]

Bendixen, Kirsten, 'The First Merovingian Coin-Treasure from Denmark', *Med. Scandinavia* 7, 85–101 [includes two Kentish sceattas]

Blunt, C. E., 'The Coinage of Athelstan, King of England 924–939', *BNJ* 42, 35–160

'The Mint-Name Searrum on a Coin of Edward the Confessor', *Seaby's Coin and Medal Bull.* 1974, 191–2 [legend altered to produce a variant of *BMC* 1192]

Dolley, Michael, 'Towards a Revision of the Internal Chronology of the Coinages of Edward the Elder and Plegmund', *ASE* 3, 175–7

'En Gotländsk Silverskatt med en Grupp av Pseudo-Iriska Mynt Påträffad vid 1800 – Talets Början', *Fornvännen* 69, 30–3

'Two Anomalous Pacx Pennies Attributed to Edward the Confessor', *Numismatic Circular* 82, 239 [Hild. 555 and 556 shown to be Danish copies with Edward's name]

'A Forgotten Hiberno-Norse Find from Rathlin Island', *Seaby's Coin and Medal Bull.* 1974, 39–40 [seven or eight Hiberno-Norse pieces found in 1916 and concealed *c.* 1040]

'Further Light on Early Nineteenth-Century Finds on [*sic*] Eadgar Pennies from Co. Dublin', *Seaby's Coin and Medal Bull.* 1974, 145–8 [two hoards from Bullock near Dalkey: 1838, three Anglo-Saxon pennies; 1840(?), sixty-five pennies of Edgar]

Dolley, Michael, and Tuukka Talvio, 'An Unpublished Hoard-Provenance of Hedeby', *NC* 7th ser. 14, 190–2 [two of the rare anepigraphic coins with stag and facing bust type now associated with Hedeby identified in the British Museum trays as from the 1840 Cuerdale hoard]

Finn, P., 'Forgeries of English Hammered Coins', *Numismatic Circular* 82, 242–4 [illustrates fourteen Anglo-Saxon forgeries of Seaby numbers: 598, 456, 444, 482, 492 B, 498, 481, 474, 628, 600, 506, 460, 353 and 355]

Grierson, Philip, 'The Sutton Hoo Coins Again', *Antiquity* 48, 139–40

*Heywood, Mary H., 'Hereford City Museum Report, 1971', *Trans. of the Woolhope Naturalists' Field Club* 40.2 (1971), 294–5 [includes accessions of Anglo-Saxon coins]

Hunter, Michael, see sect. 1

Jonsson, Kenneth, 'Ethelred II First Hand Pennies with Left-Facing Bust in Swedish Public Collections', *Numismatic Circular* 82, 100–1

*Kent, J. P. C., 'The Aston Rowant Treasure Trove', *Oxoniensia* 37, 243–4

Laing, Lloyd, 'British Coin Jewels', *Seaby's Coin and Medal Bull.* 1974, 111–15 [mentions early Anglo-Saxon coin-ornaments from Kent and the south-east]

*Mack, R. P., *R. P. Mack Collection: Ancient British, Anglo-Saxon and Norman Coins*, Sylloge of Coins of the Brit. Isles 20 (London, 1973)

Malmer, Brita, *King Canute's Coinage in the Northern Countries*, The 1972 Dorothea Coke Memorial Lecture (London)

*Miedema, H. T. J., see sect. 2

Pagan, H. E., 'Anglo-Saxon Coins Found at Hexham', *Saint Wilfrid at Hexham*, ed. D. P. Kirby (Newcastle upon Tyne), pp. 185–90

Rhodes, John, 'Money, Mints and Moneyers: Reflections on The Sylloge', *Bristol Archaeol. Research Group Bull.* 5, 3–4

Rigold, S. E., see sect. 8*e*

Talvio, Tuukka, 'A Finnish 19th Century Collection', *Numismatic Circular* 82, 383 [Johan Fredrik Stichaeus (d. 1853) collection, present whereabouts unknown; including at least thirty-three Anglo-Saxon coins, presumed to be from Finnish hoards]

Thompson, R. H., 'Publications and Papers of Christopher Evelyn Blunt', *BNJ* 42, 11–33

8. ARCHAEOLOGY

a. General

[Anon.] 'Wiltshire Archaeological Register for 1972', *Wiltshire Archaeol. Mag.* 68, 126–39 [Anglo-Saxon sites and finds, pp. 135–6]

Benson, Don, and David Miles, *The Upper Thames Valley. An Archaeological Survey of the River Gravels*, Oxfordshire Archaeol. Unit Survey 2 (Oxford)

*Bishop, Philippa, 'The World of the Saxon Kings', *Apollo* 98 (1973), 138 [reviewing an exhibition in the Holburne of Menstrie Museum, Bath]

Brothwell, Don, and Wojtek Krzanowski, 'Evidence of Biological Differences between Early British Populations from Neolithic to Medieval Times, as Revealed by Eleven Commonly Available Cranial Vault Measurements', *Jnl of Archaeol. Science* 1, 249–60

Brown, David, 'Problems of Continuity', *Anglo-Saxon Settlement and Landscape*, ed. Trevor Rowley, Brit. Archaeol. Reports 6, 16–19

Council for British Archaeology, *Archaeological Bibliography for Great Britain and Ireland 1972* [contains a full bibliography covering national and local periodicals and dealing with all periods]

Brit. Archaeol. Abstracts 7 [covers material published 1 July 1973–30 June 1974]

Council for British Archaeology, Group 1 (Scottish Regional Group), *Discovery and Excavation in Scotland 1973* [information on post-Roman period, *passim*, and bibliography for 1973, pp. 78–80]

Council for British Archaeology, Group 8, *West Midlands Annual Archaeol. News Sheet* 17 (Department of Extramural Studies, University of Birmingham) [includes Anglo-Saxon sites and finds]

Council for British Archaeology, Groups 12 and 13, [*Wessex*] *Archaeol. Rev.* 8 [surveys work done in 1973, including (sect. 7) early medieval *c.* 450–1000]

Department of the Environment, *Archaeological Excavations 1973* (London) [brief accounts of all excavations undertaken with state aid in 1973]

Bibliography for 1974

Dickinson, Tania M., *Cuddesdon and Dorchester-on-Thames, Oxfordshire: Two Early Saxon 'Princely' Sites in Wessex*, Brit. Archaeol. Reports 1

*Dodwell, C. R., see sect. 1

Drewett, Peter, *Rescue Archaeology in Sussex* (Institute of Archaeology, London)

Dymond, D. P., *Archaeology and History. A Plea for Reconciliation* (London)

Edwards, K. J., see sect. 6

Farley, Michael, 'Archaeological Notes from the Buckinghamshire County Museum', *Records of Buckinghamshire* 19, 344–51 [Saxon and medieval discoveries in 1973, pp. 347–51]

Fowler, P. J., and J. Bennett, ed., 'Archaeology and the M5 Motorway', *Trans. of the Bristol and Gloucestershire Archaeol. Soc.* 92, 21–81 [includes Anglo-Saxon sites and finds]

*Gough, Michael, see sect. 1

Griffiths, Richard, and Josie Southerwood, 'Archaeological Notes from Newton Longville, 1964–72', *Records of Buckinghamshire* 19, 317–28 [late Saxon pottery from the village]

Harcourt, R. A., 'The Dog in Prehistoric and Early Historic Britain', *Jnl of Archaeol. Science* 1, 151–75

Hill, David, 'Offa's and Wat's Dyke: Some Exploratory Work on the Frontier between Celt and Saxon', *Anglo-Saxon Settlement and Landscape*, ed. Trevor Rowley, Brit. Archaeol. Reports 6, 102–7

'The Inter-Relation of Offa's and Wat's Dykes', *Antiquity* 48, 309–12

*Holzapfel, Otto, see sect. 1

Hume, Kathryn, see sect. 3*bi*

Hunter, Michael, see sect. 1

Imber, Donald, 'Excavations for Stane Street in the Clapham Area 1966–71', *Trans. of the London and Middlesex Archaeol. Soc.* 25, 235–50 [includes discussion of the bounds of P. H. Sawyer, *Anglo-Saxon Charters* (London, 1968), no. 1036]

*Larsen, Johan, 'Nogle bygningstekniske Synspunkter på Jærnalderens og Vikingetidens Huse', *Aarbøger for nordisk Oldkyndighed og Historie* 1972, 151–86

Marjoram, John, 'Archaeological Notes, 1972', *Lincolnshire Hist. and Archaeology* 8, 35–49 [Anglo-Saxon sites and finds, pp. 41–2]

Medieval Village Research Group, *Report* 20/21 (for 1972 and 1973) [includes Anglo-Saxon sites]

*Ordnance Survey, see sect. 1

Owles, Elizabeth, 'Archaeology in Suffolk, 1973', *Proc. of the Suffolk Inst. o, Archaeology* 33, 94–102 [includes Anglo-Saxon discoveries]

Rutland, R. A., and J. A. Greenaway, 'Archaeological Notes from Reading Museum', *Berkshire Archaeol. Jnl* 66, 129–34 [sites and finds 1971: Saxon, pp. 132–3 and 134]

Schmidt, Holger, 'The Trelleborg House Reconsidered', *MA* 17, 52–77

*Tewkesbury District Council, *Tewkesbury District. A Preliminary Archaeological Survey* (Tewkesbury, 1973)

Thorp, F., 'The Yorkshire Archaeological Register: 1973', *Yorkshire Archaeol. Jnl* 43, 141–53 [Anglo-Saxon sites and finds, p. 146]

Webster, Leslie E., 'Medieval Britain in 1972: I. Pre-Conquest', *MA* 17, 138–52 [survey of archaeological work]

Wells, Calvin, and Charles Green, 'Sunrise Dating of Death and Burial', *Norfolk Archaeology* 35, 435–42

Wilson, David M., *The Viking Age in the Isle of Man: the Archaeological Evidence* (Odense)

b. Towns and other major settlements

Addyman, P. V., 'New Slants on Old Angles: Problems in the Archaeology of York', *Interim* [*Bull. of the York Archaeol. Trust*] 1.4, 20–3

'York, The Anatomy of a Crisis in Urban Archaeology', *Rescue Archaeology*, ed. Philip A. Rahtz (Harmondsworth), pp. 153–62

Bacon, Stuart R., 'Underwater Exploration at Dunwich, Suffolk', *Nautical Archaeology* 3, 314–18

*Baker, David, 'Bedford Castle: Some Preliminary Results from Rescue Excavations', *Château Gaillard* 6 [Venlo, 1972], 15–22

Benson, Don, and David Miles, see sect. 8a [for Dorchester on Thames]

Biddle, Martin, 'The Future of the Urban Past', *Rescue Archaeology*, ed. Philip A. Rahtz (Harmondsworth), pp. 95–112

'The Archaeology of Winchester', *Scientific American* 230.5, 32–43

Buckland, P. C., 'Archaeology and Environment in York', *Jnl of Archaeol. Science* 1, 303–16

Buckland, P. C., J. R. A. Greig and H. K. Kenward, 'York: an Early Medieval Site', *Antiquity* 48, 25–33

Carter, A., and J. P. Roberts, 'Excavations in Norwich – 1972. The Norwich Survey – Second Interim Report', *Norfolk Archaeology* 35, 443–68

Coppack, Glyn, 'The Excavation of a Roman and Medieval Site at Flaxengate, Lincoln', *Lincolnshire Hist. and Archaeology* 8, 73–114 [includes Middle Saxon and Saxo-Norman pottery]

Davis, R. H. C., '[Oxford:] The Ford, the River and the City', *Oxoniensia* 38, 258–67

Dickinson, Tania M., see sect. 8a

Down, Alec, *Chichester Excavations* II (Chichester)

Rescue Archaeology in Chichester (Chichester Civic Society, Chichester)

Fasham, P. J., 'Excavations in Banbury, 1972: First Report', *Oxoniensia* 38, 312–38

Griffiths, Michael, 'Recent Work by the Exeter Archaeological Field Unit', *Proc. of the Devon Archaeol. Exploration Soc.* 32, 167–70

Hassall, T. G., *et al.*, 'Excavations at Oxford, 1972: Fifth Interim Report', *Oxoniensia* 38, 268–98

Heighway, Carolyn M., *Archaeology in Gloucester. A Policy for City and District* (Gloucester District Council, Gloucester)

Hurst, Henry, 'Excavations at Gloucester, 1971–1973: Second Interim Report', *AntJ* 54, 8–52

Kittredge, Selwyn, 'Digging up Viking and Mediaeval Dublin', *Archaeology* 27, 134–6

Platt, Colin, 'Colonisation by the Wealthy: the Case of Medieval Southampton', *Proc. of the Hampshire Field Club and Archaeol. Soc.* 29, 29–35

Rowley, Trevor, 'Early Saxon Settlements in Dorchester on Thames', *Anglo-Saxon Settlement and Landscape*, ed. Trevor Rowley, Brit. Archaeol. Reports 6, 42–50

*Shoesmith, R., 'Hereford City Excavations 1970', *Trans. of the Woolhope Naturalists' Field Club* 40.2 (1971), 225–40

'Reports of Sectional Recorders: Archaeology, 1971', *Trans. of the Woolhope Naturalists' Field Club* 40.2 (1971), 280–2 [excavations in Hereford, p. 280]

Shoesmith, R., *The City of Hereford. Archaeology and Development* (West-Midlands Rescue Archaeology Committee, Birmingham)

'Reports of Sectional Recorders: Archaeology, 1972', *Trans. of the Woolhope Naturalists' Field Club* 40.3, 391–3 [includes excavations in Hereford]

Williams, John, 'Northampton', *CA* 4, 340–8

c. Rural settlements, agriculture and the countryside

Adams, A. W., 'Nether Hambleton, Rutland', *Trans. of the Leicestershire Archaeol. and Hist. Soc.* 48, 64 [Anglo-Saxon settlement]

Addyman, P. V., and D. Leigh, 'The Anglo-Saxon Village at Chalton, Hampshire: Second Interim Report', *MA* 17, 1–25

Avery, Michael, and David Brown, 'Abingdon Addenda', *Oxoniensia* 38, 387 [cf. *Oxoniensia* 37, 66–81]

*Baker, Alan R. H., and Robin A. Butlin, ed., *Studies of Field Systems in the British Isles* (Cambridge, 1973)

Benson, Don, and David Miles, 'Cropmarks Near the Sutton Courtenay Saxon Site', *Antiquity* 48, 223–6

see sect. 8*a*

Branigan, Keith, 'Latimer – Some Problems of Archaeological Interpretation', *Records of Buckinghamshire* 19, 340–3 [replies to reviews and includes comments on post-villa structures]

Chenevix-Trench, John, 'Coleshill and the Settlements of the Chilterns', *Records of Buckinghamshire* 19, 241–58

Clayton, N. B., 'New Wintles, Eynsham, Oxon.', *Oxoniensia* 38, 382–4

Coppack, Glyn, 'Low Caythorpe, East Yorkshire – the Manor Site', *Yorkshire Archaeol. Jnl* 46, 34–41 [occupation begins in Middle Saxon period]

Cunliffe, Barry, 'Chalton, Hants: the Evolution of a Landscape', *AntJ* 53, 173–90

Drury, P. J., and W. J. Rodwell, 'Excavations at Gun Hill, West Tilbury', *Essex Archaeology and Hist.* 5, 48–112 [*Grubenhaus*, pp. 66–9; Anglo-Saxon pottery, pp. 86–7; discussion, p. 100]

Everson, Paul, 'An Excavated Anglo-Saxon Sunken-Featured Building and

Settlement Site at Salmonby, Lincs., 1972', *Lincolnshire Hist. and Archaeology* 8, 61–72

Faull, Margaret L., 'Roman and Anglian Settlement Patterns in Yorkshire', *Northern Hist.* 9, 1–25

Fowler, P. J., 'Hedged About with Doubt', *Bristol Archaeol. Research Group Bull.* 5, 35 9 [comments on dating of hedgerows by species count]

Gray, Margaret, 'The Saxon Settlement at New Wintles, Eynsham, Oxfordshire', *Anglo-Saxon Settlement and Landscape*, ed. Trevor Rowley, Brit. Archaeol. Reports 6, 51–5

Harvey, John H., 'Hedges and Local History', *Local Hist.* 11, 80–1 and 235–6 [reply by M. D. Hooper, pp. 81–2]

Hirst, S. M., and P. A. Rahtz, 'Cheddar Vicarage 1970', *Somerset Archaeology and Nat. Hist.* 117, 65–96

Huggins, P. J. and R. M., 'Excavations of Monastic Forge and Saxo-Norman Enclosure, Waltham Abbey, Essex, 1972–73', *Essex Archaeology and Hist.* 5, 127–84

Jones, M. U., 'An Ancient Landscape Palimpsest at Mucking', *Essex Archaeology and Hist.* 5, 6–12

Jones, M. U., and W. T. Jones, 'An Early Saxon Landscape at Mucking, Essex', *Anglo-Saxon Settlement and Landscape*, ed. Trevor Rowley, Brit. Archaeol. Reports 6, 20–35

Kirby, D. P., 'The Old English Forest: its Natural Flora and Fauna', *Anglo-Saxon Settlement and Landscape*, ed. Trevor Rowley, Brit. Archaeol. Reports 6, 120–30

Miles, David, 'Abingdon and Region: Early Anglo-Saxon Settlement Evidence', *Anglo-Saxon Settlement and Landscape*, ed. Trevor Rowley, Brit. Archaeol. Reports 6, 36–41

Nash, S. G., 'A Deep Water Inlet at Highbridge', *Somerset Archaeology and Nat. Hist.* 117, 97–101

Rowley, Trevor, ed., *Anglo-Saxon Settlement and Landscape*, Brit. Archaeol. Reports 6 [papers presented at a symposium at Oxford, 1973]

Sawyer, Peter, 'Anglo-Saxon Settlement: the Documentary Evidence', *Anglo-Saxon Settlement and Landscape*, ed. Trevor Rowley, Brit. Archaeol. Reports 6, 108–19

Steane, J. M., *The Northamptonshire Landscape: Northamptonshire and the Soke of Peterborough* (London)

Swanton, M. J., 'A "Lost" Crop-Mark Site at Westenhanger', *Archaeologia Cantiana* 88, 203–7

Taylor, C., 'The Anglo-Saxon Countryside', *Anglo-Saxon Settlement and Landscape*, ed. Trevor Rowley, Brit. Archaeol. Reports 6, 5–15

Wade, Keith, 'The Anglo-Saxon Settlement of Bonhunt, Essex: an Interim Note', *Anglo-Saxon Settlement and Landscape*, ed. Trevor Rowley, Brit. Archaeol. Reports 6, 74–7

'Whither Anglo-Saxon Settlement Archaeology?', *Anglo-Saxon Settlement and Landscape*, ed. Trevor Rowley, Brit. Archaeol. Reports 6, 87–92

West Stow Environmental Archaeology Group, 'Experiment and the Anglo-Saxon Environment', *Anglo-Saxon Settlement and Landscape*, ed. Trevor Rowley, Brit. Archaeol. Reports 6, 78–86

d. Pagan cemeteries and Sutton Hoo

Brown, David, 'The Site of Stephen Stone's Saxon Cemetery at Standlake', *Oxoniensia* 38, 233–8

Bruce-Mitford, Rupert, *Aspects of Anglo-Saxon Archaeology. Sutton Hoo and Other Discoveries* (London)

Carr, R., Catherine Hills and Peter Wade-Martins, 'First Interim Report of the Excavations at Spong Hill, North Elmham (1972)', *Norfolk Archaeology* 35, 494–8

Cramp, R. J., see sect. 3*bii*

Detsicas, A. P., 'Excavations at Eccles, 1972. Eleventh Interim Report', *Archaeologia Cantiana* 88, 73–80 [Anglo-Saxon cemetery, pp. 78–80; cf. pp. 212–13]

Detsicas, A. P., and Sonia Hawkes, 'Finds from the Anglo-Saxon Cemetery at Eccles, Kent', *AntJ* 53, 281–8

Dickinson, Tania M., 'Excavations at Standlake Down in 1954: the Anglo-Saxon Graves', *Oxoniensia* 38, 239–57

see sect. 8*a*

Evison, V. I., 'Anglo-Saxon Grave-Goods from Mucking, Essex', *AntJ* 53, 269–70

Frere, S. S., and J. K. St Joseph, 'The Roman Fortress at Longthorpe', *Britannia* 5, 1–129 [Anglo-Saxon cemetery, pp. 112–13, with a note on the Anglo-Saxon pottery by J. N. L. Myres, pp. 115–21, and a note on the Anglo-Saxon glass by Dorothy Charlesworth, pp. 121–2]

Hills, Catherine, see sect. 8*i*

Hinton, David A., 'Anglo-Saxon Burials at Postcombe, Lewknor', *Oxoniensia* 38, 120–3

Hogarth, A. C., 'Structural Features in Anglo-Saxon Graves', *ArchJ* 130, 104–19

Kennett, David H., 'Seventh Century Cemeteries in the Ouse Valley', *Bedfordshire Archaeol. Jnl* 8, 99–108

'An Anglo-Saxon Grave from Biscot', *Bedfordshire Archaeol. Jnl* 8, 133

Ketteringham, L., 'Purley: Skeleton, Believed to be Saxon, on Russell Hill (TQ 306622)', *Bull. of the Surrey Archaeol. Soc.* 108 [p. 5]

Price-Williams, David, and James Barfoot, 'Excavation of Galley Hills Saxon Barrow', *London Archaeology* 2, 127–30

St Joseph, J. K., 'Air Reconnaissance: Recent Results, 35', *Antiquity* 48, 213–15 [probable Anglo-Saxon cemetery at Eastry, Kent]

Shaw, M., and Lilian Thornhill, 'Coulsdon: Saxon Knives from Cane Hill Cemetery', *Surrey Archaeol. Collections* 69, 189

Wells, Calvin, 'Probable Trephination of Five Early Saxon Skulls', *Antiquity* 48, 298–302

Wells, Calvin, and Charles Green, see sect. 8*a*

West, Stanley E., and Elizabeth Owles, 'Anglo-Saxon Cremation Burials from Snape', *Proc. of the Suffolk Inst. of Archaeology* 33, 47–57

e. Churches, monastic sites and Christian cemeteries

Alcock, Leslie, '*Fenestrae obliquae*: a Contribution to Literate Archaeology', *Antiquity* 48, 141–3

Box, K. D., 'The Chancellor Collection of Architectural Drawings in the Essex Record Office, Chelmsford', *Essex Archaeology and Hist.* 5, 202–24 [includes details of drawings of Greensted church, 1889]

*Burrow, Ian C. G., 'Tintagel – Some Problems', *Scottish Archaeol. Forum* 5 (1973), 99–103

Chambers, R. A., 'A Cemetery Site at Beacon Hill, near Lewknor', *Oxoniensia* 38, 138–45

*Cramp, Rosemary, 'Anglo-Saxon Monasteries of the North', *Scottish Archaeol. Forum* 5 (1973), 104–24 [includes Burgh Castle, Suffolk, as well as Tynemouth, Whitby, Monkwearmouth and Jarrow]

Drewett, P. L., 'Note on a Human Skeleton from Old Windsor', *Berkshire Archaeol. Jnl* 66, 61–3

Fletcher [Eric], Lord, 'Brixworth: Was There a Crypt?', *JBAA* 3rd ser. 37, 88–96

Gilbert, Edward, 'Saint Wilfrid's Church at Hexham', *Saint Wilfrid at Hexham*, ed. D. P. Kirby (Newcastle upon Tyne), pp. 81–113

Godfrey, J., 'The Emergence of the Village Church in Anglo-Saxon England', *Anglo-Saxon Settlement and Landscape*, ed. Trevor Rowley, Brit. Archaeol. Reports 6, 131–8

Gould, Dorothy and Jim, 'Excavations on the Site of the Old Church at Shenstone, Staffs. and the Identification of Saxon Stonework There', *Trans. of the South Staffordshire Archaeol. and Hist. Soc.* 15, 43–9

*Gray, M., 'Excavations at Eynsham Abbey, 1971', *Oxoniensia* 37, 246

Green, C. J. S., 'Interim Report on Excavations at Poundbury, Dorchester, 1973', *Proc. of the Dorset Nat. Hist. and Archaeol. Soc.* 95, 97–100

*Hassall, T. G., 'Excavation at the Saxon Church at Waterperry, Oxon.', *Oxoniensia* 37, 245

Hickmore, M. A. S., *St Paul's Church Jarrow* (Newcastle upon Tyne)

Horn, Walter, 'On the Origins of the Medieval Cloister', *Gesta* 12, 13–52

Lewis, J. M., and B. Knight, 'Early Christian Burials at Llanvithyn House, Glamorgan', *Archaeologia Cambrensis* 122, 147–53

Parsons, D., 'An Investigation of the Light-Transmitting Properties of Early Medieval Splayed Windows', *Archaeometry* 16, 55–70

Radford, C. A. Ralegh, 'Pre-Conquest Minster Churches', *ArchJ* 130, 120–40

*Rahtz, Philip, 'Monasteries as Settlements', *Scottish Archaeol. Forum* 5 (1973), 125–35

Rigold, S. E., 'Further Evidence about the Site of "Dommoc"', *JBAA* 3rd ser. 37, 97–102

Rodwell, Warwick, and Kirsty Rodwell, 'Excavations at Rivenhall Church, Essex. An Interim Report', *AntJ* 53, 219–31

Searle, Sidney, 'The Church Points this Way', *New Scientist* 3 January, pp. 10–13 [the orientation of churches and variations in magnetic declination]

*Small, Alan, Charles Thomas and David M. Wilson, *St Ninian's Isle and its Treasure* (London, 1973)

*Sturdy, D. A. M., 'Excavations in St Peter-in-the-East Church, Oxford', *Oxoniensia* 37, 245

Taylor, H. M., 'The Architectural Interest of Æthelwulf's *De Abbatibus*', *ASE* 3, 163–73

'The Anglo-Saxon Chapel at Bradford-on-Avon', *ArchJ* 130, 141–71

Thomas, Charles, *Bede, Archaeology and the Cult of Relics*, Jarrow Lecture, 1973 (Jarrow [1974])

Thompson, N. P., and H. Ross, 'Excavation at the Saxon Church, Alton Barnes', *Wiltshire Archaeol. Mag.* 68, 71–8

Wilson, D. M., 'Benty Grange', *Reallexikon der germanischen Altertumskunde*, ed. Johannes Hoops, 2nd ed. II.2–3, 337

f. Ships and seafaring

[Anon.] 'Saxon Boat Found in the City', *London Archaeology* 2, 180

*Ellmers, Detlev, 'The Earliest Report on an Excavated Ship in Europe', *Nautical Archaeology* 2, 177–9 [discovery of probable Roman ship at Verulamium by Ealdred, abbot of St Albans]

Müller-Wille, M., 'Boat-Graves in Northern Europe', *Nautical Archaeology* 3, 187–204

g. Sculpture on bone, stone and wood

[Anon.] 'An Interesting Stylistic Link: Bristol and Botkyrka, Sweden', *Bristol Archaeol. Research Group Bull.* 5, 13 [with reference to 'the harrowing of hell' in Bristol cathedral]

Beckwith, John, *Ivory Carvings in Early Medieval England, 700–1200* [catalogue of an exhibition in the Victoria and Albert Museum, London]

Coatsworth, E., 'Two Examples of the Crucifixion at Hexham', *Saint Wilfrid at Hexham*, ed. D. P. Kirby (Newcastle upon Tyne), pp. 180–4

Cramp, Rosemary, 'Early Northumbrian Sculpture at Hexham', *Saint Wilfrid at Hexham*, ed. D. P. Kirby (Newcastle upon Tyne), pp. 115–40, with hand-list on pp. 172–9

Galbraith, K. J., 'Further Thoughts on the Boar at St Nicholas' Church, Ipswich', *Proc. of the Suffolk Inst. of Archaeology* 33, 68–74

Marks, Richard, 'The Tympana of Covington and Thurleigh', *Bedfordshire Archaeol. Jnl* 8, 134–5

Musty, John, K. Wade and A. Rogerson, 'A Viking Pin and Inlaid Knife from Bonhunt Farm, Wicken Bonhunt, Essex', *AntJ* 53, 287

Osborn, Marijane, see sect. 3*biii*

Pritchard, V., 'A Carved Stone in Ripon Cathedral', *AntJ* 53, 265

Swanton, M. J., 'A Pre-Conquest Sculptural Fragment from Rochester Cathedral', *Archaeologia Cantiana* 88, 201–3

Wilson, David M., 'Men de ligger in London', *Skalk* 1974 nr 5, 3–8 [sculptured rune-stone from St Paul's churchyard]

h. Metal-work and other minor objects

Avent, Richard, 'An Anglo-Saxon Variant of a Merovingian Rounded-Plaque Buckle', *MA* 17, 126–8

Bailey, Richard N., 'The Anglo-Saxon Metalwork from Hexham', *Saint Wilfrid at Hexham*, ed. D. P. Kirby (Newcastle upon Tyne), pp. 141–67

Bradley, S. A. J., 'An Anglo-Saxon Cross Brooch', *Interim* [*Bull. of the York Archaeol. Trust*] 1.4, 36–9

Bruce-Mitford, Rupert, see sect. 8*d*

Detsicas, A. P., and Sonia Hawkes, see sect. 8*d*

Evison, V. I., see sect. 8*d*

Graham-Campbell, James, 'The Ninth-Century Anglo-Saxon Horn-Mount from Burghead, Morayshire, Scotland', *MA* 17, 43–51
  'A Fragmentary Bronze Strap-End of the Viking Period from The Udal, North Uist, Inverness-shire', *MA* 17, 128–31

Harbert, Bruce, see sect. 3*c*

Hauck, K., 'Zur Ikonologie der Goldbrakteaten, v', *Geschichte in der Gesellschaft: Festschrift für K. Bosl* (Stuttgart), pp. 92–159

Hawkes, Sonia, 'Some Recent Finds of Late Roman Buckles', *Britannia* 5, 386–93

Hinton, David A., *A Catalogue of the Anglo-Saxon Ornamental Metalwork 700–1100 in the Department of Antiquities, Ashmolean Museum* (Oxford)

*Holzapfel, Otto, see sect. 1

Jessup, Ronald, *Anglo-Saxon Jewellery* (Aylesbury)

Laing, Lloyd, 'British Coin Jewels', *Seaby's Coin and Medal Bull.* 1974, 111–15

Musty, John, K. Wade and A. Rogerson, see sect. 8*g*

Shaw, M., and Lilian Thornhill, see sect. 8*d*

*Swanton, M. J., *The Spearheads of the Anglo-Saxon Settlements* (Royal Archaeological Institute, London, 1973)

Swanton, M. J., *A Corpus of Pagan Anglo-Saxon Spear-Types*, Brit. Archaeol. Reports 7
  'Finglesham Man: a Documentary Postscript', *Antiquity* 48, 313–15

i. Inscriptions

Hills, Catherine, 'A Runic Pot from Spong Hill, North Elmham, Norfolk', *AntJ* 54, 87–91

Miedema, H. T. J., see sect. 2

Wilson, David M., see sect. 8*g*

j. Pottery and glass

Biddle, Martin, and Katherine Barclay, 'Winchester Ware', *Medieval Pottery from Excavations*, ed. V. I. Evison, H. Hodges and J. G. Hurst (London), pp. 137–65

Carr, R., Catherine Hills and Peter Wade-Martins, see sect. 8*d*

Chambers, R. A., 'A Deserted Medieval Farmstead at Sadler's Wood, Lewknor', *Oxoniensia* 38, 146–67 [Anglo-Saxon pot, p. 162]

Charlesworth, Dorothy, see under Frere, S. S., and J. K. St Joseph, sect. 8*d*

Coppack, Glyn, see sect. 8*b*

Cunliffe, B. W., 'Some Late Saxon Stamped Pottery from Southern England', *Medieval Pottery from Excavations*, ed. V. I. Evison, H. Hodges and J. G. Hurst (London), pp. 127–35

Dickinson, Tania M., see sect. 8*a*

Drury, P. J., and W. J. Rodwell, see sect. 8*c*

Evison, V. I., 'The Asthall Type of Bottle', *Medieval Pottery from Excavations*, ed. V. I. Evison, H. Hodges and J. G. Hurst (London), pp. 77–94

Evison, V. I., H. Hodges and J. G. Hurst, ed., *Medieval Pottery from Excavations. Studies presented to Gerald Clough Dunning, with a Bibliography of his Work* (London)

Hills, Catherine, see sect. 8*i*

Jones, M. U., and W. T. Jones, see sect. 8*c*

Kennett, David H., 'Some Anglo-Saxon Pottery from Luton', *Bedfordshire Archaeol. Jnl* 8, 93–8

Myres, J. N. L., 'An Anglo-Saxon *Buckelurne* from the Mucking, Essex, Cemetery', *AntJ* 53, 271

see under Frere, S. S., and J. K. St Joseph, sect. 8*d*

Parsons, D., see sect. 8*e*

Rahtz, Philip, 'Pottery in Somerset, AD 400–1066', *Medieval Pottery from Excavations*, ed. V. I. Evison, H. Hodges and J. G. Hurst (London), pp. 95–126

Rodwell, K. A. and W. J., 'Prehistoric, Roman and Saxon Finds from Stanford le Hope', *Essex Archaeology and Hist.* 5, 123–6 [Anglo-Saxon grass-tempered pot]

Williams, J. H., 'A Saxo-Norman Kiln Group from Northampton', *Northamptonshire Archaeology* 9, 46–56

k. Musical instruments

Bruce-Mitford, Rupert, see sect. 8*d*

9. REVIEWS

Adamus, Marian, *Tajemnice sag i run* (Wrocław, 1970): Leopold Zatočil, *Germanistik* 15, 337

Addleshaw, G. W. O., *The Pastoral Structure of the Celtic Church in Northern Britain*, Borthwick Papers 43 (1973): Kenneth Harrison, *Yorkshire Archaeol. Jnl* 46, 160

Alcock, Leslie, *Arthur's Britain: History and Archaeology, AD 367–634* (London, 1971): Richard Avent, *Carmarthen Ant.* 10, 129; Wendy Davies, *AntJ* 54, 119–20; Donald A. White, *AHR* 79, 768–70

'By South Cadbury is that Camelot...'. *Excavations at Cadbury Castle 1966–70* (London, 1972): S. C. Hawkes, *ArchJ* 130, 334–5; Brian Hope-Taylor, *Antiquity* 48, 72–3; Roland Mathias, *Anglo-Welsh Rev.* 22, 242–4; Richard Reece, *Bull. of the Inst. of Archaeology London* 11, 173–4; A. L. F. Rivet, *EHR* 89, 649

Alexander, Michael, *Beowulf: a Verse Translation* (Harmondsworth, 1973): *TLS* 1 February, p. 100; N. K. Sandars, *Agenda* 11, 112–17; E. G. Stanley, *N&Q* 21, 402

Autenrieth, Johanne, and Franz Brunhölzl, ed., *Festschrift Bernhard Bischoff* (Stuttgart, 1971): J. M. Wallace-Hadrill, *EHR* 89, 145–6

Baetke, Walter, *Kleine Schriften* (Weimar, 1973): Werner Affeldt, *Deutsches Archiv für Erforschung des Mittelalters* 30, 234

Baker, Alan R. H., and Robin A. Butlin, ed., *Studies of Field Systems in the British Isles* (Cambridge, 1973): W. O. Ault, *AHR* 79, 771–2; J. A. Chartres, *EconHR* 27, 469–71; G. C. F. Forster, *DUJ* 67, 106–7; Nigel Harvey, *Geographical Jnl* 140, 124–5

Barber, Richard, *The Figure of Arthur* (London, 1970): Leslie Alcock, *AntJ* 53, 321; Raymond J. Cormier, *CCM* 17, 156–9; Ann Dornier, *ArchJ* 130, 332–3; A. G. Dyson, *Jnl of the Soc. of Archivists* 5, 49–50; P. A. Wilson, *Archaeologia Cambrensis* 122, 193–4

Barlow, Frank, *et al.*, *Leofric of Exeter* (Exeter, 1972): V. H. Galbraith, *EHR* 89, 152; M. R. Godden, *Archives* 11, 46–7; T. A. Shippey, *YES* 4, 244–5

Barrow, G. W. S., *The Kingdom of the Scots* (London, 1973): H. R. Loyn, *Scottish Hist. Rev.* 53, 78–80

Bech, Gunnar, *Das germanische reduplizierte Präteritum* (Copenhagen, 1969): Lars-G. Hallander, *SN* 46, 530–3

Becker, Alfred, *Franks Casket. Zu den Bildern und Inschriften des Runenkästchens von Auzon* (Regensburg, 1973): Torsten Capelle, *Deutsches Archiv für Erforschung des Mittelalters* 30, 326–7

Beckwith, John, *Ivory Carvings in Early Medieval England* (London, 1972): Sandy Heslop, *Burlington Mag.* 116, 413

Ivory Carvings in Early Medieval England, 700–1200 [catalogue of an exhibition in the Victoria and Albert Museum, London] (1974): P. Lasko, *Burlington Mag.* 116, 426–7

Benson, Don, and David Miles, *The Upper Thames Valley: an Archaeological Survey of the River Gravels* (Oxford, 1974): Graham Webster, *Antiquity* 48, 246–7

Beresford, M. W., and H. P. R. Finberg, *English Medieval Boroughs: a Hand-List* (Newton Abbot, 1973): Derek Keene, *Archives* 11, 220–1; S. E. Rigold, *MA* 17, 198–9

Beresford, Maurice, and John G. Hurst, ed., *Deserted Medieval Villages: Studies* (London, 1972): H. P. R. Finberg, *Population Stud.* 1972, 323; M. G. Jarrett, *Geographical Jnl* 138, 91–2; Fr Verhaeghe, *Helinium*, 14, 196–7

Bergmann, Rolf, *Verzeichnis der althochdeutschen und altsächsischen Glossenhandschriften* (Berlin and New York, 1973): Henning von Gadow, *Erasmus* 26, 130–1; Sigrid Krämer, *Deutsches Archiv für Erforschung des Mittelalters* 30, 259–60; Hartwig Mayer, *Germanistik* 14, 544–5

Bill, E. G. W., *A Catalogue of Manuscripts in Lambeth Palace Library* (London, 1972): Andrew G. Watson, *History* 58, 417

Birkeli, Fridtjov, *Norske Steinkors i tidlig Middelalder* (Oslo, 1973): Per Sveass Andersen, *Historisk Tidsskrift* (Oslo) 1973, 344–6

Bibliography for 1974

Bishop, T. A. M., *English Caroline Minuscule* (Oxford, 1971): K. R., *Deutsches Archiv für Erforschung des Mittelalters* 29, 619–20

Bolgar, R. R., ed., *Classical Influences on European Culture AD 500–1500* (Cambridge, 1971): M. L. Clarke, *Classical Rev.* 23, 203–6

Brière, Pierre, 'La Restauration du Monastère de Saint-Paul de Clairvaux en Rouerque (Aveyron) en 1060', *Mélanges Offerts à Szabolcs de Vajay* (Braga, 1971), pp. 119–34: D. J., *Deutsches Archiv für Erforschung des Mittelalters* 29, 576

Brodribb, A. C. C., A. R. Hands and D. R. Walker, *Excavations at Shakenoak Farm, near Wilcote, Oxfordshire. Part III: Site F* (Oxford, 1972): Leslie Alcock, *MA* 17, 189–90; P. D. C. Brown, *Britannia* 3, 376–7

Brown, R. Allen, *Origins of English Feudalism* (London and New York, 1973): C. Warren Hollister, *AHR* 79, 124–5

Brown, T. J., *et al.*, ed., *The Durham Ritual*, EEMF 16 (Copenhagen, 1969): A. C. Campbell, *MÆ* 42, 259–60

Bruce-Mitford, Rupert, *The Sutton Hoo Ship-Burial: a Handbook*, 2nd ed. (London, 1972): Peter Hunter Blair, *MÆ* 42, 301–2

Burgschmidt, Ernst, and Dieter Götz, *Historische Linguistik: Englisch* (Tübingen, 1973): Wolfgang Blumbach, *Kratylos* 18, 96–8; Manfred Görlach, *Anglia* 92, 408–12; W. Meid, *Die Sprache* 20, 206

Campbell, A., ed., *Anglo-Saxon Charters. I: Charters of Rochester* (Oxford, 1973): Bernard Wigan, *Archaeologia Cantiana* 88, 229–30

Carnicelli, Thomas A., ed., *King Alfred's Version of Augustine's Soliloquies* (Cambridge, Mass., 1969): R. Derolez, *ESts* 55, 496

Chaney, William A., *The Cult of Kingship in Anglo-Saxon England* (Manchester, 1970): Cecily Clark, *ESts* 55, 463–4; Richard Drögereit, *Historische Zeitschrift* 216, 134–6; Hanna Vollrath-Reichelt, *Archiv für Kulturgeschichte* 55, 489–91

Chibnall, Marjorie, ed. and trans., *The Ecclesiastical History of Orderic Vitalis* II–IV (Oxford, 1969–73): P. C. Boeren, *Tijdschrift voor Geschiednis* 87, 571 [IV only]; John Le Patourel, *JEH* 25, 203–4 [IV only]; H. R. Loyn, *AntJ* 54, 124–5 [III only]; D. J. A. Matthew, *History* 59, 87–8 [III only]; Robert B. Patterson, *Speculum* 49, 320–1 [II and III]; Karl Schnith, *Historisches Jahrbuch* 92, 420 [II only]; John K. Yost, *Church Hist.* 43, 391–2 [III and IV]

Clark, Cecily, ed., *The Peterborough Chronicle 1070–1154*, 2nd ed. (Oxford, 1970): Raymonde Foreville, *CCM* 16, 237–9

Clemoes, Peter, *et al.*, ed., *Anglo-Saxon England* 1 and 2 (Cambridge, 1972–3): *ArchJ* 130, 336 [1 only]; *Speculum* 49, 174–5 [1 only]; Frank Barlow, *Theology* 77, 99–100 [1], and 661–2 [2]; J. E. Cross, *N&Q* 21, 186–91; H. R. Loyn, *JEH* 25, 309–10 [2 only]; J. N. L. Myres, *AntJ* 54, 120–1 [1 only]; Janet L. Nelson, *History* 59, 85–6 [1 only]; Richard W. Pfaff, *Church Hist.* 43, 97–8 [1], and 389–90 [2]; Karl Schnith, *Deutsches Archiv für Erforschung des Mittelalters* 30, 315–17; Celia Sisam, *RES* 25, 66–7 [1 only]; E. G. Stanley, *ASNSL* 211, 418–21 [1 only]; Dorothy Whitelock, *Antiquity* 48, 162–3 [2 only]; R. M. Wilson, *MLR* 69, 367–8 [1 only]

Bibliography for 1974

Coetsem, Frans van, and Herbert L. Kufner, ed., *Toward a Grammar of Proto-Germanic* (Tübingen, 1972): Eduard Kolb, *Beiträge zur Namenforschung* 9, 305–7

Crépin, André, *Histoire de la Langue Anglaise* (Paris, 1967): Jaroslav Macháček, *Linguistics* 82, 126–8

Cunliffe, Barry, *The Regni* (London, 1973): A. L. F. Rivet, *Britannia* 5, 490–1; J. S. Wacher, *Antiquity* 48, 76–7

Darby, H. C., ed., *A New Historical Geography of England* (Cambridge, 1973): D. J. Gregory, *Hist. Jnl* 17, 652–4

Darby, H. C., and I. B. Terrett, ed., *The Domesday Geography of Midland England*, 2nd ed. (Cambridge, 1971): W. O. Ault, *AHR* 79, 771–2

Dodgson, J. McN., *The Place-Names of Cheshire* i–iv (Cambridge, 1970–2): Dirk P. Blok, *Beiträge zur Namenforschung* 9, 201–4; Gillian Fellows Jensen, *Northern Hist.* 7, 136–7 [i and ii]; Dorothy Sylvester, *Geography* 56, 168 [i], and 57, 78 [ii and iii]

Douglas, David C., *William the Conqueror* (London, 1964, etc.): Fritz Trautz, *Historische Zeitschrift* 219, 387–8

    The Norman Achievement, 1050–1100 (London, 1969): Massimo Oldoni, *Studi Medievali* 14, 1174–5; Fritz Trautz, *Historische Zeitschrift* 219, 387–90

Dumas-Dubourg, Françoise, *Le Trésor de Fécamp et le Monnayage en Francie Occidentale pendant la Seconde Moitié du Xe Siècle* (Paris, 1971): Michael Dolley, *CCM* 17, 257–9; J. Yvon, *Archéologie Médiévale* 3/4, 437–40

Elrington, C. R., and N. M. Herbert, *The Victoria History of the County of Gloucester* x (London, 1972): David Walker, *History* 58, 417

Els, T. J. M. van, *The Kassel Manuscript of Bede's 'Historia Ecclesiastica Gentis Anglorum' and its Old English Material* (Assen, 1972): Raymond Schnittlein, *Revue Internationale d'Onomastique* 25, 304–6

Farrell, R. T., *Beowulf Swedes and Geats* (London, 1972): A. J. Deverson, *AUMLA* 41, 79–80; T. F. Hoad, *N&Q* 21, 267–8; T. A. Shippey, *MLR* 69, 144–5

Fellows Jensen, Gillian, *Scandinavian Settlement Names in Yorkshire* (Copenhagen, 1972): G. W. S. Barrow, *Northern Hist.* 9, 170–1; Eduard Kolb, *Beiträge zur Namenforschung* 9, 398–403

Finberg, H. P. R., ed., *The Agrarian History of England and Wales* 1.2 (Cambridge, 1972): W. O. Ault, *AHR* 79, 1163–4; H. R. Loyn, *History* 59, 80–2; J. N. L. Myres, *EHR* 89, 845–9; J. A. Raftis, *Speculum* 49, 559–61; Timothy Renter, *ArchJ* 130, 312–13; David Walker, *Anglo-Welsh Rev.* 22, 246–52

Fowler, P. J., ed., *Archaeology and the Landscape: Essays for L. V. Grinsell* (London, 1972): David Dymond, *AntJ* 53, 293–4

Fowler, Roger, ed., *Wulfstan's Canons of Edgar*, Early Eng. Text Soc. 266 (1972): Dorothy Bethurum Loomis, *MÆ* 43, 151–5

Frank, Roberta, and Angus Cameron, ed., *A Plan for a Dictionary of Old English* (Toronto, 1973): André Crépin, *Études Anglaises* 27, 221–2

Galster, George, *The Royal Collection of Coins and Medals, National Museum, Copenhagen. Part III, A–C, Anglo-Saxon Coins, Cnut*, Sylloge of Coins of the Brit. Isles 13–15 (London, 1970): S. E. Rigold, *AntJ* 53, 319–20

Gardner, John, *Grendel* (New York, 1972): Carl T. Berkhout, *Notre Dame Eng. Jnl* 7, 55–8

Garmonsway, G. N., trans., *The Anglo-Saxon Chronicle* (London, 1972): Veronika Kniezsa, *Acta Linguistica Academiae Scientiarum Hungaricae* 23, 433–5

Gatch, Milton McC., *Loyalties and Traditions: Man and his World in Old English Literature* (New York, 1971): Janet M. Bately, *Anglia* 92, 443–4; Patrizia Lendinara, *Annali, Sezione Germanica* (Naples) 15, 315–17

Geipel, John, *The Viking Legacy* (Newton Abbot, 1971): Michael Barnes, *SBVS* 18, 381–3

Gneuss, Helmut, *Hymnar und Hymnen im englischen Mittelalter* (Tübingen, 1968): Sergio Rossi, *Studi Medievali* 12, 540–1

Göller, Karl Heinz, ed., *Epochen der englischen Lyrik* (Düsseldorf, 1970): Wolfgang Weiss, *Anglia* 92, 223–7

Geschichte der altenglischen Literatur (Berlin, 1971): Patrizia Lendinara, *Annali, Sezione Germanica* (Naples) 15, 317–18; E. G. Stanley, *ASNSL* 210, 359–63

Gough, Michael, *The Origins of Christian Art* (London, 1973): J. M. C. Toynbee, *Antiquity* 48, 70–1

Gradon, Pamela, *Form and Style in Early English Literature* (London, 1971): *TLS* 8 November, p. 1265; Phil Rogers, *Humanities Assoc. Rev.* 25, 348–50

Greenfield, Stanley B., *The Interpretation of Old English Poems* (London and Boston, 1972): J. E. Cross, *MÆ* 43, 42–6; T. P. Dolan, *Studies, An Irish Quarterly Rev.* 62, 352–4; R. E. Kaske, *MP* 72, 190–4; Burton Raffel, *Notre Dame Eng. Jnl* 9, 31–3; Phil Rogers, *Humanities Assoc. Rev.* 25, 348–50; T. A. Shippey, *YES* 4, 242–4

Gretsch, Mechthild, *Die Regula Sancti Benedicti in England und ihre altenglische Über-setzung* (Munich, 1973): E. G. Stanley, *N&Q* 21, 344–7

Grünberg, Madeleine, *The West-Saxon Gospels: a Study of the Gospel of St Matthew with Text of the Four Gospels* (Amsterdam, 1967): James Rosier, *Anglia* 92, 229–31

Gunstone, A. J. H., *Ancient British, Anglo-Saxon and Norman Coins in Midlands Museums*, Sylloge of Coins of the Brit. Isles 17 (London, 1971): S. E. Rigold, *AntJ* 53, 319–20

Hahn, E. Adelaide, *Naming-Constructions in some Indo-European Languages* (Cleveland, 1969): Wolfgang Meid, *Anzeiger für die Altertumswissenschaft* 25, 346

Harding, Alan, *The Law Courts of Medieval England* (New York, 1973): Margaret Hastings, *AHR* 79, 494–5

Hartung, Albert E., ed., *A Manual of Writings in Middle English 1050–1500* III (New Haven, 1972): Norman Davis, *RES* 25, 67–9; R. M. Wilson, *MLR* 69, 146

Hawkes, Christopher and Sonia, ed., *Greeks, Celts and Romans: Studies in Venture and Resistance* (London, 1973): T. G. E. Powell, *Antiquity* 48, 74–5

Heusler, Andreas, *Kleine Schriften* II (Berlin, 1969): Lawrence S. Thompson, *Amer. Notes and Queries* 11, 75

Holthausen, Ferdinand, *Altsächsisches Wörterbuch*, 2nd ed. (Cologne and Graz, 1967): Heinrich Tiefenbach, *Beiträge zur Namenforschung* 9, 286–8

[Hoops, Johannes] *Reallexikon der germanischen Altertumskunde*, 2nd ed. 1.1 etc. (Berlin, 1968–): Karl J. Narr, *Germanistik* 15, 16

Hughes, Kathleen, *Early Christian Ireland: Introduction to the Sources* (London, 1972): L. Bieler, *JEH* 25, 91–2

Hunter Blair, Peter, *The World of Bede* (New York, 1971): Michael Paulin Blecker, *CHR* 60, 477–8

Hurt, James, *Ælfric* (New York, 1972): M. R. Godden, *MÆ* 43, 46–7; John C. Pope, *Speculum* 49, 344–7; Fred C. Robinson, *Medievalia et Humanistica* 4, 223; Alexandra Smith, *Humanities Assoc. Rev.* 24, 221–3; Robert D. Stevick, *JEGP* 73, 111–13

Isaacs, Neil D., *Structural Principles in Old English Poetry* (Knoxville, 1968): Klaus Weimann, *Anglia* 92, 227–9

Jones, Gwyn, *Kings, Beasts and Heroes* (London, 1972): Felix Braendel, *Carleton Miscellany* 13, 168–70; Moira Dearnley, *Anglo-Welsh Rev.* 22, 241–4; Roberta Frank, *Humanities Assoc. Rev.* 24, 220–1; Edward B. Irving, Jr, *Anglia* 92, 441–3; Bill Manhire, *SBVS* 18, 390–1; Alice S. Miskimin, *Yale Rev.* 62, 299–305; Lotte Motz, *Med. Scandinavia* 6, 208–10

Kispert, Robert J., *Old English: an Introduction* (New York, 1971): Joseph B. Trahern, Jr, *General Ling.* 13, 123–8

Klingenberg, Heinz, *Runenschrift – Schriftdenken – Runeninschriften* (Heidelberg, 1973): Alfred Ebenbauer, *BGDSL* (Tübingen) 96, 125–33

Knowles, David, C. N. L. Brooke and Vera C. M. London, ed., *The Heads of Religious Houses: England and Wales 940–1216* (Cambridge, 1972): R. Gilyard-Beer, *AntJ* 53, 322; Bennett D. Hill, *Speculum* 49, 575–7; C. J. Holdsworth, *History* 59, 451; Kurt-Ulrich Jäschke, *Archiv für Kulturgeschichte* 56, 223–6; L. Milis, *Tijdschrift voor Geschiednis* 87, 89–90

Knowles, David, and R. Neville Hadcock, *Medieval Religious Houses: England and Wales*, 2nd ed. (London, 1971): Michael Richter, *Welsh Hist. Rev.* 6, 380–1

Köbler, Gerhard, *Lateinisches Register zu den frühmittelalterlichen germanischen Übersetzungsgleichungen* (Göttingen, Zürich and Frankfurt, 1973): Elfriede Stutz, *Beiträge zur Namenforschung* 9, 281

Kohl, Norbert, *Bibliographie für das Studium der Anglistik I: Sprachwissenschaft* (Bad Homburg, v. d. H., 1970): Helmut Gneuss, *Anglia* 92, 402–7

Krämer, Peter, *Die Präsensklassen des germanischen schwachen Verbums* (Innsbruck, 1971): Ingerid Dal, *Kratylos* 17, 96–100; Fredrik Otto Lindeman, *Bulletin de la Société Linguistique de Paris* 68, 235–6

Krüger, Karl Heinrich, *Königsgrabkirchen der Franken, Angelsachsen und Langobarden bis zur Mitte des 8. Jahrhunderts* (Munich, 1971): Wolfgang Metz, *Historisches Jahrbuch* 92, 416–17; K. Schäferdick, *Zeitschrift für Kirchengeschichte* 85, 98–9

'Königskonversionen im 8. Jahrhundert', *Frühmittelalterliche Studien* 7 (1973), 169–222: W. H., *Deutsches Archiv für Geschichte des Mittelalters* 30, 271

Leighton, Albert C., *Transport and Communication in Early Medieval Europe* (New

York, 1972): Gordon East, *Geographical Jnl* 63, 589–90; M. M. Knight, *Jnl of Economic Hist.* 33, 892–3; Lynn White, Jr, *Speculum* 49, 577–9

Lindemann, J. W. Richard, *Old English Preverbal 'Ge-': its Meaning* (Charlottesville, 1970): M. M. Makovskij, *Voprosy Jazykoznanija* 1972, 153–6; Ruta Nagucka, *Linguistics* 137, 108–11

Lockwood, W. B., *Indo-European Philology: Historical and Comparative* (London, 1969): Oswald Panagl, *Linguistics* 90, 97–106

Lowe, E. A., *Codices Latini Antiquiores* ii, 2nd ed. (Oxford, 1972): Peter Hunter Blair, *EHR* 89, 111–13
Palaeographical Papers 1907–1965, ed. L. Bieler (Oxford, 1972): Peter Hunter Blair, *EHR* 89, 111–13; Wesley M. Stevens, *Church Hist.* 43, 536–7

Mack, R. P., *R. P. Mack Collection: Ancient British, Anglo-Saxon and Norman Coins*, Sylloge of Coins of the Brit. Isles 20 (London, 1973): Michael Mackensen, *Britannia* 5, 481–2

Marckwardt, Albert H., and James L. Rosier, *Old English: Language and Literature* (New York, 1972): T. F. Hoad, *N&Q* 21, 63–6

Markman, Alan M., and Erwin R. Steinberg, ed., *English Then and Now: Readings and Exercises* (New York, 1970): Jon L. Erickson, *General Ling.* 13, 128–33

Matthews, C. M., *Place-Names of the English-Speaking World* (London and New York, 1972): Gillis Kristensson, *ESts* 55, 302–3; David Parry, *Anglo-Welsh Rev.* 22, 237–9

Mayr-Harting, Henry, *The Coming of Christianity to Anglo-Saxon England* (London, 1972) and *The Coming of Christianity to England* (New York, 1972): William A. Chaney, *CHR* 60, 475–6; Howard J. Happ, *Jnl of the Amer. Acad. of Religion* 42, 387–8; Peter Hunter Blair, *EHR* 89, 146–7

McKisack, May, *Medieval History in the Tudor Age* (Oxford, 1971): Bernard Guenée, *Revue Historique* 249, 185–6; Giuseppe Sergi, *Studi Medievali* 13, 1115–16

McNamee, Lawrence, *Ninety-Nine Years of English Dissertations* (Commerce, Texas, 1969): Helmut Gneuss, *Anglia* 92, 399–401

McNeill, John T., *The Celtic Churches: a History, AD 200 to 1200* (Chicago, 1974): Bernard McGinn, *Church Hist.* 43, 268

Meid, Wolfgang, *Das germanische Präteritum* (Innsbruck, 1971): Fredrik Otto Lindeman, *Bulletin de la Société Linguistique de Paris* 68, 236–43

Mellinkoff, Ruth, *The Horned Moses in Medieval Art and Thought* (Berkeley and Los Angeles, 1970): David Freedberg, *Burlington Mag.* 116, 337–8; Adelheid Heimann, *Zeitschrift für Kunstgeschichte* 37, 284–8

Menzies, Gordon, ed., *Who are the Scots? A Search for the Origins of the Scottish Nation* (London, 1971): R. G. Cant, *Scottish Hist. Rev.* 53, 76–8

Millward, Celia, *Imperative Constructions in Old English* (The Hague, 1971): Janet Bately, *Anglia* 92, 198–200; Bruce Mitchell, *ESts* 55, 387–9

Moeller-Schina, Ute, *Deutsche Lehnprägungen aus dem Englischen von der althochdeutschen Zeit bis 1700* (Tübingen, 1969): Helmut Gneuss, *Beiträge zur Namenforschung* 9, 290–2

Morris, John, *The Age of Arthur* (London, 1973): Keith Bailey, *London Archaeology*

2, 161–4, 204 and 207; H. R. Loyn, *ArchJ* 130, 331–2; C. A. Ralegh Radford, *Britannia* 5, 487–9; Donald A. White, *AHR* 79, 768–70

Morton, Catherine, and Hope Muntz, ed., *The 'Carmen de Hastingae Proelio' of Guy, Bishop of Amiens* (Oxford, 1972): R. Allen Brown, *History* 59, 251–2; Kenneth E. Cutler, *Speculum* 49, 364–5; H. R. Loyn, *CCM* 17, 265–6; G. Orlandi, *Studi Medievali* 13, 196–222; Karl Wührer, *Historische Zeitschrift* 217, 407–8

Müller-Wille, Michael, *Bestattung im Boot: Studien zu einer nordeuropäischen Grabsitte*, Offa 25–6 (Neumünster, 1970): Jan Peder Lamm, *Germania* 51, 639–43

Munske, Horst Haider, *Der germanische Rechtswortschatz im Bereich der Missetaten. I: Die Terminologie der älteren westgermanischen Rechtsquellen* (Berlin, 1973): D. H. Green, *JEGP* 73, 73–5

Musca, Giosuè, *Il Venerabile Beda, Storico dell'Alto Medioevo* (Bari, 1973): D. W. Robertson, Jr, *AHR* 79, 493–4

Myres, J. N. L., and Barbara Green, *The Anglo-Saxon Cemeteries of Caistor-by-Norwich and Markshall, Norfolk* (London, 1973): Heli R. Roosens, *Antiquity* 48, 248–9; David M. Wilson, *JBAA* 3rd ser. 37, 124–5

National Maritime Museum, *Three Major Ancient Boat Finds in Britain* (1972): Peter Marsden, *ArchJ* 130, 315; H. Hazelhoff Roelfzema, *Nautical Archaeology*, 3, 350–1

Newton, Robert R., *Medieval Chronicles and the Rotation of the Earth* (Baltimore and London, 1972): Edward Grant, *Medievalia et Humanistica* 4, 225–6; Kenneth Harrison, *EHR* 89, 412; Nicholas H. Steneck, *Speculum* 49, 365–8

O'Faolain, Julia, and Lauro Martines, ed., *Not in God's Image: Women in History from the Greeks to the Victorians* (New York, 1973): Ann Robson, *Histoire Sociale – Social Hist.* 7, 121–3

Okasha, Elisabeth, *Hand-List of Anglo-Saxon Non-Runic Inscriptions* (Cambridge, 1971): O. von Feilitzen, *Jnl of the Eng. Place-Name Soc.* 4, 63–7; Fred C. Robinson, *Medievalia et Humanistica* 4, 223–5; R. Dean Ware, *Speculum* 49, 584–6

Oppel, Horst, *Englisch–deutsche Literaturbeziehungen* (Berlin, 1971): A. Closs, *MLR* 69, 689–91

Pächt, Otto, and J. J. G. Alexander, *Illuminated Manuscripts in the Bodleian Library, Oxford* III (Oxford, 1973): C. R. Dodwell, *EHR* 89, 871–2

Page, R. I., *Life in Anglo-Saxon England* (London, 1970): Cecily Clark, *ESts* 55, 64–5

An Introduction to English Runes (London, 1973): Bruce Dickins, *Antiquity* 48, 152–3; John McN. Dodgson, *JBAA* 3rd ser. 37, 128

Pearsall, D. A., and R. A. Waldron, ed., *Medieval Literature and Civilisation: Studies in Memory of G. N. Garmonsway* (London, 1969): Mechthild Gretsch, *ASNSL* 210, 363–6

Penzl, Herbert, *Methoden der germanischen Linguistik* (Tübingen, 1972): Alfred Bammesberger, *Anglia* 92, 407–8; Heinrich Beck, *Beiträge zur Namenforschung* 9, 230; Daniel Brink, *Lingua* 33, 169–72; Paul Valentin, *Kratylos* 17, 214–15; John Weinstock, *JEGP* 73, 280–1

Piirainen, Elisabeth, *Germ. '*frōð-' und germ. '*klōk': eine bedeutungsgeschichtliche Untersuchung* (Helsinki, 1971): John L. Flood, *MLR* 69, 211–12; August Scaffidi-Abbate, *Beiträge zur Namenforschung* 8, 377–80

Platt, Colin, *Medieval Southampton: the Port and Trading Community, AD 1000–1600* (London, 1973): Martin Biddle, *Antiquity* 48, 247–8

Ploss, Emil Ernst, ed., *Waltharius und Walthersage: eine Dokumentation der Forschung* (Hildesheim, 1969): Massimo Oldoni, *Studi Medievali* 13, 1140–1

Plotkin, V. Y., *The Dynamics of the English Phonological System* (The Hague, 1972): Allan R. James, *Kratylos* 17, 194–8; Horst Weinstock, *SN* 46, 267–70

Porter, H. M., *The Celtic Church in Somerset* (Bath, 1971): Wendy Davies, *History* 58, 80

Prins, A. A., *A History of English Phonemes* (Leiden, 1972): Ulf Magnusson, *Studia Linguistica* 28, 115–31; A. R. Tellier, *Bulletin de la Société Linguistique de Paris* 68, 256

Ramat, Paolo, *Grammatica dall'Antico Sassone* (Milan, 1969): Paul Valentin, *Bulletin de la Société Linguistique de Paris* 68, 243–4

Reszkiewicz, Alfred, *Synchronic Essentials of Old English: West Saxon* (Warsaw, 1971): Angus Cameron, *Anglia* 92, 412–13

  A Diachronic Grammar of Old English I (Warsaw, 1973): Jerzy Wełna, *Kwartalnik Neofilologiczny* 21, 130–4

Richter, Michael, ed., *Canterbury Professions*, Canterbury and York Soc. 67 (1973): H. S. Offler, *DUJ* 67, 107–9

Ris, Roland, *Das Adjektiv 'reich' im mittelalterlichen Deutsch: Geschichte – semantische Struktur – Stilistik* (Berlin, 1971): D. H. Green, *MLR* 69, 215–16

Robinson, Fred C., *Old English Literature: a Select Bibliography* (Toronto, 1970): Helmut Gneuss, *Anglia* 92, 439–41

Rosenthal, Joel T., *Angles, Angels, and Conquerors* (New York, 1973): Ralph V. Turner, *AHR* 79, 492–3

Royal Commission on Historical Monuments (England), *An Inventory of Historical Monuments in the County of Cambridge* II (London, 1972): M. W. Thompson, *MA* 17, 200–1

  An Inventory of Historical Monuments in the County of Dorset IV (London, 1972): Charles Thomas, *MA* 17, 201–2

  An Inventory of the Historical Monuments in the City of York II (London, 1972): A. P. Baggs, *ArchJ* 130, 342; Lawrence Butler, *Yorkshire Archaeol. Jnl* 46, 167; M. W. Thompson, *Antiquity* 48, 67–8; Jarosław Widawski, *CCM* 17, 169–70

  An Inventory of the Historical Monuments in the |City of York III (London, 1972): R. Gilyard-Beer, *MA* 17, 202–3; George G. Pace, *AntJ* 54, 135–7

Ryding, William W., *Structure in Medieval Narrative* (The Hague, 1971): Massimo Oldoni, *Studi Medievali* 14, 1209–10

Samuels, M. L., *Linguistic Evolution with Special Reference to English* (Cambridge, 1972): A. J. Bliss, *N&Q* 21, 182–6

Sandgren, Folke, ed., *Otium et Negotium: Studies in Onomatology and Library Science presented to Olof von Feilitzen* (Stockholm, 1973): Barrie Cox, *Antiquity* 48, 159–60; Anthony Faulkes, *MLR* 69, 834–5; Karl Inge Sandred, *Namn och Bygd* 62, 177–81

Sawyer, P. H., *The Age of the Vikings*, 2nd ed. (London, 1971): Else Roesdahl, *SBVS* 18, 403–9

Scardigli, Piergiuseppe, *Filologia Germanica*, 2nd ed. (Florence, 1971): R. Gendre, *Archivio Glottologico Italiano* 57, 161–6

Schibsbye, Knud, *Origin and Development of the English Language. I: Phonology* (Copenhagen, 1972): Torben Kisbye, *SN* 45, 437–9

Schmitt, Ludwig Erich, *Kurzer Grundriss der germanischen Philologie bis 1500. II: Literaturgeschichte* (Berlin, 1971): Gerhild Geil, *Kratylos* 17, 217–19

Schmitt, Rüdiger, *Indogermanische Dichtersprache und Namengebung* (Innsbruck, 1973): Gottfried Schramm, *Beiträge zur Namenforschung* 9, 261–2

Schramm, Percy Ernst, *Kaiser, Könige und Päpste* i–iv (Stuttgart, 1968–71): Arne Odd Johnsen, *Med. Scandinavia* 6, 198–205

Schwab, Ute, *Die Sternrune im Wessobrunner Gebet* (Amsterdam, 1973): Heinz-Joachim Graf, *ASNSL* 211, 98–9; Klaus Grinda, *Beiträge zur Namenforschung* 9, 311–15

See, Klaus von, *Germanische Heldensage* (Frankfurt, 1971): R. G. Finch, *SBVS* 18, 383–7; Joseph Harris, *Scandinavian Stud.* 46, 185–90; Stefan Sonderegger, *Skandinavistik* 4, 72–4

Die Gestalt der Hávamál (Frankfurt, 1972): G. Turville-Petre, *SBVS* 18, 387–9

Seebold, Elmar, *Vergleichendes und etymologisches Wörterbuch der germanischen starken Verben* (The Hague, 1970): Hartmut Beckers, *Amsterdamer Beiträge zur älteren Germanistik* 5, 171–9

Seltén, Bo, *The Anglo-Saxon Heritage in Middle English Personal Names, East Anglia 1100–1399* (Lund, 1972): Hartmut Beckers, *Beiträge zur Namenforschung* 9, 278–9; Karl Inge Sandred, *Namn och Bygd* 61, 83–92 and *SN* 46, 262–7; R. M. Wilson, *MLR* 69, 368

Settimane di Studio del Centro Italiano di Studi sull'Alto Medioevo 17, *La Storiografia Altomedievale* (Spoleto, 1970): E. Ladewig Petersen, *Med. Scandinavia* 6, 223–5

Shippey, T. A., *Old English Verse* (London and New York, 1972): Robert B. Burlin, *Speculum* 49, 758–60; M. R. Godden, *JEGP* 73, 108–11; J. R. Hall, *Notre Dame Eng. Jnl* 8, 110–13

Shores, David L., *A Descriptive Syntax of the Peterborough Chronicle from 1122 to 1154* (The Hague, 1971): Cecily Clark, *MÆ* 43, 47–50

Small, Alan, Charles Thomas and David M. Wilson, *St Ninian's Isle and its Treasure* (London, 1973): James Graham-Campbell, *History* 59, 450–1; Thomas M. Y. Manson, *Aberdeen Univ. Rev.* 45, 161–5; R. B. K. Stevenson, *Antiquity* 48, 324–5; M. J. Swanton, *ArchJ* 130, 335–6

Smith, Eric, *Some Versions of the Fall: the Myth of the Fall of Man in English Literature* (London, 1973): J. M. Evans, *N&Q* 21, 114–16

Smith, T. P., *The Anglo-Saxon Churches of Hertfordshire* (London and Chichester, 1973): David Parsons, *ArchJ* 130, 336–7

Starck, Taylor, and J. C. Wells, *Althochdeutsches Glossenwörterbuch mit Stellennach weis zu sämtlichen gedruckten althochdeutschen und verwandten Glossen* I and II (Heidelberg, 1972–3): H. von Gadow, *ASNSL* 211, 99–105; Heinrich Tiefenbach, *Beiträge zur Namenforschung* 9, 222–6

Stenton, F. M., *Anglo-Saxon England*, 3rd ed. (Oxford, 1971): Guy Fourquin, *Revue Historique* 249, 497–8; H. R. Loyn, *CCM* 17, 279–81

Strang, Barbara M. H., *A History of English* (London, 1970): Jerzy Wełna, *SAP* 5, 204–8

Szenci, Miklós, Tibor Szobotka and Anna Katona, *Az angol irodalom története* [History of the English Language] (Budapest, 1972): László Orszagh, *ZAA* 22, 209–11

Thomas, Charles, *Britain and Ireland in Early Christian Times, AD 400–800* (London and New York, 1971): Laurence Keen, *Bull. of the Inst. of Archaeology London* 11, 175–6; Robert T. Meyer, *CHR* 60, 125

The Early Christian Archaeology of North Britain (London and New York, 1971): Robert T. Meyer, *CHR* 60, 474–5; C. A. Ralegh Radford, *MA* 17, 190–2

Tinkler, John D., *Vocabulary and Syntax of the Old English Version in the Paris Psalter* (The Hague, 1971): J. Rosier, *MÆ* 42, 260–1

Trapp, J. B., ed., *The Oxford Anthology of English Literature* (gen. ed. Frank Kermode and John Hollander) I (London and New York, 1973): Basil Cottle, *RES* 25, 318–23; S. G. Kossick, *UNISA Eng. Stud.* 12, 73–5; Duncan Macrae-Gibson, *Aberdeen Univ. Rev.* 45, 409–10; Sergio Rossi, *Studi Medievali* 14, 1213–15; Roger Sharrock, *DUJ* 35, 335–8

Traugott, Elizabeth Closs, *A History of English Syntax* (New York, 1972): Ernst Burgschmidt, *Anglia* 92, 194–8

Uecker, Heiko, *Germanische Heldensage* (Stuttgart, 1972): Jacqueline Simpson, *Med. Scandinavia* 6, 225

Valentin, Paul, and G. Zink, ed., *Mélanges pour Jean Fourquet* (Paris, 1969): Werner Schröder, *BGDSL* (Tübingen) 94, 249–55

Viator: Medieval and Renaissance Studies 2 (1972) and 3 (1973): R. J. P. Kuin, *Amer. Notes and Queries* 11, 125–7, and 12, 43–7

Visser, F. Th., *An Historical Syntax of the English Language* III.1–2 (Leiden, 1969 and 1973): Martin Lehnert, *ZAA* 22, 202–5

Vollrath-Reichelt, Hanna, *Königsgedanke und Königtum bei den Angelsachsen bis zur Mitte des 9. Jahrhunderts* (Cologne and Vienna, 1971): Eric John, *EHR* 89, 611–14; G. Köbler, *Historische Zeitschrift* 216, 375–7; Giovanni Tabacco, *Studi Medievali* 14, 886–91

Wagner, Karl Heinz, *Generative Grammatical Studies in the Old English Language* (Heidelberg, 1969): Klaus B. Grinda, *IF* 77, 120–4

Wallace-Hadrill, J. M., *Early Germanic Kingship in England and on the Continent* (Oxford and New York, 1971): Boyd H. Hill, Jr, *AHR* 79, 1160–1; Stanisław Russocki, *Czasopismo Prawno-Historyczne* 24, 263–4; Hanna Vollrath-Reichelt, *Historische Zeitschrift* 217, 400–3

Bibliography for 1974

Warnicke, Retha M., *William Lambarde: Elizabethan Antiquary, 1536–1601* (Chichester, 1973): John H. Gleason, *AHR* 79, 1549

Weber, Gerd Wolfgang, '*Wyrd*': *Studien zum Schicksalsbegriff der altenglischen und altnordischen Literatur* (Bad Homburg, v. d. H., 1969): Milton McC. Gatch, *Speculum* 49, 771

Welldon Finn, R., *The Norman Conquest and its Effects on the Economy, 1066–1086* (London, 1971): R. Allen Brown, *AntJ* 52, 389–90; R. Drögereit, *Historische Zeitschrift* 216, 489–90; Guy Fourquin, *Revue Historique* 250, 477–80

The Making and Limitations of the Yorkshire Domesday (York, 1972): Janet Cooper, *Archives* 11, 45–6; Edward Miller, *Northern Hist.* 9, 171–2

Domesday Book: a Guide (Chichester, 1974): *TLS* 5 July, p. 733

Winterbottom, Michael, ed., *Three Lives of English Saints* (Toronto, 1972): J. W. Binns, *MLR* 69, 614; Servus Gieben, *Collectanea Franciscana* 44, 224; Joseph F. Kelly, *Church Hist.* 43, 391; J. N. L. Myres, *JTS* 25, 197–8

Wolff, Philippe, *Les Origines Linguistiques de l'Europe Occidentale* (Paris, 1971): Charles R. Barrett, *CCM* 16, 352–3

Western Languages, AD 100–1500 (London, 1971): Denys Hay, *History* 58, 425–6

Wrenn, C. L., ed., *Beowulf with the Finnesburg Fragment*, rev. W. F. Bolton (London and New York, 1973): *TLS* 1 February, p. 100

Wright, C. E., *Fontes Harleiani: a Study of the Sources of the Harleian Collection of Manuscripts Preserved in the Department of Manuscripts in the British Museum* (London, 1972): R. W. Southern, *EHR* 89, 113–16

Zöllner, Erich, *Geschichte der Franken bis zur Mitte des sechsten Jahrhunderts* (Munich, 1970): Rudolf Schützeichel, *Beiträge zur Namenforschung* 9, 186–94

Zweig, Paul, *The Adventurer: the Fate of Adventure in the Western World* (New York, 1974): John Gardner, *New York Times Book Rev.* 22 December, p. 7